Big Business and the State

Changing Relations in Western Europe

Written under the auspices of The Center for International Affairs, Harvard University

Big Business and the State

Changing Relations in Western Europe

Raymond Vernon, Editor

HD3616
.E82V37

Harvard University Press   Cambridge, Massachusetts   1974

Library of Congress Catalog Card Number 73–91784
ISBN 674–07275–8
Printed in the United States of America

Preface

This book is the product of a rare adventure in intellectual partnership. Most of us who contributed to the book were strangers to one another when the exercise began. We came from seven different countries; we bridged two generations; we came out of economics, politics, and business administration; we wrote in four different languages. But as the intellectual interaction progressed, none of these differences seemed to matter very much. A hard core of ideas, shared, refined, and reinforced, emerged out of the process. It is doubtful that each of us would subscribe to all the nuances in the analysis of the others; indeed, some important differences of view are clearly to be seen in some of the articles. But the scope of the shared impressions and conclusions has proved impressive.

The process began in 1969, when a number of researchers in the Center for International Affairs and in West European Studies at Harvard began to voice the uneasy feeling that some major trends were developing in the political economy of Western Europe which they did not quite understand. There were some who articulated this uneasiness in terms of the direction of Europe's industrial policies, some in terms of the drift of its labor relations, some in terms of social change of a more amorphous kind. The upshot was that the Center for International Affairs and West European Studies invited a group of scholars from both sides of the Atlantic to spend a few days at Harvard in seminar discussion exploring the problems of European society on which they happened to be working. The first round of discussions was wide-ranging and uninhibited, covering politics, labor, social systems, business, and a variety of other topics. The consensus seemed to support the conclusion that major changes were in the air in western Europe, though the articulation of the changes seemed difficult and elusive.

In the year or two that followed, the problems and the questions began to sort themselves out. One cluster of problems seemed to involve labor organizations, labor markets, and welfare issues; another cluster was detected in the problems of lagging sectors and lagging regions; still another in the changing relations between big business and national governments, the subjects of the present publication. No doubt other clusters of issues will develop as the process of trans-Atlantic collaboration continues.

In any case, once it became evident that the interactions between business and government offered a promising field for study, the problem of developing a study design and a team of researchers still remained. While in Europe in the spring of 1972, I undertook to assemble such a team. Some had been involved in the earlier sessions at Harvard, but some had not. All, however, attended a final three-day session at Harvard in January 1973, where preliminary drafts of their papers were presented.

The entire operation was undertaken on a remarkably austere budget. Moderate support came from a Thyssen Foundation grant to the Center, and from a Ford Foundation grant in support of Harvard's international studies. In addition, I took advantage of my location in western Europe, while working on a Harvard Business School study of the world's multinational enterprises, to enlarge my own research activities somewhat and to create some of the basis for my introductory article. The Business School project was financed by a separate Ford Foundation grant.

The timely preparation of the book made especially heavy demands on two key persons: the Center's editor, Dorothy W. Whitney; and my secretary, Claudette Manancourt-Dubin. As expected, they responded to the challenge with intelligence, skill, and commitment.

Raymond Vernon
Cambridge, Massachusetts
February 25, 1974

Contents

Figures

Part I

Synthesis

Enterprise and Government in Western Europe

Raymond Vernon

In the early 1970s, the major countries of Western Europe were launched on an exciting and uncertain phase of their national development. Moving in fits and starts through the 1960s, six of them had managed to advance a long distance toward economic union. Nevertheless, though the perspectives of each had been greatly modified in the process, their separate national identities were still much in evidence, deeply affecting the content and the style of their public policies.

The focus of this book is on one area of public policy in which the differences were particularly powerful. Every country of Western Europe had spawned its own crop of very large enterprises; each government had developed a distinctive style in using those enterprises and being used by them. In some nations, public ownership was extensive; in others not. In some, cooperation across the public-private boundary was intimate; in others less so. For certain countries, the relationship between business and government was a major issue in the national political process; for others, a matter of indifference.

As the European integration movement reached out to cover other countries in the early 1970s, the existence of these differences raised certain formidable questions. Were there signs of convergence among the major countries, suggesting the eventual possibility of common attitudes and common policies toward their large national enterprises? If differences seemed likely to remain, what did these differences imply for the economic and political policies of Europe?

Drawing on the observations of my colleagues in this volume, I am led to several major conclusions. One is that the national policies of the leading European countries toward their large enterprises have taken on greater similarities than they had a decade or two earlier. Moreover, the similarities have included not only those of substance but also those of process and of style. In brief, there has been a growing tendency to use large national enterprises in an effort to solve specific problems, as if they were agencies of the state. And there has been a related tendency to develop methods of governance that have reduced the role of the parliamentary process and elevated the role of specialized groups such as large enterprises and large unions.

Raymond Vernon is Director of the Center for International Affairs, Harvard University, and Herbert F. Johnson Professor of International Business Administration, Harvard Business School.

Despite the convergence in the content and style of the policies of major countries, however, it is not clear that the process of European integration has been greatly helped. The new policies and style seem as much oriented to national objectives as the policies and style of earlier years. Some of the major purposes for which the European integration movement was launched are no better served; indeed some are even more imperiled.

To see the reasons for these conclusions, however, it is useful to turn back to the situation in the early 1950s, when the foundations of the integration movement were being laid.

Targets and Instrumentalities in the 1950s

National varieties. Even in the early years following World War II, the various states of western Europe already shared certain important common characteristics. All the leading countries were parliamentary democracies, with some sort of political commitment to private ownership of the means of production. At that time, the industrial structures of the leading countries exhibited the similarities that are found in highly developed modern states. For example, in most of the countries concerned, about one third of the work force was in industry and a somewhat smaller proportion was in agriculture.[1] Moreover, though the order of priorities in national policy was a bit different from one country to the next, all were concerned with essentially the same set of problems.

First, foremost, and overwhelmingly, each nation was concentrating upon its own national economy, not upon the joint economic problems of Europe. Even small open economies such as the Netherlands and Sweden were attempting to apply independent national policies through such measures as price and wage restraints.[2] Some of the larger economies, naturally enough, seemed even more strongly committed to independent policies. When restraint was practiced in the application of restrictions at the border, the main reason seemed to be to avoid a cycle of mutually destructive retaliation.

Though each European nation displayed a narrow national focus in its economic objectives, in the 1950s, the targets that the nations sought exhibited some strong similarities: achieving a satisfactory national growth rate, which was generally identified as being on the order of 5 or 6 percent; developing or maintaining some basic stability in prices, employment, and foreign exchange earnings; and dealing with the social and political problems of lagging regions and lagging sectors within the national economy. Latent at the time but due to exhibit itself more obviously in the succeeding decade was another aim, namely, that of reducing the dependence of the national economy on foreign-controlled sources of key inputs, notably technology and scarce raw materials.

Where the national differences manifested themselves was not so much in the list of goals, therefore, as in the ordering of those goals and in the trade-offs between conflicting goals. The Germans, for instance, were deeply preoccupied with maintaining price stability and avoiding the nightmare of hyper-inflation that they had suffered in the 1920s and the 1940s. The British placed a heavy emphasis on employment stability, reflecting their national memory of the desolate 1920s and 1930s. Until de Gaulle's ascent in 1958, the French were concerned first and foremost with national growth, leaving the problems of internal price stability and exchange rate stability for some later stage.

Other differences existed as well. One was a general public attitude toward the right and proper use of governmental powers. In Britain and Germany, the expectation that government should be responsible for managing economic change was fairly weak; only in times of manifest emergency was the government expected to take a very strong hand. In France, on the other hand, the general expectation was that significant national initiatives should normally be inspired by the government. And in Italy the question was rendered largely irrelevant by the widespread feeling that no Italian government was in a position to carry out a strong national policy.[3] All these differences played a hand in determining the relations between business and government.

Business as an instrumentality. In practically every country, considerable variety could be found in the relationships between business and government. Nevertheless, the typical patterns of different countries were quite distinct in some respects. These differences are illustrated well enough by two general areas of policy: the national approach to monopoly and competition; and the national approach to public ownership and public control of industry.

As for the issues of monopoly and competition, Great Britain and Germany represented one end of a spectrum. After the first postwar phase of reconstruction, both these countries turned to center-liberal governments, and both professed to be committed to a strong reliance on the market economy. Consistent with that commitment, each exhibited a strong distaste for rules or practices that consciously selected among firms for penalty or for favor. In both countries, individual firms might avail themselves of some general provision of law, such as a statute granting preferential tax treatment or capital grants to enterprises that settled in lagging areas. But the selection of a given enterprise for treatment that would not be available to others similarly placed was usually avoided.

The historical antecedents that led to this common attitude in Britain and Germany were probably quite different. The British attitude was one of very long standing, and was almost surely related to the deep-seated principle in British jurisprudence which places heavy emphasis on formal equality before the law. The German view seems to be identified with a few economists in key positions who were strongly associated with the liberal classical tradition, as well as a few political figures who were still reacting in revulsion against the authoritarianism of the Hitler era.[4]

Despite the emphasis on the efficiency of market forces, neither the British nor the Germans felt a strong need to challenge the hold of enterprises that had managed to achieve a dominant position in their national economies. A tolerance for concentration was exhibited in many ways. For instance, though both countries in the 1950s adopted laws to curb restrictive business practices in their economies, neither country was prepared to control mergers or to limit the activities of dominant firms.

Many of the elements of British and German public policy were to be found in other European countries as well. That combination of policies, for instance, could fairly be said to have existed in Sweden and the Netherlands during the 1950s. To be sure, it was unavoidable in small countries such as these that the intervention of the authorities often had the explicit and conscious purpose of influencing a single firm. Individual enterprises were wheedled, coaxed, or threatened on a case-by-case basis either to settle in backward areas, or to hold down prices, or to slow down on a program of mass layoffs, or to pursue various other policies in which the state had an interest. Yet all this could be done side by side with an enduring respect for the ideal of an open competitive market in which all entrants were on an equal footing.

That ideal, however, enjoyed less status and vitality in France and in Italy. In Italy, the vital issues of the 1950s that bore on the state's relation to large enterprises were mainly of two sorts.[5] One was the struggle for influence and position between the big private enterprises and the big firms that the state had absentmindedly acquired in the two decades preceding World War II. The other question, not unrelated to the first, was that of fashioning the appropriate instrumentalities for the development of the lagging south of the country. Emphasis on issues of a more general nature regarding the relations of the state to business enterprises was relatively rare.

In the state's relations with enterprise, however, it was the French who represented the opposite extreme from the Germans and the British, both in style and in theory. The French government, playing its role as the initiator of change and the guardian of harmony in the French economy, had long since grown accustomed to dealing with enterprises branch by branch; and where firms were relatively large, even firm by firm. Numerous explanations have been offered for this national preference. Some stress sociological factors, such as the fact that the elite of big business and the elite of government agencies are drawn from the same social classes and trained in the same schools. Whatever the reasons, the historical preferences of the French seemed as strong in the 1950s as they had ever been.[6]

Accordingly, when the French government had some clear-cut target that could best be performed through the instrumentality of some given firm or consortium, there was no ideological barrier to singling out the firms for the chosen task. Moreover, the firms themselves were quite prepared to accept the existence of tutelary ministries, which concerned themselves as a matter of course with the production plans, the pricing policies, and the financing needs of the enterprise. Though the influence of the ministries varied from one industry to the next, the legitimacy of their exerting such influence was never in serious question.[7] Besides, whatever the individual firms may have thought of the legitimacy of governmental involvement, they had to reckon with the fact that most of the sources of credit in the country were owned or controlled by the government, and that stringent capital controls were in effect at the French border.

Public ownership and control. Another characteristic that distinguished the style of the European states from one another in the 1950s, it will be remembered, was their policies toward the public ownership and operation of business enterprises. Practically every European state entered the 1950s in possession of a number of large public enterprises. Some of these enterprises had been acquired before World War II, such as the predecessors of the Anglo-Iranian Oil Company in Britain, Compagnie Française des Pétroles in France, Ente Nazionale Idrocarburi in Italy, and Volkswagen in Germany. More companies were taken over as enemy property at the end of the war, including Renault and Francolor in France.

In terms of ideology, Germany stood out as a case by itself. In that country, the very question of public ownership was seen as a doctrinal issue: public ownership was a bad thing, creating formal differences in the position of potential competitors and interfering with the play of the market. Not even the German parties with socialist orientation were prepared to make an issue on this point.

In Britain, the issue of public ownership was very much involved in the political process. The test of strength in Britain was applied mainly to the steel industry, which was successively nationalized and denationalized during the 1950s as political fortunes changed. But the ideological division suggested by the struggle over steel was not all that strong. For instance, once the coal industry had been nationalized, it remained so without anything like the struggle that involved the steel industry. Moreover, the fact that the British government owned a controlling interest in Britain's largest oil company, British Petroleum, was allowed to go largely unnoticed throughout the debate; and the enterprise itself was allowed to operate very much as any large private enterprise would have done.

In France and Italy, the ideological aspects of the public-private dichotomy were also fairly subdued. In France, as was suggested earlier, private enterprises worked hand in glove with the ministries, while state-owned enterprises ran on lines that did not readily distinguish them from those in private hands. In Italy, too, the ideological element in the expansion of public sector enterprises was of no great importance. Where some national objective might be served, such as rescuing the ailing shipyard industry, or expanding investment in the south, or controlling foreign sources of petroleum for the Italian market, the public sector was allowed to expand in order to perform the job.[8]

As Europe began the decade of the 1960s, therefore, there were both similarities and differences among the countries that were worth stressing. The economic objectives of most European states were narrowly national, concentrating on stability, growth, and balance among regions and sectors within each nation. The instrumentalities chosen to achieve these objectives were quite diverse, stemming from different ideological preferences and sensitivities. But the period of the 1960s produced some very new emphases.

A Kind of Convergence

At first glance, the policies of the various European states toward their business sectors during the 1960s seem to have very little in common. But the essays of my colleagues in this volume have persuaded me that strong elements of commonality existed. Those elements can be stated boldly in a few propositions.

France played a leading role. Bolstered by strong political leadership and a self-confident bureaucracy, France tested a number of different approaches to its national problems. The first approach, visible through the early 1960s, was the emphasis upon the comprehensive, rational plan, the efficient vehicle for the satisfaction of national demand; the second, ascendant through the middle 1960s, was the growing preoccupation with solving key sectoral and regional issues of a narrower and more specific sort, such as the question of catching up in a lagging technology or bolstering a lagging region; and the third, quixotically and unexpectedly visible in the late 1960s, was a rediscovery of the power of the market, together with a new emphasis on costs, benefits, profits, and losses.

The record suggests that French experience with the first two stages of this three-stage evolution had a very considerable influence on other countries in Europe. Each in its own way and under its own timetable set out to copy some elements of the French pattern. The third phase was something else again; in the early 1970s, that phase was too new for France and too old for the others to suggest many conclusions about its likely course. One could question how long or how deeply France would follow its new leanings; and one could speculate whether France could continue to exercise its role as leader and innovator by espousing a policy that the others had professed for a much longer time. In any event, France's leadership had already developed a kind of convergence in the 1960s which merits a few more words of elaboration.

The comprehensive plan. The French experiment with the comprehensive national plan began with the end of World War II. From the first, French policymakers had no worries about the adequacy of their internal demand to absorb all that their economy could produce; the main task, as far as they were concerned, was to produce more efficiently. With Jean Monnet's modernization plan of 1946, France began experimenting with the formulation of explicit output targets and with the conscious activation of chosen enterprises to achieve those targets. During the 1950s, the characteristic French concern for rationality and coherence pushed its planners toward more detailed targets, as well as more complete tests of their internal consistency. In the end, of course, this approach culminated in the concept of a comprehensive national plan, including targets for domestic outputs, estimates of the imports needed to realize those outputs, identification of the exports needed to finance the imports, and so on. At the same time, the French administrators formalized and extended their practices of consulting with the leaders of industry in formulating the targets and identifying the means of achieving those targets.

During the late 1950s and early 1960s, as the new apparatus of capitalist planning was being put in place in France, the country prospered. Economic growth was rapid; and for once economic growth was achieved without much inflation. From the point of view of other countries with seemingly similar problems, France appeared a model worth emulating.[9]

By 1962, numerous countries had been influenced by the French example enough to adopt some of its features; Belgium, Norway, Italy, and Britain were among those affected. But each adapted France's approach to its own national setting. As a result, though Britain's efforts to create a system of national planning were inspired in part by the French example, they had very little in common with the inspirational source. In the first place, unlike France, Britain was as much concerned with the demand side as with the output side of her economy. Much more than France, Britain saw the need to restrain its national demand from time to time in order to ensure that Britain would remain competitive in world markets and would earn sufficient foreign exchange to support the pound sterling.

In the second place, Britain proved reluctant to introduce a planning system that would be controlled by an official bureaucracy. As the British laboriously built up their national planning machinery in the early 1960s, the topmost body—the National Economic Development Council—emerged at first as a structure in which government, business, and labor had equal representation, together with a secretariat that was independent of the government apparatus. (Later on, it is true, the independent secretariat would disappear; but the tripartite political structure of the NEDC would remain unchanged.) Moreover, British planners had nothing like the powers of implementation of their French counterparts; control over the flow of credit to British industry, for example, was far less complete and less effective than control over credit to French industry.[10]

As other countries drew on the example of French planning during the early 1960s, the great differences in national backgrounds and national propensities became evident once again. For the Italians, French planning had to be interpreted and adapted in light of the fact that governmental efforts to influence the level of national demand could not be expected to work very well. Even so, a consensus in favor of some sort of national planning seemed briefly to appear. For the Dutch and the Swedes, comprehensive planning à la française had to be modified in order to take into account the inescapable openness of their economies and the need to remain upright and watertight in a heaving international sea; for them, therefore, the problem was one of selecting the devices of stabilization that were in harmony with their national social objectives. For the Germans, too overt an adoption of the French approach ran the risk of heresy. The government could deviate from ideological purity to the extent of tolerating a statistical exercise, such as a projection of aggregate demand by industries. But the development of explicit output targets was something else again, a gross interference with the process of the market.[11]

Nonetheless, with all the caveats, the basic point was clear. Most European countries came to realize that there was some utility in looking at the various elements of the national economy all at once, in observing whether internal consistency existed, and in considering how more efficient combinations of national activity might be brought about.

The functional approach. Overall rationality may have its virtues; but no country of Europe, not even France, was convinced that it could solve all its problems by means of a general national plan. Accordingly, even as these countries placed heavier emphasis on the importance of such rationality, none altogether abandoned the practice of dealing ad hoc with narrower problems, problems associated with some specific industry or region or element of the labor force. Here again, it is fair to

say that France seemed to take the lead. Its long tradition of intervention in this case made the leadership role fairly easy.

The efforts of European states to achieve some degree of independence in the fields of high technology illustrate well enough how
problems of this sort were handled.

In the middle and late 1960s, the United States still appeared to be
well ahead of Europe in its ability to command and control the sources
of high technology on which it relied. As Europeans interpreted the
sources of strength of the science-based enterprises in the United States,
two factors were thought to be crucial: the help such enterprises were
getting from the U.S. government;[12] and the strength they seemed to
derive from their very large size. Though some scholars on both sides of
the Atlantic were skeptical that size went hand in hand with efficiency,
official circles usually took the relationship for granted. On the basis of
that assumption, the idea of developing a national champion—an enterprise responsive to its national government's needs and entitled to its
national government's support—began to take root.

The concept of the national champion, of course, was not altogether
new. Situations had existed in earlier decades in which European governments had found it useful to create and equip national enterprises to
do battle against the foreigners. Perhaps the clearest cases were those of
the Anglo-Iranian Oil Company's predecessor and the Compagnie
Française des Pétroles—the first created in 1908, the second in 1924,
with the mission of holding the U.S. oil companies in check and reducing Europe's reliance on American-controlled oil supplies. And there
were other cases as well.

The version of the national champion that appeared in the 1960s,
however, manifested itself in other ways.[13] In addition to creating some
new state-owned or state-financed enterprises, various governments in
Europe set about trying to encourage their existing firms to merge into
large units. As the studies in this volume suggest, the techniques differed
from one country to the next, according to national traditions and governmental powers. The French, with few ideological problems and with
well-developed machinery for the promotion of mergers, were especially
vigorous in developing programs for fusing their national leaders into
effective national champions. In Great Britain efforts to generate
mergers were more awkward and self-conscious, partly because they ran
counter to the traditional grain of government practice. Still, a British
Labour government, operating under somewhat lesser inhibitions than a
Conservative government might have done, overrode usual practice and
created an Industrial Reorganisation Corporation (IRC); and by the
middle of the decade the Corporation was trying to cajole, coerce, or
bribe weak enterprises to join in larger units so that employment could

be ensured, efficiency increased, or innovation stimulated. The Italians displayed similar tendencies; in their case, since the governmental machinery itself was incapable of launching any strong policies, the implementation took place without benefit of direct government support, mostly in the form of new mergers and alliances between the large private firms and the semi-independent public enterprise sector. Germany as usual was odd-man-out, refraining from an official encouragement of mergers; but even in the German case, there was evident satisfaction in official circles at the efforts of leading manufacturers of electrical equipment and leading steel companies to merge themselves into larger units. Special legislation to support the German nuclear power industry, the aerospace industry, and the computer industry was placed on the books. Though German officials continued their ideological affirmations, German policies in the advanced-technology industries and in petroleum began to reflect some of the emphases to be found in France, Britain, and other large countries.[14]

The technique and style by which governments pursued their objectives were quite varied. As usual, the French exercised greater flexibility and ingenuity than the others. Among other things, they very early developed the concept of formulating specific contracts between the government and specified branches of industry. These contracts laid out production targets that the branches agreed to try to achieve, as well as pricing guidelines.[15] So flexible was the French approach that it could offer extraordinary inducements to conforming sectors, such as reduced income tax payments and even (exceptionally) free television time on the state broadcasting system. Practically all countries, however, shared some common techniques. Providing capital on favored terms was one typical device; discriminating in government procurement policies was a second; subsidizing research programs a third. Whatever the method, it implicitly or explicitly embodied one important factor: the exercise of public power to discriminate in favor of chosen national champions. Moreover, since oligopolistic industries were often involved and since the number of large firms in these industries was very small, several countries pursued a policy of limiting the role of foreign-owned firms in the country in order to give their own champions greater opportunities.[16]

The emergent frustrations. The upshot of these ad hoc emphases, alas, was not quite what the national policymakers intended. At least, that is how I read the evidence of my colleagues. One reason for the seeming miscarriage of intentions is the fact that the formulation and execution of ad hoc policies have demanded a certain slackening of control from the center and a considerable diffusion of power: diffusion in planning, in direction, and in execution of the various disparate policies. That diffusion has taken somewhat different forms in different countries of Europe. But it is in evidence practically everywhere. And

the diffusion generally has led to a breakdown of the boundaries between the traditional ideology-oriented groups in the various national
economies.

In France, the diffusion was especially visible, since it was embodied
in the tutelary relationships between business and the ministries. The
manifold contracts, loans, purchases, and other arrangements between
each of the ministries and its clientele have been a feature of French
governance for a very long time. In Britain, the special deals epitomized
by the operations of the IRC and the deliberations of various committees under the NEDC have been an Anglicized version of the French
machinery, albeit a pale and ineffectual one. In Germany, the methods
of diffusion have been more arcane, but no less real: the intervention of
banking interests, of extraparliamentary committees, of alliances between business and labor groups in various industries. In Italy, new
alliances have bracketed the public enterprises with private enterprises
in unprecedented combinations. In Sweden, one saw a different process,
an actual sharpening of traditional ideological boundary lines; but
Sweden was the exceptional case.

Processes of this sort, it was once supposed, could create the *économie concertée,* the efficient national apparatus based on some sort of
consensus as to goals as well as the means for their achievement. If I am
interpreting my colleagues correctly, however, a different kind of outcome seems to have been common in Europe. The principle of the
squeaking wheel seems to have prevailed. An inordinate share of effort
and of treasure has been poured into ad hoc programs that were essentially palliative in nature. Programs that were intended to modernize and
strengthen the economy were starved, while public resources were
directed mainly to support ailing shipyards, declining coal mines, and
uncreative mechanical industries. Though public subsidies sometimes
went to the support of more dynamic sectors, these proved to be much
the lesser part of the largesse coming from the public purse. What is
more, some of the industry studies in this volume support a painful
generalization: even when the subsidies seemed directed toward the
more dynamic sectors, they often made little or no contribution to the
growth of those sectors.

There are hints in some of the studies, though no more than hints,
that the diffusion of political power and political control may have
benefited one other group in European industry. In the oligopolistic
industries, the process of negotiating with national governments may
well have produced higher prices and higher wages than an impersonal
and unrestricted European market would have afforded. In any event,
whatever the underlying process may have been, both prices and wages
in these industries tended to rise faster throughout Europe than the
national authorities had intended. And it was commonly observed that

insofar as genuine competition existed in European markets, it did not appear very often either in the lagging sectors of the Continent or in the sectors in which strong national oligopolies existed.

By the late 1960s, according to my interpretation of my colleagues' studies, the expectations which had inspired the concept of the *économie concertée* were not being realized. Stuart Holland's analysis of Europe's public enterprises reflects his wistful hope that these enterprises could have turned the trick, if only they had had the proper political guidance. But the analysis of the others offers little support for that view. Instead, they seem to suggest that the diverse activities of the individual sectors, whether dominated by public enterprise or by private, were not adding up to a consistent pattern. Public authority had been parceled out among committees, organizations, and enterprises throughout the economy; public oversight and public control had been diffused and diluted; parliamentary powers had been weakened. And the results had not been encouraging in social terms. Perhaps that is why, when the 1970s began, France seemed on the verge of a new flirtation with the well-worn ideas of Marshall and Pareto.

The European Approach

What did all these developments, which were essentially national in their focus, have to do with the evolution of a European movement? The relationships were not simple. But, on the whole, it appears that many of the national developments just described were at odds with the idea of a pan-European economy, and that many of the measures taken by national governments have handicapped the future development of that idea.

Europe and the national plan. One of the first appearances of major conflict came in the early 1960s, with the elaboration of consistent national plans. During that period, while the individual countries of Europe were preoccupied with developing sharper tools for the management of their national economies, Europe itself was changing rapidly. The consequences of the creation of the European Economic Community (EEC), and to a lesser extent of the EFTA, were becoming visible in the rapid growth of foreign trade and investment. Though the internal national transactions of the economies of Europe were also expanding at an impressive rate, their foreign transactions—especially their transactions with other Europeans—were expanding faster still.[17]

The growth in the relative importance of foreign trade and investment ran counter to a basic premise that underlay most national planning. In the case of French planning, for instance, it was assumed that the spark which would generate the necessary flame for national growth would be lit inside the economy. Changes in imports and exports and in foreign investment, according to this conception, would be a controllable consequence, not a moving cause, of the process. Otherwise, of course, both the dimensions of national growth and the composition of such growth would be hard to control.

To be sure, French planners in the early 1960s had not altogether overlooked the possibility that the increasing openness of national borders might make difficulties for the French planning process, nor the possibility that outside forces might also prove to be a source of unplanned dynamism for the economy. But the strength of the outside forces seems to have been underestimated, just as it was misjudged in Britain, Italy, and various other countries. For instance, the success of the French automobile industry in building up its exports during those years is said to have been unanticipated, hence disconcerting, for French national planners.[18]

During the early and middle 1960s, various countries tried out a succession of responses to the problems generated by the increasing porosity of their borders. One such response, visible in several countries, was a tightening up in the screening of foreign investment. However, the trouble with the response, as France learned soon enough, was that any country which sought to follow a policy of controlling the foreign firms ran a risk: the risk that the firms would set themselves up in another location and would export their products to the regulated area. In short, the limitations that any one country sought to place on foreign investment were counterproductive unless the country was in a position also to restrict its importations.[19]

France had a special problem with foreign direct investment.[20] The particularistic approach by which the French bureaucracy undertook to implement its plans required in effect that the bureaucracy should be able to communicate readily and effectively with the leaders of industry. Foreign-owned enterprises, needless to say, were somewhat less sensitive than French firms to messages from the national bureaucracy, and were sometimes well positioned to ignore the messages they received. The access of such enterprises to alternative sources of financing outside the French economy, for example, deprived the bureaucracy of a potent lever in affecting business decisions.

The responses of each of the European states to the problems presented by foreign-owned enterprises were unique in certain respects. For the Germans, the problem was not very acute, since they professed an ideological preference for identifying problems in general terms and for applying general measures of response. Accordingly, the fact that foreign-owned enterprises might not be easily amenable to some prescribed set of output goals had no great bearing. The British too were inhibited by a long-standing ideological distaste for ad hoc regulation. Despite that leaning, there were some signs in the middle 1960s that foreign-owned enterprises, such as Chrysler and Westinghouse, might be obliged to accept a number of limitations on their management prerogatives; but on the whole, the British reactions were relatively restrained. Italy's responses were obscure or nonexistent, probably because of the general inability of the government to introduce any major innovations in policy at the time.[21] As for the smaller countries, they tended to see the direct control of foreign investment as irrelevant or downright harmful, given their general conviction that small countries dared not employ autarchic measures without the risk of social loss.

Confronted with the need to deal with the foreign investment problem while maintaining open boundaries in Europe, France responded characteristically. The government proposed a common policy on the subject for the whole EEC area, but a policy that would not reduce the autonomy of French planners. What France was looking for was a European-wide system of assurances that if France laid restrictive conditions upon a foreign investor, the others would not undercut the French position by offering better terms. Philosophically, that sort of relationship between France and the others in the EEC was quite in accord with de Gaulle's larger conception at the time of a *famille des patries,* and it illustrated the well-known point that the harmonization of national policies in Europe did not necessarily contribute to European integration.

In the perspective of the 1970s, it is obvious that none of these efforts of the middle 1960s to shore up the idea of the independent comprehensive national plan had much chance of succeeding; the contradiction between independent national plans of that sort and open national boundaries was simply too strong. On the other hand, though the EEC had the power to undermine national plans, it did not have the capability to substitute a pan-European planning device that would supplement or supersede the national plans. The EEC had no structure through which the political interests and the pressure groups could express themselves. It had no effective powers by which to persuade or coerce either individual firms and sectors *à la française* or broad classes of firms *à l'anglaise.* It could dispose of neither credit nor subsidies nor tax exemptions nor procurement contracts nor the sense of shared values of the old boys' clubs that were to be found in the individual countries of Europe.

Some of these tools might perhaps have been provided to the EEC if the ground had been prepared and the will existed. The EEC treaty itself, for instance, could conceivably have offered philosophical and administrative guidelines applicable to the planning process. But the drafters of the treaty had consciously avoided such issues where they could, concentrating mainly on the elimination of national barriers to economic union. The most relevant section of the treaty, Articles 85 to 89, dealt merely with the avoidance of restrictive business practices and the abuse of dominant positions. And though the articles were quite remarkable in scope and content, it was clear that their purpose was limited mainly to ensuring that the internal market of the EEC was not partitioned by private agreements.

Besides, at least in the early 1960s, there were the political views of de Gaulle to be reckoned with. Partly in response to those views, the concept of the European atomic energy policy had been stopped dead, the concept of a European energy policy had been placed in deep freeze, and the application of a European competition policy had been slowed to a crawl.[22] For the time being, therefore, the EEC had to be thought of as an unlikely agent through which the emerging frustrations over the limitations of national planning could be overcome.

Europe and the functional approach. When the European nations began to realize that the national plan was unlikely to contribute much to the solution of particular problems of a functional sort, one might have hoped that the time for a pan-European approach was at hand. In fact, the development of a common agricultural policy in the EEC, an outstanding political achievement, offered a certain justification for that expectation.

On the whole, however, the shift to functional problem-solving seemed to create fresh obstacles to a European approach. Each nation inevitably tended to identify such problems in terms of its own national political environment. The problems with highest priority tended to relate to a region or a class in the national economy that possessed some special measure of political clout, or to some psychic need that other countries did not necessarily share. The usual solution involved the selection of some reliable national agents who would carry out spot investments in a lagging region, or fix a price in some key commodity, or undertake some other task of importance to the state. As it became evident that the EEC itself was unlikely to be allowed to respond to needs of this sort, the desires of individual nations to provide for these needs were strengthened even further.[23]

The institutions that European states developed to deal with their functional problems seemed on the whole to pose some added obstacles to the pan-European approach. The committees and alliances that were given a quasi-public role in solving national problems could hardly be expected to coordinate their activities with other European groups unless there was a strong compulsion to do so. And the individual firm in the role of national champion appeared even more nation-oriented in concept and purpose.

The Champion and Europe

During the 1960s a number of European states had developed national champions in order to deal with various national problems. One such problem had been to create independent sources of technology in the advanced industries.

The studies in this volume as well as numerous independent sources indicate that the results of these efforts have been exceedingly spotty.[24] As various failures became apparent in the late 1960s, governments and enterprises cast about for new policies which might respond to some of their needs. Out of this search, a number of collaborative efforts developed in Europe, bordering at times upon a pan-European approach. Once again, however, the failures have been much more in evidence than the successes.

One problem throughout has been that of motivation. The disposition toward pooling on the part of the Europeans has been weak and wavering. Even when European governments have been willing to attempt some limited measure of collaboration in the high-technology fields, as in the case of Concorde, Airbus, and ESRO, they have been reluctant to pool their producing organizations or their national markets. Industrial innovation, they have generally insisted, should be handled by organizations that are national in character; and no prospective innovator should be entitled to think of his market as the whole of Europe. As long as the buyers were largely from the public sector, the markets were cut up in watertight national units.[25]

The result has been that the European entrants in the high-technology race have been badly handicapped. The Americans and the Japanese ordinarily develop their innovations mainly as a result of the stimulus offered by their home markets rather than by Europe. With the costs of innovation largely covered by sales in the home market, their fortunes in Europe are not absolutely critical to the innovation process. That lesson is driven home time and again: in aircraft, in nuclear reactors, in computers, and so on. The Europeans, by contrast, often find the prospect of a small national market insufficient to stimulate the innovation that their governments hope they will pursue. Even when two or more European firms join together in order to innovate, the partnership does very little to enlarge market opportunities. Technological innovation, an EEC report on the aerospace industry observes ruefully, "has no real effect unless, at the market level, it responds sufficiently to explicit or underlying needs."[26]

A second problem is related to the first. European enterprises, sensing the hesitation of their national authorities, are quite unwilling to merge their identity with European enterprises of another nationality. Instead, they generally prefer to look for more equivocal alliances: for partnerships that will allow them to exploit some of the potential economies of scale without merging their corporate strategies and corporate identities. To the extent that corporate strategies are coordinated, they are carefully designed to preserve and protect the identity of the participants in the agreement. For the most part, therefore, they represent mainly commitments not to compete.[27]

As a result, corporate partnerships across national boundaries, such as Dunlop-Pirelli and Fiat-Citroën, have often combined some of the less useful aspects of several different worlds. They have reduced the uncertainty that each of the partners previously confronted, thereby lowering rather than increasing the stimulus that often lies at the root of industrial innovation. At the same time, they have not greatly enlarged the perceptions of market opportunity that each of the partners confronted; at best, they have offered a more specialized market to each of the partners.

Of course, partnerships of this sort, if they survive for very long, do not stand still. By nibbling away hesitantly at various cooperative ventures over a long period of time, such partnerships may gradually evolve into an integrated enterprise, as has happened over the decades with Unilever and with Royal Dutch–Shell and as seems gradually to be happening with Agfa-Gevaert. But that process, if history is any guide, is slow and uncertain.[28]

The responses of large European enterprises and their governments to the possibilities of transnational mergers, therefore, have been ambivalent. Projects for collaboration in the high-technology fields have had the air of improvisation and tentativeness that goes with one-shot undertakings. The key figures in these projects could not assume that they might continue in their roles indefinitely. Accordingly, there has been very little incentive to develop an organizational store of knowledge and an organizational memory that would survive beyond the termination of the project. It is as if Europe had deliberately taken on itself the Sisyphean burden, every time it launched a high-technology project, of reproducing the whole learning process that every complex organization must experience.

That unfortunate feature of Europe's transnational projects has been buttressed by another: the notorious principle of *le juste retour*. On the insistence of France, but with the quiet support of other countries, each nation has been guaranteed that it would receive some proportion of the business generated by individual projects, according to a formula that reflected the financial commitment of each of the states. As a result, some of the economies of scale that otherwise might have been achieved have been lost; and some of the anxieties that otherwise might have spurred competing participants have been eliminated.

These aspects of persistent nationalism in the high-technology industries have been exacerbated when the participants were state-owned enterprises. Stuart Holland's analysis of the role of public enterprises in this volume confirms the obvious, namely, that enterprises of this sort are concerned mainly with national issues. Difficult as the problem of collaboration and merger might be in the privately owned enterprises, therefore, it has been even a bit more difficult when the stockholders of the enterprises were the several states and the managers were the servants of their respective states.[29]

With the centripetal forces so weak in Europe among the leading high-technology firms, the centrifugal forces have had a greater impact.[30] Europe's leading firms, searching for allies to help them in the internal jockeying in the European market, have tended to take on the strongest partners they could find. These often have been the Americans. In the computer industry, firms such as Honeywell and General Electric were useful in this role; in the aerospace industry, notably in the development of power plants, General Electric, and Pratt and Whitney; in the nuclear power industry, Westinghouse and General Electric; and so on.[31]

The tendency to reach outside of Europe for partners, it sometimes seems, has been strengthened by the preferences of European governments and European businessmen themselves.[32] Confronted with the choice of an American partner or a European partner, many firms in Europe appear to prefer the American. The preference may be based in part upon the assumption that an American partner, being an *auslander* in the European community, is more readily subject to the control of the government in whose territory it is situated and less able to claim the privileges of an unambiguous European. Whatever the reason, that preference has been visible at times in Italy, Germany, and France, and it shows no sign of declining in the years immediately ahead.

The tendency for Europeans to create alliances with interests outside of Europe has been fortified by the nature of modern technology in the more advanced sectors. Technology of that sort has become so complex and so specialized that few economies can hope to generate all the elements for a successful end-product from sources within their borders. For some seemingly mature technologies, such as the large-scale generation and transmission of high-voltage electricity, the economy of Europe itself may no longer be sufficient.[33] The issue that is raised, therefore, is whether a European-wide policy of self-sufficiency with respect to many of the fields of high technology is any longer a feasible alternative. It may be that events have overrun a hesitant and reluctant Europe; that the instrumentalities which are used to promote the high-technology industries of Europe in the end will have to be worldwide in structure. Some of my colleagues are not so sure of this conclusion, anticipating that effective European collaboration, perhaps even leading to a European champion, may still be possible. But I do not see much evidence to support that hope, at least not so far.

The idea of the European champion, however, is not limited to the high-technology industries. Europeans also harbor a strong desire to control their own basic industrial activities, whether or not high technology is involved. In industries such as petroleum, copper, steel, aluminum, and paper, the barrier to entry that newcomers must hurdle is not the mastery of an esoteric technology. Though technology may have been the hurdle in an earlier era, the present barrier to entry in such industries is that of sheer scale—the difficulties of assembling the capital, establishing the sources of raw material, developing the organization, and capturing the markets necessary for any major facility. At the present stage of their development, industries of this sort tend to be capital-intensive; and major additions to the industry are generally accompanied by substantial rearrangements of materials and markets.

The sheer size of the production facilities in such industries gives them a special place in national planning. With very few producers in the world, national planners do not wish to be dependent on oligopolists of other nationalities. At the same time, a single national facility can represent a major source of employment or exports, a veritable *pôle de croissance*.

Europe's response to this situation, as noted earlier, might once have been pan-European in its approach. For instance, in 1950 the European Coal and Steel Community represented a European response to a European problem; eight years later, the European Economic Community and Euratom were framed in the same spirit; and in 1964 a European energy policy was proposed in very much the same mood. But the mood was perishable. As J.E.S. Hayward's study in this volume indicates, the policy of the European Coal and Steel Community was rapidly reshaped into a negotiated truce among the national coal and steel industries, a truce whose national character was underlined by the unambiguously national identity of most of the companies concerned. Euratom came into existence in name only, and the European energy policy was stillborn. More recently, as shortage and surplus have appeared in one raw material or another, the every-man-for-himself instinct has repeatedly surfaced among the European countries.[34]

Another major problem has interfered with the concept of pan-Europeanism in these industries. In the postwar period, as the industry studies show, leading American firms became well entrenched inside the economy of Europe. What is more, a complex system of partnerships, alliances, and conventions generally developed between the American and the European leaders in some of these industries, aimed at ensuring that they would move in step with one another and would avoid any outbreak of virulent competition. The threat of ruinous competition was especially strong for industries of this sort because of their capital intensity and their attendant economies of scale. With high fixed costs and low variable costs, there was always the chance that some undisciplined member of the industry might break away from the prevailing patterns of market behavior in order to improve his position in the market. Occasional disruptions in the world markets of these basic industries have reminded the participants that these risks were not merely theoretical.

The motivations that have led major European firms to form alliances with the American intruders have also encouraged them to make investments outside of Europe. In oil, the British, French, Dutch, Belgian, Swiss, American, and Italian firms are to be found all over the world, engaged in complex maneuvers that reflect their interdependency. Sometimes they are found in partnerships, sometimes as parties to long-term contracts, sometimes in a common allegiance to a set of pricing conventions. At other times in the search for stability, the leading firms have followed strategies analogous to the exchange of hostages or to the follow-the-leader principle. Partly as a result of such strategies, the extra-European investments of the leading European firms in the oil, aluminum, and copper industries had come by the early 1970s to represent a considerable fraction of their total investment.[35]

Whatever the exact motives, the strategies of some European enterprises are becoming global in scope. Producers from the United States, Canada, Japan, and even at times the Soviet Union, are integrally involved in their planning. Occasionally, the Europeans have approached the outsiders with a coordinated European position. That sort of approach, for instance, has recently been apparent in steel. But coordination has been exceptional; and even where it has existed, it has been the coordination characteristic of a loose alliance of interests, not of an integrated European entity. To some extent, however, the looseness of the alliance has been unavoidable. As long as outside suppliers or outside investors were permitted to have a role in the European market in these products, each nation could be expected to see its interests in rather a different light.

European governments, it should be noted, have sometimes given their enterprises positive encouragement in setting up outposts in other economies. But there has been no disposition to allow national enterprises to dilute their national identity. Though cooperative ventures with enterprises of different countries may be acceptable, schemes that would place the identity of a national enterprise in jeopardy, such as bids by foreigners to take over local enterprises, have been increasingly resisted by European governments. That resistance has applied not only to the take-over bids of Americans, but also to those of other Europeans.[36] So the search for global solutions has not been synonymous with a willingness to submerge the national identity of business enterprises in a European or global organization.

Still, the need for global solutions has been repeatedly recognized. The European response to an oversupply of aluminum in 1972 has been to activate an organization that sought to include Japanese interests within its structure and that enlisted the cooperation of Soviet exporting interests.[37] The oil crisis of 1970 was dealt with at Teheran through an agreement that included the major multinational enterprises of the noncommunist world. Accordingly, even though European governments find it hard to develop and support pan-European positions in some of their basic industries, they still tend to look benignly on the global arrangements in which their leading enterprises commonly participate.

A European Industrial Policy

So far, the development of a European industrial policy has been inhibited by many factors. The variety of national approaches to questions of market competition and of public ownership, which this collection of papers illustrates, represents a major obstacle. So does the unwillingness of the individual states to pool the powers on which they rely to execute their national purposes.

So far, if the past experience of the European movement is any guide, these problems do not present unsurmountable obstacles; the movement toward European unity is better described by the Hegelian paradox than by a straight line.

There is one kind of problem, however, whose solution may require more than the simple surmounting of national obstacles. As the last few pages have suggested, the time may well have passed when policies can any longer be made effectively at the European level without taking into account Europe's deep interdependencies with other parts of the world. The problem of interdependency is particularly evident in the mature oligopolistic industries. Any European regime that seeks to influence the competitive behavior of those industries—whether in pricing, production, investment, or innovation—will have to take into account the extensive entanglements of European firms with leaders headquartered outside of Europe. The costs and benefits of a European policy will always have to be weighed in terms of the outside repercussions. So oil, copper, aluminum, nickel, paper—perhaps also heavy chemicals, standard machinery, and automobiles—become industries in which anything less than a global approach to industrial policy can generate consequences that may defeat the purpose of the policy. Though the studies in this volume were completed before the stark emergence of the oil crisis in the winter of 1973–74, the evolution of that crisis simply serves to fortify that general point.

A similar observation may be made about the high-technology industries. Europe's pace and style in creating a European technology policy have been so slow and so inhibited that few European enterprises are likely to count upon such a policy for strong sustenance and support. Besides, the nature of modern technology often demands networks larger than Europe can provide: a network for the assembly of relevant information on design and production; and a network of market outlets sufficiently large to absorb the development costs of the product. Accordingly, any EEC-wide policy for the high-technology industries may have to confront the fact that the European-based enterprises cannot effectively implement an autarchic policy for the EEC.[38]

These observations point in a common direction. A Europe of Nine represents one of the largest markets of the world, a market that is badly in need of common internal industrial policies. But autarchic tendencies in its industrial policy would involve considerable costs. To avoid such costs, extensive measures of harmonization and coordination with other countries of the world are likely to be indicated.

Europe's New Public Enterprises

In the early 1960s it appeared that a first postwar wave of nationalizations in Europe had come to an end, and that the use of the public enterprise had given way to other and more flexible forms of public intervention in the modern capitalist economy. Nationalization of the first-generation type had taken whole sectors into public ownership or had salvaged failing concerns in the private sector. To all intents and purposes such first-generation nationalization seemed dead and buried. Many of the nationalized concerns had failed to show profits at all or at least profits comparable with those secured in the private sector. The substitution of public for private ownership had not resulted in a difference in worker-management relations, and it had not inspired a new ethos in the operation of enterprise.

Secondary Roles for First-Generation Public Enterprise

Most of the public enterprise which had been created by 1950 was concentrated in secondary sectors, such as mining, power generation and distribution, transport, telephone and postal communications, steel, and heavy engineering. These were sectors that derived their demand from the stimuli applied by other parts of the economy. The primary initiation of demand lay partly with private consumers but mainly with the downstream manufacturing sectors and modern service sectors, and these remained for the most part in private ownership.[1] In practice this meant the servicing of mainly private enterprise by public enterprise.

The pattern of employing public enterprise to serve the private enterprise sector was not altogether accidental. Several of the basic industrial and service sectors had been brought into public ownership to limit the monopoly power that was being applied to the detriment of manufacturing and service consumers or the general public. The intention was to have the nationalized enterprises operate more in the interest of the rest of the economy.

A primary motivation within the socialist or social democratic parties of the Left had been the takeover of these sectors at a time when they could be said to have constituted the "commanding heights" of the economy. But, in fact, by the time the main parties of the Left had any

Dr. Stuart Holland is a member of the Faculty of the School of European Studies, University of Sussex, Brighton, England.

chance to nationalize them, such sectors had already been overtaken by the more elevated heights of modern manufacturing and services. Moreover, even when the nationalized sectors had secured a monopolistic hold on their domestic markets, this had not prevented the rise of entirely new industries whose products or services could be substituted for the older monopolistic concerns, such as oil for coal, road for rail transport, and aluminum and plastics for steel.

In some cases, the enterprises that were taken over had suffered from long periods of undercapitalization and insufficient modernization. As a result, some of the immediate prewar and postwar nationalization amounted to a salvage operation. The objects of the salvage were remnants of the commanding heights of the late nineteenth century rather than flourishing up-to-date concerns. In other cases, such as the nationalization of the holdings of some of the main joint-stock banks in Italy in 1933, the public takeover was a salvage operation pure and simple, designed to prevent economic collapse.[2]

Another reason for nationalization in the immediate postwar period was punitive. In France, enterprise was nationalized when it had been clearly identified with collaboration, as in the case of Renault and Berliet. A further reason was to promote growth and technology—in particular to assure that research and development in advanced technology were maintained within national frontiers. This was most clearly the case with nuclear-power engineering in Britain, but also to a certain extent the case in the same countries in airframe and aero-engine design and manufacture.

Not all of the nationalizations before 1950 resulted in the creation of state monopolies substituting for private monopolies. In France the punitive nationalizations of the immediate postwar period generated ambiguous patterns. The enterprises involved did not constitute monopolies, nor did their identity suggest other economic reasons for nationalization. They were mainly a consequence of the commitments of the wartime resistance movement (in which the Communists had played a crucial part). A number of mixed public-private enterprises also had been created in France from 1924–25 onward, including international transport, pipelines for oil transport, and railway and other construction projects overseas.[3] In Italy, the state holding company, Istituto per la Ricostruzione Industriale (IRI), by taking over the assets of the three nationalized banks in 1933, found itself in control of a wide-ranging number of companies. These companies accounted for major proportions of the employment and output in particular sectors such as steel, shipbuilding, electricity generation, and telephone services, but only minor proportions of other sectors such as engineering. In both West Germany and Italy, ministers still exercised ultimate formal control but made use of holding companies like the United Industries Companies and IRI; that fact tended to place distance between management and ministers, thereby reducing ministerial intervention in the day-to-day running of the companies.

There were, then, five main reasons for the first generation of nationalizations in Western Europe: socialist economic policy; social or consumer interests; salvage of uncompetitive concerns; punitive nationalization of wartime collaborators; and promotion of advanced technology. Only the second and fifth of these reasons gave clear general guidelines for the role of public enterprise. The first reason, to promote a socialist ideology, might have meant more if the Labour government had not lost power in Britain in 1951 and if the Communists had not left the postwar coalition government in France. But the incoming Conservative government clearly had no vested interest in promoting public enterprise as a socialist instrument in the 1950s, and the variety of Fourth Republic governments in France did not hold power long enough to pursue a coherent public enterprise policy. In West Germany and Italy the conservative Christian Democratic governments regarded their prewar public-enterprise inheritance as something which should be sold to private shareholders as soon as possible; or, where this was not possible because of poor profit performance, something which should by and large be managed like private enterprise. In addition, a high proportion of the British Labour party, which had pushed through the nationalization program of 1945–1951, was losing confidence in the desirability of further extensions of public ownership, and this lack of confidence was shared by many Social Democrats in West Germany, Benelux, and Scandinavia.[4]

The Postwar Primacy of Keynesian Policies

One of the reasons for declining confidence in public enterprise was the "Keynesian revolution," the acceptance of a new policy approach to management of the economy. This basically entailed two main instruments for coping with the underemployment of resources: direct government expenditure and indirect stimulation of private expenditure through monetary and fiscal policy. In the immediate postwar period, the reconstruction of infrastructure and basic industry in most of western Europe necessitated major public expenditure. But after the end of the 1940s, direct public expenditure gave way in most West European economies to the increasing use of monetary and fiscal stimulants.[5]

A variety of factors appear to have influenced this change of emphasis in government policies. In West Germany, one of the most important was the identification of direct public expenditure with Nazi economic policy. Both Nazi policy and socialist Left policy, to the extent that they were committed to extending public ownership, saw such a step as helpful to a centrally planned economy. For the Nazis, state enterprise would complement private enterprise in what would remain essentially a market economy. For the Left in Italy and France, the market mechanism would have to be replaced in due course by a centrally planned socialist system.

Central planning means controls, and one of the main features of the immediate postwar economies in western Europe had been the maintenance of controls over commodities in short supply. But the pressure to relax controls and revert to allocation through the market was extremely strong. Most governments gave way to it either through lack of conviction in the merits of controls or through conscious endorsement of liberalization of resources.[6] The initial difficulties in managing some of the newly nationalized industries, exacerbated by postwar shortage conditions, helped further erode the public-enterprise approach to economic management. In addition, it rapidly grew clear that monopolistic public enterprise confronted a dilemma. When prices were kept relatively low for consumer-welfare or public-interest reasons, the flow of internal funds available for future investment was reduced. This increased external borrowing, entailing added costs that had to be met in one form or another by the public. Besides, when costs were not covered from receipts, investment criteria became more difficult. The techniques which were available for estimating the real return to the investments of public monopolies could provide effective guidelines for single projects; but they were much less effective when the interrelationship of various projects—both public and private—had to be estimated. Lacking a conventional market in which to test their proposals, the public-enterprise planners were put in the position of trying to work out what a market mechanism would have done to provide a guideline for their investment decisions.[7] On top of that, the planners had to take into account not only the benefits to the enterprise but also the social benefits of their proposed investments.

While public-enterprise pricing and investment were running into difficulties in sectors such as power generation and distribution, the private sectors in the main European economies on the Continent were experiencing a boom in investment and productivity on a scale virtually unprecedented in western Europe. Without doubt the Marshall Plan was of considerable direct help immediately after the war in enabling the main economies to secure key investment goods. But one of the most important factors in the high and sustained growth of most of the continental European countries was the indirect role of OEEC, which coordinated the European Recovery Program. That organization spread the new Keynesian orthodoxies that governments could manage aggregate demand through fiscal and monetary policies and could thereby prevent a repetition of the interwar slump.

New Problems: Trade Liberalization, Regional Imbalance, and the Multinational Challenge

The postwar reconstruction boom was intensified by the Korean War and came to a peak in the mid-1950s. By 1958 there had been a marked fall in the "miracles" represented by the growth of West Germany, Italy, and France. If the opening of the European Economic Community (EEC) in January 1959 had not.provided a stimulus to investment, these economies might have experienced a severe and prolonged slump. On the other hand, the liberalization of trade by the EEC and the reduction of barriers to the movement of capital and labor entailed costs for some of the member countries. These included the reduction of control over the national balance of payments and countercyclical policy, the aggravation of the difficulties of persuading private-enterprise companies to locate in lagging regions and areas, and an intensification of the challenge to national economic sovereignty from multinational enterprises.

In practice the degree of control which some of the main member countries had been able to exercise over their trade balance had been relatively limited. But in France, in particular, the use of tariffs as instruments for balancing trade is said to have played an important part in the first three national plans from 1947 to 1961. The instruments, according to various reports, had operated through the leading national companies. Such companies were under the constant threat that trade in their sector would be liberalized if they did not follow the wishes of their tutelary ministry. Such a tactic clearly involved an element of bluff since trade liberalization in the sense of allowing more imports would tend to aggravate the trade-balance problem itself. But the tactic was apparently used with success. After the opening of the EEC in 1959 this was no longer possible because of the agreement to reduce common internal tariffs by stages and progressively to substitute a common external tariff for the member states' individual tariff systems.[8]

Both Italy and France ran into major balance-of-payments problems within four or five years of the opening of the EEC. For Italy this was the first payments problem since the early 1950s. Though rectified within eighteen months, it served notice that the "miracle" growth rate of the fifties could encounter payments problems, and it warned the Italian government of the need to secure more effective instruments for both balance-of-payments and countercyclical policy. In France the government also found itself obliged to impose a deflationary policy. Though the decision was incompletely applied and though some of the major long-term projects of the planning officials were spared, the incident served notice that new approaches would be needed to maintain equilibrium in the country.

In the early years after the opening of the EEC the problem of unequal regional growth in economies such as Italy and France does not appear to have been aggravated to any major extent. If savings were being siphoned from the poor areas and leaving labor behind in those areas, the process was not immediately visible. But the opening of the EEC did offer increased leverage to private firms that wished to resist being pushed into such areas. These firms were in a position to insist that they either would take measures to cope more effectively with the trade challenge in the Community, or they would set up new plants in peripheral national regions, but not both. The unwillingness of the French authorities to take a tough line on regional policy with their national champions in the face of EEC competition was reflected in the laxness of their controls over the expansion of plant in the greater Paris region. In Italy it was reflected in the low degree of pressure brought on Fiat and other leading private companies to locate more jobs in the South.

The other main problem from trade and factor liberalization policies in the EEC economies was the intensification of the multinational enterprises' challenge to national economic sovereignty. Such a challenge by multinational enterprises based in the United States has already been widely recognized as a paradox. United States companies' know-how and management frequently challenged the security of national oligopolies and contributed to higher exports. There were a variety of negative effects implicit in their operations as well. According to a 1969 report of the EEC Commission, the high credit-worthiness of such enterprises in the Eurodollar market meant that they could circumvent a policy of monetary restraint within individual national economies. By transfer pricing, or the setting of prices in transactions between different affiliates of the same enterprise in different countries, they could avoid taxes. Because their production in any plant was geared to an international division and specialization among different subsidiaries, they could not be easily integrated into a national industrial policy. At the same time, they could preempt the development of a national industrial capacity in a particular area, especially in high-technology fields, and they could buy out a leading national company and remove it from the traditional sphere of government economic influence. They commonly set off one government against another in such a way as to secure unusual concessions on taxation and capital assistance. When transfer prices were used to reduce profits, the practice also had a negative influence on the balance of payments, including both the understatement of exports and the overstatement of imports; and the absence of competition between subsidiaries could blunt the effect of devaluation as an export stimulant.[9]

Whatever the relative weight of the positive and negative factors involved, there is no doubt that by the early 1970s governments had increasingly come to realize that there were both benefits and costs in the multinationalization of enterprise. They also had come to appreciate that the cost side of the equation had been increased by the international liberalization undertaken in the EEC.[10]

The Policy Response: Primary Roles for
Second-Generation Public Enterprise

The new problems of economic management and government economic sovereignty posed by the opening of the EEC and the intensification of the multinational challenge resulted in the 1960s in new roles for public enterprise. One role was as the instrument for offsetting the effects of the liberalization of trade, by providing more specific import-substituting and export-promoting investment. Another was to supply a channel for government expenditure to offset recessionary trends and sustain high aggregate growth. A further role was to ensure the location of more investment and jobs in regions of low employment growth or actual employment decline. Other roles included: undertaking long-term, high-risk projects which private enterprise was unwilling to venture; maintaining effective competition in oligopolistic sectors not exposed to foreign competition; and, finally, coping with multinational enterprises.

These factors assumed different degrees of importance and public-enterprise response in the particular West European economies.

Italy. The pace-setting economy in using public enterprise as a policy-response instrument was Italy.* Even before the creation of IRI in 1933, Italy had nationalized insurance, the railways, and the post office. But, in general, until the latter 1950s, the IRI companies were dependent on demand from private enterprises for the bulk of their output. The same was the case for ENI, formed in 1954, which secured a monopoly on exploitation of natural gas in Italy and used its profits to finance the importation, refining, and distribution of oil and petroleum products.[11]

As long as IRI and ENI (Ente Nazionale Idrocarburi) were concentrated in the basic industrial and natural-resource sectors, their potential as instruments for fulfilling some of the half-dozen tasks just mentioned was relatively limited. But both groups eventually gave a new dimension

---

* For a rather different interpretation of Italian public enterprise, see the chapter by Romano Prodi in this volume.

to the use of public enterprise in support of government economic policy. For instance, in a country with virtually no raw materials for steelmaking, IRI built shore-based, integrated steel plants which were in a position to secure iron ore and coking coal at the lowest world prices and to effect major balance-of-payments savings by reducing the imports of finished steel. This lesson was to be later applied to more sophisticated sectors such as telephone equipment, computers, nuclear power plants, satellite components and tracking stations, and passenger aircraft; in all these cases, the government employed the IRI or ENI holdings to produce and develop equipment which otherwise would have been imported, frequently developing joint ventures with leading foreign companies as the means of securing the needed technology.

The Italian government also has used its holding companies as direct instruments for countercyclical policies. During recession, the companies have been required to maintain or accelerate some of the investment on which they had already agreed as part of the national economic plan covering 1971 to 1975. By the early 1970s the Italian state holdings were still not large enough to have been able to prevent an overall recession in the Italian economy. But from 1968 to 1971 public investment rose from a third to a half of gross fixed capital formation in industry, with a clear countercyclical effect. The most important implication of the Italian government's experience was that state enterprise gave a more direct vehicle for the channeling of government expenditure than did private enterprise. The contrast was between using a lever and pushing a piece of string. Private enterprise would not readily risk the creation of added capacity during a recession for fear it might be unneeded; but this helped reinforce the recession itself. The state could offset this trend because it had a broad range of companies in the main manufacturing sectors. The larger the scope and spread of the state companies, the more effective this counterrecessionary policy could be.

The third new function for public enterprise which the Italians have pioneered has been the use of state companies as a direct instrument of regional development policy. Other countries have used state expenditure on infrastructure and on the general improvement of facilities as a regional development measure. The Tennessee Valley Authority and the federal roadbuilding expenditure programs during the New Deal period in the United States are examples of such measures. But the Italian government realized by the late 1950s that improvements in infrastructure and financial incentives alone were not attracting anything like the number of new private enterprises in the South necessary to prevent a worsening of the regional problem.

The government response in July 1957 was to introduce legislation which obliged the state holding companies to locate in the South 60 percent of their investment in new plant and 40 percent of their total investment over a ten-year period. Since the South at the time constituted nearly a third of national population, the 40 percent figure would not have been likely to lead to a dramatic improvement in the region's share of national investment over the decade. Also, since the state holdings in manufacturing enterprise were mainly capital-intensive—represented by steel, petrochemicals, heavy engineering, and so on—the policy would not be likely to have a significant effect on employment.

Nevertheless, in the period from 1950 to 1967, the South did improve its relative position in some sectors, almost invariably those sectors in which state holdings were heavily represented.[12] Also, as the state's holdings became diversified through the 1960s, more labor-intensive manufacturing enterprises became available for location in the South, including plastics, pharmaceuticals, food processing, aircraft assembly, automobiles, electronics, and computers. In 1968 the government raised the location requirements on the state holdings, requiring that 100 per cent of investment in new plant and 60 percent of total investment should be placed in the South and scheduled depressed areas elsewhere in the country.

A fourth new dimension in Italy's public-enterprise activities has been the launching of long-term and relatively high-risk ventures, of the sort that private enterprise has been unwilling or unable to undertake. In areas of advanced technology this has been a common enough policy in West European economies. But the Italian state enterprises, especially IRI, have been notable for the range of activities in which they have assumed the risk-taking function. These have included the production of steel from ore instead of scrap, the exploitation of natural gas deposits and the development of petroleum refining and distribution, the maintenance of an Italian electronics industry against the competition of international companies, the production of nuclear-power equipment for electricity generation, and the maintenance of a civilian passenger aircraft industry. Such initiatives have entailed planning over a ten- or twenty-year time horizon of a kind which private enterprises have rarely been in a position to undertake in Italy.

The Italian state enterprises also have supported a competitive market in sectors which otherwise would have been dominated by oligopolistic national companies. One of the clearest examples was the cement industry, which until the development of an IRI company had been dominated by one private concern. On similar lines, one of the effects of Alfa Romeo's new automobile facility at Naples has been to create a challenge to Fiat in the medium-priced vehicle range.

But the main competitive challenge which Italian enterprise has had to sustain through the 1960s has been from multinational rather than national companies. In this respect, as in the others, Italian public enterprise has pioneered a direct response to a pressing problem. One of the most important instances has been in electronics. As in other cases of this sort, IRI tried to build up a national champion against the threat of a multinational enterprise by entering into a joint venture with a rival multinational firm. The threatening firm had been IBM, the rival multinational enterprise Raytheon. IRI's participation in Italian Edison in 1962 along with Fiat and Raytheon provided the necessary vehicle. In 1969 Raytheon ran into difficulties at its Palermo plant and decided to withdraw. But the base in electronics already assured through these joint ventures enabled IRI to take over the Raytheon holding and to integrate the Palermo operation into a new ten-year program. IRI employed the joint-venture formula in other areas as well. In 1973 a joint venture between Boeing and IRI's Aeritalia was working on the design, development, and production of a new short-haul, quiet-jet passenger aircraft.

But the Italian state companies have been employed in more indirect ways to counter the multinational challenge. For instance, Westinghouse attempted to preempt the Italian nuclear engineering field in the 1960s by bidding on contracts to build the government's proposed nuclear power stations. The government assigned the contracts to IRI, which was already established as the country's major producer of conventional generating plants.[13] In the case of another industry of major interest to the government—food processing—U.S. multinational companies in the late 1960s made bids for the Motta, Alemagna, and Cirio food companies, three of the largest and most modern food-processing and frozen-food companies in Italy. When the government learned that the U.S. companies had no plans for the expansion of the companies' plants in the South, IRI was encouraged to make a bid for control of the companies. Having acquired interests in all three, IRI undertook to ensure that the companies would locate the bulk of their new employment in the South.[14]

The policies of the Italian state companies have given new dimensions to public enterprise. By developing a mixed economy, Italy has strengthened its national economic sovereignty. What is equally interesting, however, is the extent to which similar policy needs have prompted comparable extensions of public enterprise in other European countries. Though some of the extensions were still in the infant or adolescent stage in the early 1970s, nonetheless they were clearly identifiable.

France. The basic public-enterprise sectors of France, including electricity, mining, gas, and rail transport, played an important role in the first postwar national plan. Throughout the 1950s these sectors, particularly electricity and gas, were allowed to set their prices and raise their capital funds on terms that imposed no restraint on growth. Other public enterprise—such as Renault, which had been nationalized for punitive reasons and brought into the public sector without any formal economic rationale—were largely left to their own devices, with only an occasional demand that they should set the pace in the improvement of labor relations.[15]

With the opening of the EEC, France's fourth plan aimed at meeting an anticipated increase in demand through capacity expansion. The policy misfired, resulting in serious trade-balance problems by 1962 and imposition of deflationary policies. A much greater concern developed over the threat of price increases, and various restraints were imposed on public enterprises. The result was predictable enough: by 1965, the basic public enterprises were operating at large deficits. The subsidy to the French railways in 1966 was equal to all the state credits for the military nuclear program and to three times the state assistance to motorway construction. The direct budget costs of the state coal mines were one and a half times the credits for urban renewal and regional development. The subsidy to the state petroleum consortium, RATP, was equal to twice the credits for the national computer plan, five times the aids for the decentralization of enterprise from Paris, and twenty times the regional aid in support of lagging Brittany.[16]

A prime ministerial committee was established in April 1966 to inquire into the problems of French public enterprise. Its terms of reference indicated that the prime minister's office was already aware of some of the main roles for public enterprise mentioned earlier, and that it wished the inquiry to consider more than the financial issues alone. The committee was told:

> By their activities, particularly in terms of sales and pur-
> chases, public enterprises can:
> —contribute to improving the structure of those sectors with
>   which they are related;
> —facilitate their rationalization and stimulate their research
>   and innovation efforts;
> —act as a conduit for governmental measures to influence the
>   level of national activity;
> —contribute more effectively to the policy of regional develop-
>   ment.[17]

The committee's report, the so-called Nora report, was presented in April 1967. It argued that the passive role of public enterprise in the first four national plans had to change if the national aims of higher productivity, greater industrial concentration, heavier investment, and the innovation necessary for EEC competitiveness were to be secured in the future. To cope with the problems of the increased openness of France's borders, and to ensure new and effective planning instruments at the national level, public enterprise in France would have to be "enfranchised": "Because of the opening of frontiers and the new rules of the game accepted in the framework of the Common Market, state intervention must more and more employ forms which preserve the market mechanism."[18]

The report concluded that the aims of securing such competitive public enterprise in modern manufacturing sectors could best be attained through the establishment of new state holding companies. Sectoral holding companies should be established, and the possibility of a central holding organization on the lines of the Italian IRI be considered. If such a central holding mechanism were established, rather than a variety of separate holdings at the sectoral level, the government could use the state companies more effectively as instruments of national planning. At the same time, the principle of the state holding organization would overcome the confusion that might arise from maintaining central planning and decentralized public enterprise side by side.[19]

As a result, a new state agency was established in March 1970. The Industrial Development Institute (IDI) was structured as a state holding company rather than a development bank. It was given a capital endowment of 1,000 million francs (U.S. $181 million) for an initial four-year period, half of which was subscribed by the government and half by the various state credit institutions such as the Crédit National and the Caisse National de Crédit Agricole. It was intended to operate mainly on a state shareholding basis, but it also was empowered to make loans, and it had no obligation to secure a majority holding in the companies in which it intervened.

Once established, IDI moved slowly and in a manner altogether different from the dynamic policies recommended by the Nora report. Though approached for assistance by four hundred concerns in its first year of operations, it took financial participation in fewer than twenty companies. Its first controlling shareholding, which involved a combine-harvester company, was not acquired until January 1972, in response to a threat that the company might be taken over by a foreign multinational enterprise. The same motivation explained the largest single financing operation that IDI executed in its first two years of operation—a loan of 90 million francs ($18 million) to the government-owned computer company CII. Nevertheless, IDI was criticized for its timorous response in supporting companies faced with competition from imports or companies faced with penetration by multinational enterprises.[20]

In the early 1970s, the main French advocates for the extension of public enterprise into strategic sectors were the opposition Socialist Party and the Communist Party. In June 1972 they published a common nationalization program, proposing three main categories for added public ownership.[21] The first was made up of industries which should be completely nationalized; these included mineral resources, nuclear power, armaments and pharmaceuticals, and would entail bringing into public ownership such leading companies as Dassault, Rhône Poulenc, and Roussel-Uclaf. The second was composed of industries which would be nationalized in greater part; these included chemicals and computers and involved such companies as ITT-France, Thomson-Brandt, Honeywell-Bull, Péchiney-Saint Gobain, and the Compagnie Générale d'Electricité. The third group contained enterprises in which state ownership would not be quite so dominant, including steel, oil, air and sea transport, water distribution, and motorway construction.[22] Altogether the program would require the acquisition of control in at least thirteen leading national companies. The program can be seen as a specification of the kind of structure which could give a future socialist government in France the ability to fulfill the main objectives of growth promotion, avoidance of recession, innovation, scale, and productivity which had been set out in the Nora report.

Belgium. The fate of the Nora report in France may imply that only left-wing governments would be likely to introduce sufficient new public enterprise to fulfill the kind of role undertaken by the state holding companies in Italy. That assumption would certainly receive some corroboration from the history of a new state holding agency introduced in Belgium in 1962.

Throughout the 1950s Belgium was the laggard in the European Community growth league, achieving only a 2.6 percent annual increase in gross national product. Belgian companies in general adopted a defensive wait-and-see investment posture and hesitated to undertake major investment projects. The country also was preoccupied with the political problems of decolonialization, and relatively little focus was given to a more coherent industrial policy. In the 1960s the emergence of the EEC had a great effect on the Belgian economy. The annual growth rate of gross national product nearly doubled; leading companies became aware of the challenge offered by the larger EEC market.

A shortage of capital could have offered an obstacle to the larger-scale investment needed to meet this challenge. In 1962 the government established the Société National d'Investissements (SNI), with power both to make loans and to take shares in industrial companies. It was anticipated that it would fulfill a role comparable with that which later was assigned to the British Industrial Reorganisation Corporation, and that it would in general assist with the regrouping of Belgian companies into larger, more competitive units. However, very much like the French IDI, the SNI got off to a slow start. It failed to take industrial initiatives. In practice, it emerged as an industrial development bank rather than the joint bank and holding company which had been intended. As a result, beginning in 1965, the Belgian socialist parties pressed for the establishment of an Agency for Industrial Development (Office de Promotion Industriel, or OPI) which would be a paragovernmental agency with the right to create new public-enterprise firms as well as promote mergers between existing companies. These could be either public or private companies, or mixed public and private. The financial instrument would be the Société National d'Investissements. The royal decree establishing OPI was passed in July 1971, and the agency started operations in 1972.[23]

Germany. In 1959, the Social Democratic Party (SPD) of the Federal Republic had formally abandoned a commitment to extensive nationalization of the means of production. Against this background the proposal by the SPD's federal finance minister in April 1970 to reorganize federal public enterprise was of considerable interest. The existing United Industries Companies (VIAG) would be revamped. It would become a superholding company for the various other holding companies remaining from the Christian Democrat government's denationalizations of the 1950s. The new top company would include not only VIAG itself, operating in electricity and aluminum, but also the already partly denationalized VEBA, with holdings in electricity, petroleum, chemicals, glass, and shipping. In addition there would be included the Salzgitter group, with holdings in steel, shipbuilding, and truck production; IVG, with holdings in research and development, and motor vehicles; DIAG, in machine tools; and the Saarbergwerke, in mining, petrochemicals, and chemical products. It was hoped that the reorganization of the state holdings would facilitate the raising of more private finance for their expansion and diversification.

One of the most interesting factors in the proposal to reorganize federal public enterprise in a new superholding agency was the report of a background government study which appeared to be comparable with the Nora report in France. This document—the Pothoff memorandum—was widely shown to journalists but not published. It appeared to consider very much the same problems and prospects for public enterprise as those in the Nora report. Its areas of concern included countercyclical policy, regional development, international trade, the promotion of advanced technology, and the maintenance of national control of key industrial sectors in the face of multinationalization. Like the Nora report, it also appeared to concentrate the bulk of its analysis on the problems of financing and pricing in existing public enterprise, and to conclude that a more systematic use of the holding-company principle would allow the federal government the opportunity to secure private finance for the expansion and diversification of federal public enterprise without loss of strategic control over the companies concerned.

The proposals for a superholding company were still under consideration in the early 1970s despite the resignation of the finance minister who had generated them, and despite the reorganization of his ministry within a new joint ministry of finance and economics.[24] Moreover, there had been significant pressure within the SPD for an extension of the terms of reference of the proposed holding company beyond the question of better coordination of the existing state-owned enterprises. The proposal, following Italy's example, was to widen the functions of such enterprises. The prospects for these proposals would rest heavily on the future political orientation of Germany, as well as on the policies of the European Economic Community.

Sweden. By the late 1960s it was evident that Sweden was facing problems similar to those confronting other West European industrial countries—a rapid rise in the rate of foreign investment, inflationary pressures, and a persistent regional imbalance. Sweden's publicly owned companies also faced a loss of competitiveness. Several delegations from Sweden visited IRI installations and examined the working of the holding company in some detail. Subsequently, the Swedish minister responsible for state enterprise declared publicly that Sweden could frankly admit to having learned from the IRI experience.

In January 1970, a bill was introduced in the Swedish parliament for the establishment of a single state holding company, the Statsföretag, which would in future be responsible for practically all state companies. (The railways, the post office, and the national telecommunications administration were left outside the new structure). The twenty-five companies involved in the arrangement were found in mining, shipbuilding, banking, distilling, tobacco, catering, and various other sectors. All told, in 1970, they employed close to 60,000 people.

The first annual report of the Statsföretag showed a financial loss, a fact which was taken by some financial newspapers as an indication of failure. But one of the main reasons for the institution of the Statsföretag had been the earlier loss-making trend in some of its constituent companies. To overcome any such trend, it was clear, would require better and improved financial planning, all of which was bound to take more time.[25]

Britain. From various points of view, Britain might well be considered a leading prospect for the adoption of policies favoring new public enterprises as an instrument of growth. Keynesian policies in Britain had failed to achieve their objectives in the postwar era; after 1950, Britain's growth rate had been only about half that achieved by the continental EEC countries. Management in the manufacturing sector had failed to emulate the aggressive investment policies of Britain's continental counterparts. Productivity increases were relatively low, and the stimulation of demand tended to generate balance-of-payments deficits rather than to increase domestic supply. With periodic episodes of Keynesian stimulation and Keynesian restraint, managers learned not to risk long-term investment because it could easily result in excess capacity.

By the end of the 1950s the British government realized that Keynesian monetary and fiscal policies alone were not sufficient to cope with the low-growth, stop-go syndrome. The Conservative government's reaction was to introduce one lone instrument from the French planner's armory of policies—the National Economic Development Committees, based on the French sectoral Modernization Commissions. The incoming Labour government of 1964 attached the wider framework of a National Plan to the operations of these new committees.

The trouble with the new plan was the lack of direct policy instruments to make a reality of specific objectives. The National Economic Development Committees functioned as businessmen's seminar groups, rather than as operational instruments. An Industrial Reorganisation Corporation (IRC) was established to rationalize the structure of British firms. It was authorized to inject funds either on a loan or shareholding basis. The IRC marked up a certain number of successes in its dealings with individual firms. It was concerned, for instance, in two of the three cases involving computers.* By the time the IRC was brought to an end by the Conservative government in 1970, it had made major loans to, or taken an equity interest in, at least eight major companies, with board representation in each.[26] Nonetheless, IRC was too small to have made significant impact on the economy. Its original capital of 150 million (U.S. $420 million) would have been swallowed up in the capital program of a single Italian state steel company. Nor was it in a position to initiate large-scale investment projects on its own. Instead, it had to await the initiative of the enterprises concerned, and had to content itself with providing some added financial support in response to their initiative.

The only major nationalization act undertaken by the Labour government concerned steel, which was brought into public ownership on a state monopoly basis.† This measure amounted to nothing more than the fulfillment of a fifteen-year-old undertaking to reverse the Conservative government's denationalization of steel. No new dimensions in the use of public enterprise were created.

Nonetheless, it appeared that by the late 1960s the Labour party was learning the lessons to be drawn from the ineffectiveness of the IRC as a planning instrument. It also appeared to have been learning one of the lessons underlined in the Nora report and epitomized by Italian experience, namely, that new public enterprise could be used as a national and regional planning instrument. In its election background policy statement, the Labour party declared that "the dynamism and growth which

* See the chapter by Nicholas Jéquier in this volume.
† See the chapters by J. E. S. Hayward and Trevor Smith in this volume.

characterizes the Italian public industrial structure is completely missing from the British scene, and it is in order to develop this that over the past few years the Party has considered the establishment of a new State Holding Company along the lines of the Italian IRI."[27] The election defeat of 1970 put an end to the prospects of introducing such a holding company. Nevertheless, the Labour party endorsed the concept again in its October conference of 1972 and made it a major item in its 1973 annual program.

The incoming Conservative government in 1970 found itself forced to reverse its rigorous free-enterprise philosophy well before it had reached the midpoint of its period in office. One of its most notable reversals involved Rolls Royce, which it nationalized in 1971. Another concerned the Upper Clyde Shipbuilders yard, which the government was reluctantly obliged to finance following a spontaneous seizure by the workers. Both cases resulted from the incompetence of private management: the Rolls Royce collapse was of course directly linked with the failure to control costs in the Tristar RB-211 engine project; and the Upper Clyde problems reflected the difficulties of introducing modern production techniques. In other words, the failure of private enterprise to assure entrepreneurship of sufficient competence prompted state intervention.

Conclusions

Most West European governments introduced new public enterprises in the late 1960s which were devoted either to the management or the financing of industry. In general these second-generation public enterprises contrasted with earlier nationalizations in that governments consciously sought participation in viable rather than failing concerns. From a Marxist viewpoint, some of these measures might be seen as an attempt to spread the social risks and costs inherent in a purely private capitalist system. Various types of social need were addressed. There was the need to undertake long-term investments with a time horizon which private enterprise might not hazard; the need to protect national industry from the challenge posed by foreign direct investment; the need to redress persistent regional imbalances; the need to offset a persistent investment stagnation; and the need to maintain growth in the face of unrestrained threats from inflation and balance-of-payment deficits.

Some of these problems were heightened by the opening of the EEC and the restriction or abolition of some of the main policy instruments, such as tariffs, on which national governments previously had relied. The problems were exacerbated by the trend toward increasing multinationalization of leading capitalist companies and their penetration of West European markets after the opening of the Community. This bolstered the case for national champions to meet the new multinational challenge. There was a danger that response to the multinational challenge would breed a second generation of European multinationals which were neither responsive to national governments nor to the new EEC institutions.

One way out of the problem of controlling a new generation of European multinational companies might be sought in joint ventures with public enterprises and in mergers at the EEC level. But by the early 1970s this prospect had hardly been opened, and no serious attempt appears to have been made to relate the aims of new public enterprise at a national level with Community policy.

Governments cooperated in a few international joint ventures such as Concorde, but not in more conventional undertakings with sustained sales and employment potential. In principle, a potential existed for multinational joint ventures to be developed among public enterprises in fields of advanced technology, to countervail multinational private enterprises, especially where national financial or technological resources alone were insufficient to carry the project.

The political federalists maintained that the difficulties of adapting national public enterprises to Community tasks only showed the need for political integration as a parallel to economic integration. In fact, a closer degree of political integration could not be achieved overnight. Its success would depend on a degree of political acceptance which education programs in Europeanness alone would not be likely to promote. Quite apart from the degree of national chauvinism which might underlie opposition to political union and the transfer of decision-making to Community institutions, there were real questions of agreement over the kind of society which major parties wanted to promote in western Europe as a whole. Liberal capitalism, state capitalism, and socialism represented quite different choices. The difference was already apparent in Italy, the most developed state-capitalist economy in the Community, where the socialist unions had been able to erode profitability and self-financing through wage demands which in substantial part were designed to bring the system to a halt. The need to choose would be increasingly evident in those economies whose governments or opposition parties were fostering new public enterprise to cope with problems which private enterprise either could not solve or had initially caused.

Part II

Public Policies

Italy   Romano Prodi

Italy's industrial development has been supported by the public sector to a degree that has few equals among the nations that operate on the basis of a market economy. Italian capitalism was born and developed through a continuous series of privileged relations with the state. The role of public intervention was extremely important long before the Fascist period; it dates back to the beginning of industrial development. Though the image may not be wholly accurate, one can say that the Italian economy passed from tariff protectionism to financial protectionism.[1] Eventually, the state's economic role led it into the direct management of a wide range of economic activities.

In the history of all the European industrial systems, there have been periods of strong state intervention. But these have usually alternated with periods of pronounced "laissez faire." In Italy, on the other hand, the close tie between the public and private sectors developed permanent elements even though there were continuous institutional changes. It is important to remember the origin of this public intervention, because it still influences the conduct and expectations of the entrepreneurs in ways that distinguish them from entrepreneurs in other Western economies.

This does not mean that Italian industry was bending to a socialist ideology. In Italy, as in other countries, despite the intimate ties with the public sector, industrialists and financiers continued to be the leaders in the game; the growing ties between public power and private enterprise, therefore, were not directed toward changing existing institutions. The only major decisions in which a socialist ideology appears to have played much of a role concerned the nationalization of the railroads in 1907 and of electric power in 1962. Nevertheless, even in these instances, the institutional changes that followed nationalization were much less important than had been anticipated.

Apart from these cases, the major institutional innovations that increased public ownership and public influence in industry have taken place without a specific ideology. The innovations, for instance, have not been taken in response to some political demand for state ownership of the means of production as in Britain, or for state protection of the

Romano Prodi heads the Centro di Economia e Politica Industriale at the University of Bologna, Italy.

consumer as in Sweden. Instead, the innovations have arisen out of circumstances peculiar to the Italian economic system.

The "Italian Way" to Industrial Development

From time to time since the early 1960s, it has been evident that some deep-seated inconsistencies existed between the concept of a European Community and the operations of the Italian economy. As time goes on, it becomes more and more apparent that many of these difficulties have stemmed from the peculiar relations between government and industry in Italy. To shed light on that question, one has to know something of the influence exercised in recent years by the public sector on the structure, conduct, and performance of the Italian industrial system. In the early 1960s, three distinctive characteristics of great importance could be seen: the difference in levels of income and development that sharply distinguished the South of Italy—the Mezzogiorno —from the rest of the country; the high level of unemployment in the country; and the diffused and pervasive presence of public enterprise. The problem of the Mezzogiorno, rather than diminishing in importance, has been playing an increasingly central role in Italian industrial policy, guiding it toward decisions and instruments of intervention more and more divergent from those adopted by other countries of the European Community. The necessity to look for a "national way" to economic development has been amply justified by the unique character of Italy's situation.

Italy's response to its problems since the early 1960s has not been to strengthen the process of overall national planning but rather to intervene with a series of particularistic, fragmented programs aimed at developing the depressed areas and at rescuing enterprises and industries in situations of special difficulty. In this process, public enterprise has played a dominant role. As a result, the relations between government and the industrial system and among the most important protagonists within the industrial system have been greatly modified.

One reason why the Italian system has generated highly selective means for dealing with its problems of the Mezzogiorno and with its endemic unemployment has been its gradual loss of confidence in macroeconomic policies as a means of achieving its key national objectives. "In recent years," says an official Italian report published in 1972, "the cyclical character of the Italian economy has become accentuated, accompanied by an increasing sluggishness in the upswing phase. Though public expenditure cannot be managed as a countercyclical tool, the slowing down of productive and investment activity due to the stabilization policy generates a vicious circle of falling demand, which further affects the level of production. This is mainly due to the recognized impossibility of managing public expenditure in an anticyclical way."[2] The repeated failures of Italy's macroeconomic policy have made it difficult or impossible for industrial enterprises to plan for the medium term. State intervention in the life of enterprises has proved increasingly necessary. Therefore the role of the market has become more and more restricted.

The belief that countercyclical Keynesian policies would not work in the Italian economy was one of the major factors contributing to the transformation of the productive framework in the 1960s. All elements seem to have subscribed to that conclusion: private entrepreneurs, trade unions, and leaders of public enterprises. There also appears to have been near unanimity among these groups that therefore a myriad of instruments of intervention of a microeconomic type was justified. The same tendency can be recognized in the governmental reports on Italian national planning, which have shown an increasing attention to specific subsidies and projects by which the government supports individual industrial enterprises.

To the extent that wider national planning has emerged, it has been planning of the main industrial sectors. From consideration of individual cases, the government has broadened its focus to include the consistency and the location of investments in some sectors as a whole. Where industry-wide plans have been in effect, a "declaration of conformity" has been required by the Interministerial Committee for Economic Planning (CIPE). Through such declarations, individual enterprises have received authorization for the building of specific facilities. This authorization has become a condition for obtaining public loans at a low rate of interest. The authorization has been indispensable in most of the cases covered, since at market rates of interest it would not ordinarily have been profitable to build plants in industries with medium or high capital intensity.

Although CIPE has been charged with issuing declarations of conformity, it should not be supposed that CIPE has always felt bound to the national plan. In fact, CIPE has sometimes authorized enormous deviations from the plan. In some instances, the investment authorized by CIPE has been almost double the quantity envisaged by the plan. In this peculiar situation, the interaction between CIPE and the individual entrepreneurs has been extremely active. The possibility of breaking out of the general planning framework has led entrepreneurs to work hard on their relationships with the public authorities.

The sketchy data analyzed so far suffice to emphasize the great weakness of the structures of Italian economic planning. Indeed, not only disinterested observers but the very protagonists themselves assert that planning has shaped economic choices infrequently and marginally. A report made early in 1973 by the secretary of the Planning Commission states: "The economic plan for 1966–1970 has been defined as 'a book of dreams.' If by this, one meant that the plan's proposals had no relation to concrete problems, he would be contradicted by the plain fact that the problems identified by the plan have been crucial to recent political, social, and economic events. If, on the contrary, one meant that the plan was impotent, that is, lacking in operational instruments, he would be perfectly supported by facts. It is sad but nevertheless true that the Planning Commission has always been in a very weak position vis-à-vis the central administration and the enterprises, public and private. In other words, the political system has prevented the innovative potentialities of planning from becoming a permanent and strong conditioning factor of policymaking."[3]

The problems arising from the reorganization of the textile industry are a case in point; they have been assessed and analyzed by the Planning Commission, but when action has been taken by the Ministry for Industry, it has been completely independent and patently divergent from the solutions proposed by the Commission. The difficult and frustrating role of the Planning Commission is also well illustrated by the Chemical Plan, which supposedly was designed to regulate both the private and public chemical industry by coordinating investments.[4] In this instance, too, the industries concerned have resisted successfully, and through CIPE they have introduced important changes in the original proposals of the Commission.

The influential position of industry in the realization of investment in Italy has been increased by the fact that labor unions have played so passive a role. In the evolution of modern industrial systems, trade unions have generally been cast in the role of a countervailing force. In Italy, however, it was only in the late 1960s that trade unions became important policymakers. By 1973 this role was too new for the unions to be sure either of their direction or their strength. But there were certain clear contrasts between union behavior in Italy and that in, say, Great Britain or Sweden.

In Britain, unions have concentrated their activity on the objective of preserving jobs; and in order to achieve this purpose they have been prepared at times to refrain from pushing their wage demands so that inefficient enterprises could survive. In Sweden, on the contrary, the strategy of the unions has been to demand higher wages, while accepting the need for continuous restructuring of the enterprises. In Italy, the labor movement has refused to choose between these two strategies. Instead, in the hope of achieving both higher wages and stability, it has supported the extensive and complex series of governmental programs to bolster enterprises in difficulty.

The execution of the Italian government's policy of intervening to support firms in crisis has been almost exclusively in the hands of Italy's public enterprises. In the 1950s these rescue operations were a source of opposition and controversy in the private sector. In the early 1960s such practices came to be tolerated as a part of the legitimate strategy of large industrial groups. By the end of the 1960s and in the beginning of the 1970s, they were widely regarded as the only means of avoiding a chain of bankruptcies.

There are numerous examples of the change in public opinion with regard to these rescue operations. In the 1950s when Pignone, a medium-sized engineering firm near bankruptcy, was rescued by the publicly owned Ente Nazionale Idrocarburi (ENI) under political and social pressures, there were endless discussions both in the press and in the parliament concerning the consequences of the expansion of public corporations in a market economy. A few years later, the absorption of a fairly big textile concern (Lanerossi) by the same ENI passed almost unnoticed and was commented on only by the financial press. Similar examples may be drawn from many other industries, such as mining, shipbuilding, engineering, and food. By 1973 there was widespread agreement among government, trade unions, and private industrialists that the public sector should take control of the mounting number of ailing firms that otherwise would fail.

The large number of precarious situations in Italian firms in the early 1970s has been associated with the longest period of stagnation in the Italian postwar economy. The size and duration of the downswing led to the establishment of a public financing agency with the specific purpose of providing financial and organizational support to enterprises in difficult situations. The financial organization, Gestioni e Partecipazione Industriale (GEPI), was established in 1971 with resources of 60 billion lire (U.S. $98 million), later to be increased to 156 billion lire ($268 million). The task of GEPI has been to increase and speed up the number of rescue operations among ailing firms.

The establishment and growth of GEPI have found wide favor within the Italian political system, for the agency represents an answer to the common needs of entrepreneurs, trade unions, and the political parties. It is also wanted by the public holding companies, especially by Istituto per la Ricostruzione Industriale (IRI) and ENI, in order to soften the unremitting political pressure for absorbing sick enterprises.

In principle, the scope of GEPI's operations as an instrument of intervention appears unlimited. The interventions carried out by 1973 have in fact covered only part of the demands of the entrepreneurs, and pressures for further increase of GEPI's resources seem barely controllable. Moreover, GEPI's emphasis on guaranteeing employment rather than developing the industrial system represents a critical strategic choice. The number of jobs has become the prime objective of industrial policy. Lacking any more general social policy, the country seeks to use GEPI's rescue activities in the industrial sector as a substitute.

Originally, to be sure, the conception of the role of GEPI was quite different. Whereas IRI, ENI, Ente Partecipazioni e Finanziamento Industria Manifatturiera (EFIM), and the Ente Autonomo di Gestione per le Aziende Minerarie e Metallurgiche (EGAM) were regarded as state-owned holding companies, GEPI was thought of as a financial agency whose objective was to restore aided enterprises to financial health and self-sufficiency. GEPI's purpose was to prevent the increasing mass of firms in difficulty from being eventually incorporated in the public sector. Whenever the financial agency has attempted to act in conformity with its legal purposes, however, it has been overwhelmed by pressures from political representatives and trade unions to repeat the traditional Italian form of rescue—takeover by the public sector. The fact that the GEPI concept was inspired by the British Industrial Reorganisation Corporation, which contemplated only temporary support for ailing industries, has been brushed aside or denied.

Moreover, all this has received strong support from private entrepreneurs, for they too are favorably inclined toward avoiding market risks. At the same time, however, the disappearance of the traditional threat of bankruptcy for medium and large firms appears to have greatly restricted the dynamism of Italian business, raising serious questions as to their will to struggle. In the general tendency toward the freezing of the productive factors of the Italian economy, the so-called "managerial factors" must be taken into consideration. The search for security has come to prevail over the entrepreneurial drive, a fact that has further prejudiced the long-run development of the industrial system.

It would be difficult to overstate the importance of Italy's public enterprises in bringing about the situation of the early 1970s. Until the end of the 1950s, the contribution of the public sector to the creation of new business (and above all to a new technostructure) was undoubtedly enormous. Apart from the public sector, the industrialists of Italy at the time consisted of a few Lombard and Piedmont families, dedicated to traditional lines of manufacturing activity. It was principally the public enterprises that exhibited a capacity to form a new technostructure and to imbue that structure with a sense of responsibility for industrial growth. But that dynamism was short-lived. The vigor of the public enterprise seemed to diminish in the 1960s, infiltrated and bogged down by the process of bureaucratization which had long been characteristic of other areas of Italian life.

Large Enterprises, Italian Style

In order to grasp the situation in Italian industry by 1973, one has to be aware of some major shifts in the composition of that industry during the late 1960s and early 1970s.

The most striking fact was the increase in relative importance of the foreign-owned companies, coupled with a considerable increase in the importance of public enterprises inside the Italian economy. At the same time there was a sharp drop in the presence of independent Italian firms as well as private Italian groups.

Table 1 compares Italy's 194 leading firms in 1963 with the same

Table 1. Largest Italian enterprises, classified by ownership pattern, 1963 and 1971

| | 1963 | | 1971 | | |
Ownership	Number of firms	Sales as % of total sales of the 194 leading firms	Number of firms	Sales as % of total sales of the 194 leading firms	Changes in sales percentage, 1963–1971
IFI-Fiat	9	17.5%	8	15.8%	−1.7%
Montecatini[a]	9	6.7	16	12.1	+0.9
Edison[a]	8	4.5			
Autonomous Italian firms	48	14.9	37	10.3	−4.6
Other Italian private groups	50	21.8	37	16.2	−5.7
IRI	16	13.6	25	15.6	+2.0
ENI	5	3.1	5	2.9	−0.2
Other Italian public groups	3	0.7	6	1.2	+0.5
Foreign-owned firms	46	17.2	60	25.9	+8.8
Total	194	100.0%	194	100.0%	

Source: G. L. Alzona, "Crisi delle grandi concentrazioni industriali," *L'Impresa* (November-December 1972), p. 419.
[a] Montecatini and Edison were merged into a single company during the period.

number in 1971. The choice of 1963 as a base year is significant for two reasons. In that year the process of nationalization of the electric power industry was practically accomplished. Simultaneously the period of the so-called "economic miracle"—characterized by an industrial development without precedent and by the entry of many new firms into the market—came to an end. The entry of new enterprises into the market declined after 1963 to extremely low levels, and in this relatively static framework the processes of business reorganization assumed much more importance.

As the table shows, the private Italian firms (excluding Fiat and Montecatini-Edison) moved from 36.7 percent of the total sales (of the first 194 firms in 1963) to 26.5 percent in 1971. The public enterprises moved from 17.4 percent to 19.7 percent, and the enterprises owned by foreign capital from 17.2 percent to 25.9 percent. By 1971, the major enterprises were grouped in four classes of similar size: the public enterprises; the foreign-owned enterprises; the Fiat and Montedison groups; and finally the remaining private Italian enterprises. If the Montedison group is considered in the public sector, the importance of public companies would be greatly increased, coming to 31.8 percent. In fact, at the end of the 1960s, ENI and IRI were authorized to buy a substantial part of Montedison shares. In spite of a long-standing dispute, by 1973 no decision had been taken on the Montedison case, in which there was still a delicate balance between private and public forces. In any event, Montedison was no longer among the wholly private groups. All in all, the level and trend of public ownership, which were quite unlike those of other industrialized countries, were the result of the industrial policy referred to earlier.

There were various indications in 1973 that the most dynamic of the four groups were the foreign-owned firms. A comparison of the levels of profitability of Italian-owned firms and of those owned by foreign capital suggests that the latter have been the more profitable and that, unless profound structural changes occur, the foreign enterprises will represent the major countervailing force to the power of the state-owned firms. The enterprises owned by foreign capital, as Table 2 indicates, even showed a reasonably satisfactory level of profitability during the difficult years of the late 1960s and early 1970s when the profits of Italian firms disappeared.[5]

The rapid growth of foreign-owned firms in Italy has created an added reason for continuous expansion of the public sector. This type of reaction is clearly not the only possible one. Other countries in Europe have reacted to the same stimulus by strengthening their private enterprises, whereas the Italian response has been a continuous expansion and reinforcement of the public enterprises.

The nature of the industrial credit and banking structure of Italy has contributed to this trend. Reorganized after the great depression by public resources, that structure in effect has executed Italy's industrial policies. Industrial credits have come only from public institutions; what is more, they have been directed chiefly to new investments, while practically disregarding all the other important financial needs of industry. Meanwhile, the private banks have confined their loans to short-run

Table 2. Profitability of 194 largest Italian enterprises, classified by ownership pattern, 1963 and 1971

Ownership	Net profit (or loss) as a percentage of capital and reserves	
	1963	1971
IFI-Fiat	7.1%	(0.4)%
Montecatini[a]	1.0	
Edison[a]	3.7	(27.7)
Autonomous Italian firms	6.1	1.8
Other Italian private groups	1.3	(2.6)
IRI	5.2	(9.8)
ENI	0.4	(2.3)
Other Italian public groups	(8.8)[b]	(91.2)
Foreign-owned firms	0.4	4.0
Foreign-owned oil companies[b]	(10.6)	(10.3)
General average	3.5%	(9.8)%

Source: G. L. Alzona, "Crisi delle grandi concentrazioni industriali," p. 220.
[a] Montecatini and Edison were merged into a single company during the period.
[b] The negative performance is said to be due mainly to economic relations with the companies' holdings abroad.

commitments in the safest and most conventional areas. Firms have been obliged to maintain relations with many banking institutions simply in order to cover their ordinary short-term financing needs. Because of their relative weakness, none of the banks has been prepared to take on large obligations, let alone finance new major initiatives in industry. Confining themselves to the safest and most conventional credits, Italian bankers have failed to develop much of the expertise needed to satisfy the necessities of a modern industrial structure.

The historical root of Italy's extraordinarily conservative banking behavior may lie in its experiences during the depression years. For Italian industry, this period generated a situation of extreme difficulty from the financial and productive point of view. The bankers themselves, being ill-trained, found themselves especially unable to cope; the same was true of Italy's industrialists. The creation of the public institutions was in part a consequence of this serious shortage of high-level entrepreneurs.

The war and the necessity of reconstruction again strengthened the public presence. That presence also played an important role in providing for the survival of Italian industry in a period when tariff barriers were being eliminated or reduced and international competition was being strengthened. Therefore, practically all the special tasks of the postwar period were entrusted to public industry.

The weakness of the large private Italian enterprise, contrasting with the superior performance of the multinational enterprise in Italy, had a deep influence on Italian industrial policy in the early 1970s. It gave a distinctive character to the Italian approach to the creation of national champion companies. The first explicit articulation of the strategy of creating the champion companies in Europe goes back to France's Third Plan, published in 1958. Here, a clear framework of relations between government and industry was set up with the purpose of favoring the creation of large French companies in every significant industry. Subsequently, other European countries adopted the same policy. In Great Britain, Holland, Germany, and Italy the authorities tried to reach the same result, though with different instruments of intervention. Spurred by similar goals and interests, the major European countries have tended to favor the creation of a national quasi-monopoly in every field, in the hope of being able through this instrument to counteract the power of foreign producers and foreign investors in local markets.[6] As governments have urged the champions on to the achievement of national dominance, the enterprises themselves have come to demand forms of support and intervention from the public sector that would once have been regarded as undue interference with their autonomy.

The Italian situation, even though similar to that of other countries in terms of the goals of the public sector, has been unique in certain respects. Mergers have been relatively infrequent, public enterprises and state-controlled financial institutions have been dominant, and American firms have played an especially important role. Though Table 1 has already reflected these points, they deserve further elaboration.

In the food, mechanical, pharmaceutical, chemical, oil, and electromechanical industries, some Italian firms have joined together in mergers or alliances, while other firms have been absorbed by U.S. enterprises. In order to prevent Italy's interests in these industries from declining sharply, Italy's public enterprises have stepped in. The examples are numerous. One can mention the takeover of the food firms Motta, Alemagna, and Star by Società Meridionale Finanziaria (of the IRI group), as well as parallel operations carried out by ENI in the textile industry and by IRI in the machine tool industry.

The importance of the public sector is larger than appears from the data reported in Table 1, since in some instances public support has come through the interventions of state financial institutions, which have thereafter exercised decisive influence over the firm's internal and external growth. For instance, Istituto Mobiliare Italiano (IMI), a publicly owned financial institution, had a guiding hand in the merger of a number of firms which created the largest European group in the field of household appliances, Zanussi-Rex; it also was responsible for the development of a new leader in the Italian chemical industry, the SIR-Rumianca group. Moreover, even though SIR and Zanussi are included among "Italian private groups" because the controlling shares are privately owned, it is clear that the quantity of long-term loans supplied by IMI has been so substantial as to influence deeply all the major decisions of the firms. Finally, joint ventures and other forms of co-operation between public and private industry have added even further to the public role. For in these joint ventures, the financial resources of the public partner have generally conditioned any future development, as illustrated most clearly by the case of Aeritalia, a joint venture between Fiat and IRI.

One worrisome aspect of the growth of the public sector should not be overlooked. Though the size of many of Italy's public enterprises has been large enough to match their adversaries in the European market, there have been various legal and political factors that have obliged them to concentrate their production and sales in the national market. Because of these restraints, public industry has tended to concentrate its growth potentials on becoming the leader in the national field. This market isolation has sometimes become an element of weakness in comparison with foreign firms. When contact has been established with such firms, the relation has often been one of technological dependence rather than of actual partnership; the creation of Terninoss, a joint venture by Italsider and U.S. Steel, is illustrative of that type of relationship.

In effect, the strength of public industry in the domestic Italian context has been transformed into elements of weakness in the international framework. The tie with political power has constituted in a certain sense the seal of legitimacy of the public enterprise, provided the field of action has been the domestic economy. To retain that legitimacy, the public enterprise must concentrate on increasing domestic employment and developing depressed areas at home. In the foreign field, success has depended on capabilities of a different sort. Moreover, success has not brought a direct return to the political apparatus. Accordingly, the public enterprise has had little incentive to invest significant financial resources in achieving success abroad.

The difficulties that public enterprise has found in playing the game of international competition have not arisen from these causes alone, however. There are other factors involved which are indicated by a closer examination of how public enterprises operate.

The Operation of Public Enterprises

In many respects, Italy constitutes the most important and original example of public entrepreneurship in western Europe. The system of public intervention in the economy, however, is less the result of rational political decisions than of a series of particular historical and economic circumstances.[7] Even before the period when public enterprise started its expansion, well before the 1930s, very close relations existed between enterprises and government.

As in Germany, these relations were mediated by the banking system. Unlike Germany, however, the relative weakness of private banking structures required them to fall back on large-scale public banking for support in time of crisis.[8] In the situation of the 1930s, it was not sufficient for the public sector merely to increase the credit and widen the discount operations in support of the private sector. The only way to prevent the bankruptcy of a considerable number of the big industrial firms was for the state to intervene as a shareholder. This kind of operation first brought IRI into being in the 1930s and then provided the basis for its expansion at least until the mid-1950s. IRI became the most important Italian holding company, with interests in some of the principal banks and producing firms in Italy. In order to realize the importance of IRI in Italian economic life, one need only note that IRI's enterprises in 1968 accounted for 6.3 percent of fixed gross national investment, for 3.1 percent of GNP at factor cost, and for almost 3 percent of the labor force employed in the country.[9] IRI's expansion has continued both in the fields in which it was present from the beginning and in new fields; in 1973 its importance in the Italian economy was increasing not only in absolute terms but also in relative terms.

The expansion of IRI was accompanied by tension and dispute in Italy until the early 1960s. Thereafter, however, the continued expansion evoked almost unanimous approval. This wave of consensus is explained by a complex tangle of economic, political, and social circumstances.

The first reason must be found in the undisputed success of IRI in carrying out some of its major objectives, such as the development of the iron and steel industry, and the speedy and efficient construction of a first-class network of motorways. In the second place, one needs to note IRI's ready support, in contrast to private industry, in trying to solve the main problem of the Italian economy, the development of the Mezzogiorno. Finally, an element of its success has been the creation and formation of an entrepreneurial class that is altogether new—a class with social and cultural bases completely different from those of the traditional private businessman of Italy. This new public manager, while a match for private industry in his entrepreneurial instincts, has had a more highly developed social conscience as well as stronger ties with the political structure of the country.

The philosophy of Italy's public sector is well expressed in the writings of Pasquale Saraceno. Saraceno presents the view that structural inadequacies, monopolistic tendencies, and other deficiencies in the market mechanism hold Italian development well below its potential growth path. The Italian economy, in Saraceno's analysis, is unable to respond positively to Keynesian stimuli of demand; therefore it needs structural reforms which only the public sector is in a position to offer, be it through direct intervention in the economy or through an adequate planning policy. These same concepts constitute the basic element in the speeches and writings of the management of IRI, and they form the nucleus of a well-developed "philosophy" of public enterprise which has had an important influence not only within Italy but also in other European countries.[10]

It should be emphasized that the establishment of this philosophy on the part of IRI did not grow out of the Italian political process but was almost completely elaborated from inside the group. IRI's definition of its own tasks, in fact, constitutes the fundamental justification for its proclaimed independence from the Italian government.[11]

The other condition for the independence of public enterprises has been financial self-sufficiency, based on the ability to generate a profit. Though the primary purpose of public industry was not profit maximization, nevertheless the achievement of a profit has permitted it to resist the pressures coming from the political structure.

As an instrument for dealing with the key problems of the Italian economy, namely, diffused unemployment and the underdevelopment of the South, the public enterprise sector proved a useful mechanism from the beginning. Its continued utility, however, depended on continued liberty of action for the managers of the public industry, including continued financial autonomy. That objective was not easily reconciled with the potential sensitivity and economic cost of the social problems which these enterprises addressed. Accordingly, over the years, political and financial autonomy have become increasingly difficult to maintain. Recourse to public financing has increased and has carried with it a similar increase in the political price to be paid.

One major form of such public financing has been the so-called "endowment funds," appropriated annually out of the national budget. As such funds have been appropriated, the enterprises accepting them have been assigned a series of social tasks that could not be financed by the market, either because they did not promise much economic profit or because the profits appeared remote in time. With the intensification of the relations between the political machinery and public industry, the endowment fund has become a critical factor.[12] In 1971, financial sources supplied by the state reached 550 billion lire (U.S. $897 million), which represented about 23 percent of total needs, whereas in 1970 state sources covered only 10 percent of these needs. Meanwhile, the contribution through self-financing to the needs of public industry as a whole declined; the 446 billion lire (U.S. $728 million) of self-financing in 1971 met only 19 percent of its financial needs as compared with 29 percent in 1970, and 45 percent in 1968 and 1969.

The outlook in 1972 was bleak in this regard. The report of the Ministry of Public Holdings did not foresee any improvement.[13] Because of the uncertain pattern of the economy, according to the ministry, it was not anticipated that self-financing would constitute "a substantial share of the process of accumulation." At the same time, other nongovernmental sources had dried up. The contribution of private shareholders and bond buyers to the resources of public enterprises had been sharply reduced, so that the most important source of credit by far was that of government-subsidized loans. In 1971, medium- and long-term subsidized loans provided 828 billion lire (U.S. $1,350 million), equal to 35 percent of the firms' total needs, while short-term loans through the banking system were around 535 billion ($873 million).

The financial pillars of state-owned industry have therefore come to rely in turn on state-supplied endowment funds and subsidized loans. It could hardly be otherwise, given the increasing losses in manufacturing and the almost nonexistent profits in the service industries. In 1970 only the petroleum and cement industries had a profit, while all other industries recorded losses.

In 1972, it was clear that the original Saraceno philosophy governing public enterprise had been placed in major jeopardy, threatened by an increasing reliance on the political structure. To be sure, the idea of pumping funds into the productive sectors in years of depression could readily be justified, as an interesting attempt to introduce into the Italian economy an instrument of cyclical stabilization. The trouble was that the use of public enterprise for this purpose had produced great distortions in the country's industrial structure. And it had sharply reduced the independence of the firms' industrial operations. Aid in the form of subsidized loans had undermined the financial markets, creating interest rates on the order of 3.5 percent to 4 percent, with which private financial intermediaries could not compete. Moreover, the availability of the endowment funds had generated almost a race toward higher and higher deficits, accompanied by efforts to obtain or to increase access to the funds. A typical case, under intensive discussion in Parliament in 1972, was that of the Ente Autonomo di Gestione per le Aziende Minerarie e Metallurgiche (EGAM), one of the youngest among the institutions of state industry. With sales on the order of 150 billion lire (U.S. $258 million) and losses of 40 billion ($69 million) a year, EGAM requested and, after a skillful political battle, got, an endowment fund of 330 billion ($567 million). The earlier process, therefore, was completely reversed. Whereas the object of the public enterprises had once been financial autonomy, by 1972 they seemed to be courting financial difficulties in order to be able to increase their claim on public funds.

In evaluating the role of public industry in Italy in the 1962–1972 decade, one gets the impression that expansion at any cost became an end in itself, independent of content and motivation. This change in approach was not so much associated with enterprises in the IRI group, which constituted the original nucleus of Italian public enterprise. It appeared rather to have originated within the ENI nucleus, whose growth in the postwar period was based on the explicit public objective of achieving autonomy for Italy in the field of energy. ENI's financial resources came from its right to collect and use the rents associated with the sale of petroleum in Italy. ENI's access to a monopoly rent and ENI's need to respond directly to objectives of a political nature later became characteristics of all firms with state participation, irrespective of their different historical origins. In time, these characteristics weakened the firms. Whereas ENI in its early years had been guided by the genius of Enrico Mattei's strategy, the other public enterprises had no such source of support. The effort of these public enterprises to produce a synthesis between the objectives of the firm and those of society was undermined by the fact that there were no precise criteria for evaluating the social demands which the firms faced.[14] Even more important was the fact that public industry was in no way penalized for its management errors.

Not only were standards lacking for the evaluation of the political and social results of public enterprises; also lacking were the measures of performance to which the managers should be subjected. Extended periods of losses were being tolerated even in areas in which these losses did not have any economic justification, and this without exposing the responsible managers to a process of evaluation and dismissal. The minority private shareholders, if any, had no voice in the matter (though, at times, the endowment fund was used to give them a form of payment which compensated for the operating losses). The invulnerable position of the managers hastened the bureaucratization process in large public firms, which faced the prospect of becoming as complicated and authoritarian as government ministries.

To be sure, efforts were made to prevent this trend through various organizational reforms. But in practice it was useless to try organizational innovations in a situation in which managers could not be dismissed. Moreover, the problem of rigidity applied not only to the individuals concerned but also to the organizational structure of the public groups. For instance, the transfer of firms from one group to another, even when this fact would be consistent with economic logic, remained an exceptional event. It was easier to reorganize and regroup private firms than public firms.

Notwithstanding the existence of these rigidities, the weakness of Italy's industrial system and the progressive enlargement of the share of public enterprise have tended to place the public enterprise sector in the position of the principal policy instrument for reaching the objectives set out in the national plan. In the 1950s Italy first began to see the possibility of using public enterprises as the universal instrument of public objectives. This was a period in which the objectives assigned to such enterprises were clearer, even if they were not totally accepted by public opinion. The entry of the public sector into shipbuilding was intended to maintain a high level of employment. Unambiguous public objectives also explained the creation of a public presence in cement, steel, and fertilizers, where the purpose was partly to break a private monopoly and to bring Italian prices into line with those of other countries.

In the 1960s, however, the strategy was much more complicated, and it is impossible to reduce the behavior of public enterprise to simple formulae. The opening of international markets tended to undermine the monopolistic situations in Italy and the possibilities of exploitation that had always existed in Italian industry. Accordingly, the task of keeping prices in check in the key areas previously listed was rendered somewhat easier.

To be sure, two clear objectives still remained. One was to prevent the collapse of Italian industry in the face of fierce international competition and the rise of Italy's labor costs; but that effort was flawed by the fact that with heavy government subsidies available, success was no longer determined by the production costs of the enterprise. A second objective, as in the case of roadbuilding, was to provide services and infrastructure that the public administration apparently was less able to manage; but this too was a vicarious function because it placed public enterprises outside of the market process.

The "Double Market" in the Italian Industrial Economy

From the perspective of 1973, external circumstances rather than conscious strategy have been pushing Italy's public enterprises outside of the market's framework. The result has been a relationship between the state and the enterprises which is much like the military-industrial complex that some Americans profess to see in their country. The fact that the Italian enterprises are public and that American firms are private is of little importance in this context. What is important is the relative size of large firms and their privileged relations with the state. When this relation is strengthened and becomes general, political-economic groups arise which threaten to dominate the life of a country.

Considered from the perspective of 1973, the spirit of financial independence that represented the most original source of strength in the early years of existence of public enterprises has been declining in Italy, especially since the late 1960s. The hybrid tie between the political apparatus and public industry has provided the motive force which has shaped Italian industrial policy and has greatly modified the working of the market economy in Italy. The rules of operation have become discretionary rather than automatic; and the discretion has been placed increasingly in the hands of political forces.

Because political forces have become dominant, the incentives for industrialization in southern Italy have focused almost totally on the incentives to capital, where selectivity and discrimination can easily be exercised, rather than incentives to labor, where selectivity is much more difficult to apply. The result is that the public objective of alleviating or solving the employment problems in the Mezzogiorno has not been achieved. Instead, perverse policies have been pursued that attract enterprises with high capital and low labor intensity to the South.

In recent debates on the problem of development of the chemical industry in Italy, the tendency to place capital-intensive activities in the South has been the object of repeated complaints. Yet such seemingly irrational decisions are the logical consequence of the relationship between the state and big business: the political structure wants to retain its discretionary powers to pick and choose among the interests, and big business is quite willing to fall in with a situation in which it negotiates for favors with the political structure. These tendencies have always existed in Italian industry. But the latest changes in state participation have pushed such tendencies to the extreme by incorporating publicly owned enterprise in the relationship.

The irony is that one of the key instruments in obliterating the distinction between the operations of public enterprises and private enterprises is an entity that was intended to distinguish and differentiate such operations. The creation of a Ministry of Public Holdings was meant to ensure that the social purposes of public enterprises would be paramount. In practice, however, the ministry has seldom performed a managing role with respect to the firms. Its main purpose has been to act as a spokesman for the demands of public industry. The ministry has not represented a strengthening of rational planning activities; instead, following a long-established Italian tradition, it has contributed to the further fragmentation of political power.[15]

But the perversion of the relationship between enterprise and government has not been confined to public-sector enterprises. While public enterprises have developed a relationship with the Ministry of Public Holdings that might be called "patronage without political purpose," private enterprises have developed the same sort of relationship with the Ministry of Industry.

The policy of the Ministry of Industry has been focused on doling out subsidies to the private sector rather than on designing and pursuing a specific industrial policy.[16] The ministry has supported private firms through the provision of several types of subsidized long-term loans. In addition to the special measures to encourage investment in the South, there have been no less than twelve laws providing credit subsidies for other purposes, mainly for small and medium-sized firms. As a matter of fact, the big firms have managed to benefit from these subsidies as well, simply by subdividing their investment projects in several pieces in order to stay within the prescribed limits of such programs. The dispensation of subsidized credit, however, has not been automatic; it has been subject to discretionary decisions, which have provided one more indication of a governmental process based on favor and patronage. A number of consequences have followed: the entrenchment of the existing institutions, the reduced mobility of productive factors, the survival of inefficient firms.

A second parallel has been evident between the behavior of the Ministry of Industry and that of the Ministry of Public Holdings. Traditionally the research office of the Confindustria (the Italian national employers' association) has played the role of ghost-writer to the Ministry of Industry, while the same kind of relationship has existed between public industry and the Ministry of Public Holdings. This relation has been legitimated by reason of the public character of the ministries. They, in their turn, have rarely asked for a more active role, being content to accept the advantages they have enjoyed as a result of their privileged relations with their respective groups of enterprises.

When the public enterprises and the private enterprises of Italy began in effect to comprise a single system with common methods of operation and common purposes, some sort of national integrative procedure would have been desirable in order to reduce the tendency toward the application of dual standards, one for the public sector, the other for the private. As long as the two systems had different goals, different financial sources, and different norms of conduct, and as long as the public system represented a small share of the national production apparatus, the absence of some integrative apparatus did not matter. But its absence was of great consequence when the growth of the public sector increased the necessity for interaction with the private system. At that stage, a form of Gresham's Law became evident in the Italian industrial system, according to which the existence of the privileged channel made more and more difficult the development of an efficient market structure. The influence was felt above all in the financial field, where different starting conditions led to dualism in the conduct of the enterprises; the principle of "equality in diversity," which had formed part of the philosophical basis for public enterprises, was obviously being violated. As that fact became evident and as competition by large private firms began to appear impossible, an attempt was made to offset the dualism by extending special privileges to the private entrepreneurs as well.

The Montedison case, already mentioned, has been symbolic of the trend. Montedison's ownership structure and its history have left the firm in a sort of intermediate position between the public and private sectors. That case also has emphasized that the need for financial resources outside of normal business channels is just as acute in the private sector as in the public. In practice, the private capital market has dried up and scarcely any alternatives to public intervention have remained.

By 1973 the Montedison case had become a political issue because the existence of a major share of capital in the hands of ENI suggested strongly that Montedison would end up as a public enterprise. Even when the public holdings were in the form of debt rather than risk capital, as in the case of IMI-SIR and IMI-Zanussi, the control by the public sector was practically as great; the same results were achieved even though the firms involved still were listed nominally in the private sector. Only foreign groups could avoid this process, due to the ties they had with external credit sources. From one point of view, their sources of finance also were privileged, at least in relation to the Italian financial market.

Just as there was a dual system of access in finance, so too dualism existed in Italy's labor market. Labor contracts entered into with public firms represented the reference point for further agreements with private firms. When this occurred, the economic and financial basis of private firms, already very weak, was often threatened further.

At a time when public enterprises had become as important as they were in Italy, it was impossible to maintain dual markets in any field. The privileged market in the end prevailed and imposed its own rules on the whole economic system. Should these rules be too burdensome for the private sector, it would become necessary to further enlarge the public sphere of action, either through the takeover of the firm itself or through the supply of funds on privileged terms. This picture suggested the need to rebuild the unity of Italy's economic system by applying rules and conditions that were alike for all the firms operating in the market. Such a principle appeared as a necessary condition for setting up a flexible and efficient industrial system, able to adapt itself to changes in the economic environment.

Germany   Georg H. Küster

In only a little more than twenty years, the Federal Republic of Germany ran the gamut from a war-ravaged economy to a prosperous welfare state. In 1973 it stood on the threshold of being an "affluent society." The economic policy shaping this German "economic miracle" did not, I think, undergo a basic transformation during that period, though a considerable shift of accent could be observed. In the poverty economy of the 1950s, liberal market conceptions prevailed, embodied in the concept of a "social market economy." Its basic elements were private ownership of the means of production, free entrepreneurial initiatives, unrestricted competition, and the guarantee of a certain social stability. At the beginning of the 1960s, increasingly acerbic criticisms of this concept made themselves felt. By the mid-1960s, in response to the view that the model was outdated and naïve, another conception of economic policy was developed, that of the "enlightened market economy."

A Policy Model in Flux

Two so-called basic laws of Germany represented the two stages of German economic policy. The Act against the Restriction of Competition, generally called the Cartel Act, was enacted in 1957; it stood for the liberal conception of the 1950s. The Act for the Promotion of Stability and Economic Growth, placed on the statute books in 1967, represented the influence of the 1960s. Both laws also marked a particular constellation of parties and politics, and each reflected the personal stamp of the economics minister concerned. The Cartel Act had been supported by a government of the Christian Democrats, with their economics minister, Ludwig Erhard, while the Stability and Growth Act had been passed under a coalition government of Christian Democrats and Social Democrats, in which the Social Democrats provided the minister of economic affairs, Karl Schiller, the architect of the law.

Erhard's early introduction of a "social market economy" was experimental, since an open economic system of the sort which the phrase implied was by no means the system desired by the majority of the voters or by the economic experts. The system survived the initial

Georg H. Küster is a member of the Faculty of the Department of Economics, Goethe University, Frankfurt-am-Main, West Germany.

postwar crises of inflationary price increases and unemployment. During the 1950s, as the economy became stable, the policies enjoyed growing popularity because they presented the citizens with a previously unknown combination of increased productivity and individual freedom.

The German "economic miracle" was remarkable not only with regard to the rapid reconstruction of industry and the growth of the standard of living. It was also remarkable because it presented Germany for the first time in its history with a capitalist economic system. In contrast to the German industrialization of the nineteenth century, the postwar economic prosperity of West Germany was above all the independent work of nongovernmental economic institutions. Though certain restrictions had to be imposed by any state in the mid-twentieth century, the state did not consider its task to include the control and supervision of economic enterprise.[1]

One must emphasize, however, that the recovery of the economy was greatly helped by two factors: by substantial initial state aids for private industry; and by the fact that the old prewar structure of capital and wealth in Germany was almost wholly retained. In 1948, the Federal Republic began with a private economy "whose structure was the same as, and whose degree of concentration was only minimally lower than, that under the rule of National Socialism; and this private economy was left to the 'free play of forces.' " The experiment of the social market economy, therefore, involved an element of reversion and restoration: "When the Germans began to reconstruct their economy, they built upon the familiar structural foundation and plan, much of it invisible to the naked eye, as if guided by an archaeologist who could pick his way blindfold about some favourite ruin."[2]

The shift of emphasis in German economic policies in the early 1960s was caused by numerous factors. In the economic field, the acceleration of price increases after 1960 was the first occasion for social and political uneasiness. The government was compelled in its Annual Economic Report of 1963 to qualify its earlier goal of absolute price stability. This was caused, among other things, by the rising scarcity of labor, which induced the trade unions to give up the passive attitude toward wage increases that had previously been observed in support of German industrial reconstruction, and to demand a bigger share of the gains from growth. The decisive factors contributing to the change of economic policy, however, were doubtless the decline of the growth rate and the incipient recession of 1966–67. That recession, induced by antiinflationary measures, led not only to economic stagnation but to a government crisis as well.

In the early 1960s there were already some liberal economists who realized that it was time to emphasize the social aspects of the social market economy instead of the simple growth objectives of the 1950s.

The opportunity for a discussion of economic planning was created by the introduction of a major document in the EEC: the Commission's "Memorandum on the Community's Program of Action for the Second Stage." Inspired by the French experience with indicative planning, the memorandum suggested that the Community's economic policy should be oriented toward the long-term planning of economic development. This suggestion led to sharp controversy between Economics Minister Erhard and the German president of the EEC commission, Walter Hallstein, who like Erhard was a Christian Democrat. Erhard again expressed, in accordance with the liberal philosophy, his rejection of any kind of economic planning.[3] Despite Erhard's rejection, the German government thereafter cooperated in the shaping of the EEC's medium-term economic policy.

In 1965, an election year, Erhard developed the social content of the social market economy in the form of an explicit revision of the official doctrine of the competitive economy. Erhard's point of departure was an emotional expression of his doubts whether an economy made up of large concerns and large interest groups was able to achieve an adequate development of its economic and social structures. Accordingly, he was drawn to the idea of a cooperative society, in which conflicts of interest were harmonized in accordance with some nebulously defined standards of group responsibility. But Erhard was not the man to carry out such a program. In 1966 he was deposed as the head of government by his own party, putting off the modernization of German economic policy to the period of the coalition government.[4]

The new economics minister, Karl Schiller, made Erhard's rather vague ideas more precise. The purpose of his "enlightened market economy" was to develop a compatible system which could reconcile systematic consideration of national problems with economic freedom and with an international outlook on the part of socioeconomic groups and economic units. Schiller perceived modern economic society as an "aggregative economic society organized on a group basis," in which the government had to enter into a continuous dialogue with the organized interest groups in order to render its economic policy effective. Answering his critics' reproach that his conception implied a new interventionism, Schiller insisted that the greater the rationality of the autonomous socioeconomic groups, the less the government would intervene in economic life, and the greater the likelihood of the state's being transformed into an information and orientation center which governed with arguments rather than commands. Recognizing the threat that the state might become the agent and executor of less enlightened interests at the centers of economic power, Schiller foresaw and accepted the involvement of oligopolies and organized groups in economic decision-making but did not favor giving them control over it.[5]

Schiller's proposals represented a new level of pragmatism. Certain technological and economic facts necessitated conscious national planning in the rich nations. To achieve this planned development one could not rely on the market mechanism alone. The market economy, therefore, was no longer to be regarded as an independent political value in its own right, but merely as one of the possible instruments of economic policy. Schiller understood the optimum mixture of the instruments of policy to consist "in the combined application of the principle of free competition for microeconomic relations and of global policy for macroeconomic relations."[6] German economic policy thus reached a stage of greater rationality, in which the criteria of social science gained increasing importance in political decision-making.

Besides the emphasis on macroeconomic policy, Schiller recognized the increasing importance of policy aimed at dealing with structural changes in society. Starting from the realization that adequate economic growth cannot be ensured without conscious governmental structural policy, Schiller began to enlarge and refine his kit of policy tools in this area. It seemed high time. The country's GNP was dropping; some of the crises which had appeared in the early 1960s were becoming more acute, especially in the German hard-coal-mining industry, once the engine of the economic miracle; and West German industry's adaptation to the technological imperatives of a modern industrial society was inadequate. The awareness of a technological gap between western Europe and the United States served to galvanize Europe, as Sputnik had previously galvanized the United States. State programs were instituted for the science-based industries, and state programs were stepped up to deal with the palpable crisis—not to say disaster—in the educational system.

Despite the changes in German economic policy from 1950 to 1970, the basic structure of ideas remained; the shifts were questions of accent. Common to the structure throughout was a pluralist view of society and a neglect of social antagonisms. Society was seen as a collection of interests and groupings of equal rank, no group being able to dominate another, each group being limited by countervailing power. In other words, the idea of equilibrium in the economic-political field was raised to the status of dogma. Seen in this way, the road from the social market economy to the enlightened market economy can be understood as a development toward increasing social integration and toward the control of existing power structures in the economic and political fields. Expressing "the German longing for synthesis," the ascendant pattern must be interpreted as a means to channel and prevent conflict.[7]

Nevertheless, the structural features of a society, reflected in income distribution, the distribution of wealth, and division of labor, are manifested in social classes. These distinctions continued in German society.

The statistics on income and wealth distribution showed just as clearly as the official statements on economic goals that in much of the postwar period the distribution aims had been sacrificed by all elements to the stability goals of the nation.[8] The markedly low propensity for conflict displayed by German trade unions in comparison with the unions of other nations, as measured by the number of days lost by strikes, indicated that fact. It was not until the first wildcat strikes in the fall of 1969 and spring of 1973 that one could begin to discern the gap between the trade union leaders as integrators and cooperators in the German economy and the trade union members as neglected elements in the national economy.

Schiller had hoped that if the functions and basic principles of economic policy were modernized, "if we reshape them in accordance with the demands of the technostructure of our society and our industrial state, then we will not only execute the mandate of the younger generation, but we will execute the mandate of history."[9] In view of the keen criticism of his policy, by both the younger generation and the New Left and the older generations of liberals, it can hardly be said that his hope was fulfilled. This criticism emphasized above all the political emptiness of Schiller's technocratic and pragmatic concept, obscuring the relationship between state authority and economic power in the process of concerted action. In the final analysis, as Schiller's critics saw, his conception aimed at stabilizing existing power structures by means of integration and at harmonizing the claims of the various established socioeconomic groups by means of information and communication.

Government-Enterprise Relations: The Macroeconomic Level

The change in the concept of economic policy in the 1960s had decisive consequences for the relations between government and enterprise. The relations that were actually going on were brought out of their unofficial obscurity and were declared an integral part of the official program. One reason for this shift was the situation of the Social Democrats when they first participated in government in 1966. Unlike the Christian Democrats, their leaders had few connections with industry. Moreover, the Social Democrats were ambivalent in their relation to big business because of their traditional bonds with the workers. Apart from the special problems of the Social Democrats, government-enterprise relations were doubtlessly intensified in the 1960s by the participation of organized groups in the official discussions of economic policy, and by cooperation between the government and large enterprises in certain industrial branches. The traditional boundary between state authority and private economic initiative had become blurred.

All of these factors were evident at the macroeconomic level, that is, the level at which the performance of the economy as a whole was at issue. In the early 1960s, declining growth rates, a tense labor market, and rising rates of inflation led to the realization that Germany's aggregate demand would have to be subjected to conscious national management. Though control by competition might apply at the level of the individual firms, the postulates of Keynes would have to be applied at the macroeconomic level.[10] Discussions about the feasibility of Keynesian policies had three essential results: first, the professionalization of economic policy; second, the provision of a modern set of tools for fiscal policy, provided by the Stability and Growth Act; and third, the introduction of concerted action under the same law.

The growing professionalization of economic policy was above all expressed by the formation of an independent five-man Expert Council. The council, it was hoped, would come to scientifically based conclusions and would use moral suasion against inflationary income demands, such as demands by the unions for wage increases. At the same time, guidelines would be provided for a stability-oriented economic policy. The importance of this Expert Council was different from that of other advisory councils working for the different ministries. The publication of its annual report did not require governmental approval. The council was free to conduct special studies of its own choice. And in actual practice, the council operated "at arm's length distance from the government."[11]

The advocates of the Stability and Growth Act, promulgated in 1966, believed that it provided an ideal set of tools for global demand management. Discussions of the law continued for more than two years under Erhard before the first draft of the act was formulated. The delay was due partly to the government's technical incompetence in this field. The economic boom of 1964 to 1965 and the imminent election in 1965 also contributed to procrastination. It had been Erhard's intention originally to use the act mainly to restrain demand. But with the beginning of recession in 1966, the growth target was added both to the title and to the contents of the draft.

The act directed that the Federal and state governments should pursue policies "that contribute, in the framework of a market economy, simultaneously to achieving price-level stability, a high degree of employment, and external equilibrium, together with steady and adequate economic growth." Three groups of measures were enacted. The first related to the information and coordination functions of the state in an enlightened market economy; the second contained instruments for countercyclical variations of public expenditure; and the third included a number of new tax measures.[12]

The importance of the measures contained in the Stability and Growth Act was not that they were novel for Germany, but that they provided a coordinated set of tools. The financial independence of the states and the local authorities was reduced in favor of the Federal authorities, requiring a constitutional change. Furthermore, the concept of macroeconomic equilibrium was introduced into a modern constitution for the first time. The government's right to apply countervailing measures to maintain the equilibrium against threat was almost free of parliamentary control.[13] The considerable independence which this gave to the Federal executive was usually defended with the argument that a high degree of flexibility was necessary and desirable.

Of special importance for Schiller's new economic policy and for the relations between government and private industry, however, was another provision of the Stability and Growth Act. This key measure stipulated that in case one of the overall aims of the act was endangered, "the Federal government should provide the orientation data for simultaneous and mutually agreed upon measures [concerted action] on the part of Federal, state, and local authorities, labor unions and employers' associations," in order to remove the threat.

Concerted action on incomes policy had previously been proposed in mid-1965 by the Expert Council, which had obviously drawn its inspiration from the French model of the *economie concertée*.[14] Both the unions and the employers' associations declared themselves ready for such cooperation, but the Erhard government rejected the idea on the ground that it violated their liberal philosophy. Not until the coalition government was formed in 1966 could concerted action be sanctioned by law. After that, under Schiller's theatrical management, concerted action gained in political importance and became the basic model for economic policy on all levels.

Concerted action to achieve the aims of stabilization policy was described by one of its inventors as a "code of behavior," as a "kind of multilateral gentlemen's agreement controlled by an enlightened public."[15] Unified conduct by government and socioeconomic groups in the field of income policy was to be reached through the conviction and insight of group representatives. The result, it was hoped, would be agreement on guidelines for budget, wage, and price policy. These guidelines, however, were not absolutely binding: they represented indicative data for orientation, not for command. Concerted action was regarded as complementing monetary and fiscal stabilization measures, not as a substitute for them.

What effects had concerted action actually had on German economic policy by 1973? One aspect of that question has to do with the relationship of the state to private groups in the formation of economic policy, and particularly with the question of participation. There is no official list of the regular participants in the concerted action process; but it can be assumed that the government representatives had included the economics minister as chairman, as well as the finance and labor ministers and representatives of the Federal Chancellor's office. Participating as "independents" were representatives of the Expert Council, the president of the Federal Cartel Office and, after 1968, representatives of the Federal Bank. The organized groups invited to participate were "two central unions and six top entrepreneurs' associations—that is, eight organized groups."[16]

In view of the seemingly arbitrary selection, the criteria for participation in the process have been questioned. In principle, the economics minister had been left to judge which associations were to be included. The privileged position of especially powerful interest groups was explained by the statement that the selection had been made according to whether the associations "caused one to expect optimum participation in the concerted action in consideration of their size and importance."[17]

Though Schiller had expressed a strong desire to give oligopolies access to decisions relating to the economy as a whole, the Federal Ministry of Economics stated that representatives of single large enterprises had never taken part in the meetings.[18] But the unrepresentativeness of the selected group could scarcely be disputed. Neither the consumers nor the state and local authorities, as stipulated in the Stability and Growth Act, were represented in the concerted action process; and though the association of small- and medium-sized enterprises had actually applied for membership in the group, its initiative had been rejected.

The strong sense of exclusivity in the concerted action process was intensified by its secrecy. No official list of regular participants existed and no detailed account of actual proceedings was made public; this of course stood in stark contrast to Schiller's asserted desire for a "transparent economic policy."[19] This attitude was explained by pointing to the advantages of secret negotiations, which were said to permit frank statements of views, and positions free of narrow sectarian interests.

Nonetheless, the legitimacy of the operation by democratic standards was exceedingly questionable. The leadership of the business groups represented in the process had not been selected by standards appropriate to a democratic state; internal voting rights were generally determined by the companies' sales or the amount of their membership contributions. Schiller accordingly achieved his objective of participation by the oligopolies, but through an institutional channel that had been intended for another purpose.

Indeed, the elitist cooperation between government authorities and organized groups in the concerted action program had developed into a quasi-parliament for economic policy. Its participants discussed not only guidelines for income policy but also matters of competition policy, trade policy, and wealth policy. Subcommittees and study-groups were formed to deal with the problem of revising the Cartel Act and with questions of codetermination, that is, workers' representation on corporate boards. Accordingly, the decision processes in economic policy were transferred from open parliamentary discussions to extraparliamentary secrecy. Organized groups were given a say in the state's political decisions, while retaining their freedom of action in civil law. At the same time, the state achieved its purposes, while hiding behind the anonymity that was ordinarily reserved to private parties.[20]

The advocates of Schiller's new economic policy defended these ambiguities by stressing that the responsibility of the executive to the legislature could not be said to have been diminished, and by observing that the process of concerted action was formally covered by constitutional law. However, as one liberal critic put it, concerted action in reality resembled "the power-structure of a social oligarchy, that is, of an oligopolistic constitution applied to politics." In the terminology of the New Left, "the government becomes the executor of the hopes of the monopolistic groups."[21]

From an economic point of view, the actual consequences of concerted action by 1973 were of special interest. As far as the price stability objective was concerned, concerted action seemed to have worked only when it was not needed, that is, in recession. And it has failed to work when it was needed, that is, during the boom. The policy of concerted action was first applied in the recession of 1966–67. At that time, the interests of the employers' associations, the unions, and the Federal government were almost identical; all were agreed on Schiller's policy of "controlled expansion." In the boom of 1968–69, however, the interests of the different groups were in conflict. The upshot was that the Federal Republic experienced the highest price increases in more than a decade.

By 1973 it had become clear that concerted action in the sense of indicative guidelines could only be successful as long as the participants had similar interests. If interests parted company, the process of concerted action simply papered over the cracks; those taking part either were not influenced at all or else they lost the power to keep their constituency in line. As that realization began to dawn, there came also a growing recognition that the fiscal policy instruments of the Stability and Growth Act, on which such great hopes had been placed, suffered from major shortcomings. The combination of disappointments shook deeply the early hopes that the act and its related policies would provide effective solutions for the Federal Republic.[22]

Government-Enterprise Relations: The Sectoral Level

In addition to operating at the macroeconomic level, the Federal Republic of course was concerned with many problems that related to explicit branches or sectors of the economy. In the 1950s, ad hoc measures were relied upon to deal with such problems. Between the mid-1960s and the early 1970s, however, there was an attempt to coordinate structural policy. Growth had slowed up in some sectors, labor was scarce in others. Markets had expanded and shrunk as the EEC had developed. Worries over the technological gap had left their imprint.

Significant steps toward the coordination of structural policy were signaled by the publication under Schiller of the "Principles of Sectoral Policy" in 1966 and the "Principles of the Federal Government's Sectoral and Regional Economic Policy" in 1968. One major principle was to avoid creating a special set of tools to deal with the peculiarities of each sector and branch of the industry. The aim was to solve similar problems in different branches with a common set of instruments, oriented to common principles and aims. In that spirit, five general principles were enunciated:

> Structural intervention was only justifiable when the difficulties concerned the whole sector and were based on lasting economic changes.
>
> The entrepreneurs and managers were to be primarily responsible for the necessary structural adaptation.
>
> The government's role was to support measures of self-help, provided these measures promised to strengthen, on some lasting basis, the competitiveness of the enterprises concerned.
>
> Special governmental aids or other interventions could only be considered if the individual sectors were undergoing major changes at a rapid rate, and if the changes would generate undesirable economic and social consequences.
>
> The aids should be temporary, should be gradually withdrawn, and should not cripple the competitive process.[23]

In practice, of course, these liberal principles were often ignored. Political and social goals were the dominant factors, and economic goals took a secondary place.

More specifically, German structural policy had three aims. The first was to stabilize and improve the income to employers and employees in the lagging industries. The second was to help in the process of adaptation on the part of industry; in practice this meant slowing up the process of shrinkage on the part of declining industry much more than it meant accelerating the growth of industries that could profit from expansion. Toward the end of the 1960s a third aim received growing attention: the promotion of research and development in the high-technology industries. The aim in this case was to put the results of research into industrial practice with the least delay possible. But the weights assigned to the three objectives were very different. The political priority of the respective aims can be adduced from the fact that in 1970, 66 percent of the total amount of Federal subsidies and tax allowances was spent on the aims of conserving declining industries, 28.5 percent on easing the adaptation of industries, and only 5.5 percent on the aims of boosting productivity.[24]

Though a multiplicity of measures were introduced by the government to promote sectoral policies, a few of these are especially relevant for understanding the relations that developed between government and enterprise.[25]

In 1965, the Federal income tax law was amended in order to remove an impediment to the movement of funds from one type of enterprise to another. Corporations were permitted to exchange old shares for new without in the meantime revealing the existence of hidden reserves that previously would have been subject to taxation. A 1969 law eased the tax problems that had been involved in mergers of privately owned companies and of public corporations, as well as problems associated with converting enterprises from one legal form to the other. Another measure cleared the way for close organizational relations between independent, privately held enterprises, such as the pooling of research efforts in a single organization without incurring additional tax burdens.

The government's efforts to establish a favorable climate for innovations also found expression in a number of different tax concessions. Special depreciation allowances were offered for machinery and buildings devoted to industrial innovation. Going beyond mere tax concessions, the government in 1969 extended a subsidy of 16 percent to certain investments associated with industrial innovation.

Of considerably greater importance than the general measures for industrial promotion, however, were the special measures applied to certain problem industries. One of the most persistent problems in the 1960s was the question of support for the German hard-coal-mining industry. At the end of the 1950s, this industry was in great trouble, due to increased imports of coal and fuel oil. To deal with the problem, the oil companies were persuaded to restrict their imports "voluntarily"; restrictions of this sort were in effect from 1965 to 1971. In addition, the supplying of fuel oil and refinery gas to the electric power companies was made subject to the consent of the economics minister. Supporters praised the "voluntary" agreement as a model of pragmatic economic policy, emphasizing that such self-limitations were to be preferred to state interference in the market.[26]

But the government-initiated cooperation of the oil companies had dubious results. In order to increase the effectiveness of the agreement, the independent fuel oil importers, being outsiders in the arrangement, were choked off. The government introduced a requirement that importers must stockpile a certain amount of oil as a national security measure, a requirement that was not financially feasible for the small firms. The retail price of fuel oil almost doubled from 1965 to 1968. The added profits in the fuel oil market allowed the big oil companies to push independent gas stations out of the retail market. The consequence of the voluntary agreement for consumers, therefore, was increased coal and fuel oil prices, together with an increase in the degree of concentration for the already highly concentrated fuel oil and gasoline market.

The process of concerted action was highlighted by the technique of the voluntary agreement. Agreements of this sort came into being through government initiative, in close cooperation with big oligopolists. The government in effect made itself the abettor of oligopolistic arrangements by assuring the agreement's immunity from the Cartel Act and by putting pressure on the small outsiders, who had no effective legal protection. Public functions were thus transferred to large enterprises, and the special state competencies of the public and private sectors were confused.[27]

It was generally assumed that the self-limitation agreement would "have a firm place among the various forms of market regulation in the foreseeable future."[28] The agreement in the oil industry was not the first case and was followed by others. An agreement among the big department stores to refrain from expanding their market in medium-sized towns to the disadvantage of the small retailer was another case in point. In 1966, large enterprises in the cigarette industry made an agreement to limit advertising, and in 1970 they renewed the agreement. Another field in which the voluntary agreement technique was being considered in 1973 was that of environmental protection. In all these cases, speed and simplicity were seen as the great virtues of the approach as compared with legal regulation.

The changed relationship between government and private industry was especially evident in the 1968 enactment in support of Germany's hard-coal-mining industry. The aim of the law was "to get the hard-coal-mining industry into a state in which it can hold its own in the market economy."[29] To that end, a Federal official was designated whose task it was to influence the mining companies to adapt their capacities to the limited market and to concentrate their production in the mines with highest productivity. These measures were complemented by steps to promote the mobility of labor as well as a special system of social security and financial support for the areas in which the coal mines were clustered. While remaining within the framework of the requirements of the European Coal and Steel Community, there was a deliberate effort to promote the concentration of the industry, culminating in the foundation of the Ruhrkohle A.G. in 1968 as well as the application of the concerted-action process to the industry.

The sponsors of the 1968 law in support of Germany's hard coal industry had emphasized from the very beginning that the fractionation of the industry was a major handicap. It was said to impede the process of planning, to prevent the achievement of optimum firm size, and to block technical progress. In accordance with these ideas, the 1968 statute provided that govermental subsidies should be cut off from those companies "which do not prove to have a firm size desirable for the achievement of optimum productivity." Applying general standards of this sort, the economics minister was empowered to define and apply the concepts in the act, by means of legal decree.[30]

When the decree of the economics minister emerged, it was couched in such a way as virtually to force all mines in a given region to develop a so-called regional branch.[31] The Ruhrkohle A.G., the most important of the regional branches, covered the Ruhr district. Ruhrkohle was operated in a pattern of close cooperation among the economics minister, the enterprises, and the unions concerned.

Ruhrkohle was formed from twenty-six mining companies, which turned over their mining assets, together with the debts involved, and received an interest-yielding obligation of Ruhrkohle A.G. in compensation. The obligation and interest were guaranteed by the Federal government and by the state government concerned. In effect, the former owners, while retaining some measure of influence and control, traded their uncertain claim to future profits for a government-guaranteed stream of income.

The implementation of the hard-coal act had all the characteristics of concerted action at the sectoral level. Bypassing the Federal official created to administer the act, the economics minister preferred to negotiate the details of merger directly with private industry. In these negotiations, the examination of conditions that would be attached to state subsidies and the concept of gradual reduction of the subsidies were not even considered. The power stations of the old mining companies were left outside the merger. Contracts were concluded with the electrical power industry and the steel mills, on terms which in effect subsidized the coal industry. Other direct and indirect subsidies for coal, such as special transport rates, a tax on competing fuel oil, and tariffs and other limitations on coal imports, were all left untouched. In effect, the law was avoided in substance but was not formally violated. Moreover, various aspects of the operation justified the generalization that it was a "classic example of the usurpation of political decisions by oligopolies and organized groups."[32] The secrecy of the decision-making process pointed in this direction. So did the occasional hints regarding the balance of power in decision-making: witness the Thyssen group's threat in 1973 to withdraw from the Ruhr group if the government did not increase its coal subsidy.

A similar project for industry mergers was initiated in the petroleum industry in 1968. The lack of a domestic source of crude oil and the limited financial strength of German companies compared with those of other nations induced the government to promote closer cooperation among the existing enterprises in order to provide the Federal Republic with more secure and cheaper supplies of petroleum.[33] A secure system of procurement, it was thought, would be one in which at least 25 percent of Germany's crude oil supply came from German firms. To achieve this objective the government initiated a joint venture by seven German-owned oil firms, to search for new sources of oil. The government granted state aid to the new company for a period of six years in the amount of DM 575 million (U.S. $144 million). Part of the aid was in the form of subsidies, part in the form of loans. Independently of these measures there was an inquiry into tax benefits provided to foreign-owned crude oil companies, in order to determine whether they placed German firms at a disadvantage.

In the advanced technology industries, the tendency to encourage concerted action and to foster mergers or cooperation between the leading companies was also apparent. Government support for these industries was justified with three arguments: the inability of enterprises to finance the necessary expenditures out of their own resources, in light of the high risks involved; the need to match the many direct and indirect measures of support that other nations were extending to competitors of the German firms, and the gap between the companies' short-term profit goal and the long-term social benefits of investments in research.[34] By 1973, the German government's support of science-based industries had been concentrated on aeronautics and space, computers, and nuclear energy.

In the aeronautics and space industry, following a resolution passed by the German parliament in 1968, the government successfully brought about the merger of five firms, each with 6,000 employees. Out of the process, there appeared in 1970 two firms with 20,000 employees each and one firm with 6,000. Since the aeronautics and space industry depended on the government for 75 percent of its sales, the government had a very strong position in the negotiations.* The process of concentration in the nuclear energy industry and the computer industry was also expressly provided for in programs, and probably it was actually

* For a detailed discussion of the aerospace industry see M. S. Hochmuth's chapter in this volume; for the electronic data processing industry see Nicolas Jéquier's chapter.

initiated by the government. In these cases, too, there was close cooperation between government and large enterprise, as the government's orders accounted for a considerable percentage of the industries' sales.[35]

German economic policy at the sectoral level in the 1960s, therefore, was characterized first of all by attempts to introduce a coordinated set of principles and aims. But these general principles were very often disregarded in a process of direct cooperation among government, enterprise, and unions. Concerted action at the sectoral level was especially important in the ailing industries. Nonetheless, acting under the stimulus of the technological gap and recognizing that other governments were giving extensive support to their advanced technology industries, the German government began consciously to develop national champions in these industries as well.

Government-Enterprise Relations: The Firm Level

On the level of the individual firm, official and semiofficial sources throughout the 1960s continued the theme that had dominated in the 1950s: a fundamental affirmation of support for the competitive market economy. In 1967 the government stated: "Competition is and remains the basis of our economic system. Effective competition ensures as much individual freedom as possible for consumers and entrepreneurs and at the same time the best possible economic results."[36] But despite the similarity in the semantics of the two decades, a considerable change could be observed in both the aims and means of competition policy. The stimuli for these changes came on the one hand from a change in economic circumstances and on the other from the work of the political economists themselves.

The contribution of the theorists was especially important. In the 1950s, the ideal of competition policy was—implicitly or explicitly— perfect competition. The actions of individual firms and governments were measured by that yardstick. This orientation of competition policy was shaken by the positions of Schiller and Erhard Kantzenbach. Schiller took a first step at a very early stage when he stated: "One must not regard planning and competition—if the two are to be combined— as goals of economic policy. A policy with two such goals is bound to fail . . . But if one merely regards both as instruments of economic policy, as means of guidance, then the first rocks have been circumnavigated."[37] Competition was no longer a political end in itself and a manifestation of individual freedom; it had to be viewed in more pragmatic terms.

The theoretical foundation of a new competition policy appeared in a book by Kantzenbach, published in the same year that Schiller took office as economics minister. Following Schiller, Kantzenbach held that the decision in favor of competition was primarily a political decision, one which "by no means prejudges the decision of economic policy in choosing among various forms of the competition process." He dwelt on certain functions of competition, emphasizing above all the functions of adaptation to structural change and the development of innovations in products and processes. Perfect competition, he demonstrated, was not able to fulfill these functions in an optimum way. Accordingly, Kantzenbach came to the conclusion that "the optimum intensity of competition is not realized in atomistic markets but in broad oligopolies with homogeneous products and ready market information."[38]

This hypothesis gave rise to passionate discussions of competition policy. Whereas the liberal school placed most emphasis on the competitive condition of the market, as indicated by structure and conduct,[39] Kantzenbach and the government saw market performance as the main criterion of the workability of competition; market performance in this context was meant to include not only price performance but also the quality of products and the technical progress of the industry. Concentration could be justified, therefore, on the simple ground that it led to larger company units, which permitted the realization of economies of scale in production and in research and development; thereby technical progress and economic growth might be enhanced.

Kantzenbach's competition concept was quickly adopted by the government, the Federal Cartel Office, and the industrial associations. His views, very much in the Schumpeter tradition, also drew strength from Galbraith's *The New Industrial State* and Servan-Schreiber's *Le Défi Américain*. Moreover, they could hardly fail to impress politicians and big business, in face of the challenge of the Common Market and the technological gap hypothesis.

When Schiller took office in 1966, these views were given added support. Thus, the Federal government's comment on the Federal Cartel Office Report of 1967 stated: "The Common Market and the trend to world-wide economic integration have created new premises for competition. Larger markets demand in many ways larger and more efficient company units . . . The Federal government is concerned to remove obstacles which stand in the way of concentration of enterprises now blocked by cartel law, so that the development of firms of optimum size will not be hindered."[40] This conclusion led to the various revisions in tax law mentioned earlier.

The support of the theorists for the promotion of concentration was matched by action in the business community itself. A Concentration Inquiry of the parliament had already come to the conclusion that from 1954 to 1960 industrial concentration in the Federal Republic had increased. After the mid-1960s, moreover, the tempo of concentration had visibly accelerated.[41] From 1966 to 1970, 646 mergers were reported to the Federal Cartel Office. In the years 1969 and 1970 alone, the Cartel Office noted 473 company mergers, 69 more than the 404 reported for the entire decade of 1958–1968.

Above all, the so-called big mergers increased considerably, especially among firms whose sales were measured in billions of deutschemarks.[42] Most significant was the process of horizontal concentration between big companies, 116 such cases being reported between 1966 and 1970. Conglomerate mergers also grew in importance, with 66 reported in the four-year period, 50 of them in the last year of the period alone. These were mostly mergers in which production facilities in one branch could be joined with selling outlets in another. On the other hand, vertical concentration played a minor role, only three cases being reported in the four years.

In the concentration euphoria of the mid-1960s the connection between enterprise size and export potential played a special role. The opening of the European market and the expansion of American direct investments in western Europe were thought to be overwhelming the German economy. Government and industry saw in the promotion of concentration an effective instrument of adaptation to the international situation. Unusual significance was attached to an expert report on enterprise size and international competitiveness, financed by the interested branches of industry. Although the report was not commercially available, members of parliament concerned with the subject carried it under their arms during the relevant debates, citing it as a bible. The report assumed that the German export trade was to a disproportionate extent conducted by large enterprises, and that the degree of concentration in German industry was relatively low. It concluded that larger units would be needed for the long-term competitiveness of Germany, "because only they can create the adequate counterweight to foreign competition."[43] The superiority of American companies was explained by the higher intensity of capital, the higher quality of management and organization, and the scale effects of a larger home market.

In actual fact, of course, in the early 1970s West German industry led all other EEC nations in its degree and increase of concentration. As early as 1966, the four largest firms accounted for the following proportion of sales in their respective industries: oil and gas, 83.7 percent; automobiles, 81.3 percent; shipbuilding, 54.2 percent; electric power, 49.5 percent; chemicals, 49 percent; electrical engineering, 47.4 percent; and rubber and asbestos, 45 percent. Presumably these ratios had increased by 1973. The EEC Commission's fostering of transnational concentrations and investments, therefore, though apparently parallel to that of German policy, actually had the opposite effect as far as concentration in the German economy was concerned. Whereas concentration of the big enterprises at a national level carved up the European market into rigid power-structures, transnational mergers diffused the influence of any given group operating in a national market.[44]

Germany's new competition policy, when stressing the desirability of concentration, characteristically referred to the small and medium-sized firms rather than to the leaders. Where too many small and medium-sized companies existed, competition had first of all to be fostered by creating efficient firm units and, if need be, efficient joint units among the firms. The idea of cooperation among small and medium-sized companies was expressed in a so-called "Cooperation Primer," which defined the areas for cooperation that would not run afoul of the Cartel Law. Permission to make specialization agreements, as provided in a Cartel Act amendment of 1965, was facilitated.

Other measures were also taken to encourage cooperation between medium-sized companies. Through special financial and advisory programs the government tried to ease the formation of small and medium-sized enterprises, to facilitate their adjustment to changes in the market situation, and to help them apply technical innovations. According to a study published in 1971, the advisory programs proved to be a much better means of overcoming the problems of small and medium-sized firms than the financial assistance programs. Moreover, as an added sign of the strengths and needs of such firms, various medium-sized firms very successfully took part in innovative competition with large enterprise, in both domestic and international markets.[45]

Despite all the emphasis on the virtues of concentration, the rapid concentration of industry in the Federal Republic toward the end of the 1960s eventually stirred up the public, the government, and the Federal Cartel Office. The simplified thesis of the advantages of concentration gave way to a more qualified attitude in the field of competition policy. In conformity with Kantzenbach's view of some optimum degree of concentration to achieve effective competition, the authorities recognized that concentration could be overdone. The Federal government stated in 1969: "Recently, there has been a series of mergers which have created or extended strong market positions in key sectors of the economy. The question of how such concentration processes affect the whole economy is difficult as a rule to estimate; for it cannot be asserted that technical progress always requires concentration, and that larger enterprises are especially helpful in promoting progress. It may be that concentration helps to facilitate the adoption of cost-saving methods, technical progress, and enhanced competitiveness on international markets. But concentration can also lead to a decline of workable competition."[46]

Insights such as these led at the end of the 1960s to discussions over changes in the Cartel Act. As it stood, the Cartel Act could not effectively block undesirable concentrations. The main emphasis in the act was on the prohibition of cartels, and even that was limited by numerous exemptions. Thus, according to judicial interpretations, collusive market conduct or price leadership, even if they served the same purpose as a cartel, could not be touched by the cartel prohibition. And abuses committed by companies by virtue of their simple dominance of the market were placed by court interpretation essentially outside the reach of the act. That market power in the economy might be increased by company mergers was not reflected in the act; mergers need only be reported to the Cartel Office.[47] And if the enterprises did not exceed a certain size and position in the market, they risked nothing but a hearing.

The Federal government's comments of 1969 on the drawbacks of excessive concentrations were noteworthy in another respect. They stressed for the first time "that the Cartel Act no longer does justice to the changed economic reality. The number one problem of economic policy is no longer cartel formation but the concentration of enterprises." Beginning at that time, the government prepared an amendment to the Cartel Act, the main emphases of which were the introduction of a system for the control of mergers, improvements in the control of enterprises in a dominant market position, and further facilitation of cooperation among small and medium-sized companies.[48] In 1971 the government finally introduced its bill. The election victory of the Social Democrats and Free Democrats in 1972 heightened the probability that some such enactment would eventually take place.

To sum up, a new concept of competition policy was developed by the official policymakers in the 1960s. Appealing to the need for improved performance in technology and for greater international competitiveness, it fostered a concentration trend that was already apparent in the economy. This had two decisive consequences for government-enterprise relations. First, competition itself became an instrument in a national planning process, that process being undertaken cooperatively by the economic centers of power. At the same time, the officially sanctioned concentration process provided the basis for the development of more and more powerful enterprises, through which cooperation between government and large enterprise could be extended and intensified.[49] Whether or not the government's intentions to restrain concentration in the 1970s could impede or even reverse these tendencies, however, was doubtful. Even if the means for combating concentration that were under consideration in the early 1970s should be applied, they seemed scarcely sufficient to measure up to the job.

Policy Formulation in the Federal Republic

Germany's new economic policy of the 1960s represented a complex effort to integrate a number of different strands of economic policy into a consistent whole. The Stability and Growth Act, with its emphasis on Keynesian policies and the management of aggregate demand, represented one key element of the national approach. The structural policies epitomized in the government's Principles of Sectoral Policy represented a second. And the emphasis on the free market system, laid down in the Cartel Act, represented a third. The Federal government's efforts to interrelate all three in a common national program was evident from its enactments. The Stability and Growth Act contained references to structural ends and means, while the official Principles of Sectoral Policy referred to Germany's familiar quartet of macroeconomic goals—internal stability, high employment, external equilibrium, and growth. Both the Stability and Growth Act and the Principles of Sectoral Policy made their obeisance, of course, to a competitive market economy.

These laborious affirmations of the interrelatedness of the three lines of policy, however, proved to be of no real consequence. What was decisive for German economic policies in the 1960s, as has already been pointed out, was the increasingly direct cooperation among governmental authorities, organized interest groups, and large enterprises. The new economic policy must therefore be regarded as an attempt to overcome the monolithic policy of the 1950s, which had identified the maintenance of the market system as the sole end and means of economic policy. In the 1960s it was realized that one could limit the market's performance in various ways without being pushed to the other extreme, that of the command economy and the central plan. It began to be understood that in modern industrialized societies there were four basic social processes relevant for policy coordination: the price system, the interaction in the hierarchy, the electoral process, and the play of bargaining among interest groups.[50] Each system had its strengths and limitations; and various combinations had to be applied to solve different social tasks.

In linking the three different levels of economic policy, Germany combined the various social decision systems, relating the electoral process in government and in interest groups with elements of the market mechanism, and these in turn with bargaining among the representatives of government, the interest groups, and the large enterprises. The object was to achieve a coordinated, harmonious policy at the macroeconomic, the sectoral, and the firm level—"a homogeneous economic policy," in Schiller's words. But it is doubtful that anything of the sort had actually been achieved by the early 1970s.

In order to analyze the outcome of this process, certain simplifying assumptions have to be made. The government, we may assume, has the paramount aim of being re-elected. According to Anthony Downs' theory of representative democracy, a limited number of political parties are in competition for the largest number of votes.[51] The formal equality of voters at the ballot box, however, does not imply that the government attributes the same political weight to the interests of all citizens.

The disparity in political importance between different groups of citizens is due to the fact that most political decisions on the part of both government and voters alike are made under conditions of uncertainty. Some voters are in possession of more information than others, or can acquire information at lower cost than others. This is simply a consequence of the fact that each voter is better informed about the area of his specialty than about other areas in which his interest is more dilute. The cost of information may be relatively high in areas of dilute interest. Thus there are groups of citizens who can rationally afford to influence governmental policy on any particular issue, and others for whom it is rational to remain ignorant. For governmental parties this means: "Economically speaking, government policy in a democracy almost always exhibits an anti-consumer, pro-producer bias."[52]

The same rationality principle applies to groups. Mancur Olson has demonstrated why large unorganized groups of voters have almost no chance to establish powerful organizations.[53] According to his theory, organized groups will only be established if the group members are rewarded by the hope of achieving special advantage, typically an increase in the real incomes of their membership. If the group's leadership succeeds, it increases its chances of remaining in office as well as its chances of attracting more adherents to the group. All of these general propositions, whatever their validity might be in other times and places, seemed to apply well enough to the Germany of the 1960s.

However, the concerted actions fostered by the government were, above all, bargaining situations between the leadership of organized groups and government officials. The question arises, therefore, what special benefits the group leadership had to offer to the government. Here again one must stress the conditions of uncertainty under which government officials have to decide on policy matters. They cannot be sure what effect a particular policy will have on a certain sector of the economy and how the welfare of the income-receivers of this sector will be affected by the measure. The industrial associations and the unions, however, are in a position to place special information at the disposal of the government at almost no extra cost.[54]

Apart from information, there is also the question of the market power of organized groups. If an organized group or a single large enterprise possesses considerable influence in the market, it can affect not only its own group members but also outsiders who have similar interests, such as customers and suppliers. One of the reasons for the large sustained subsidies in favor of the German hard-coal-mining industry can be seen in the extraordinary market power of the industrial associations and the unions of that industry. In the 1960s, employment in the industry was high and was concentrated in a few regions; the industry was both a supplier and customer of the steel and electrical power industries; and it could affect the price and supply of those key products. For other countries, one might have added, too, that the coal-mining industry could finance political activity and could threaten the use of strikes; but for the Germany of the 1960s these were less important considerations.[55]

Factors of this sort indicate what a strong position organized groups had both in the political process and in the process of concerted action. Schiller pragmatically accepted these facts: "The associations are nowadays an expression of our group-aggregated society. Experience shows that whoever gets into a basically negative relationship with these organized groups can no longer govern." In light of that acceptance, his asserted desire also to pit "the laws of rational economics . . . against the demands of the lobbies" might be described as rather quixotic.[56]

It is not at all surprising, therefore, that the macroeconomic decisions generated by the concerted action process exhibited a palpable anticonsumer bias. The preferential treatment of producers' interests was reflected by the administration's successes in combating the recession of 1966–67 and by its failure to reduce the inflation during the five-year boom that followed. Concerted action, it was supposed, would contribute to the total stability of the economy by direct global planning of the macroeconomic aggregates, especially the national wage bill. Actual rates of pay and wage structures were to be left to the determination of the market or of wage settlements. The two levels were to be linked by the promulgation of projections and guidelines issued with the joint blessing of the participants in the concerted action process. But the critical question still remained: How were such guidelines translated into actual decisions of the market?[57]

If one takes a closer look at the organized groups involved in the concerted action process, one discovers that as a rule only the men at the very peak of the interest-group pyramids took part. Although they were in a position to perform some of their role as suppliers of information and advocates for their group interests, they were far removed from the associations representing specific industry sectors and from the individual unions. The ability of the advocates at the summit to deliver the cooperation of these remote groups, where issues of wage determination and price determination were involved, was probably quite limited.

There was one level of economic policy, however, in which the concerted action process generated results attractive to all concerned. This was the policy for the sectoral level. Considering the fact that producers' associations representing sectoral interests were relatively efficient units for generating information with respect to their own sectors, they were superior as a rule to the individual firm.[58] Their collective financial resources and their ability to exercise collective bargaining power in the interests of the sector were also superior. In oligopolistically structured industries, their limited number and their habits of cooperation added to their strength.

That strength was one of the reasons for the common observation that "sectoral economic policy in the Federal Republic of Germany has greatly undermined general economic policy." At the firm level, the government could defend its basic policies, if it wished, by referring to the Cartel Act; at the macroeconomic level, it could appeal to the Stability and Growth Act. The government's so-called Principles of Sectoral Policy, however, did not possess the force of law. Though a Structural Adaptation Act had been proposed in order to diminish the dangers of giving benefits to certain organized groups to the disadvantage of the whole of society, no such law had been placed on the books by 1973.[59]

One major incentive that the German government had for resisting sectoral demands was that such demands generally added fuel to the inflationary process. The special sensitivity of the German public to inflation suggests that a government which gave way to these inflationary pressures indiscriminately might run a major risk of losing its mandate. On the other hand, the ailing branches of industry generated such acute unhappiness among workers, owners, and managers directly affected that governmental help in these sectors was more likely to generate political strength than political loss. Assuming that the asymmetry of producers' and consumers' interests was realistic, it would generally pay a government to support such industries.[60]

This line of argument suggests that expanding industries would be less likely to get the support of a politically conscious German government than the branches that were declining. The science-based industries, however, were a special case. These industries were greatly dependent on governmental orders. Accordingly, the workers, owners, and managers could relate a deterioration of their situation directly to the lack of governmental support. This might generate the same political calculation and the same political response as for the ailing industries. Indeed, that could well have occurred in Germany if the employment and output of the industries concerned had been larger. As it was, the German government gave those industries only half-hearted support. Despite the official proclamations, therefore, sectoral economic policy in the Federal Republic in the 1960s and early 1970s was largely protectionist in flavor and contributed to retardation rather than growth promotion. And the process that generated this result was one that detracted from the power of the parliamentary process and the democratic system on which it was based.[61]

The United Kingdom

Trevor Smith

The early 1950s exuded something of an air of economic optimism, a rare enough event in the mood of Britain after 1945. If this optimism was not based on the firmest foundations it was at least understandable. Despite the failures of government policies to achieve their goals, and despite fuel crises and other debilitating setbacks, the immediate post-war years had avoided the kinds of economic and social problems which had beset the country in the years after 1919. High employment had been maintained and a welfare state more or less consolidated; wartime rationing and other controls had finally been lifted; and a far-off Korean war had stimulated something of a boom, however short-lived. By 1954 the Chancellor of the Exchequer felt able to predict a doubling of living standards within twenty-five years. An era of mid-century prosperity appeared to have been launched: the 1951 Festival of Britain, emulating the Great Exhibition promoted exactly a century before, symbolized that such was the hope.

In the ensuing years and up to the early 1970s this hope was sustained, albeit on the meager diet of relatively slender achievement. The symbolic trappings of a rapidly fading imperial grandeur and the compensatory vaunting of the so-called special relationship with the United States may have been necessary bromides to assuage the trauma of facing up to a new reality which was already dawning. The 1954 *Economic Survey,* for example, "was one of the first published documents to draw attention to Britain's falling share in world trade."[1] Despite such portents, however, government economic policy remained largely a matter of relying on the Keynesian techniques of demand management with the intention of maintaining high employment levels, containing excessive inflation, and safeguarding both the nation's balance-of-payments position and that of sterling as an international reserve currency. British economic policy in the 1950s consisted essentially of pursuing as far as possible a general nondiscriminatory approach in the belief that this was the best way of fostering a climate favorable to economic stability and industrial expansion. There were two main departures from this. The investment program of the nation-

Trevor Smith is Senior Lecturer in Government and Political Science, Queen Mary College, University of London, England. This chapter is based partly on research carried out for the Acton Society Trust and supported by a grant from the (British) Social Science Research Council.

alized industries were used as short-term policy instruments for effecting changes in government public expenditure decisions, often with little regard for the long-term implications for the industries' future development. In a more positive way, selective investment incentives were used to attract new industrial development in the more sluggish regions of the economy.

Toward the end of the decade the reliance on broad, macroeconomic techniques began to be questioned. The main source of doubt sprang from the growing habit, which later was to reach epidemic proportions and which ought really to have been classified as a contagious public disease, of comparing Britain's economic, industrial, and social performance with that of other industrialized nations and particularly those in the EEC. The remorseless construction of such comparative data poignantly illustrated the fact that, following the loss of empire, the international reference group had become the major determinant of Britain's economic psychology.

Once it had been established that Britain's performance, especially the ability to promote faster growth, lagged behind those of other countries and was, moreover, in danger of slipping still further, the causes of this state of affairs had to be diagnosed and remedies suggested. In terms of Britain's own experience during the 1950s there was a near-unanimous consensus that the reason for its poor performance lay in trying to maintain a balance among the competing goals of full employment, balance-of-payments considerations, and the combating of inflation. Because these could not be balanced successfully for any appreciable length of time, the government perforce had retreated to dealing with them sequentially, rather in the manner of an oriental juggler spinning plates on bamboo sticks, but without the same dexterity. This approach had resulted in a series of enervating stop-go cycles, whereas the need seemed to be for a broad-spectrum remedy. In terms of other countries' experience, a swift glance at the Continent was enough to point to the solution, or, more accurately, an amalgam of solutions. The indicative planning practices of France, the industrial relations system of Sweden, and the commercial orientation of Italian state enterprise were among the favorite examples which commentators urged Britain to follow. If a fundamental change in attitudes and behavior was to come about, it was argued, a start had to be made with the government.

The Government

The Conservative government, 1951–1964. As the 1950s drew to a close, the government began to exhibit signs that some modifications were needed to improve its regulation of the economy. Alarmed at the continuing domestic inflation, resulting in part from overgenerous pay settlements, it created an independent Council on Productivity, Prices, and Incomes in August 1957. The Council's task was to pontificate at regular intervals on the state of the economy in the hope of educating public opinion toward a more sober appreciation of economic reality. A more substantive reform followed the publication of the Plowden report on public expenditure in 1961, which recommended the incorporation of a variety of management techniques, including medium-term forecasting, into the Treasury's armory. The report also prompted the creation of the Centre for Administrative Studies to furnish civil servants with an elementary acquaintance with economics and statistics. But its greatest impact, perhaps, was in stamping the notion of *management* on the public service in place of the more traditional concept of *administration*. This was no mere substitution of nomenclature: it signified the beginning of the attempt to move away from the relatively detached and passive stance of government toward the adoption of a more interventionist and assertive role in economic and industrial affairs.

From Plowden onwards, reformist fervor swept through Whitehall like a bushfire, with an eager corps of technocratically inclined academics and journalists fanning the flames.[2] In 1961 the Conservatives, who since the end of the war had doggedly opposed planning as a piece of socialist dogma, embraced it overnight, although they took pains to distinguish between their new indicative variety and what they regarded as the old idea of centralized state direction. Harold Macmillan, the prime minister, had been one of the leading Conservative supporters of planning when it was first suggested in the 1930s: then he had been in a small unorthodox minority whose members were drawn from all political parties. In the early 1960s he was in a position to implement his earlier nostrums, particularly in view of the apparent French success with planning which had been initiated under the direction of Jean Monnet.

This sudden conversion resulted in the creation of the National Economic Development Council (NEDC), that was to provide an independent tripartite forum at which representatives from government, business, and the unions could meet as equal partners to discuss in broad outline what future direction the economy should take. Attached to the NEDC was the National Economic Development Office (NEDO), consisting of a planning staff (mainly economists drawn on a temporary basis from industry, the universities, and the civil service), and an industrial staff. The planning staff was to begin to draw up national economic plans and related programs, while the industrial staff was to provide a liaison network—principally through the Economic Development Committees (EDCs)—by which the three contracting parties and their constituents could communicate with one another.

The deliberations of the NEDC were intended to produce a realistic consensus as to the desired future development of the economy to which all three partners would broadly subscribe. It was hoped that this consensus, embodied in five-year plans, would reduce uncertainty, eliminate stop-go cycles, and enable government and industry alike to look ahead with greater confidence and knowledge. The effective motive power behind the new experiment in planning was expected to be generated by the independent technocrats in the NEDO as they went about exercising an uninhibited intellectual, political, and entrepreneurial flair in a manner akin to their French counterparts in the Commissariat du Plan: an authoritative and articulated "NEDO view" would serve, additionally, to promote a consensus within the NEDC which would be endorsed, eventually, by a wider audience.

There were three reasons which required the NEDO staff to perform an initiating role. First, because the NEDC members (ministers, union leaders, and industrialists) met only once a month, they were not well placed to make much of a substantive contribution to the formation of planning programs. The NEDC, on the other hand, was placed at the apex of the planning machinery and could function as a sounding board as well as a legitimizing agency. Secondly, even if the industrialists and unionists were disposed to contribute significantly to the production of plans within the NEDO-NEDC arena (as opposed to making the more conventional ad hoc representations directly to the government on specific items of economic management), neither the Confederation of British Industries (CBI) nor the Trades Union Congress (TUC) could compete with the specialist resources of the NEDO. And the government, which was better equipped, was effectively under a self-denying ordinance to safeguard both the principle of equality established for the tripartite forums and the independent status of the NEDC-NEDO structure. Thirdly, the NEDO staff, in the absence of a more positive role definition, were expected to emulate the French.

In the years between 1961 and 1964, when the Conservatives made their dash for planning, the NEDO published a plan for achieving a 4 percent annual growth rate, entitled *Growth of the U.K. Economy to 1966,* and a supplement *Conditions Favorable to Foster Growth.* In the same period they created the National Incomes Commission (NIC), in the face of strong union opposition, to adjudicate on wage settlements; passed the Industrial Training Act, which placed a statutory obligation on firms to undertake systematic training schemes supervised by a variety of Industrial Training Boards (ITBs); and, against considerable opposition from their own backbenchers, outlawed price-fixing agreements by pushing through the Resale Price Maintenance Act.

The Labour government, 1964–1970. The new Labour government of 1964 carried on, for the most part, where the Conservatives had left off; but though the general direction remained the same, the pace quickened perceptibly. Shortly before the election the first batch of EDCs had been set up, covering chemicals, the distributive trades, most of the engineering industries, woollen textiles, paper, and confectionery. Other industries were added until in 1967 twenty-one EDCs existed. They spanned four fifths of the private-sector labor force and the post office, the one state industry to be included within the EDC network. To complement the vertical antennae which the EDCs constituted, the government established tripartite Economic Planning Councils in each of the newly defined English regions, together with similar councils for Wales, Scotland, and Ulster, to form a network of horizontal antennae.

A major departure from the Conservative practice of maintaining the independent status of the NEDC-NEDO structure was taken when the Labour government transferred the bulk of the NEDO's economic staff to the newly created Department of Economic Affairs (DEA), which was to be primarily responsible for constructing national plans. The NEDC was to remain as a consensus-building, legitimizing forum, but henceforth the NEDO, acting through the medium of the EDCs, was to be mainly concerned with improving the flow of communications between government and industry, with stimulating industries' awareness of their own deficiencies, and with encouraging them to come up with solutions which would then be widely disseminated. The founding of the DEA was intended to place the formulation of plans squarely within the machinery of government, thus releasing the government from its self-denying ordinance. The DEA was also intended to provide a countervailing perspective within Whitehall to that of the Treasury, whose established modes of operation were thought to give too low a priority to growth and which would have inhibited the hortatory style necessary to arouse a widespread commitment to the objectives of planning.[3]

The DEA, together with the NEDO, the EDCs, and, to a much lesser extent, as it turned out, the regional Economic Planning Councils, comprised the government's planning machinery. These agencies, recognizing the need for swift production of an official and reasonably comprehensive document if the momentum in favor of planning, which had been building up since 1961, was not to be dissipated, produced and published *The National Plan* in 1965. In July 1966, however, the government felt obliged to introduce vast deflationary measures in order to deal with the current crisis of that year and to avoid devaluation. In doing so, it moved into a direction wholly contradictory to the spirit and substance of the Plan, effectively scuttling its major objective of growth. After the demise of the Plan, the reformist critics—armed with hindsight and in a mood analogous to *post-coitum tristesse*—competed with one another to expose the shortcomings in its underlying assumptions, its mode of preparation, the speed of compilation, and its lack of internal consistency.[4] Such critics failed to understand the complex and necessarily imperfect nature of planning. Whatever the regime, planning, whether coercive or indicative, seems to require a judicious balance between extensive exhortation and symbol manipulation on the one hand and a definitive program, however sketchy, on the other. Planning, with a capital P, by definition contains a large unrealistic element, and perhaps for this reason should not be attempted; but if it is, the impossibility of achieving perfection should be recognized both before and after the event.

The abandonment of the Plan seriously undermined the planning agencies despite official protestations to the contrary. The DEA began a lingering death, succumbing finally in 1969. The EDCs carried on, but even the careful nursing of the NEDO staff could not prevent the process of erosion. Some EDCs continued to busy themselves, for example, those in chemicals, the distributive trades, and most of those in engineering; others, such as those in printing, knitwear, and building, later broke up with varying degrees of acrimony; while still others, like those in the post office, rubber, and paper, seemed to quietly peter out. By 1971 only nine EDCs remained intact.

Although the deflationary package of July 1966 undermined the rationale of the planning agencies, it gave added impetus and status to the work of the government's new interventionist instruments: the Ministry of Technology (MinTech), which, like the DEA, had been set up in 1964; the National Board for Prices and Incomes (PIB), which had been created in 1965 as a successor to the National Incomes Commission; and the Industrial Reorganisation Corporation (IRC), which had been formed early in 1966 to speed up the process of industrial restructuring.

MinTech represented the Labour government's commitment to forge a new and modernized Britain "out of the white heat of the technological revolution." To begin with, it was given the task of looking after the fortunes of four industries: computers, electronics, telecommunications, and machine tools. It also had responsibility for atomic energy, the National Research Development Corporation (NRDC), and various government research establishments. After a generally warm press reception, its first two years, with Frank Cousins as minister, were nevertheless somewhat inauspicious; indeed, only a year after its formation it was censured by the House of Commons Estimates Committee for being too top-heavy, for overlapping too much with the DEA, and for making slow progress in reviewing the four industries in its charge. Like all new agencies it had teething problems, particularly in establishing a clear role for itself. In December 1965 its tasks were extended to cover the electrical and mechanical engineering industries, and it was given general oversight of the engineering profession. By February 1966 its future direction was well charted. After the deflationary measures taken by the government in July it gained further prestige at the expense of the DEA, and in the same month Cousins was replaced as minister by the energetic Anthony Wedgwood Benn. Within a few months MinTech expanded again, absorbing the Ministry of Aviation and taking over responsibility for shipbuilding.[5]

As an earnest of the government's intentions to encourage technological progress, the borrowing power of the NRDC was raised from £25 million (U.S. $60 million) to a ceiling of £50 million ($120 million) in 1967, which was used *inter alia* to subsidize computer developments and experiments with numerically controlled machine tools. The Shipbuilding Industry Act of 1967 provided loans of £400 million ($960 million) at preferential rates, which led to the formation of Upper Clyde Shipbuilders, merging four previous shipyards. In 1968 the role of MinTech was further enhanced by the passage of the Industrial Expansion Act. That act released £100 million which could later be raised to £150 million to enable the government to make loans, grants, and guarantees and to underwrite losses in order to support industrial schemes that would improve efficiency or profitability, create or expand productive capacity, or promote technological improvements.[6] Under the act the government initiated the computer merger which culminated in the formation of ICL, and it also provided aid for the building of three aluminum smelters.*

Another interventionist agency, the IRC, had originally been the brain child of MinTech although it was launched under the paternity of the DEA in 1966. Its formal terms of reference were

(a) to promote or assist the reorganisation of development of any industry; or

(b) if requested to do so by the Secretary of State, to establish or develop, or promote or assist the establishment or development of any industrial enterprise.

Its creation reflected the government's desire to quicken still more the speed of industrial restructuring which, through mergers and takeovers, was already fairly rapid. The IRC was expected to give priority to schemes that promised to reduce imports or stimulate exports, and it was enjoined to take cognizance of regional needs. It was given initial funds of £150 million ($420 million) and a board of eleven members consisting mainly of industrialists and merchant bankers together with a lawyer and a "statutory" trade unionist. The board, representing as it

* See in this volume Nicolas Jéquier's chapter on computers and Zuhayr Mikdashi's chapter on aluminum.

did established and distilled wisdom, was complemented by a relatively youthful team of full-time staff which never numbered more than thirty.[7]

The IRC began cautiously, for like most of the new agencies its role was not clearly delineated. It was also obliged to act circumspectly to disarm its critics. The Confederation of British Industries (CBI), the Institute of Directors, and ICI had all expressed hostility when its creation was first announced. ICI condemned it as a means of extending state interference and furthering "the policy of the public ownership of the means of production." The Institute of Directors called it "trap door nationalisation"; and the CBI promised to make sure that the government did not "envisage nationalisation by the back door."[8]

Like MinTech, the IRC soon gained confidence and built up a formidable workload. Within eighteen months of its inception it had committed about a third of its money to finance schemes covering seven sectors of industry; in addition it had made confidential contacts with some four hundred companies. Using either its influence or its cash, it participated in a number of major amalgamations, including the series of electrical mergers that led ultimately to an enlarged General Electric Company (GEC). The IRC also assisted in rationalizing part of the mechanical engineering industry, encouraged the formation of the British Leyland Motor Corporation, and helped to ward off the bid of a Swedish company, Skefco, for a larger share of the British ball-bearing industry. Nevertheless, the IRC was abolished in 1971. On its abolition, it reported that it had "been substantially involved in about 90 projects at least 75 of which are turning out as expected. Rolls Royce is a special case. The remainder, though labouring to some extent, are still operating in the direction intended."[9]

It is difficult to evaluate the work of the IRC. In 1970 its chairman, Sir Joseph Lockwood, thought it would be another four or five years before an overall assessment could be made. But, even then, given the nature of mergers and the difficulty of monitoring their effects, only a very general judgment would be possible. Taking a narrow view of the IRC and judging it on its own terms a number of conclusions, mainly favorable, can be drawn. It is true that it failed inevitably to secure "early returns in terms of increased exports or reduced import requirements." On the other hand, whatever its economic shortcomings, it had a measure of political success: most notably, the CBI became converted to its cause. It was emulated by the French Institut du Développement Industriel (IDI) and was, in a certain sense, resurrected by the Conservatives in 1972 in the form of the Industrial Development Executive (IDE). The influence of the IRC was still felt in 1973 when moves were made to effect a merger that it had urged unsuccessfully four years earlier.[10]

When one takes the broad rather than the narrow view and looks at the IRC against the wider background of the totality of economic policy, a more cautious judgment must be made. The use made of the IRC and its performance must then be compared with the use and performance of two other interventionist instruments—the National Board for Prices and Incomes (PIB) and the much older Monopolies Commission (MC).

Complaints were often voiced about the apparent contradiction in having both a merger-fostering IRC and a monopoly-investigating MC. But their simultaneous existence in no way offended the canons of indicative planning. The reverse was the case. One of the principal aims of such planning is to bring about a more sensitive, tailor-made approach to policy at the level of the firm. Accordingly, some mergers— even those leading to a monopoly situation—might be deemed necessary in the public interest and thus be candidates for encouragement and support from the IRC. Others, alternatively, might on balance seem detrimental and should be closely scrutinized by the MC and, if judged unfavorably, subsequently prevented.[11] The problem for government was how to use both agencies; how, in other words, to differentiate between potentially beneficial and potentially harmful mergers, and how to coordinate the activities of the IRC and MC.

The Labour government clearly intended, early in its life, to police mergers effectively, for it passed the Monopolies and Mergers Act in 1965. This act considerably strengthened the MC by enlarging both its size and its terms of reference. It also incorporated some of the proposals considered by the previous Conservative administration. The subsequent operations of the MC were something of an anticlimax. From 1965 to 1969 the Board of Trade considered some 430 proposed mergers but referred only twelve to the MC for further consideration: and one of these (Associated Fisheries and the Ross Group), which the MC rejected, was later promoted by the IRC. The Board of Trade agreed, usually at the instigation of the IRC, not to refer eight other major proposals to the MC in return for certain assurances as to the future structure or behavior of the amalgamated enterprises.[12] What needs to be explained in the light of these figures is why, given the government's original intention, the MC was used so sparingly. An answer to this question can best be attempted by making comparisons among all three interventionist agencies: the MC, the IRC, and the PIB.

In the first place, the differential use made of the MC on the one hand and the IRC and PIB on the other was due to the circumstances molding government policy in the latter half of the 1960s. The collapse of the Plan virtually dictated that a greater emphasis would be placed on the work of the interventionist agencies, while the implementation of a prices-and-wages freeze as part of the deflationary measures elevated the role of the PIB. In the case of the IRC, political considerations apart, the preponderant mood of industry was one which favored amalgamations. Despite the reservations which the CBI had harbored at its creation, the IRC had the good fortune to be working in the favorable climate of what might be called merger mania. Expectations and attitudes are clearly an important factor in determining the successful outcome of economic policy. Thus, neither the business world nor the government was likely to restrain the IRC's efforts; indeed the government, to emphasize the IRC's independence, had given it a virtually free hand from the outset.

Secondly, there were differences in the time scale of operations between the MC and the other two agencies. It took the MC all of six months to adjudicate a merger referred to it by the Board of Trade, whereas the IRC could act as quickly as it wished. And the PIB reported within three months on the prices or wages proposals referred to it. In the somewhat frenetic atmosphere of the times the ponderous deliberations of the MC counted against it.

Thirdly, the enlarged MC found itself in a *Catch 22* predicament. As a *Times* leader observed:

Its role, hitherto perhaps, owes too much to a crude political suspicion of concentrated private industrial power . . . But it also owes too much to a static economic theory which was originally developed to explain price levels in a given market situation.

The theory is not valueless as such. But it takes little account of dynamic factors: for example, research and development costs, long-run economies of scale, international competition in a rapidly changing industrial world, the scarcity of first class management. Thus the more the Monopolies Commission tries to be modern and dynamic in its thinking, as in a number of its better recent reports, the more it seems to cut the ground from under its own feet.[13]

Extravagant though this criticism was, it faithfully reflected, in its citation of R&D, rapid industrial change, paucity of good management, and other modish shibboleths, the prevailing wisdom.

Fourthly, and perhaps most starkly, the MC differed from the PIB and IRC in the approach it adopted to its task. It was presided over by a lawyer rather than by a business executive. Sixteen of its twenty-three members were over fifty. Some of its permanent staff of sixty-nine members had been with it from the start in 1948. It is not surprising, therefore, that it acted on a traditionally British ad hoc basis. As the *Times* reported: "Sir Ashton Roskill, QC, refuses to talk about the philosophy of the Monopolies Commission, of which he is chairman. 'It is enshrined in the reports which we have published. You must read those. Each case is different.' " This contrasted totally with the brash and buoyant outlooks which both the PIB and IRC generated. The PIB chairman, Aubrey Jones, and its first secretary, Alex Jarratt, ensured that the PIB had an impact on the mass media considerably greater than that which it had on inflation. Jones's forceful, publicity-seeking style was complemented by the energy and flair of Jarratt, an untypical civil servant who later forsook Whitehall to become a prominent businessman and influential in the CBI. The PIB's mode of operation, particularly in its first years, was highly organic as opposed to mechanistic. A similar style was adopted by the IRC with its specially selected staff, most of whom were in their fifties. As Andrew Graham has observed: "The IRC's vague terms of reference meant that the personnel who operated it were crucial in determining its shape. In practice, its approach seemed to consist largely of finding good management and then backing it, either in a merger or takeover."[14] Though the agency was outwardly circumspect, a high level of internal excitement must have been generated in playing the clandestine game of real-life *Monopoly* with £150 million of other people's money.

In the circumstances it is little wonder that the MC was upstaged and outflanked by both the PIB and the IRC.

In its last months of office the Labour government announced its intention to combine the PIB and MC into a single Commission on Industry and Manpower (CIM). Although the move was never consummated, the ostensible reason behind it was rationalization: the PIB's concern with monopoly pricing encroached on a part of the MC's preserves. But apart from eliminating the overlap in functions of the two bodies, such a reform might also have led to a more vigorous policing of monopoly formation, which was clearly needed: the chances were that the philosophy, style, and methods of the CIM would have resembled those of the PIB rather than those of the MC. One of the errors of economic management in the late 1960s was the failure to maintain a reasonable balance between the influence of the IRC and the MC.

The Conservative government, 1970–1972. The result of the 1970 election not only prevented the creation of a CIM but also led to the abolition of the IRC and the PIB. The Conservatives' manifesto contained a strong element of economic liberalism, and it appeared from this that the new government intended to pursue policies which would increase the degree of competition in the economy and reduce the interventionist role of the state. They promised to strengthen the MC though they abolished the Consumer Council; to limit severely the flow of subsidies and grants from the government to industry; and to eschew the use of selective fiscal instruments of the kind introduced by Labour, in favor of a return to measures of a more general, nondiscriminatory nature.

In two areas of policy the Conservative government pushed ahead where Labour had halted. First, it passed an Industrial Relations Act, similar to the one which its predecessor had withdrawn in 1969 in the face of massive trade union pressure. The act attempted to bring industrial relations within the framework of the law. It involved the creation of a National Industrial Relations Court, and it formally enhanced the status of the Commission on Industrial Relations (CIR) which had been established in 1969; the CIR was the one agency initiated by the Labour government which was not formally abolished.

Secondly, MinTech was expanded into a full-blown Department of Trade and Industry (DTI) through the addition of what was left of the old Board of Trade. It was hoped that the DTI would be better placed to produce an integrated and comprehensive national industrial policy, the main features of which presumably were to be the fostering of more competition and a disengagement from much of the government's involvement in industry.

Within the space of two years these and most of the government's other economic tenets had been abandoned. In the face of mounting unemployment and inflation, lagging investment, and the spectacular bankruptcies of Rolls Royce and Upper Clyde Shipbuilders, the government reversed its course of action and returned to a policy of intervention in individual cases.

In March 1972 a White Paper announced the introduction of an Industry Bill which would provide the DTI with funds of up to £550 million ($1,435 million) to assist the financing of industrial development;[15] in the previous year the government had repealed Labour's Industrial Expansion Act whose provisions appeared excessively modest even allowing for inflation. The bill also resurrected an IRC of sorts in the form of an Industrial Development Executive (IDE). The main differences between the IRC and the IDE were that the IDE was to be under the direct control of a minister and to be located within the DTI; it was to have regional branch offices; and it was to concentrate its efforts on getting local industry to expand in the depressed regions rather than tempting new industries to move into such areas.[16] As under Labour, computers, shipbuilding, and machine tools were among the industries singled out for special assistance under the new legislation.

Larger and subject to greater governmental restraint, the IDE was likely to be slower and less dynamic than the buccaneering IRC. Indeed, only nine months after its announcement the *Times* warned that: the IDE was "already developing a bureaucratic intention . . . The hope was that a new sense of urgency would be injected into the business of getting projects off the drawing board and on to the ground. It is a melancholy fact . . . that the new, local tiers of advisers mean additional delay, before approval for projects of any substance is obtained in Whitehall."[17]

There were other major departures from stated Conservative policies. For example, the decision was made to float the pound sterling for an indefinite period. Then, after tripartite talks among representatives of business, government, and labor failed to reach agreement on a voluntary system of restraining wage and price increases a ninety-day standstill was imposed, to be followed by two further periods of restraint. During this time the government worked out proposals for creating two new tribunals—one for prices and the other for incomes—to examine proposed increases in much the same way as had the defunct PIB.

At the same time, late in 1972, the government published a Fair Trading Bill which was designed to improve consumer protection and to recast the policing of monopolies. On the consumer side an Office of Fair Trading was to be established with a director general, working directly under a new minister for consumer affairs who was part of a revamped DTI ministerial team. To deal more effectively with monopolies, the MC was to be restyled the Monopolies and Mergers Commission (MMC). Five guiding principles were laid down to assist the commission to decide whether or not a monopoly was in the public interest; in addition, a stricter definition of monopoly was enunciated, reducing the criterion from a third to a quarter of the market share.

Whether or not the Conservatives would be able to achieve a better balance between the operations of the IDE and the MMC than Labour had managed to attain between those of the IRC and the MC only time would tell. The *Guardian*'s assessment of the Fair Trading Bill was that while it afforded a better deal for protecting consumers it contained little that would promote competition.[18]

Business Enterprise

It is difficult enough to follow the twists and turns of the economic and industrial policies pursued by successive governments, but it is a considerably more intimidating task to analyze the multifarious elements which together constitute British business. A diligent and comprehensive exposition would take into account the differences in attitudes and behavior of firms resulting from a range of factors, including size, age, capitalization, technological base, and so on. No such undertaking has ever been made, but its absence has not daunted a host of commentators from making sweeping generalizations about the attitudes, behavior, and performance of British business. However unrevealing and cavalier these commentaries may have been, British business has gone some of the way toward accepting the commentators' recommendations. In certain respects, and especially in the field of organized industrial representation, the situation in the early 1970s was less chaotic than it had been before 1960.

At the beginning of the 1960s industrial representation was vested in three organizations—the Federation of British Industries (FBI), the British Employers' Confederation, and the National Association of British Manufacturers. In 1965 these bodies combined to form the Confederation of British Industries (CBI) so that industry could speak with a single voice. The possibility of a unified organization had been under discussion for some time, and its realization was a major manifestation of the changing stance of industry toward the formulation of public policy. The move, when it finally came, was induced by the part which the FBI had played in promoting the idea that Britain should adopt French-style indicative planning.[19] Once the government had accepted this and had set up the requisite tripartite machinery, it was clearly desirable for industry to be represented in much the same way as the Trades Union Congress (TUC) represented labor.

Like most of the institutions which were thrown up by the innovative upsurge of the 1960s the CBI had its share of early troubles. In an attempt to cast its net as wide as possible it offered membership to the state industries, first as associates and later, in 1969, as full members. On the same tack it courted the financial institutes of the City of London but received a rebuff; thereafter it sought to recruit the banks, insurance companies, and other financial enterprises on an individual basis and met with greater success.

Seeking the broadest representational span was not without its problems. It was not easy for the CBI to maintain a united front with a diverse membership: the interests of its private-sector firms did not always harmonize with those from the state sector; the needs of small firms did not always square with those of larger concerns; there might well be conflicts between the requirements of new, expanding industries and those of the older ones which might be relatively static or in decline; and the interests of industry and commerce might diverge at times. These and other conflicts are endemic to organizations, like the CBI, which seek to serve as extensive a constituency as possible. It was to be expected that the CBI would find difficulty in articulating and maintaining a consistent policy, and that it would suffer from regular bouts of schizophrenia. As the *Times* put it: "The result . . . has sometimes been rational behaviour at one level, contrasted with statements of stark Poujadism."[20]

The record of the CBI on the question of incomes policy is a case in point. It "tentatively supported"[21] the Labour government's standstill in July 1966 but took umbrage when the government froze laundry prices without consulting the CBI in the following October. In 1970 it withdrew from the early warning system for notifying the government of impending price increases in protest against the proposed Commission on Industry and Manpower (CIM). By July of the following year, however, in the face of the refusal of the Conservatives to introduce an incomes-and-prices policy, it seized the initiative and embarked on a voluntary twelve-month scheme whereby its members agreed to limit price increases to 5 percent.

There were two manifestations of disenchantment with the way in which the CBI operated. The first was the formation of the Industrial Policy Group (IPG) in 1967 to promote the virtues of free enterprise. Its first chairman was Sir Paul Chambers, from ICI. In 1966 he had criticized the IRC for bringing Britain to the verge of communism, but a year later he "compared the government's methods of managing the economy with those of the Nazis."[22] The IPG consisted of twenty-four prominent businessmen drawn from such major companies as Dunlop, Beechams, Shell, Unilever, Guinness, and Tate and Lyle. The CBI's president and director general were made ex-officio members, presumably to camouflage the degree to which the IPG dissented from CBI mainstream policies. The IPG attracted those companies which, unlike older declining industries, such as textiles, or newer, high-risk, high-technology ones, such as computers, were less reliant on government assistance. Its aim was to commission research in depth and to use "the outstanding business knowledge and experience of its members for the development of a contribution to public debate on economic issues."[23] While adding to the CBI's difficulties in trying to create industrial consensus on economic affairs, the IPG made little impact: it was an uninfluential group of influential businessmen.

Another reaction to both the emergence and focus of the CBI was to be seen in the formation of the Smaller Businesses Association (SBA) in 1968 by some dissident members of the former National Association of British Manufacturers. To avoid being outflanked by the SBA, the CBI created its own Smaller Firms Council to deal with the needs of small firms.

Despite the challenge of the IPG and the SBA, the CBI persevered with its aim of becoming as representative of business as it could, and it met with increasing success. It joined with the Association of British Chambers of Commerce (ABCC) in appointing an inquiry under Lord Devlin into the state of industrial and commercial representation. The subsequent Devlin report, published late in 1972, recommended the creation of a single peak organization in the form of the Confederation of British Business (CBB), merging the CBI and the ABCC, to which it hoped the other major representative bodies like the Retail Consortium and the Chamber of Shipping would belong. Among other proposals, the report suggested a new representational system in which most individual firms would belong to product associations, which in turn would join trade associations; these trade associations would be affiliated to the CBB together with the largest companies. Within seven weeks of its publication the ABCC announced its acceptance in principle of the Devlin proposals; but the CBI subsequently rejected a merger with the ABCC.[24]

Apart from continuing to expand its membership the CBI also managed, under the influence of its new director general, to forge a different and more consistent approach to its work. It took the initiative in declaring a twelve-month limitation on prices in 1971, and it tried to disguise its primary role as a protector of business interests by projecting itself as being concerned with the plight of low-paid workers, the old, and the homeless.[25] Whatever the future pattern of tripartite relationships, the CBI's endeavor was to ensure that a collective business voice would make itself heard.

There are strong Rousseauesque overtones in the articulation of a collective business voice on many issues of policy. It is easy enough to secure general agreement in the advocacy of measures for reducing profits tax or increasing depreciation allowances which benefit the whole of business, but it is virtually impossible to get a common commitment to measures which, for example, discriminate between different sectors of industry or commerce. Inevitably, for the most part, sectoral policy is dealt with in bilateral discussions between governmental agencies and the firms most closely concerned.

Left to their own devices, though with ample encouragement from the government, individual firms freely exercised a penchant for merging in the 1960s. The government favored amalgamations which would raise efficiency by, for example, improving the R&D capacity of firms. Later in the decade the emphasis was broadened; enterprises were created in what were regarded as strategic sectors in order to avoid an undue reliance on foreign suppliers. One would not be justified in using the term "national champions" in the British case, however, for that would impute an almost Gaullist type of xenophobic determination to British policymakers.[26] As the decade progressed, businessmen's motives for merging seemed also to change. In manufacturing, for instance, the largest twenty-eight companies held 39 percent of the net assets in 1961; by 1968 their holding had increased to 51 percent. By 1969, however, a preference for concentration appeared to have been superseded by one which favored diversification.[27] Whereas the earlier amalgamations could be carried out under the guise of promoting efficiency through rationalization, the later wave of mergers was unashamedly motivated by one of two impulses which were not necessarily mutually exclusive: either the pursuit of quick returns available from asset-stripping (buying undervalued corporations and later selling off parts of them at a profit); or else seeking protection against takeover bids by building up a large powerful corporation either unilaterally or in association with other firms which also felt vulnerable.

In the early 1970s the events and circumstances of the past decade or so, and the policy responses they evoked, were still too recent to be put into a well-rounded perspective. Although an overall assessment of the changing nature of government-business relations during the period would be a premature undertaking, two observations, one political and the other economic, might legitimately be ventured.

Commentaries on British economic policy have tended to play down the political element in decision-making. This tendency has been manifested by ignoring both the nature and the effects of the system of two-party competition.[28] Perhaps it has had something to do with the associations which the word "competition" has for those whose analytical focus is grounded in the discipline of economics, which leads them wrongly to infer that British government is based on the rivalry of two roughly similar parties, subject equally to the same constraints and opportunities. In fact British politics is not an equal struggle in terms of the differential circumstances in which the parties are elected to office: historically, the Labour party has only been returned with a majority at a time of crisis, and it has mattered little whether the crises have been real or imagined. This has been as unfortunate for Labour as for the good ordering of public affairs, economic or otherwise, for it has conditioned both the conduct of Labour governments and the expectations of the general public. In order to achieve electoral success Labour campaigning has had to stress Labour's claim to be the superior party for implementing needed reforms, with the consequence that it has been saddled with an overambitious program and a climate of public opinion which is over-optimistic about the results the government can deliver. The course of history from 1964 to 1970 can be explained partly in terms of this "iron law" of electoral fortunes, and it is not surprising that in economic affairs, as in other policy areas, the Labour government overextended itself.

Whatever other long-term results may flow from the work of the IRC, two have already been suggested by other scholars. First, the recent rise of large *national* corporations enjoying sectoral domination in their home economies may inhibit the development of pan-EEC amalgamations. Secondly, part of the *raison d'être* for encouraging such corporations has been the hope that they will capture a reasonable share of the international market, which frequently involves considerable investment in foreign economies and generally increases the internationalization of capital. To the extent that this occurs, the effectiveness of national governments in controlling their domestic economies is impaired.[29]

In the early 1970s the direction of relations between government and business in Great Britain during the next decade was difficult to predict. In the high-risk, capital-intensive, high-technology sectors—in which the government was necessarily involved both as a provider of funds and as a participant in policymaking—it seemed likely that there would be an increase in the amount of intra-EEC cooperation, both bilaterally and multilaterally.

Government policy toward any further encroachment of foreign firms into the economy was more problematical. Much would depend on what was offered by the EEC to stimulate the more depressed regions of the kingdom. If EEC regional policy was judged to fall short of what was considered necessary or equitable, then the government would be less inclined to discourage American corporations, or any other foreigners, willing to establish factories in the depressed regions. If the amount of help offered by the EEC to those regions was deemed to be too little, it would be likely to become an important political issue. Rightly or wrongly, a reasonable slice of EEC regional development funds was seen as an essential quid pro quo for the payments made by Britain to subsidize continental farmers under the common agricultural policy.

As to the likelihood of effectively policing mergers and of developing a coherent policy with regard to the operations of multinational corporations, one could only remain skeptical. The odds were that the government would look to the EEC to devise new policy initiatives in these fields, even though the chances that such initiatives would be forthcoming in the foreseeable future were slight. On the broad strategic issues, therefore, the government would be relieved if it could shift the onus to the EEC institutions, while on specific issues it would tend to react pragmatically and self-interestedly as it had in the past.

France
Charles-Albert Michalet

Any attempt to interpret the relations between the state and the big enterprises of France in the early 1970s presents a formidable challenge. In recent years, there have been some profound changes both in the country's policies and in the country's structure.

The traditional statist doctrine of the nation, so long embedded in its history, has been called into basic question. Frenchmen, deeply involved in the development and application of the economic decisions of the state, have been searching for more coherent policies and rules of conduct to guide the economy. These efforts are so new that it is hard to say what will come of them in the end. Still, certain imperatives exist, notably the changes in the external environment.

Before examining the changes in the rules of the game, however, it is necessary to define the actors with precision: government on the one hand, large enterprises on the other. One might suppose that the concept of a large enterprise would be relatively unambiguous. Yet in actual application it proves to be hazy. In the context of the French economy, the word "group" would come closer to describing some of the national business interests that are thought of as the large enterprises of France. Unfortunately, existing information does not, in the majority of cases, allow us to take into consideration the interrelations and mixed participations that help to define a group. Moreover, the expansion of multinational enterprises since the early 1960s has brought about an increase in France of another type of large enterprise, the offspring of foreign companies. Finally, one has to determine how the publicly owned enterprises of France—some of which are certainly large by any standards—are to be considered.

The definition of the other actor—the government—demands even more care. In the strict sense, "government" indicates the political organism consisting of the president, the prime minister, and the rest of the ministers and secretaries of state. Even this definition will no doubt appear too broad to specialists in constitutional law. Yet in trying to understand relations with large enterprise, the definition of government still seems to be restrictive. That is why I would rather refer to the state. The terms take in not only the government, as just defined, but also the rest of the administration, including the Commissariat du Plan

Charles-Albert Michalet is a member of the Economics Faculty of the University of Paris, Nanterre, France.

as well as public enterprises to the degree that they are directly under the control of the administration. The classification may be imperfect; but within the limited framework of this study, it seems sufficient.[1]

The definition of the state, as it turns out, is at the very heart of the subject of this volume. For in the course of the last ten years the frontier between the public sector and the private sector has again been put into question. This is particularly true in the case of France, given the extensive role of the state. In the early 1970s the financial flows passing through the budget represented 25 percent of the gross national product; and, what is no doubt more important, almost half of the investments of the private sector were financed directly or indirectly by public funds. The composition of the public sector and the private sector were in endless movement and their relations were complex.

These complexities are all the more difficult to handle because of the lack of an adequate theory of the state that relates to contemporary France. Two major lines of theory do in fact exist, although they are of little help. One is represented by the neoclassical school, the other by neo-Marxist doctrine.[2] Those who support the neoclassical view reduce the state to the role of producer of collective goods and services, thereby viewing it simply as one more enterprise responding to microeconomic stimuli and goals. The neo-Marxist approach assigns a double function to the state, that of the agent for the absorption of capital surplus, and that of the agent of monopoly capitalism. In this approach, the state is nothing more than an adjunct of the great monopolistic enterprises. Both these points of view share a common attribute: the state is not allowed to assume a separate identity with its own distinctive character. Neither of these approaches helps in an understanding of modern France.

It is not my intention to propose a new theory of the relationship between the state and the big enterprises. This chapter rests upon the assumption that the state enjoys a certain degree of autonomy that permits it to be analyzed and described. Moreover, the interrelationships between the state and the large enterprises of France seem to have fallen into three successive patterns, the third of which was still only potential in the early 1970s.

In the first phase, the relations between the two actors could be viewed within a structure determined by French economic reconstruction. The rate of growth was rapid, and the main imperative was that of developing some kind of internal coherence between the private sector and the public sector. The state played the private role, but the enterprises were not in a subordinate position. They freely accepted and supported the objectives fixed by the state within the structure of the plan. This was a period of concertation par excellence.

A second situation was created when the economy was opened to the

rest of the world. From that point on, a new imperative emerged: the
need to be effectively competitive. The agreements between the state and
the large enterprises more frequently took the form of bilateral agreements. These aimed essentially at creating sectors which, through the
formation and arming of national champions, could hold their own in
foreign markets.

The very success of this policy led to a third phase. The national champions aspired to become multinational enterprises. As a result their
strategy began to take on world dimensions. A new type of rapport developed between the enterprises and the state in which these enterprises
had originated; the state appeared simply as one among several, even if
a bit more privileged. The earlier equilibrium was broken, this time for
the benefit of the firm.

The Statist Tradition

The French state has a well-founded reputation for authoritarianism,
going back to Colbert and the First Empire. It was that characteristic of
authoritarianism which permitted an English observer of French economic life to refer to the domination in France of a "statist tradition."[3]
The tradition has been characterized by economic interventionism and
by a resistance to the free play of market forces. It has also been
marked—and this point is most important for my purpose—by the
affirmation of the superiority of the state over other economic entities in
the determination of the general interest.[4] Among other things, this has
meant that the determinations of the state could not be subordinated to
the operations of the market. Logically, the result of this tendency should
have been the institution of authoritarian planning. In actual practice,
however, that has not been the outcome in the French case.

Patterns of state intervention. In a formal sense, one can say that the
statist tradition dominated the relations between state and enterprise
from the end of World War II to the opening of the Common Market.
After that, the exercise of state power was modified, at least in form.

One means of intervention by the state that permitted it to influence
the choices and activities of enterprises of the private sector was the
kind of universal measure that is traditional to all states, such as
measures related to monetary and fiscal policies. Because measures of
this sort are universal in developed economies, it is not necessary to
consider them in detail as applied in France.[5] In any event, because of
their lack of selectivity, these instruments had obvious limitations for
France, since they were not suited for any precise purpose limited to
some given industrial sector. Nevertheless, their use had important indirect effects on the life of large enterprises.

The instruments of banking policy, for instance, were used essentially for the struggle against inflation. Increases in interest rates discouraged the incentive to invest on the part of French entrepreneurs, especially because their rates of self-financing were relatively low in comparison with those of U.S. enterprises.

General measures of price control also were used effectively as a means of dampening investment. As long as inflation existed unchecked, the high price of borrowed money was easily recovered in the sale of goods. Generalized price controls were intended to put an end to this particular channel of financing. Enterprises were really pinched when these measures were reinforced by restraints on the rate of increase of the loans extended by banks. Giscard d'Estaing's stabilization plan of 1963 incorporated that feature. The plan also placed a limit on the government's financing of its budgetary deficit by the sale of bonds, a procedure that had drained an important part of the nation's savings, to the detriment of private borrowers. Instead, taxes were increased and the Treasury's debt was held within limits.

In contrast to generalized policies of this sort there were some measures that were directed more explicitly toward the support of enterprises. Supports of this type consisted essentially of financial aid in one form or another.[6] The business activities for which such aid was available were quite varied. For example, a short-term or medium-term loan to finance exports could be obtained from the Compagnie Française d'Assurance pour le Commerce Extérieur (COFACE), together with guarantees against the risks of shipping and other hazards, including insolvency on the part of the buyer. For large exports such as generators, locomotives, and plants, the guarantee of COFACE enabled exporters to get advance financing from the banks. Firms that were developing or expanding plants in France were offered all sorts of financial help, including tax exemptions, interest-rate subsidies, and capital grants.

Public assistance to private enterprises in the fields of research and development was particularly important; in fact such assistance amounted to approximately 35 percent of the expenditures of the private sector on R&D. From 1965 on, the state offered subsidies to encourage innovation, which covered up to 50 percent of the total cost of the operation. If the operation succeeded commercially, the subsidy was repayable by being transformed into a loan. At times, programs of this sort benefited individual firms; at other times, as in the atomic area, groups of firms were brought together to act on a concerted basis.

In the late 1960s, certain fiscal measures were taken to simplify mergers of enterprises and to make them less costly. These included exemptions from capital gains that might result from a merger, the right to transfer to the surviving enterprise the debts of businesses that were being absorbed, and a number of other technical measures of some importance.

The regrouping of French enterprises was also stimulated by the activities of a "marriage bureau" in the Ministry of Industry, and by the creation of the Institut de Developpement Industriel (IDI), on the model of the English IRC. The mission of the IDI, 40 percent of whose capital was provided by the state, was to facilitate the restructuring of industry. It aided chiefly medium-sized enterprises that were profitable and expanding, including not only financial support but also advice on administration; but even dynamic small industrial enterprises could obtain its support. Financial aid also was involved in the state's relations to supplying enterprises, especially large enterprises that sold to public authorities.

All told, the state's contribution to private investments is hard to estimate. Relying on budgetary data, it is possible to evaluate the portion of the funds received by the private sector at about one quarter of the total of all investments financed through public funds.

Through these various general instruments of economic policy, the state clearly influenced the actions of private enterprises, though the influence remained very diverse and general. Before the middle 1960s, the purpose of the measures was fairly traditional: to promote a stable economic environment, favorable to enterprises. After the middle 1960s, however, both the means and the objectives of intervention seemed to change The means grew more selective, and the objective of growth acquired greater emphasis.

As most observers point out, it is extremely difficult to summarize the special interventions of the state.[7] These interventions did not follow a common strategy. They seemed to be the results of crises and special circumstances. They took place in the framework of a sector or a division, acting only indirectly on a particular corporation. Nonetheless, the relations between the state and large enterprises can be analyzed according to three purposes: assistance to declining sectors; aid to sectors with a rapidly changing technology; and support for enterprises that were international in character. These three themes undoubtedly tend to oversimplify the past actions of the public authorities. On the other hand, they reflect quite well the tendency of the state to try to develop some order and rationality in the field of industrial policy.

The declining industries that led to the intervention of the state were, notably, coal, naval construction, and steel.

The case of coal was distinctive in the sense that the principal enterprises affected were public or nationalized enterprises: Electricité de France (EDF), Gaz de France, Energie Atomique, and a group of petroleum companies of mixed ownership. The major problem in the case of coal was to manage a reduction of production after the over-optimistic development of the postwar period, which had led to a record level of production in 1958. The Jeanneney Plan of 1960 was designed to institute a necessary cutback in view of the competition of the other forms of energy. The cutback set off a grave social crisis, including a strike of the miners in 1963. Production continued to decline neverthe-less, though price supports and subsidies grew. Electricité de France was obliged to sign a contract which bound it until 1978 to a price very much above the international price. (In contrast, after 1967, coke was sold to the steel mills at the international price.) The principal objective of the state in the coal sector has been well defined by McArthur and Scott: "to slow down the rate of retreat."[8]

Another declining sector, naval construction, belonged entirely to private industry in France. By its very nature, it constituted a sector integrally committed to international competition. In this case, the action of the state after 1951 consisted entirely of extending a subsidy to the enterprises corresponding to the protective customs duty that existed for the other sectors of French industry. This policy ran into trouble after the creation of the Common Market with the decision of the Commission in April 1965 drastically to limit various forms of state aid beginning in mid-1968. As a result, the French state adopted a new policy toward the shipbuilding industry. In July 1968, the objective became that of concentrating the five main enterprises into two groups: one controlled by Schneider, the other by Compagnie Financière de Paris. At the same time, the state exempted the supplies of the sector from customs duties, and it liberalized the conditions of credit associ-ated with the export of ships so that they matched those of competing producers in other countries.

Steel is a good illustration of a sector which did not know how to take into consideration the effects of the product cycle.[9] In 1966, the steel industry was operating above capacity, on the basis of technically out-dated equipment. The industry was heavily burdened with debt. In July 1966, after long negotiations between the industry's council and the state, a plan to finance the restructuring of the industry was agreed upon. This restructuring involved a regrouping of five existing enter-prises into two: Usinor-Lorraine-Escault and De Wendel-Sidelor-Mosellane de Sidérurgie. The state also participated in a plan for the retraining of the personnel discharged in the process, which amounted to almost a quarter of the workforce, and for the encouragement of new installations in Lorraine. In 1968, the plan was extended to special steels, through the absorption of Imphy by Forges du Creusot, and the rescuing of Pompey. Thus the state, in the end, simply participated financially in an operation of modernization that the steelmakers would have had to undertake in any case in order to remain competitive.

Like the declining industries, the technologically advanced industries also maintained privileged relations with the state. The aeronautical construction industry in France was composed of public and private enterprises, with a curious division of labor between them. The private sector was the principal supplier of military matériel, while the public sector was for the most part devoted to the construction of civil aircraft. In 1967 and 1969, imitating the tendency of the private sector toward concentration, the state regrouped its public enterprises into three units, and then one: the Société Nationale Industrielle Aérospatiale (SNIAS). At the same time, the economic basis of the aeronautical industry came to be dominated by the multinational contracts between European firms for the construction and marketing of the Airbus and the Concorde. The Concorde operation had several objectives: to promote technological advance, to develop a commercial market, and to achieve national independence and prestige.

The nuclear industry belonged entirely to the public sector. It operated under the double sponsorship of the Commissariat à l'Energie Atomique and Electricité de France. The national character of this sector was at the heart of the arguments concerning the choice of the producing unit.

The communications industry offers a pointed illustration of the relations between the state and large enterprises, as a result of the famous Bull affair. Without engaging in postmortems over the errors of that operation,* it is useful to point out certain lessons that can be drawn from the case.

In the beginning, when the intervention of the state began, Bull, a private French company, was in very serious difficulty. The veto by the French government of General Electric's proposal to buy 20 percent of Bull suddenly presented the French company with the need to engage in a process for which it was utterly unprepared. The institution of a coherent policy did not come until the middle of 1966 with the creation of a general commission for the industry, and with the launching of a program, the so-called Plan Calcul. The negotiations, led by the head of the Plan Commission, seem to have been arduous; to some degree, the state had to force the hand of the industry. The refusal of the U.S. government to authorize the delivery of two huge computers to the Commissariat à l'Energie Atomique at the beginning of 1966 played a determining role. The Plan Calcul was based principally upon the idea of achieving national independence.[10] The agency designated for executing the plan, the Compagnie Internationale pour l'Informatique (CII), was created by a merger that involved an offspring of Schneider.[11] Half of the capital of CII was provided by the state, which agreed also to

---

* But see the sections on the elements of a computer policy and on the emergence of national champions in Nicolas Jéquier's chapter in this volume.

make CII its almost exclusive supplier. Despite the state's role in founding the company, it denied having any desire to create a new public organism. According to one commentator, "It deliberately chose to play the card of private industry."[12] Though the view is no doubt right, one is entitled to be more skeptical about another view of the same commentator that the new operation was to be conducted entirely in the spirit of an industrial venture.[13]

The remaining area in which governmental intervention was commonly found consisted of enterprises having an international character. These included a rather heterogeneous collection, belonging to the sectors of the French economy dependent on external factors, or, to use the terminology of those who support a coherent industrial policy, to the sectors that were "exposed." In that group was found a mélange of petroleum companies, chemical enterprises, food industries, the household-appliance industry, the automobile industry, and the machine-tool industry. With the exception of the petroleum sector, the general characteristic of the relations between the state and the enterprises of these sectors can be defined as one of uneasy abstention on the part of the state, interrupted sporadically by intervention. For example, through a prohibition on price-cutting in 1965 and an imposition of quotas in 1968, the state took ultraprotectionist measures to protect French enterprises in the household-appliance industry from Italian competition. It also objected to a prospective Fiat-Citroën regrouping; and it formally prohibited Westinghouse from acquiring Jeumont-Schneider. At the same time it took no effective action to slow down the absorption of almost the whole of the food industries by English and American corporations. In other cases, as in the treatment of machine tools in the Fifth Plan, the state limited itself to rather vague promises concerning the restructuring necessary to be internationally competitive. Sometimes, this restructuring was accomplished by the private sector without state action; this occurred, for instance, in the chemical industry, through the Pechiney-Saint Gobain merger in 1961, the Ugine-Kuhlmann merger in 1966, and the Saint Gobain–Pont à Mousson merger in 1969.

Only the French petroleum companies were the object of a sustained interest on the part of the state. By 1971, three French groups—ERAP (Elf), Compagnie Française des Pétroles (Total), and ANTAR—had come to control 50 percent of the French market. This was the result of a long-term policy, first enunciated in November 1964 and taken up again in the Fifth Plan, aimed at reducing the position of foreign companies in France with regard to the importation, refining, and distribution of petroleum, as well as foreign trade in finished products.[14]

The relative inactivity of the state and the apparent indifference of the private enterprises in the sectors exposed to international competition were rather astonishing in view of France's commitment to a progressive opening of the national economy. As a general rule, the state seemed to intervene only when firms in the private sector slipped into a situation of nearly insurmountable difficulties. The enterprises in the international sectors apparently had not reached such a condition in the early 1970s, at least not in large numbers. Some, it appeared, had not yet fully faced the problem, while others had given up the struggle and allowed themselves to be bought out by foreign interests.

The role of planning. The adoption of a national economic plan in the aftermath of the war seemed to fit the statist tradition of the French economy.[15] To be sure, at the very beginning the adoption of a plan could have had diverse interpretations. The Monnet Plan could be regarded as a simple program of economic reconstruction. Indeed, in giving priority to the basic sectors of the economy, that was its obvious objective. But the Monnet Plan could also have been interpreted as the first step toward a planned economy on the Soviet model. The nationalizations in the key sectors seemed to be going in the same direction; and the political climate of the time did not make the hypothesis unrealistic.

Planning in the French style has not restricted itself to a limited program of reconstruction; but neither has it set in movement a fundamental change in the nature of the economic regime. An intermediate formula has prevailed: the plan has been indicative, not imperative; it has rested on concertation, not on subordination. The theme of concerted action has been central. This concerting process has gone on in the Commissions du Plan, and between the representatives of the different elements of the administration and of the Commissariat du Plan itself. The representatives of the workers' unions and of the consumers, on the other hand, have played only a minor role. The Commissions du Plan have contributed largely toward bringing together the state on the one hand and large enterprises on the other. The Commissariat du Plan has played a technical role at the heart of the negotiation, which Shonfield has not hesitated to classify as a "conspiracy":[16] a conspiracy between high functionaries and directors of enterprises who speak the same language, have a similar education, belong to the same social milieu, and often are destined eventually to find themselves side by side in the same administrative councils.

The ability of the representatives to reconcile interests that have sometimes been divergent has been based on a common desire to avoid the risks and hazards of an untamed, competitive capitalism. To take the formulation of one of the most prestigious heads of the planning commission, Mr. Massé, the plan has been "risk-avoiding" in purpose.[17] Its most important use has been to improve the gathering of information by the two principal sectors of the French economy: the state and the large enterprises. The object of gathering information has not been confined to the simple evaluation of a past event but has been directed toward medium-term predictions. Since the French economy has been seen as on the road to reconstruction, the projection has been deliberately optimistic, consistent with a perspective of continual increase in production. One cannot say for sure, therefore, that the Plan in itself has been the source of the expansive tendency of the entrepreneurs. But by scouting out the road ahead and by providing a responsible framework of economic analysis, the existence of the Plan has encouraged the directors of the large enterprises to play the game of growth to the limit.

It has been observed by various scholars, notably Schollhammer, that large enterprises have been influenced by the Plan much more than small. That observation is no doubt correct. Unlike Schohlhammer, however, I do not believe that the reason why large enterprises have been so strongly influenced is that the Plan imposes greater restraints upon them. Rather, the large enterprise has fallen in line with the objectives of the Plan more willingly because it has participated more than the others in the formation of the Plan. The very essence of the concertedness has rested on this dialogue. The dialogue no doubt has played a greater role between the large enterprises and the state than between the state and the small and medium-sized enterprises. To the extent that the state has renounced its power of control by engaging in the dialogue, it has been obliged to exert its influence by other means: the extremely varied range of incentives referred to earlier. Most of the incentives have been financial in nature; hence the particularly strong influence of the Plan on decisions of financing and investment revealed by Schollhammer's inquiry.[18]

The heavy emphasis on financing and investment also reflects the direction of the preoccupations of the public authorities. The stimuli have been oriented first toward the increase of production. They have been less strongly oriented toward innovation or commercial action and therefore have exerted less influence on the marketing decisions or R&D policies of the large enterprises.

The privileged position of the large enterprises in the process of planning has been related to the fact that the quantitative objectives of the Plan have been fixed at the level of the industrial division or sector. Their realization therefore has depended upon the agreement of the enterprises which control an appreciable part of the production of the sector. Recognizing that fact, Plan authorities have viewed the ideal situation as one in which 80 percent of the production comes from 10 percent of the firms.[19] The efficiency of the Plan has been reinforced by the fact that the number of participants in the process of dialogue is limited.

Nevertheless, one cannot easily say how much the planning process itself has actually affected the basic behavior of the large enterprises. One of the major conclusions of McArthur and Scott is that the Plan itself has had very little effect on the strategy of large industrial enterprises in France. To be sure, the direct interventions of the state in the industrial structures have been palpable. But these interventions have been made independently of any pre-established national strategy; so the critical issue of the influence of the formal planning process remains in doubt.[20]

Industrial Policy in an Open Economy

A critical breaking point in the relations between the state and large enterprises in France occurred some time in the late 1960s. That breaking point was associated with two converging forces: the opening of the French economy, resulting from France's entry into the Common Market; and the evolution of the basic doctrine which underlay the economic policy of the public authorities.

Changes in the rules of the game. From the end of the war to the beginning of the 1960s, relations between the state and large enterprises were dominated by the reconstruction of the economy and animated by Keynesian theory.

The first imperative was to increase production, to return to the levels of activity attained before the crisis of 1929, and then to exceed them. The mechanism for that purpose was simple: it consisted of stimulating demand and, in an economy that remained closed, looking to domestic supply to satisfy that demand.

In this context, where the increase of production took highest priority, planning provided the obvious model. The state played a predominant role in the economy, making the decisions that were needed to encourage demand. Of course, the state was not alone in controlling production. Nationalization needed to be confined to only a few sectors. The supply of consumer goods and equipment was still dominated by private enterprises. The industrial structure already in place was often archaic, and it was characterized by large numbers of small and middle-sized producers. Dialogue with them was difficult; hence the privileged relation with the large enterprises.

Paradoxically, the stress on the role of private enterprise tended to increase the economic power of the state over the basic sectors. The increase in state power was easily accepted by the large enterprises, which were familiar with the chronic difficulties of making a profit. By playing the state's game within the framework of the Plan, they benefited through public aid and in a market carefully protected from foreign competition. In a certain sense, the large enterprises were following a traditional policy; they were transposing the practice of cartel agreements from the private sector to the public sector. But these rules of the game could only be followed in a closed economy. They were soon put in doubt by the choice of a strategy based on an open economy, and by the constraints of international competition.

It is not necessary to dwell on the considerations which led the French economy to move from a highly protectionist regime to an economy open to competition. The essential elements in the change were the signing of the Treaty of Rome in 1957 and the treaty's entry into force in 1959; the return to monetary convertibility prepared by the 1958 devaluation; the development of a strong franc; the reduction in import duties associated with the Kennedy Round in the later 1960s; and the enlargement of the Common Market in 1972.

Adhering to the Treaty of Rome implied the acceptance of the free circulation of goods, of capital, and of people within the Common Market. It also implied the acceptance of common economic mechanisms, involving elements of limitation on national sovereignty.

The Common Market has been a major cause of the intensification of commercial exchanges between the member countries, and of an exacerbation of competition between European enterprises. This tendency has not been accompanied by a systematic policy of regrouping among firms across the national boundaries of Europe. Rather it has accelerated the movement toward internal concentration within each European economy.[21] At the same time, the success of the Common Market has attracted massive investments of American origin. To counter the "European challenge,"[22] American businessmen seem to have preferred production at the market rather than competition by the usual export route. This evolution has, without the slightest doubt, modified the strategy of French firms and the power of action of the state. The national market no longer constitutes a private hunting preserve; it can no longer represent the limits of the commercial interest of French firms, which have thus become more dependent on their sales in other countries.

At the same time, the position of the state has been modified by the opening of the French economy. That opening has limited the state's means of control to various forms of macroeconomic regulation, and it has loosened the state's hold on the enterprises themselves. The emphasis on the primacy of macroeconomic coherence, which originally lay at the heart of the French indicative plan, has ceased to be accepted as valid.[23]

The entry of France into the Common Market occurred at a time when the period of war-induced scarcities and the seller's market were coming to an end. Accordingly, the simple objective of a quantitative increase of production no longer sufficed. Enterprises had to begin to think about selling their merchandise. The question of productivity and of the optimal allocation of resources came to be the issue of the day.

Sooner or later, this transformation of priorities was bound to show itself in a decline of Keynesianism. It was evidently no accident that in 1958 an economist with the classical liberal ideology of Jacques Rueff was chosen to draw up a candid diagnosis of the French economy.[24] This document was dominated by a desire to prepare the French economy to rediscover the advantages of the operation of an open market. To that end, according to Rueff, the balanced budget should again become the golden rule of public finance, subsidies should be barred, the demands of organized labor should be resisted. The new economic policy was to rest on a respect for the key "balances"—in the budget, in the balance of payments, and in supply and demand. The state should limit its interventions and allow free play to the laws of competition. Though enterprises should be under the control of the administration, they were no longer to count to the same degree on public assistance. A new type of relation would have to develop between the state and the private sector.

The so-called Rueff-Armand Plan, which was subsequently published as an outgrowth of the Rueff report, went further by proposing to root out all vestiges of corporatism and all restraints on the free play of the marketplace. But it was not followed by action. The desire to break with both the statist tradition and Keynesian economic policy was not to find expression until ten years later when the Sixth Plan was in preparation.

The so-called "Fifi" model (Modèle Physico-Financier), conceived in the framework of the preparation of the Sixth Plan, took as its point of departure the new conditions of the French economy: "the establishment of the Common Market, the liberalization of foreign exchange, the intensification of foreign competition modify significantly the economic environment. . . . The growth that is physically possible is no longer ipso facto possible to achieve; production is an effect, at least for enterprises exposed to foreign competition, determined much more by their competitiveness than by their demand."[25] As a result, price became something one could not control. Investment and production, which were functions of the financial position of the enterprise, were henceforth dependent on competition. Only sheltered enterprises continued to see their production determined by aggregate demand, and their prices fixed at an "adequate" level.[26]

For the exposed enterprises, competitiveness became a vital question. Gains in competitiveness would have to be obtained with uncontrolled prices, and, consequently, with reduced margins for self-financing. The only way to strengthen these enterprises was to improve their recourse to external financing and to reduce their costs. The latter objective could be attained by the lightening of taxes levied on them, and by controlling their labor costs. This approach broke radically with Keynesian conceptions, a fact of which the promoters of the basic concept were well aware: "Such a policy of getting supply going again is fundamentally different from that, based on Keynes, of getting internal demand going again."[27]

The play of the "competitive economy," the new dominant economic doctrine, led the public authorities to redefine the role of the state and the role of the public sector. In a very general way, it is possible to characterize this revision as a generalization of the application of the restraints imposed by the marketplace. Thereafter, it was no longer acceptable that the state should set itself outside the constraints of the market. The principles of its behavior had to be consistent with the rules that applied to the private sector.

This new conception carried a series of consequences for the relations between state and enterprise. The authority of the state in its relations with the private sector should not be too restrictive. It should not coerce; it could only seduce. It had to respect the rules of the game of economic life and "conduct itself like any other player."[28]

Under this new definition of relations between state and enterprise, some revised principles of behavior were indicated. First, the state's economic interventions would be directed toward improving economic efficiency. Its role was no longer to provide a benign push in the direction of mere growth; it was rather to encourage an optimal allocation of existing resources. This new purpose was to govern not only the state's choices of economic policy but also its own detailed economic conduct.

As a corollary, growth policy itself was left largely to the initiative of the private sector. Moreover, the state could in no way substitute for private initiative or encroach upon the private sector by extending its industrial or service activities. Its role was above all to order the national environment so as to facilitate the activities of the enterprises. The state therefore would take the responsibility for infrastructure: the telephone, the road network, the collective goods of society. When the state required the output of an enterprise, this would be achieved through a straightforward contract whose duration would not necessarily be based on that of the Plan.

Finally, to play the game of the market economy all the way, the state was obliged to apply to itself certain principles of behavior that were widely practiced by the large enterprises. In the use of public funds, it would have to follow the indications of cost-benefit analyses. A rational system of budgetary choices would become the rule throughout the administration. On the same lines, the state would have to subject the behavior of public and nationalized enterprises to the same standards of profitability and efficiency as those to which private enterprises submitted.

The Nora Report of 1967* contained a group of illuminating recom-

* See the section on France in Stuart Holland's chapter in this volume.

mendations on the new mission of the public enterprise, the mission of efficiency. Efficiency would have a double effect. First, it would allow public enterprises "to go shopping at the smallest cost to them and to society."[29] Second, it would aid the public authorities "to determine the objectives responding to the demands of the market, and not to stray from them unless they are perfectly aware of the social costs which that entails."[30] In the extreme, if it appeared that private initiative was capable of improving on the public sector's performance in certain areas, such as superhighways, hospital care, and the telephone system, the state was not to hesitate to turn over the activities in these areas to private enterprise. And private enterprises were no longer to accept a subordinate role, bearing in mind that it was the private sector which furnished the model for the state.

The principles of industrial policy. Most attempts to formulate an industrial policy in France date from 1968. Thus by the early 1970s the doctrine was still very recent, but it was a doctrine born of reflection on the past relations between the state and large enterprises.

As a result of such reflection, partisans of an industrial policy were eager to create a rational system which would govern the interventions of the state in the private sector. Stoleru spoke in 1969 "of a confused tangle of concurrent policies," of a mass "of on-the-spot interventions too much based on chance." The goal should be an industrial policy that J. Saint Geours described as "a combination of basic principles and conscious choices that shape public intervention toward clearly defined objectives."[31] Such a reorientation would require a break with old preferences, such as a preference for subsidies over reforms, for an unconcentrated industrial structure, for limited mobility on the part of the labor force. The model was that of the North American economy, founded on scale and innovation.

Besides, the choices of industrial policy had to be conceived in an international environment, hence in a competitive economy. This implied that industrial policy would not substitute for private initiative, but that it would give private initiative the means for efficient and profitable development.

What did these principles mean in terms of the general policies and the more selective actions of the state?

In relation to general policies, these principles suggested a concern first of all for the maintenance of an environment that would facilitate the activities of the enterprises themselves. For example, the high priority accorded to the telephone system and to the highway system in the Plan would be appropriate. Moreover, budgetary and fiscal policies would have to be conducted with a consideration for the priority needs of the industrial sector. Thus, the tax structure should favor the development of national savings. Moreover, in order to keep the supply and demand of financial resources in balance, the state would have to cut back certain social programs, such as state housing, the Rhone-Rhine link, and credit to farmers. The objective was to break down the partitions separating the network of financial intermediaries. The abolition in 1966 of the distinction between investment banks and commercial banks. and the provision allowing for the easier creation of new banks, fitted in with this orientation.[32] Finally, the strategy of expansion was to be ruled by "the objectives of the marketplace." Demand needed only to be consistent with supply; it was not to surpass supply. These recommendations concerning general policy appeared for the first time in the Montjoie Report of 1967.

As for the more selective actions of the state in the framework of industrial policy, these too would rest on the notion of the marketplace. The state would have the duty of intervening when the private sector appeared inadequate. Included in this category would be not only collective goods and services, whose very nature made sale on the market impossible, but also pioneering activities requiring a great deal of R&D. In this domain the state should first of all try hard to breathe life into private initiative through a certain number of incentives. For instance, in the case of new commodities, it might substitute itself completely for the private entrepreneur in order to get the product started. But the state should always have an eye on the need to turn the enterprise back to the private sector. The object was not to expand the public sector but to render the private sector more competitive in relation to the outside world.

The state also would have the mission of correcting the effects of the market when it did not function appropriately. For instance, the state would have to slow down the growth of investments in sectors which, though currently profitable, were doomed soon to be saturated. It should facilitate the rapid modernization of the sectors on the decline when that was desirable. In such cases, the state might have to move toward the concentration of existing enterprises. Saint Geours proposed a set of criteria for intervention by the state. His criteria included the relative importance of the sector, the intensity of its R&D activity, its importance for the national security, and finally its foreseeable rates of expansion—all this evaluated in light not only of the national market but also of foreign marketing possibilities.

National Champions and the Plan

The definition of industrial policy as illustrated by the policy of the state in the early 1970s revealed above all a desire to break with the traditional type of relation between the state and the enterprises. The state was no longer to play the role of fireman, to use the suggestive image of McArthur and Scott.[33] It had to take the initiative itself in any industrial sector, as required by the Plan. But the initiatives could no longer be identified in advance, even if they were to be taken within the framework of the Plan. That is perhaps the reason that the initiatives implied by the Sixth Plan were not fixed with great precision, and were regarded as subject to periodic adjustment. The problem was to ensure that the order of priorities was supported rather than being turned upside down by interventions undertaken under the name of industrial policy.

The risk that such interventions might occur increased as the instruments of a successful industrial policy, the national champions, gained in strength. The existence of such national champions and the possibility that they might grow in strength were enhanced by the fact that the state was not expected to limit itself to rescue operations alone. Though the state in the past had been the last recourse for enterprises in difficulty, it would be obliged henceforth to refuse systematically to aid the feeble, in order that it might devote still more resources to reinforcing the strong. It would be necessary for French enterprises to have international stature and competitiveness, capable of facing up to the multinational giants of the United States, or Japan, or the member countries of the Common Market. The state would have to do everything to increase the number of such firms, whether they were exporting companies or companies that located some of their production abroad. The latter possibility posed unprecedented problems just as much to the public authorities as to the enterprises themselves.

The French-based multinational enterprise. The opening of the French economy exposed it to the commercial competition of foreign enterprises. At the same time, it forced the French economy to participate in the process of internationalization of production, a process whose principal impetus came from the multinational enterprises. This transformation of the environment broke with the narrow limits of the national economy: the national champions were obliged to become large multinational enterprises.

The reports of the different commissions of the Sixth Plan alluded in several places to the necessity of encouraging French enterprises to become multinational. The development of the export field, they pointed out, still remained very important. But it had become insufficient, the more so because successful exporting was in part a function of plant installations abroad: "There is no expansion without exporting, and, more and more, exporting will depend on the importance and the quality of the commercial and industrial network abroad." Again, "the whole of the Commission on Industry thought that the essential objective on the one hand was orienting action to national development and on the other hand creating multinational enterprises of French origin."[34]

The Commission on Industry was also concerned to improve the conditions for French enterprises establishing plants abroad.[35] First of all, the process of entry into foreign environments should be eased by improving the gathering of information provided by the commercial counselors stationed abroad. Moreover, there should be an increase in the support of French banks through overseas branches or correspondents; finally, there should be more joint production ventures overseas by groups of French firms. The Commission also recommended the elimination of certain financial obstacles; the liberalization of the monetary exchange regulations; an increase and simplification of the methods of financing; a guarantee of political risks; and the lightening of taxation. Other suggestions were offered to assure improved financial facilities of French multinational enterprises: access to foreign financial markets, rights to transfer funds, unrestricted use of cash reserves, greater use of middle-term budget planning, and measures to reduce the risk of changes in exchange rates. The concern to stimulate the multinationalization of French enterprises was accompanied by an outline of sectoral priorities. Minerals and nonferrous metals, petroleum, electronics, agricultural, and food industries were high on the list.

In the early 1970s, the movement of French enterprises abroad seemed to be limited by two groups of factors. The first related to the state, and more particularly to the administration of the Treasury, which saw the development of French investments abroad first of all as a drain on the reserves of the central bank. The second related to the French entrepreneurs themselves. The results of an inquiry regarding the factors involved in the decision to invest abroad revealed the absence of a real consciousness of the phenomenon of multinationalization. The approach of French businessmen was still essentially commercial. When plants were built abroad, they constituted a defensive move to preserve part of a threatened market that had originally been acquired by exporting. The step was rarely taken in order to exploit the advantages offered by the conditions of production outside the national frontiers.[36]

The foreign-based multinational enterprise. The attitude of the state in regard to the subsidiaries of foreign-based multinational enterprises in France changed considerably in the late 1950s. In general, the public authorities moved away from a defensive regulatory approach in the matter of foreign investments toward a desire to understand the phenomenon of internationalization of production. This evolution led to a spelling out of the criteria used to screen the applications of multinational enterprises that wished to establish their subsidiaries in France.

Until 1966, the activities of multinational enterprises were regulated by the administration concerned with foreign exchange, that is, by the institutions concerned chiefly with the surveillance of capital flows. The rules in force in the early 1970s were fixed by a decree of January 1967, based on a 1966 law, which eliminated the control of foreign exchange for all financial operations except foreign direct investment.[37] Such investment was defined as the creation of branches or subsidiaries, or as the taking of direct or indirect control of more than 20 percent of the capital of a corporation. For operations of over one million francs, preliminary declarations of a desire to invest were examined by the Committee of Foreign Investment, which included representatives of the Ministry of Industry, the Ministry of Social Affairs, the Commissariat Général du Plan, and the Délégation pour l'Aménagement du Territoire et l'Action Régionale (DATAR).

After 1966, the handling of the applications became very liberal. There were few definitive refusals. Hence, the public authorities again assumed an attitude that had prevailed throughout the postwar period except for the years from 1963 to 1966. Besides, the studies in preparation for the Sixth Plan contemplated the growth of such multinational enterprises in France, a fact which found an echo in the final report for the Sixth Plan. Preparatory work for the Seventh Plan reflected the same approach.

The criteria which determined the decisions of the state regarding the requests coming from foreign firms can be classified in a number of categories. The Committee of Foreign Investment first of all took into consideration the nationality of investors. Although there was no formal discrimination, the applications of enterprises belonging to one of the member countries of the Common Market were more easily accepted.[38] In this respect, the Committee was simply applying one of the principles of the Treaty of Rome, that which established the free circulation of capital. The effects of foreign investment on economic growth were also taken into consideration, such as the number of jobs created, the contribution to the development of the economy, the methods of awarding contracts, the processes of fabrication and distribution, and the means of financing.

Special criteria were established for the means of financing. In reaction to the U.S. policy of restricting exports of capital, France required that payments by participants be made immediately and in cash. Moreover, the use of French funds could not, in principle, account for more than half of the total financing. Another criterion was related to the form of investment. If a going enterprise was being taken over, the reaction of the committee was less favorable than if a new enterprise was being created. And the committee's attitude was still more negative if the French enterprise to be taken over was profitable or could be regrouped with others to generate a "national champion." The creation of new enterprises was welcome except when it might cause an overly serious situation of dependence, as in the case of the communications industry. Finally, the last criterion had to do with the effects of foreign investment on the balance of payments. Here, the concern was essentially with the transfer of currency linked to the setting up of the installation; but this question became secondary after 1966. More important was a concern that the foreign offspring should support the exporting capability of the French economy.

Whether it was a question of multinational firms of French origin or of foreign origin, the state was playing the game of internationalization of production. Hence, it was breaking with the traditional protectionist attitude. This choice reflected a strategic orientation based on the development of the large enterprises. At the same time, it was not at all clear if the mass of small and medium-sized French enterprises would be able to sustain the shock of competition from large national and foreign firms. Accordingly, by the early 1970s the relation of the state to large enterprises had come to be of even greater importance in French economic life.

Perspectives on the Future

This analysis of the relations between the state and large enterprises in France between the early 1960s and early 1970s has brought out both the continuity of policy and the shift in balance between the two partners. The continuity of the relations between the public authorities and the private sector has been illustrated by the preservation of the idea of concertedness. From one Plan to the next, from one political regime to the next, the cornerstone of French economic growth has been that of a privileged relation between the state and large industrial groups.

That feature of French policy continued despite a noticeable modification in the balance of forces between the two parties. In the first period of relationship, which was marked by the objective of producing within the limits of a sheltered economy, the state set the rules of the game. Even if the enterprises accepted this situation without having to be forced, it was still true that the state had the initiative in the general orientation and internal coherence of the economy.

From the moment when the imperative of production was supplanted by the imperative of competitiveness, the direction of state–enterprise relations tended to become inverted. The success of industrial policy in an open economy rested less on the respect for domestic balance guaranteed by the state than on the acceleration of the movement toward concentration and on the competitive dynamism of national champions. As a result, the achievement of the macroeconomic plan within a fixed time frame grew less important, and the achievement of explicit accords between the state and the firms of variable duration grew more important. Nevertheless, despite this shift, the relation itself was maintained. Up to that point, the concertedness continued.

The period of the early 1970s may prove to be the eve of the disappearance of the concerted society. Concertedness, whether chiefly state-oriented or private, rests fundamentally on a reciprocal need for cooperation. If the state had been all-powerful, the enterprises in the private sector would certainly have been discouraged and some form of statism would have been promoted. On the other hand, the question in the early 1970s was whether the practice of concerting would decline because the firms themselves no longer felt the need for it. If France's industrial policy succeeded, would it give rise to industrial groups so large and strong that they felt able to take a course that was more or less independent of the state itself?

If current policy was to be taken at face value, the strategy of the state would be subordinated to the plans of the large enterprises. Besides, these groups would have an international character. This would come about either through an increase in the relative importance of exports in total production, or through the spread of industrial installations abroad, or both. In any case, the national market no longer would play quite so predominant a role. That development would reduce by just so much the effectiveness of any action that the state was in a position to take.

The process of multinationalization of enterprises put the problem of relations between the state and large enterprises in a light that was unfamiliar for France. The strategy of the firm had been developed on a global scale. Its financing, its production, and its personnel recruitment had also been undertaken on a global scale. Each unit of the multinational enterprise, wherever it might be, had been linked in a network of interdependence with the others. This type of organization gave firms a large degree of autonomy in relation to national public authorities.

The first group of countries to be disquieted by this development was not the home countries of these enterprises but the host countries, especially those that had a sense of being relatively weak. Later, however, many host countries that were well developed showed some uneasiness.[39]

It was perfectly possible that in the future a similar sort of disquietude would take hold in the home governments of the multinational firms. In this respect, multinational firms of foreign origin and those of national origin operated by the same principles and generated similar consequences. In both situations, the state was equally disarmed. This was an outcome that French public authorities risked if the policy of national champions was to be pursued without limit. The dilution of national sovereignty inherent in the multinationalization of enterprises could sharply reduce the desire and the need to pursue the policy of concertedness; that is, unless the difficult task of elevating that policy from the national level to the European level, and even to the international level, could be accomplished. But that is another story.

Sweden Göran Ohlin

Sweden has often been considered a socialist economy, but this reputation is undeserved if the criterion used is the ownership of the means of production. In the early 1970s, private enterprise in Sweden was more dominant than in most countries in western Europe. The public sector was almost exclusively devoted to the activities that states and local governments characteristically assumed in all mixed economies. Besides the usual public services, the government operated the railways and the telecommunications, produced about half the electric power, and ran a few industrial firms. The total employment in such publicly owned enterprises was only slightly more than 5 percent of the total labor force.

It is in the uses of GNP rather than its production that Swedish ambitions in social policy have been reflected. In 1972, total public revenue (including taxes and tax-like duties of state and local governments) was no less than 56 percent of GNP. Of this, public consumption accounted for 26 percent, investment for 6 percent, and a surplus for 3 percent. The remaining 20 percent was used for redistributive payments in the form of welfare allowances.

The fiscal pressure has thus been heavier than in any other major country in the developed world. To a large extent the Swedish formula has simply been one of high taxes, extensive public service, and generous welfare schemes. In the early 1970s, however, government intervention in private enterprise became much more extensive and ambitious than before.

New Policies for Industry

To some extent the change was induced by the impression that in the mid-1960s other European governments had assumed new responsibilities in economic policy, taking in charge such arcane subjects as the "structure" of industry and the growth of science and technology. This impression was partly fostered by the talk, at OECD and elsewhere, about science policy and high technology.

"Industrial policy" emerged as a challenging concept suggesting a new and purposeful kind of public intervention. One reason for the new concern was undoubtedly the disappearance of the tariff, which had for

Göran Ohlin is a member of the Faculty of Uppsala University, Sweden.

most countries been a principal instrument of industrial policy in the past. The call for intervention arose at both ends of the spectrum. In stagnant or contracting industries, structural problems caused widespread alarm; in dynamic and expanding sectors there was apprehension about foreign and notably U.S. superiority in advanced technology. A new wave of mergers and takeovers also swept through most countries, in some cases resulting in foreign ownership and control. Deprived of the tariff instrument, economic nationalism was bound to seek new modes of expression.

Another reason for the pressure toward industrial intervention was the spread of "stagflation," with its constellation of accelerated inflation and rising unemployment, which left any simplistic "Keynesian" approach to the short-term management of the economy hopelessly inadequate. Fiscal and monetary policy that acted exclusively on demand was stymied by the simultaneous appearance of glut and inflation. Price control and incomes policy were tried, abandoned, and tried again, without the emergence of any consistent patterns or principles.

The failure of the lodestars that had guided stabilization policy strengthened the impetus toward more ambitious policy, not confined to the management of demand but affecting production, location, employment, and exports in more direct ways. Most of these efforts could be subsumed under the heading of industrial policy.

Of course, governments had always done much to regulate, promote, or suppress industry, whether accidentally or purposefully. When attention was suddenly directed toward industrial policy, most countries were therefore able to make an inventory of a great variety of measures and claim an unsuspected vigor in the field. More often than not such inventories revealed an array of uncoordinated and often unrelated activities rather than anything that could be called a policy, but this sometimes stimulated administrative reform and the transfer of functions to new ministries or other agencies.

The Swedish response to the industrial problems of the 1960s was very similar to that in other countries except in one very important respect. The new pattern of relations between state and industry did not express a closer collaboration or a deeper sense of shared interests and concerns, but precisely the opposite. The Social Democratic party, in office since 1932, found in the theme of industrial policy an opportunity to assume a more radical posture and revive its ideological zeal. The power resources of the state were to be used more actively than before to correct the deficiencies of the market and of private enterprises and to protect wage earners, consumers, the environment, and the national interest against rapacious profit-seekers and irresponsible holders of private power.

As far as management and industry were concerned, however, these proposals from the government party were quite unwelcome. Industrialists had been made to serve as scapegoats far too often to welcome a policy which to many seemed chiefly anti-industrial and marked by hostility and suspicion rather than helpfulness and stimulation. To be sure, government spokesmen tried to strike a conciliatory note when addressing the business community, especially in private; but this did not heal the rift. There was much talk of a "crisis of confidence," and although one should not exaggerate the harmony and sweet reasonableness of the relations between industry and government in earlier years, there was a clear deterioration in the late 1960s.

Political rhetoric should not be taken entirely at face value. Actual dealings between authorities and companies were often cordial enough, especially when generous subsidies were at stake. It is nevertheless essential in appraising the industrial policy of Sweden to observe that it was launched on an aggressive note.

If a date should be chosen for the birth of the new policy, 1967 seems appropriate. In that year, a unit for industrial policy was established on a high level in the Ministry of Finance, and only a year later it became the new Ministry of Industry. But many of the strands in the new policy reached back to the early postwar years and call for a brief review of certain postwar developments.

Competition and Concentration

In the early 1970s the overwhelming bulk of Swedish industry was privately owned, and public enterprise in the industrial sector was very small by European standards. Measured by employment, public enterprise accounted for only 5 percent of manufacturing and mining. The government was a very large employer only in mining, where it accounted for 75 percent of the labor force as the result of the purchase in 1957 of the Luossavaara-Kiirunavaara AB (LKAB) iron mines in the north of the country, in which the state had been a partner since the turn of the century.

Unionization, on the other hand, was fairly complete and centralized. It covered not only wage earners and white-collar workers but higher civil servants, officers, and all conceivable employees short of business executives. Most wage earners' unions were combined in the Swedish Confederation of Labor (LO), which was closely linked to the Social Democratic party.

These circumstances have made for a constellation of interests and powers in Swedish industry quite different from that found in most of the large European countries, where the government has usually been a bigger industrialist, and where the unions have been more fragmented and have had less direct political influence.

Socialization of industry, or for that matter of the banking system, has not in the past recommended itself to the Swedish labor movement. Its influential postwar program, largely drafted by Gunnar Myrdal, stressed instead the need to maintain competition and efficiency and to fight collusion and monopoly.[1] In the immediate postwar years, a number of committees were appointed by the government to study the structural problems of individual industries, for the most part those more or less perennially troubled, such as the shoe, glass, and furniture industries. It was not very clear, however, what the government could be expected to do, and the reports were quietly shelved.

In the early 1950s, legislation against restraint of trade and competition was finally introduced. Resale price maintenance and collusive tendering were outlawed but other practices were tolerated unless proven "harmful." In spite of the recent creation of a specialized court, Swedish policy was still relatively lenient in 1973, possibly because international competition was taken to be an effective safeguard. By and large, public discussion of industrial structure was also dominated by simple-minded beliefs in the virtues of size and economies of scale, and by the suspicion that oligopolistic competition was often more wasteful than it was creative.

Increasing concentration of output did become an issue in the late 1960s when a commission appointed to study this phenomenon crowned its long labors with the publication of a whole series of reports on the structure of industry, banking, and trade in Sweden.[2] Although the commission's experts had been much preoccupied with theoretical concepts of efficiency, the concern at that time was not primarily with efficiency itself. In the mood of the late 1960s, what attracted more attention was the issue of power and influence in the private sector, as manifested by interlocking directorates and inherited wealth. No attempt was made to demonstrate that the large private power extant in industry and banking had in fact been abused, nor was there any interest in domestic or international countervailing power. The mere existence of great economic influence and decision-making responsibilities in a few private hands seemed offensive and suspect.

The Swedish economy was indeed characterized by great concentration in the banking sector. A small handful of large commercial banks were clearly dominant, and the major industrial companies were linked with few exceptions to one or the other of these banks, either as more or less dependent clients or as the result of ownership control, often exercised with relatively small holdings. Commercial banks themselves were not normally allowed to hold shares of stock as assets, but some banks were associated with investment companies.

In the most celebrated case, the Wallenberg family around 1960 not only managed and controlled the family bank—Enskilda Banken—but also had controlling or substantial holdings in many of the most dynamic industrial companies, accounting altogether for some 15 percent of total value added in Swedish manufacturing. The industrial eminence and the international connections of Enskilda had long been undisputed, and when in 1970 it merged with Skandinaviska Banken, which had even greater assets and a far more extensive branch network, the resulting Skandinaviska Enskilda Banken (SEB) left all competitors behind, both as a financial and as an industrial factor. The merger required formal government consent for technical fiscal reasons. The chief reason given by the government for sanctioning this transaction, which constituted a sensational event in Sweden, was the need for a bank of internationally competitive size.

Planning

Economic planning was a cherished concept in Swedish socialism before the war, but given the character of the Swedish economy what was occasionally referred to as planning was hardly more than an attempt—relatively timid and ineffective in the 1930s—to pursue full employment by essentially Keynesian means of fiscal and monetary policy. This was equally true in the postwar years, with the major difference that instead of the expected depression the government found itself vainly struggling with inflation.

Nevertheless, slightly more detailed documents gradually made their appearance as "plans." Annual "national budgets" grew out of some new work on national accounts. Essentially forecasts, in 1973 the budgets were still the basic instruments for the formulation of general fiscal policy. The first five-year plans had been drawn up in the context of the Marshall Plan soon after the end of World War II. Also forecasts, they were undertaken in a period in which there were obstacles to the achievement of internal consistency between supply and demand projections. The preparation of such forecasts was educational to policymakers, but it took a long time before these exercises could even be termed "indicative planning." Yet a machinery eventually emerged for the collection of plans, including unspecified amounts of wishful thinking, from such sources as local governments and industrial companies.

In the early 1960s, when French indicative planning was an exciting innovation, the Swedish authorities expressed an active interest in it and made contact with French officials. But nothing like the elaborate French system for collecting information and involving firms on a regional basis emerged. Considering that the whole of Sweden was no larger than one of the French regions, it was natural that Sweden should follow a different course. The implications of Sweden's small size were evident in many aspects of its planning style. In the preparation of the five-year plans, for instance, the crucial section on industry was contracted out to a research institute financed by Swedish enterprise and enjoying the confidence of both government and industry.

In 1973 Swedes still referred to their five-year plans as "long-term plans" although in international terminology they would be dubbed medium-term. What is more important is that they have obviously held some sway over minds both in the public and private sector, which presumably is the purpose of indicative planning. Whether the grip has been firm enough is a moot question. There is no convincing evidence that the plans have created the confidence which would make them self-fulfilling. On the other hand, they have provided a yardstick for the assessment of overall performance which has been influential in formulating short-term economic policy, and perhaps even more influential in criticizing it when growth has not followed the path laid down.

This kind of planning, however, has not produced any major change in the relationship between government and industry, short of an increasing obligation to provide statistical information and reply to questionnaires. That obligation may have forced managers to think farther ahead than they would otherwise have done. But the planning itself has not been linked to any specific technique of execution.

Manpower Policy and Old-age Pensions

Two other developments in the 1950s were to prove far more consequential for the future shape of Swedish economic policy. They provided instruments without any clear plan for their use. The first was the evolution of an active manpower policy which gave very great powers to a government agency created for the management of the labor market. The second was the introduction in 1959 of a universal supplementary old-age pensions scheme.

In the late 1940s it became apparent that regional disparities and structural change had to be taken into account in applying Keynesian policies. It was impossible to pursue full employment in the North and other depressed regions by general fiscal and monetary stimulation without creating inflation and wage drift in the rest of the country. The so-called Rehn model, which was developed around 1950 by two economists of the LO, assumed that if the government created excess demand in order to mop up unemployment in every corner of the economy, it was futile to expect unions to exercise self-restraint or employers to refrain from bidding up wages. Demand management through fiscal and monetary policy should therefore aim at restraint and price stability. Where unemployment or shortages of labor emerged, these tendencies should be met by intensive measures to enhance the mobility of labor. The basic rationale for extensive retraining and for generous subsidies to promote occupational and regional mobility was that the private cost of moving or changing occupation was likely to exceed the social cost by very great amounts.

Operational around the middle of the 1950s, the manpower policy remained for about a decade the most distinctive feature of Swedish economic policy and attracted a great deal of international attention. Institutionally, it rested on a network of employment exchanges which had evolved over a long time, though in an essentially passive role. Under dynamic leadership, the Manpower Board, with a monopoly of employment agencies, rapidly became a major factor in economic policy. Its activities were generally welcomed, and the manpower policy was widely acclaimed. Not until the early 1970s, after the task of the Manpower Board had been vastly expanded to include a great deal of job creation, did its activities become somewhat controversial.

The supplementary old-age pensions, on the other hand, were controversial from the start. Their introduction was the occasion of a pitched political battle. A major issue was whether the generous pensions proposed should be compulsory or voluntary. The technicalities of the scheme attracted less interest. Unlike the existing system of social security and old-age pensions, the new pensions were not to be carried in the state budget. Instead, in analogy with private pension schemes, a large fund was to be built up from contributions paid in by employers but referred to as the "wage earners' money" in political parlance.

Although futile attempts have been made to analyze the incidence of these payments, relatively little attention was at first paid to the implications of the rapid growth of the Supplementary Pension Fund (ATP), a new and very large institute of intermediate finance. Until 1973, legislation restricted the fund's holdings to bonds or comparable securities. In the course of the 1960s, such purchases by the ATP came to overshadow all other sources of long-term finance in Sweden. At the same time, the Central Bank was allowed to maintain its control of new issues, and the performance of the capital market settled into an argument between the two authorities, with the ATP picking up more than two thirds of all issues authorized by the Bank. Over the years, a fairly regular pattern evolved, and the ATP divided its new money fairly evenly among state, municipal, and industrial bonds. It was not much of a capital market, but then there has never been a strong feeling in Sweden that a genuine capital market would necessarily be a good thing.

Again, as in the case of the labor market, the pensions reform created a vast power in public hands waiting to be used for some purpose or other. As an indication of the magnitudes involved, the addition to ATP funds in 1972 was about 7 percent of GNP or 30 percent of total savings. The total size of the funds in 1973 was about twice the market value of the stocks of companies listed on the Stockholm stock exchange.

Industries and Regions

As already suggested, the Swedish government's involvement in the promotion or control of specific industries and specific regions has not been very extensive, at least as compared with any other countries in Europe. An obvious exception, already visible in the early postwar period, was a venture into nuclear energy. The research was done in a semipublic corporation, Atomenergi, which committed itself to a program for the development of a heavy-water technology. Sizable funds were sunk into this project until it was abandoned a decade later. Thereafter Atomenergi devoted itself to research and development and to the production of components and instruments in the nuclear field.

By and large, however, as late as the early 1960s, the rules of the game in the Swedish "mixed economy" still left industry largely to its own devices, subject to nondiscriminatory treatment. The thrust of government policy was toward social reform, with the emphasis on health and social security. The active manpower policy had a welfare aspect, but it was also a form of intervention which seemed to be in conformity with the market economy and aimed to remove rigidities which made structural change both slower and more painful than it ought to be. A remarkable feature was that the unions made no attempt to fight technological and structural change but instead argued that it should be accelerated in the interest of productivity and prosperity.

In 1961, a working party appointed by LO published a call for a "coordinated industrial policy" to assume control of the major trends of industrial development instead of leaving them to market forces.[3] This thoughtful and detailed report insisted that competitive forces were too weak to be relied on and called for energetic intervention, particularly in industrial investment decisions. Then, as later, it was unclear by which criteria the public interest was to be assessed. Nevertheless, a strong skepticism was expressed toward the growing industrial centers around Stockholm, Göteborg, and Malmö, where social costs of congestion were thought to be high. The report suggested the creation of a new ministry for industry and employment, an intensified manpower policy, and a more energetic development policy in areas of stagnation or economic regression. The document was premature, however. Quite a few years were to pass before industrial policy became a popular political topic, but in due time the report would serve as at least a partial blueprint.

The change in the relationship between state and industry, however, was not initiated by a vague vision of more purposeful planning but primarily by increasing political pressure from the depressed regions in the North. Excess labor could not be removed from these regions with sufficient rapidity: many individuals did not want to move; and, naturally enough, municipal and provincial governments were anxious to stimulate employment locally. In the 1950s, the Manpower Board had tried means of suasion and information to steer firms to labor-surplus areas, but without much success. It was only in the 1960s that it was also armed with huge financial resources for development grants and low-cost loans. The location of industry rapidly became a major part of the Manpower Board's activity.

Around the middle of the 1960s, however, the employment situation deteriorated even in regions which had previously been marked by persistent shortages of labor. As a result, the so-called support zones, where investment was entitled to subsidy, were extended. In the early 1970s even the metropolitan regions suffered from employment problems and protested angrily against the policies discriminating against them.

In addition to grants and subsidized loans, another instrument to influence the location of industrial activity was found in the "investment reserve funds" introduced after World War II for the purpose of stabilization policy. Companies were exempted from tax on such parts of their profits as they deposited with the Central Bank. In recessions, the government could stimulate private investment by an order releasing these funds for use. (If withdrawn at any other time, the normal tax would have to be paid). For investments financed in this way, depreciation could not subsequently be charged against earnings. But the benefits of timing investment in accordance with government inventions were nevertheless substantial, and the release of the funds contributed to the easing of a few recessions, notably the one in the early 1960s. The funds were also used as a regional inducement, notably in the case of large companies contemplating investment projects in the South, outside of the support zone. After bargaining with the Manpower Board, the companies would be allowed the use of tax-free investment reserves for such projects on condition that they would simultaneously undertake some minor investment in the North.

This use of regional development funds and stabilization funds amounted to a radical departure from the traditional, essentially nondiscriminatory relationship between government and business. The prizes offered in the form of cheap funds or even downright grants were too large to be neglected, particularly during the severe credit squeezes in the 1960s when industry felt starved of capital. Businessmen were increasingly seen in the corridors of power, hat in hand, and cabinet ministers proudly announced agreements on new industrial projects even when only a few dozen jobs were created.

The new style of direct ad hoc bargaining could be fitted into the Rehn model with its rejection of "general" policies for the management of the employment level. The more piecemeal approach was termed "selective" policy. Critical voices spoke of neo-mercantilism, but the sudden appearance of a balance-of-payments problem in the mid-1960s was to reinforce the government's aversion to general expansionary policies.

Almost miraculously, Sweden had been spared concern over balance of payments ever since 1949, to the point where the possibility had almost been forgotten. In 1965, it was resoundingly demonstrated that Sweden was not immune to such problems when a huge deficit in the balance of trade decimated the foreign exchange reserves. In 1973, the balance-of-payments constraint was still strongly felt, especially as the government and a large segment of the political and business community continued to regard exchange-rate adjustments as ignominious, immoral, or futile.

Apart from the objections in principle to "general" fiscal and monetary management, it is obvious that "selective" measures offered the government irresistible opportunities to respond to a variety of local situations and to emerge as public benefactors.

The Swedish Investment Bank and the Ministry of Industry

In 1966, the government party suffered a stinging defeat in the municipal elections, and Swedish politics entered a phase which the London *Economist* described as one of "exhilarating uncertainty." The government had to appear active and forceful.

Accordingly, the budget submitted at the very beginning of 1967 contained suggestions for an activation of industrial policy. It specifically mentioned the creation of a large fund for the support of industrial development projects. Only a few weeks later the proposal was changed to provide for the establishment of a new bank which was to channel money from the ATP into medium- and long-term financing of industrial reorganization and large and risky projects, especially when they promised to be of social value as well as offering private profitability. The proposed scale of operations of the new bank was of a magnitude which was bound to alarm the private banking community, the more so as the government analysis was not only rushed and perfunctory but was presented in a strident tone. It suggested that so far the government had been confined to the unrewarding task of bailing out firms in trouble whereas it would now show its mettle as a promoter. The bank, which came to be called the Swedish Investment Bank, was expected to play a leading role in this task.

The bank took a long time to get started and did not then attempt to perform as a Swedish equivalent of the British Industrial Reorganization Corporation (IRC) or to finance anything particularly large and risky. A few loans were made in the troubled textile and shoe industries, but the bulk of the lending went into fairly conventional financing, especially in the pulp and paper industry. Under conservative management the bank became nothing like the spearhead of industrial reorganization.

But new issues were soon added to the concern with employment and structural change—technology, environment, and industrial democracy. In addition, the political climate was changing rapidly. As in most of the rest of Europe, there was vigorous social criticism from the New Left, and a generational shift occurred in the Social Democratic party which brought young men into leading political positions. The great welfare reforms, and the high and progressive taxation accompanying them, had so far seemed the essence of Swedish socialism, but this "socialization of incomes" had more or less run its course, and no further wings of the welfare state were on the drawing board. Industrial policy was received as a great opportunity to continue the transformation of society in a socialist but pragmatic spirit. The party was called to an emergency meeting in the fall of 1967 at which an enthusiastic speech by the minister of economics introducing the party's industrial policy statement was met with ovations. A time of continuous creation of new institutions and agencies followed.

First of all there was the Ministry of Industry itself, which took charge of the management of state-owned industries, energy supply, and research and technology, as well as measures to promote what Swedes insist on calling *strukturrationalisering* in different industries. Then there was the Council for Industrial Policy, in which business and labor were represented. It was supposed to play a consultative role and to supervise the many studies and analyses of individual industries sponsored by the ministry. A Technological Development Board (STU) was created in 1968 to serve as top body in matters concerning research and development. The Swedish Development Corporation (SUAB) was set up at the same time with the task of promoting product innovation. In 1969, a special corporation was formed to acquire or start industries in depressed regions (SVETAB).

Regional authorities were created for regional planning, while physical planning on a national scale was initiated by a central planning office. A large body for the protection of the environment was set up. A new agency for more active consumer protection was established. Legislation was passed to put government representatives on the boards of the commercial banks. In terms of bureaucratic expansion, these years were a period of great activity.

Deals and Disenchantments

Some of the new institutions had an obvious *raison d'être*. The protection of the environment was efficiently and energetically pursued, and by 1973 it had almost ceased to be a political issue. But the new industrial policy also came to mean a stepped-up role for the government as entrepreneur and an unprecedented number of deals, purchases, collaboration agreements, and the like. Here the record was not encouraging.

The state-owned enterprises, in spite of their relatively small importance, had long been controversial. They had not been acquired or founded for their economic merit, and some had been notorious losers over remarkably long periods of time. A steel company in the North (NJA) had been kept alive for employment purposes for decades. The new Ministry of Industry, however, was anxious to demonstrate that the state could manage industry as well as anybody else, or even better since it would do it with a view to a broader social interest. For a brief period, the suggestion was entertained that when various social benefits justified operations in the red, some specific and limited subsidy would be made available to the management which would from then on operate as a profit-maximizer. But this idea of a social contract was quickly forgotten in a whirl of embarrassing business transactions.

A number of companies, acquired wholly or in part, were actually on the verge of bankruptcy. Great efforts to rescue them by introducing quixotic new product lines only resulted in growing losses, which in turn received unwelcome publicity and were not easily defended. In some cases, state intervention was said to aim at establishing workable competition. This occurred notably in the pharmaceutical industry. It also appeared as a motive in building materials, where the purchase of a smaller firm (Durox) in 1965 grew into a *cause célèbre* before the firm was closed down in 1969. In that year, too, the government suddenly stepped in to prevent the sale to Italian interests of a minor electronics company—a rare measure in Sweden and one which enhanced the impression of erratic improvisation.

A number of other initiatives were more successful. In 1968, the government joined the large private firm ASEA in the nuclear field as a 50 percent partner in ASEA-Atom. It also entered another partnership (Uddcomb) with a private company to manufacture reactor equipment under a license from Combustion Engineering, a U.S. firm. In 1969 the state took a half-share in a consortium for oil prospecting in the Baltic.

Positive terms were used at first by the new Minister of Industry to describe the pioneering role of state industries in fostering industrial democracy. This view changed at the end of 1970 when work at the LKAB mine in Kiruna was halted by an unauthorized strike. It attracted international attention and revealed that alienation and industrial unrest were not inconceivable in a nationalized industry.

After only a few years of the new industrial policy it was clear to all that it had become a political liability.

Partial Retrenchment

In the early 1970s the style of intervention became less flamboyant. The politicians and junior civil servants without business experience who had staffed the new ministry were gradually replaced by quiet executive types. Such a man even replaced the minister.

The state-owned industries were reorganized in 1970 when some thirty companies were grouped together in one holding company, Statsföretag AB (literally, State Enterprises, Inc.). It had a total employment of 34,000, and sales in 1971 were close to U.S. $800 million, which sufficed to make it the seventh largest corporate group in Sweden (after the cooperative industries, Volvo, the Johnson group, Svenska Kullagerfabriken (SKF), Saab-Scania, and ASEA. Of all industrial companies in public ownership the only ones of any importance that remained outside of Statsföretag were the distilleries, the two nuclear companies, a number of armories and other defense suppliers, and some firms producing telephone and railway equipment.

The creation of Statsföretag kept everyday problems out of the ministry. By 1973 there was less talk about the great and special tasks of the state industries, and performance and morale seemed to have improved a good deal. Even so, in 1971 less than one third of the member companies were in the black, and only two (LKAB and the state tobacco company) showed real surpluses.[4]

Although industrial policy had vanished from budget speeches and other political platforms almost as fast as it appeared, the problems of structural change and regional development had not gone away. In 1973 the sudden merger wave which had begun in the late 1960s was receding only slightly, the number of industrial closures remained at a high level, and new starts were few and far between. Some industries had been virtually wiped out and in others the number of firms had fallen to a fraction of what it had been a decade or so before.

In a few cases, the government took an active part, notably in shipbuilding. There, in tough, drawn-out negotiations it insisted on technical cooperation among leading competitors as a condition for state aid. But, by and large, reorganization had come about the hard way, and it was probable that the net effect of public intervention had been to prolong the agony. A report to the annual meeting of the Social Democratic party in 1972 complained that the last years had seen a great many rescue actions to deal with short-term emergencies but little in the way of systematic and purposeful industrial planning.

More and more was left to the Manpower Board to handle. In 1973 it disposed of 2 percent of GNP, of which about half was used for moving and training labor and half for job creation by a variety of means. But the Manpower Board had been created to cope with the specific problems of labor mobility, not with industrial policy at large or with a general unemployment situation. Although its huge bureaucracy received less public exposure than a ministry would have, it was subject to the same political pressures; and its operations were sometimes enigmatic and usually paternalistic.

In the spring of 1973, the government submitted a bill to reorganize the venerable Board of Trade and to extract from it the elements necessary to create an executive and coordinating agency for industrial policy under the Ministry of Industry.[5] In a more controversial move, which rapidly grew into one of the major issues of the campaign before the elections in late 1973, it also proposed that the ATP should be empowered to buy corporate stock. Presented as a measure to enhance the power which the public and the unions, through their representatives on the board of the ATP, might exercise over industry, the proposal was bound to raise the objection that it aimed at creeping socialization.

But it would have been too much to expect Swedish industrial policy to be very systematic. The "rationalization" of industrial structures was in most cases a euphemism for the contraction, disinvestment, and disappearance of firms, factories, and workshops as they were displaced by rising costs, changing technology, and comparative advantage. The rapidity of the industrial contraction wrecked many communities and threatened many more in an already sparsely populated country. Any government would have been under very great pressure to relieve such distress.

It could even be said that the government showed surprising restraint in two areas: in not resorting more to tariff or non-tariff protection and in not using procurement in such a discriminatory fashion as was done in many other countries. The biggest exception in the first case was the imposition of an emergency quota on knitwear from so-called low-cost producers. In the case of procurement, the government's own Atom-energi failed to secure any orders for nuclear power stations in competition with ASEA-Atom and Westinghouse, and the computer division of SAAB fared badly in competition with IBM and other foreign companies.

Policy without Objectives

From the perspective of 1973, the new, more active industrial policy has not been vindicated by experience. Unemployment has shown a steadily rising trend. Output per man-hour has continued to increase fairly rapidly in manufacturing, to a large extent by a purge of older units of production; but manufacturing output has grown ever more slowly and has stagnated. In contrast, the subsidiaries of Swedish firms outside of Sweden have been growing rapidly.

All of this should not be laid at the door of industrial policy, nor is all of it necessarily a bad thing. The share of manufacturing in the Swedish economy could be expected to decline with the move toward a "post-industrial society." Yet much of what has been done in the name of guiding and stimulating industrial change has been marred by confused and conflicting objectives, as well as by excessive expectations.

Those who had seen in industrial policy a way of giving new content to socialist aspirations have been preoccupied with the problem of wresting power from the hands of owners and managers. It has been taken for granted that, given power and influence, the government would be in a position to steer industrial change and performance in some way that better conformed with the overall public interest.

But there has been no clear conception of the public interest. The stated objective of the Ministry of Industry has been to promote efficiency and market performance through industrial reorganization, not to retard it. Like the Manpower Board, however, the ministry has been led to great efforts to move industry and jobs to the people, and the mere existence of a high-level authority for the support and promotion of industry has inevitably been an invitation to a new and elusive protectionism.

Similarly, power or influence over private companies has been pursued without any very clear notion of how to use it. Although it was sometimes presented as a step toward industrial democracy, it was not the same thing as placing power in the hands of the employees, and the claim that the state was the natural spokesman for "wage-earner interests" could be doubted.

By 1973 the government had granted itself the right to appoint public representatives to the boards of the major banks, and legislation had been drafted for government representation on boards of foundations and large investment companies. Employees were to be represented on the boards of corporations with more than one hundred employees. Curiously, the Swedish unions, which in the past had opposed proposals for profit-sharing and codetermination, had been forced into an awkward reversal of their traditional objections to a blurring of the interests. Their about-face occurred when the political opposition countered the government's plans to put representatives on the board with its own proposal for employee representation.

The political premise behind the first years of experimentation in the field of Swedish industrial policy had been the existence of deep conflicts of interest between labor and capital, producers and consumers, industry and society. Actual experience had belied that premise, however, and pointed to large elements of a community of interest as well as to conflicts along different lines, such as those between employees in two different industries.

The design of a policy which adequately identified and rectified the divergence between social and private costs and benefits had not been attained in Sweden by 1973. Nonetheless, important lessons had been learned. The government and the civil service had found business more difficult than they imagined. The business community, while not in a position to decline the subsidies offered by the public sector, had reacted against the ascendancy of political influence-mongering and erratic favoritism. Such practices were not common in Sweden in spite of its small size, perhaps because the labor movement, which had held political power for so long, had traditionally kept business at arm's length.

But even if some retrenchment was under way there could be no return to the days when the state was happy to leave industry free to mind its own affairs. The mutual dependence was too great and the public responsibilities in the labor market and the capital market far too large. Nevertheless, the relationship between companies and authorities could assume a variety of forms. It could aim at surveillance or direction, it could be based on coercion or incentives, it could be arbitrary or governed by rules. The search for a practice which is workable and reasonably efficient will undoubtedly go on in Sweden, as in any industrial state.

Part III

Industries

Aerospace

M. S. Hochmuth

Of the industries studied in depth in this work none more vividly depicts the pattern and range of government interest and influence than does the aerospace industry. Because this sector was so crucial to military power after the First World War, it became the subject of intense governmental scrutiny, support, and guidance. This preoccupation, always greater in Europe than in the United States, was heightened in the early 1960s by the recognition that a broad capability in advanced technology was more than a necessary requisite to military power; it had become essential to status as a first-rank economic power. Indeed, prowess in advanced technology was even deemed fundamental to achievement of internal social and welfare goals.[1]

The aerospace industry has been one of the most voracious consumers and instigators of advances in practically all the scientific and engineering disciplines. Because of the military, technological, and social significance of the industry, as well as the high visibility of its end products, the aerospace sector has received more attention from West European governments than its relative economic importance would seem to warrant. In 1967 the aerospace industries accounted for only 1.5 percent of the total value added by manufacture in the nine countries that were to comprise the EEC by 1973. The corresponding U.S. figure was 6.6 percent.[2] But the military and technological importance of the industry, combined with its disproportionate position in foreign trade, tended to concentrate official interest upon it. With export markets for low-technology manufactures drying up, the Western nations saw healthy trade balances increasingly dependent on export success in high-technology products. Faced with the superiority of the United States in computers and nuclear energy, the Europeans were more than solicitous of those high-technology sectors in which their competence held hope for a shift in trade patterns. Among these *secteurs de pointe,* aerospace, and in particular the aircraft segment, was perhaps the most obvious vehicle for the Europeans to demonstrate a commercial capability.

For the first three decades following the Wright brothers' flight, western Europe stayed well ahead of the United States in aircraft technology. A broadly based capability was created, including the necessary human

M. S. Hochmuth is a member of the Faculty of the Centre d'Enseignement Supérieur des Affaires, Jouy-en-Josas, France.

resources and the technological infrastructure. No such capability existed, for example, in nuclear energy in the early 1970s (despite important British progress). This early European lead was in part due to the recognition by Britain, France, and the Netherlands after World War I that civil aviation could "show the flag" and help stitch their far-flung empires together. But the advent of the Second World War saw Europe's lead in civil aviation disappear. At the end of that war, only Britain was left with a viable aircraft industry. Although Britain's aircraft production base was dwarfed by the U.S. industry, Britain was not outdone in technological capacity. In fact, with the dismantling of the German industry which had produced the first jet fighters, Britain became the world leader in gas turbine technology, which later was to revolutionize the industry.

Given this history of past capability and even eminence, it is not surprising that the goal of the West European powers after World War II, and particularly from the early 1960s to the early 1970s, was to redress the perceived disparity in industry size and share of the world market between Europe and the United States. How great this disparity loomed in European eyes is seen by comparing the total aerospace sales of the Common Market, Britain included, which were $3,817 million in 1970, with Boeing's sales of $3,667 million for that year. Moreover, at least three other U.S. aerospace firms had sales rivaling this figure, so that U.S. aerospace sales in total came to $24,850 million for 1970. The U.S. industry had an overwhelming share of the world military and space market.[3] What particularly disturbed European officials and industry leaders, however, was the U.S. share of the civil market. In 1970, 75 percent of the aircraft flying on the scheduled airlines of the world (excluding the USSR and China) were of U.S. manufacture. Over 90 percent of the acquisition costs of such aircraft were embodied in U.S. equipment.[4]

Although the West European governments have in common a long history of involvement in their aerospace industries and though they shared common goals and challenges in the early 1970s, they had reacted over the years in markedly different ways. In part their very different policies stemmed from historical and cultural differences, and in part from the personalities of the key government officials and industrialists.

This analysis will focus on the British and French aerospace industries, which have enjoyed substantial government support and are by far the most highly developed in Europe. The German aerospace industry, while slowly regaining its prewar eminence, has not occupied a position of great importance in the eyes of successive Bonn administrations. The situation in the Italian, Dutch, and Swedish industries can be deduced from the experience of the much larger industries in Britain and France.

The Nature of the Industry

The achievement that first made powered flight possible was evolution of the internal combustion engine to a point where the power-to-weight ratios permitted lift-off and sustained flight. From the inception of powered flight, progress in aircraft has continued to be paced by engine development. Because the technology and production process involved in engines differed so greatly from those of the airframe industry, a separate engine industry evolved both in Europe and in the United States. Nevertheless, there is very little difference in the nature of relations between government and industry in the airframe and engine sectors. More importantly, the choice of power plant and the overall design responsibility are always the prerogative of the airframe designer. Accordingly, this chapter concentrates on the pivotal airframe industry.

Major subsectors. As the technology of aircraft became more and more complex, the aircraft manufacturers increased their reliance on specialist suppliers of expensive accessories, such as reliable hydraulic and electrical systems, retractable landing gear, instruments, and navigation equipment. Some equipment suppliers became wholly dependent on the aerospace industry. Others were in a different industry and aerospace was only part of their business. In the United States the equipment sector rivaled the engine sector in total sales in the early 1970s, but there were hundreds of equipment firms and only four major engine firms. In Europe equipment sales were less important in relative terms.

World War II brought another major sector into the aerospace industry—rocket-powered missiles. The ensuing military and space programs boosted the importance of the new sector. The relative importance of some of these activities can be seen from the data for 1967 given in Table 1 on the following page.

Another way of looking at the industry's breakdown is by the nature of its end product rather than its inputs. Prior to World War I, the major interest in aviation, other than sport, was commercial. Yet before the war only 740 aircraft of all types were built in France, and at the onset of hostilities Britain had only 50 serviceable aircraft. By November 1918, the major European powers had each produced tens of thousands of planes. After that, military requirements and eventually military and space requirements constituted a major portion of the aerospace market. Of course, the ratio of military and space sales to total sales varied considerably from firm to firm and from country to country. But in general, such sales represented 60 to 80 percent of total sales over the decades.[5] Such governmental support provided the stimulus for the enormous technological advances of the industry. As early as 1931 a study of the U.S. industry stated that "progress is prohibitive in its cost unless it can be stimulated by military production." The Aerospace Industry Committee which prepared the Sixth Plan (1970-1975) for the

Table 1. Aerospace sales by country and sector, 1967

Country	Airframe	Space & missiles	Engines	Equipment[a]	Total
	Millions of dollars				
France	599	231	288	132	1250
Germany	167	34	60	n[b]	261
Italy	93	n	38	29	160
Belgium	11	n	16	n	27
Netherlands	60	n	n	n	60
Great Britain	764	78	608	160	1610
Total EEC & Great Britain	1694	343	1010	321	3368
United States	9238	4753	4111	5156	23258
	Percentages				
France	47.9%	18.5%	23.0%	10.6%	100.0%
Germany	64.0	13.0	23.0	0	100.0
Italy	58.1	0	23.8	18.1	100.0
Belgium	40.7	0	59.3	0	100.0
Netherlands	100.0	0	0	0	100.0
Great Britain	47.5	4.8	37.8	9.9	100.0
EEC & Great Britain	50.3	10.2	29.9	9.6	100.0
United States	39.7	20.4	17.7	22.2	100.0

Source: *Les Industries aéronautiques et spatiales de la Communauté, comparées à celles de la Grande Bretagne et des Etats-Unis*, prepared for the EEC Commission by Soris, July 1969 (Brussels: Collection Etudes, Série Industrie no. 4, 1971), II, 432.

[a] Electronic communication equipment is omitted.

[b] n = negligible

French government was no less emphatic: "the military portion of the aerospace industry is currently by far the major portion of the (French) aerospace activity . . . Experience has shown that this military portion of the total effort is the source and origin of the industry's technological progress to date and there is no significant national aerospace industry in the world that is not supported by a military product-market base of breadth and quality."[6]

The critical variables. West European governments and their aerospace industries have seen themselves as the victims of an overly powerful U.S. industry. Yet it is clear that this state of affairs has stemmed from technology and market structure rather than a deliberate U.S. strategy. One critical aspect of the U.S. lead has had to do with the time required to develop an aircraft.

At the beginning of the air age, the time from start of design to entry in service of an aircraft was measured in months. Marcel Dassault and Henry Potez, working in their spare time, are reputed to have developed a two-place fighter observation plane—the SEA-4—in less than two years at the close of World War I.[7] By contrast, the Concorde SST has been scheduled to enter service in 1975, more than twelve years after the British and French agreed to merge their designs (and these designs had already been under way for several years independently).

Although the time between design and service release of civil and military aircraft increased over the years in the United States as it did in Europe, data for the late 1960s showed the United States well ahead of the United Kingdom and France. The average development time for civil aircraft was 52 months in the United Kingdom and 62 months in France, but it was 43 months in the United States. The average time for military aircraft development was 100 months in the United Kingdom as against 75 months in the United States. (Figures are not available for France.)[8]

What these averages do not show are the wide variations in development times for specific key aircraft, variations which are more significant than the averages depicted. Development of Britain's first military aircraft capable of twice the speed of sound, the English Electric Lightning, was begun in 1949. The Lightning first flew in 1957 and entered service in late 1959. On the other hand, design of France's highly successful counterpart, the Dassault Mirage III, was begun in January 1956, with the first prototype flying less than a year later and production deliveries beginning before the end of 1958. Since technology changes rapidly and since the market for European civil and even military aircraft is necessarily worldwide and highly competitive, excessive development lead times can profoundly affect the sales success of an aircraft.

Even more significant than development time, however, is the trend of development costs. These have also risen dramatically over the years. Development costs have kept pace with the growth in technological sophistication. This is equally true for military and civil aircraft. Table 2 shows the trend in the cost of aircraft development.

Prior to World War II, development costs for both military and civil aircraft were usually risk ventures of the individual firms, whose development costs were amortized on subsequent sales or written off. After the war, governments in both Europe and the United States financed military developments.

In the United States, Boeing's 707 was made possible by the initial order for development and production of the military tanker version. Civilian airliner development continued to be financed in the United States through the resources of the producing firm, including advance payments from airline customers. From Table 2 it is clear that the development of a completely new airliner probably exceeds the means of even the largest American firms. The huge development costs of the 747 forced Boeing to require its six major subcontractors, who together manufactured 70 percent of the plane, to share the development costs and risk. United States manufacturers have not initiated full-scale development of an airliner without advance orders guaranteeing sufficient production to establish the aircraft in the market place and to assure private financial backing.

As Table 2 shows, development costs were running at levels that were much too high for any single European firm to support. Engine development was no less costly; the Rolls Royce engine for the Lockheed Tristar involved costs of about $600 million.

In Europe the state by one means or another had to pay for either the whole or an important part of airliner development. And in contrast to the Americans, European manufacturers rarely enjoyed the advantage of firm orders prior to initiation of development. Deprived of commercial financing and without substantial military programs to spread the overhead and furnish cost-free technology, these manufacturers needed government financing as a *sine qua non*. Aggravating the European situation were the compartmentalized national markets. Britain, France, and Germany harbored two major firms each, all much smaller than the leading U.S. firms. Under these circumstances there was little likelihood of adequate development orders in advance of development for any European civil aircraft. Indeed, even in the military market, increasing production costs made it more and more difficult for the major European nations to justify a purely national military production program without assurance of substantial exports.

Just as development costs mushroomed, so too did costs of the final

Table 2. Aircraft development costs between 1933 and 1974 (millions of current U.S. dollars)

Plane[a]	Time period	Development costs
DC 1/2/3	1933–1936	$1.5
Canberra (U.K. military)	1945–1951	50
Caravelle	1953–1959	140
Douglas DC-8	1955–1959	200–300
Concorde (Anglo-French) (including engine)	1962–1974	2,400
Boeing 747	1965–1969	1,000
Airbus A-300 (Franco-German)	1969–1974	500

Sources: Peter W. Brooks, *The Modern Airliner* (London: Putnam, 1961), pp. 82, 86; Great Britain, Committee of Inquiry into the Aircraft Industry, *Report,* 1965 (Cmnd. 2853), p. 6; Frédéric Simi and Jacques Bankir, *Avant et après Concorde* (Paris: Seuil, 1965), pp. 49, 106; R. G. Hubler, *Big Eight* (New York: Duell, Sloan and Pearce, 1960), passim; *Le Monde,* February 2, 1973, p. 8; Commission of the European Communities (Brussels), *A Policy for the Community for the Promotion of Industry and Technology in the Aeronautical Industry,* p. 49 (Annex III).

[a] Excludes engines except where indicated.

product. The World War II Spitfire cost about $40,000 to produce. In 1972 Dassault offered forty Mirage III's to Switzerland at a unit price of $2.5 million, probably representing no more than the marginal cost of production. A more representative figure is the $6 million cost (in "devalued" 1973 dollars) of the Anglo-German-Italian swing-wing fighter originally scheduled to be in service by 1976. United States fighter aircraft costs have varied from $3 million to more than $10 million, excluding spare parts or provision for R&D amortization.[9] As Figure 1 shows, the increase in sales price of civil airliners has been

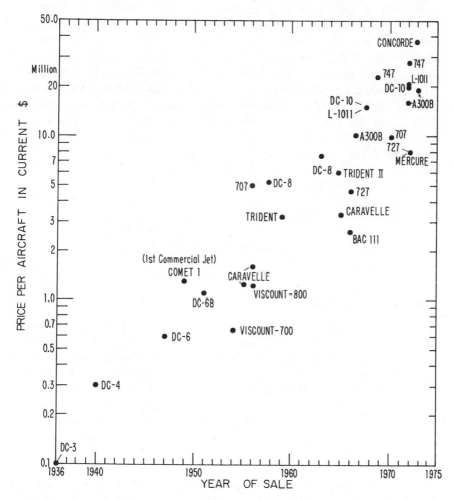

Figure 1. Commercial Aircraft Prices
Source: Current trade journals: *Aviation Week and Space Technology; Flight.* Figures are approximate and may apply to quotations rather than actual sales in some cases.

even steeper, reflecting a constant increase in size as well as in performance. The prices in Figure 1 include some provision for the amortization of development costs but do not include cost of repair parts or ground equipment.

European manufacturers have had a decided advantage over the United States with respect to labor costs. But this advantage has been more than offset by the size of the U.S. market, which has permitted U.S. manufacturers to reap the benefits of economies of scale and to spread the costs of the learning process.[10] While the phenomenon of economies of scale is well understood, the importance of the learning curve is less well known. Briefly, according to a widely accepted model, the production costs of successive lots of an aircraft can be expected to diminish by a fixed percentage, 20 percent being a commonly used figure. Thus if the production cost per plane of the first lot is C, the cost of the second lot would be 0.8 C, the third lot 0.64 C, and so on. Clearly, American manufacturers, with a home market significantly larger than the combined European home market, could set a lower average price for a given plane. Moreover, because of the national compartmentalization of the European market, European manufacturers have had to export heavily in order to achieve any degree of cost competitiveness. Though total market estimates for different classes of civil airliners have varied considerably, European manufacturers have been forced by U.S. competition to set initial prices which would require sales of 250 to 350 aircraft in order to reach the break-even point. Few European transport planes in the last twenty years have enjoyed this degree of success.

Key Elements in Change

Though most nations have applied strong internal pressures to foster military air power, these pressures have often created serious conflicts within the government. As a result there have been sharp vacillations in governmental policy, with profound effects on the aircraft industries. Vacillation was especially common because the demands of the military market were in fact politically determined. Hence, military "needs" could be rationalized radically downward by an economy-minded government as in the case of Britain, or upward as was the case in France under de Gaulle.

The special problems of national industries came not only from the volatility of demand but also from the need to deal with an extensive bureaucracy in each government. Major and even minor technical and strategic decisions were questioned and often changed by an army of government experts, which in general meant a loss of management flexibility and initiative for the firms. Such government co-management inevitably resulted in longer development times and lower profits. Finally, the ever-increasing costs of military aircraft meant that fewer military aircraft could be procured within slowly growing national budgets. Military production runs were thus reduced to "uneconomical" levels in countries with important industries. Indeed, some countries, including Belgium and the Netherlands, had to be pressured by their NATO allies to maintain a capability at all.

Accordingly, those in western Europe concerned with maintaining a production capability have come to look wistfully at the commercial aircraft market. By the early 1970s the aerospace exports of Britain and France were not much in excess of their respective imports; and as far as commercial aircraft alone were concerned, both countries had long been on a net import basis. The United States, of course, was the world's heavy net seller, with total aerospace exports of over $4 billion annually. Faced with increasingly uneconomic national military markets and shrinking military exports, the major European industries either would have to increase their share of the civil transport market or would be reduced to a point at which competition with U.S. firms would be out of the question. The statistics in Tables 3 and 4 place this problem in perspective.

Unlike the politically based military market, the commercial airliner market has been almost purely economic, a function of factor costs and

Table 3. Annual aerospace sales of selected firms, 1971 (millions of 1971 U.S. dollars)

British		Frencha		United States	
Rolls Royce	$ 650	Aerospatiale	$ 663	Boeing	$3,011
British Aircraft		Dassault-Brequet	316	Lockheed	2,852
Corporation	382	Snecma	248	McDonnell-	
Hawker-Siddeley	546			Douglas	2,069
Westland	139			United Aircraft	2,029
Total	$1,717		$1,227		$9,961
Total industry sales excluding intra-					
industry sales	$1,634		$1,418		$20,632

Sources: Annexes I and II of "Les Actions de politique industrielle et technologique de la Communauté à entreprendre dans le secteur aéronautique," EEC Commission, document III/2457/72-F, Brussels, December 21, 1973. Sales of individual U.S. firms are from Moody's Industrial Register 1972; total U.S. industry sales from *Aerospace Facts and Figures,* 1972–73.

a Excluding tax.

Table 4. Breakdown of aerospace sales of British, French, and U.S. firms by market segment, 1968-1969 average

	Percentage distribution of aerospace sales		
Market segment	British firms[a]	French firms	U.S. firms
Domestic			
Military and space R&D	12%	13%	18%
Military aircraft and missiles	29	33	57
Civil R&D	12	12	5
Civil aircraft	14	3	7
Foreign			
Civil	20	12	9
Military	13	27	4
Total	100%	100%	100%

Sources: "Les Actions de politique industrielle et technologique," EEC Commission, document III/2457/72-F, Brussels, December 21, 1973, pp. 9, 17; *Aerospace Facts and Figures,* 1972–73.

[a] Imports and re-exports included; missiles and used aircraft excluded.

consumer demand. That market can be visualized as two-tiered: a public market for transportation services, met by the airline industry; and the airline industry itself, which makes up the market for airliners.

From 1929 to 1954, the passenger-kilometers that were generated by the world's scheduled airlines increased at an annual rate of 25 percent. From 1951 to 1971 the annual rate of growth averaged about 13 percent. The nonscheduled airlines meanwhile grew even more rapidly to account for about 23 percent of the world's freight and passenger traffic in 1971.[11] Just as the cost of development and cost per plane increased exponentially, so did payload and speed. In the time taken by a transatlantic ocean crossing, a 707 or DC-8 making several trips could carry as many passengers across the Atlantic as an ocean liner and could do so at a fraction of the liner's capital and operating costs. Indeed, BOAC, BEA, and Air France had fewer airliners in their 1971 fleets than in 1951, while the kilometers per seat offered per year increased almost tenfold.[12] On the other hand, fares increased little on the average; and on the highly competitive transatlantic route they decreased between 1950 and 1971. What was disconcerting to the Europeans was that the European fleets, which had been practically all manufactured at home prior to World War II, consisted mostly of U.S.-manufactured airliners after the war.

As suggested earlier, the large size of the domestic U.S. airliner market gave the U.S. manufacturers a huge advantage over European manufacturers. Table 5 presents specific data on the constancy of this advantage over the past few decades. As the table indicates, U.S. carriers enjoyed 50 percent of the world market after the early 1930s. Further data show that most of the U.S. market was domestic (82 percent in 1971, 75 percent in 1964) as opposed to international, whereas the opposite was true for the European carriers.

Table 5. Non-freight air transport market (millions of passengers-kilometers on scheduled routes)

Country of carrier	Year			
	1932	1937	1964	1971
Britain	26	79	10,795	19,907
France	22	60	6,697	13,834
United States	236	743	94,134	215,585
World	465	1,500	171,000	494,000

Source: R. Modey and T. Cawley, *Aviation Facts and Figures, 1953* (Washington, D.C.: Lincoln Press, 1953); International Air Transport Association (IATA) and International Civil Aeronautic Organization (ICAO), *Reports,* 1964 and 1971.

In the United States the national policy has been to foster some degree of competition among carriers. Passengers in West European countries also have had a choice of airlines, despite pooling, administered prices, and other cartel-like arrangements. With rates and schedules controlled, the only major variables that could be manipulated to gain competitive advantage were speed, safety, and comfort—the variables that derived largely from the technical characteristics of the aircraft itself. Hence, as soon as a more attractive plane was developed, all of the competing airlines were forced to fly it, or its equivalent from another manufacturer to avoid losing their own market share. As a consequence, the world's major airlines have been forced periodically to replace perfectly serviceable aircraft. And because of the international nature of the competition even the government-controlled European carriers have not been completely captive markets.

The problem facing the European manufacturers, therefore, has been crystal-clear. An analysis of the data in Tables 3 and 4 points up the overwhelming advantage in scale enjoyed by U.S. industry over its British and French competitors. Sales of military and space products by the U.S. industry to the U.S. government were well over ten times the corresponding British and French sales combined. This disparity is reflected in the relative sizes of the leading U.S. and West European firms. The average sales of the five largest U.S. firms were over five times the average sales of the first five European firms. Even the sales of the second five firms in the United States were 6.5 times larger than those of the second five European firms.[13] The major U.S. aerospace firms have been in a better position to exploit their domestic civil airliner market, which represents over half the world total. To these advantages of scale must be added the additional benefits of technology transfer from the military and space effort.

Lacking sufficiently large national markets, the Europeans needed to capture a large share of the market outside the United States in order to survive. But this implied a technological and price-competitive product attractive enough also to succeed in the U.S. market. How difficult it is to achieve such success is seen from Figure 2. Of the twelve leading U.S. airframe firms only five have developed and produced civil airliners

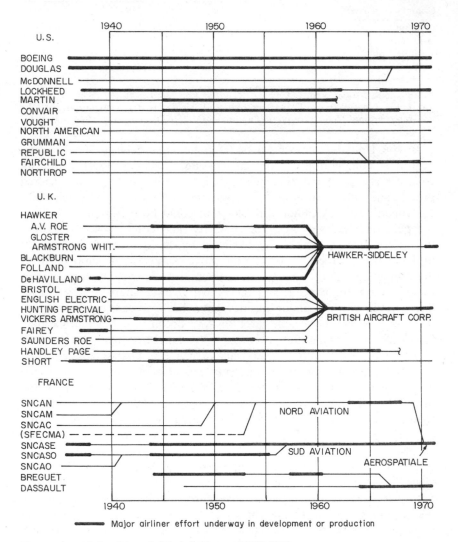

Figure 2. Major Aircraft Manufacturers, 1936–1971.

since World War II, and by 1973 only three U.S. firms remained in the airliner market, with Lockheed's success in doubt. (Fairchild produced and marketed a European plane, the Fokker F-27, in the United States.) Only four European aircraft have effectively penetrated the U.S. and world markets in the postwar period. These are the Vickers Viscount, Caravelle, BAC 111, and Fokker F-27. Of these four, only the first and last returned a significant profit to their manufacturers.

A specific example brings this European difficulty into bold relief. After the Boeing 747, the next major airliner development to reach scheduled service in fleet operations was the so-called "wide-bodied" medium-range jumbo jet represented by the Douglas DC-10 and the Lockheed L-1011 Tristar. These three-engined airliners initially had one half the range and carried two thirds the passenger load of a 747 but were offered at two thirds its price. Development of the DC-10 and L-1011 began in early 1966 with initial orders from U.S. airlines. A 1968 market estimate foresaw world requirements by 1980 of about 1200 such aircraft. But such a development was far beyond the capabilities of any one European firm. After two years of negotiations an agreement was signed in September 1967 by the governments of Britain, France, and Germany to initiate and financially support the development of the A-300 Airbus. (Britain later was to drop out.) Head-on competition with the United States was avoided by selecting a design utilizing only two engines. From the beginning of 1968 to the end of 1972, the competing designs had changed in various respects, as indicated in Table 6. Moreover, the dates for entry into service had slipped a year or two.

Table 6. Airbus models and characteristics

Plane	Number of passengers		Range (kilometers)		Cost per plane (millions of current dollars)	
	1968	1972	1968	1972	1968	1972
DC-10	250–300	250–300	4,000	6,000–10,000	15	19–20
L-1011	250–300	250–300	4,000	6,000	15	19–22
A-300	260–300	225–300	2,000	2,000– 4,000	10–11	17–19

Sources: Jane's All the World's Aircraft (London: S. Low Marston, 1968 and 1969); Proceedings of a symposium sponsored by the Association Internationale des Constructeurs Aeronautiques, London, September 13 and 14, 1967; *Les Echos* (Paris), November 27, 1972, p. 10; *Fortune,* September 1970, p. 115.

Early estimates of the break-even point for each of the two U.S. airliners were about 250 planes, estimates which rose to almost 500 planes by 1973. In light of these figures the sales registered by late 1972 were significant.[14]

DC-10:	177 sales and 47 options
L-1011:	124 sales and 60 options
A-300B:	16 sales and 22 options

The attitude of Lufthansa, one of the buyers of the A-300B, is instructive of the special problems of the European manufacturers. Although Lufthansa is 50 percent owned by the German government, and although the A-300B received almost half its financial support from the German government, Lufthansa could not be prevailed upon to place an order until the end of 1972. At that time it ordered only three planes for delivery in 1975 with options for an additional four. At the same time, however, Lufthansa, which had previously ordered four long-range DC-10s and was already flying twenty-seven Boeing 727s, purchased five additional DC-10s and three more 727s, the closest rival of the A-300B. In spite of Lufthansa's awareness of relative costs and its confidence in the performance characteristics and price of the A-300Bs, there must have been several reasons for Lufthansa's purchase of the DC-10s and 727s. Among them no doubt were Lufthansa's need to remain competitive with other airlines which were introducing the U.S. planes, its common maintenance agreements with other European purchasers of the U.S. planes, and the rapid growth of the passenger market, which necessitated early deliveries.

In summary, by the early 1970s, ballooning costs of development and production had driven the break-even production point for civil aircraft above the level that could be sustained by the requirements of any one European country. A similar situation prevailed with respect to military aircraft, although France, Britain, and even Sweden reluctantly continued in this area on the basis of national security considerations. These factors first drove the West European nations to consolidate their own industry; and when this remedy proved inadequate, they began to seek some sort of association or cooperation across frontiers. Out of this effort arose various joint ventures, mostly government-initiated. Because each of the firms involved nurtured the hope of acquiring ultimate ascendancy over national and international competitors, all such joint ventures had one common characteristic—they were temporary affairs, not permanent marriages. To understand the approach of these countries to such joint ventures, however, it will be helpful to take a more detailed look at the British and French industries.

Great Britain's Industry

Shortly after World War I three British and two French airlines were operating cross-channel commercial services. When in 1921 the competition threatened to ruin the British firms, the government began subsidizing two of them. After that the principal British carriers were under constant government control; and, from 1946 on, they were under government ownership. By early 1973, consolidation of Britain's two major airlines, British European Airways (BEA) and British Overseas Airways Corporation (BOAC), was in its final phase. A national champion was born. Of interest here is the typically British process through which this was accomplished. From the Hambling Committee, which led to the formation of Imperial Airways in 1924, through the Fisher Committee of 1935 and the Cadman Committee in 1937, a succession of committees, commissions, and parliamentary investigations led to the consolidating of the "chosen instruments" into a single nationalized firm.

Unlike the airlines, the aircraft industry appeared to fare much better in the 1930s. Though many firms dating from World War I went by the boards, de Havilland, Vickers, Bristol, Gloster, Hawker, Handley Page, A. V. Roe, Short, Rolls Royce, and Armstrong-Siddeley established themselves and made major contributions to aviation technology. In the civil transport field the need was for planes to fly the "Empire Route" to the colonies and dominions. Because of the technology then available and the primitive quality of the airports in the Empire's outposts, flying boats were required. On the other hand, in the United States, technology and market characteristics combined by 1936 to produce the record-breaking Douglas DC-3 land plane, which was to set the standard for the industry. Before the highly competent British producers could react, the war clouds gathered and the British had to concentrate on military aircraft. So great had the British and French military requirements become by 1938 that purchasing missions were sent to the United States to place large orders.

By 1943, employment in the British airframe and aero-engine industry exceeded a million workers, with production divided among about fifteen firms. Although four of these firms had been merged into the Hawker Group in 1935, they continued to maintain their separate engineering and production facilities. Such "agglomeration" rather than consolidation was characteristic of later British mergers. At the war's end, when employment in the British aircraft industry fell to 170,000, the British government still continued to support all the firms.[15] For the time being, a technological edge maintained exports and managed to keep all the firms in business. But not for long. From 1945 to 1950 nine British firms were in production on fourteen different types of large civil and military aircraft. But in that five-year period only three firms produced over a thousand such planes each: de Havilland, Gloster, and Hawker.[16] Nevertheless, all major firms, whatever their achievements, continued to receive government support for new developments. Dissolution was hardly a reward for valiant wartime service.

The British government, it is evident, was pinning its hopes not only on the military market but also on the civilian demand for aircraft. Fully aware of the future importance of commercial aviation, the British government had begun planning early in the war to assure its industry a leading role in postwar world markets. To this end Lord Brabazon was appointed in 1942 to chair a committee charged with mapping out the strategy. Two successive committees forged an across-the-board product strategy and were instrumental in launching the program as early as 1943. The cornerstone of the effort was Britain's lead over the United States in gas turbines. By early 1950 Britain had already invested as much as £70 million ($300 million) in the program.[17] Although such expenditures are difficult to assess accurately, the investment was enormous when compared to prewar expenditures. Some ten different transports in five basic categories were initially selected for development. None, however, was competitive with the far less costly "stretched" DC-6s and Constellations. These U.S. planes, in service in 1950, could lift up to ninety tourist-class passengers at take-off weights of 130 thousand pounds. Their British competitors proved smaller and slower.

What the British did succeed in doing was to enter the first jet transport in commercial service in 1952, six years before the Boeing 707. But the special risks of the radical innovator soon appeared. Accidents due to metal fatigue forced the withdrawal from service of the British plane in 1954. By 1958, when a redesigned and somewhat larger version appeared, it was too late to compete successfully with the even larger and more efficient 707, which entered airline service simultaneously.

No less than twenty-five different commercial transport developments were launched in Britain in the period 1944–1959, most with varying degrees of governmental support. Some twelve different firms, including two new entries, were competing with one another for government funds and success in a world market, over half of which was in the United States. (Meanwhile in the United States five firms were marketing only five basic airliners.) Of the many British developments only eleven types saw any production at all, and of these eleven the Viscount, which entered service in 1953, was the only major transport to have a commercial success.[18] Nevertheless, there was no consolidation or even "agglomeration" in this period. The British government continued to scatter the military and civil effort so as to keep the fragmented industry intact.

The archaic Princess flying boat was supported until 1954, four years after its only possible customer, BOAC, had abandoned the flying boat concept. Bristol Aircraft, responsible for the huge and hopeless Brabazon I and for the later Britannia, whose development had been characterized with typical British understatement as "unduly protracted," continued to receive support.[19] Paradoxically, successes like the Viscount were rewarded by giving Vickers, in 1957, the impossible task of starting development of the VC-10 (competitor to the 707) two years after massive orders for the 707 and DC-8 had already been placed. It was in 1955, while the British industry was in the throes of its problems with its pioneer jet airliner, that the French first flew their medium-range twin-jet Caravelle. Not until 1957 did the British government give de Havilland the go-ahead to develop a competitive medium-range airliner, the tri-jet Trident. Unfortunately, this plane was designed to meet specific BEA requirements with little reference to wider export market requirements. A year later, Boeing launched the more universally attractive tri-jet 727, which entered airline service in 1962, a full year ahead of the Trident. The sales statistics in Table 7 depict the British industry's plight.

Table 7. Jet transports delivered or on order to commercial carriers: number of planes of selected types

Type of aircraft	Through December 1965	Through December 1971
Boeing 707/720 (U.S.)	598	841
DC-8 (U.S.)	319	556
Boeing 727 (U.S.)	428	888
Caravelle (French)	212	278
VC-10 (U.K.)	38	54
Trident (U.K.)	48	88

Source: International Civil Aeronautical Organization (ICAO), *Annual Reports of the Council, 1971,* document 8982, A19-P/1, Montreal, April 1972; ICAO, *Annual Report of the Council for 1965,* document 8572, A16-P/1, Montreal, April 1966.

From the vantage point of the 1970s, as one surveys the complex twists and turns of Britain's producers and Britain's airlines, a final telling generalization emerges. Apart from the Viscount and BAC-111, British producers have had to rely on the captive national airline, BEA, as the major purchaser of British short- and medium-range airliners. However, BOAC's fleet, being in international competition, has always been forced to depend on U.S. aircraft in order to stay competitive.

The unhappy postwar experiences of Britain's commercial aircraft manufacturers have been matched by equally disconcerting experiences in the sales of military aircraft during the same period. British aircraft, it is true, met with considerable success in the early postwar period. The industry, fully supported by the government, initiated development of a plethora of fighters and bombers. Yet the outbreak of the Korean War in 1950 found Britain without a competitive fighter. A strong factor behind

Britain's procrastination in consolidating its aircraft industry and putting order into its commercial aircraft program was the advent of the Korean War in 1950. The overloading of the U.S. industry due to the war triggered an offshore procurement program whereby the United States purchased military equipment in Europe. In July 1952 it was announced that the United States would spend over $225 million for the procurement of European military aircraft and Britain would get the "lion's share."[20] While this windfall may have amounted to a small percentage of Britain's aircraft sales at that time, it was enough to sustain hope. At the same time British planes were being built under license in continental Europe, including France, and British prestige was high.

A host of different starts in the 1945–1950 period coupled with rising development and procurement costs proved too much for the British Treasury. Britain had to face reality, and the reappraisal was brutal. A defense White Paper in 1957 "shattered the hopes of the industry . . . There would be no long range bombers after the 'V' bombers and no high performance fighters beyond the Lightning. The rocket and guided missile were expected largely to take the place of manned aircraft" except for transports and helicopters. Out of this new look came the decision to rely for strategic uses upon the Blue Streak, a liquid-fueled, medium-range ballistic missile. All the military aircraft projects started in the 1950–1955 period were canceled. The 1957 White Paper in effect wrote off future military aircraft development.[21]

Yet the fifteen or so firms that made up the industry continued to exist with government support. Not until after the November 1959 election and strong pressure from the new government was there a move toward consolidation. Once initiated, the action was far-reaching. Two major aircraft groups replaced nine separate firms. One was Hawker-Siddeley, which at last consolidated its separate aircraft divisions and absorbed Blackburn, Vickers Armstrong, English Electric, and Hunting (as shown in Figure 2). To ease the birth pangs the government awarded a contract for a new manned bomber, the TSR-2, to BAC and Bristol-Siddeley, although only two years earlier it had been decided there would be no more manned bombers. Much later, in 1968, Bristol-Siddeley was to merge into Rolls Royce.

In addition to forcing the mergers of the early 1960s, the new government cancelled the Blue Streak project on the ground that it was too costly and had been outmoded by solid-fueled missiles such as the Minuteman and Polaris. Instead, Britain agreed to share in the development of the U.S. Skybolt air-launched nuclear missile. Unfortunately, the United States unilaterally cancelled the Skybolt two years later (in 1962). In another break with previous policy the British government entered into several European joint aerospace ventures with her European neighbors. Among these was the European Launcher Development

Organisation Agreement of November 1961 wherein Britain convinced the major continental powers to use the cancelled Blue Streak as the first stage of a multinational three-stage satellite launch vehicle. Here, Britain's participation was less a sign of a newborn willingness to be European than a strong desire to salvage jobs and know-how in her hard-pressed aerospace industry. Also in 1962 Britain signed the agreement to develop the Concorde SST jointly with the French.

Then in April 1964 the British industry received a stunning but inevitable blow stemming from the 1957 White Paper. Lacking a modern plane to replace the Royal Navy's aging Sea Vixens, the government was forced to order McDonnell Phantom jet fighters from the United States, the first of several such orders.[22] Faced with an ailing economy, with the TSR-2 development costs tripling and the Concorde costs doubling, the industry received another shock when Labour won the October 1964 elections. There ensued a traumatic belt-tightening, including the cancellation of the TSR-2 and the two other major military aircraft projects, together with an abortive attempt to pull Britain out of the Concorde program. To analyze the shambles, the Plowden Committee was appointed "to consider what should be the future place and organisation of the aircraft industry."

One of the Plowden Report's strongest recommendations was that Britain should base its future aerospace efforts on cooperative ventures with other countries, and with European nations rather than with the United States. This was easier said than done. Two joint developments for military aircraft were carefully negotiated with France. A French firm was given the leading role in the development of a light fighter. But rather than give the lead to a British firm for a swing-wing fighter, as had been arranged, France turned to Dassault to achieve the development on a purely national basis, leaving Britain to seek new partners. Joint projects, it was evident, carried their own special uncertainties.

By the early 1970s Britain had gradually and painfully shaped its industry into two airframe enterprises and one motor firm, and there had been continuing pressure from the government on BAC and Hawker-Siddeley to merge and thereby to create a single "national champion." Such a national champion would be less the result of deliberate long-range policy than the consequence of economic circumstance coupled with vacillating government policies. For over a decade after World War II the British industry induced the government to spread its limited resources widely. The result was that they were too thin to assure success in the face of a tightening world market, strong U.S. competition, and unavoidable technological hazards. When the government could no longer avoid the economic realities, there ensued a stream of ad hoc decisions rather than a realistic long-range plan. Unfortunate circumstances seem to have plagued the industry. The government added to the problem with improvident planning and an inadequate decision and control mechanism. But behind everything else lay economic realities, which made any single national response largely inadequate.

France

From the end of World War I to about 1930 France could justifiably claim the title of having the world's leading aviation industry. After 1930 the relative importance of France decreased before Britain's growing interest and strength, Germany's new and superior aircraft technology, and the growing U.S. market. At the same time, the French industry, which was just as fragmented as the British, ran into serious financial problems resulting from the lack of a long-range government procurement program and from a depression budget. In 1936 Leon Blum's Popular Front government nationalized the armament industries, including aircraft. As Figure 2 shows, the ten or so large firms were reduced to six, and then in 1941 to four. One of the survivors was the Société Nationale de Constructions Aéronautiques du Sud-Est (SNCASE, or Sud-Est). Though some of the previous owner-managers were given top positions in the nationalized firms, the resulting managerial shock was apparently not overcome by the time of the German victory in 1940. Nationalization did set the stage, however, for the continuing reorganization and consolidation that engaged the French aircraft industry after World War II.

During the war, while Lord Brabazon's committees were mapping Britain's challenge for commercial transport supremacy, the French aircraft industry languished under German occupation. France's extremely competent aeronautical engineers, most of them *Polytechniciens* (alumni of France's elite Ecole Polytechnique) and also graduates of the Ecole Nationale Supérieure de l'Aéronautique, could do little more than dream. One, Lucien Servanty (a rare non-*Polytechnicien*), was reduced to designing a jet aircraft around German engines on his dining-room table. He was later to become the chief French designer of the Concorde.

In the immediate postwar period Charles Tillon, the Communist Air Minister, compounded the near chaos in the industry by swelling employment from 40,000 to 100,000 and by placing many political appointees in executive positions. The inevitable crisis led a subsequent government to make important changes in the management of the nationalized industry. During this period Breguet and Dassault, two prewar engineer-entrepreneurs who had lost their firms in the 1936 nationalization, were able to enter into competition with the nationalized sector by means of government contracts. Though French military fears of the strong Communist influence in the nationalized firms may have played a role here, it is more likely that these experienced industrialists had a much better feel for what was needed and wanted than the disturbed nationalized companies. In turn, the aggressiveness and ability of the entrepreneurs to get things done created a competitive environment previously absent in the nationalized industry. After the 1947–48 housecleaning the new top managers of the nationalized firms had to be masters not only of bureaucracy and politics but of business as well.

One of the few top managers who managed to survive the shake-up was Georges Héreil, a lawyer and trustee in bankruptcy whom Tillon in 1946 had named president of the Société Nationale de Constructions Aéronautiques du Sud-Est. At that time Sud Est, in financial straits, was struggling to produce the government's first large postwar order for commercial transports. The company's four-engined, 35-passenger plane was of 1939 vintage, similar to the early Boeing 307, not at all competitive with the postwar DC-4. After Héreil took over he was able to get further government backing for development of a very large four-engined propeller-driven airliner, with a capacity of eighty passengers. Huge development costs and poor performance forced curtailment of the program in 1950. Completion of seven aircraft was made possible only through Marshall Plan aid. It is a tribute to Héreil's entrepreneurship that when the Air Ministry later decided to produce the British Vampire jet fighter, Sud-Est somehow managed to get the assignment.

The turmoil and meager financial support of the late 1940s forced the leaders of France's aircraft industry to fall back on characteristic French verve and ingenuity to meet their needs. Exhibiting what was to become their hallmark, French engineers learned to take calculated risks, to develop aircraft quickly and boldly, and to get prototypes flying in a minimum of time at a minimum cost. Dassault was a master of this technique, which in conjunction with superb engineering resulted in the highly successful Ouragan fighter in 1947 and its carefully evolved derivatives, the Mystère and Mirage series. These successes led the French government to give Dassault a "monopoly" on military aircraft development and production. Dassault also took full advantage of another trait of the French aircraft industry. Ever since nationalization the firms had been required to subcontract extensively to one another in order to utilize all production resources. Dassault carried this policy almost to an extreme, subcontracting most of his effort to the nationalized firms and private industry. Such tight cooperation gave the French invaluable experience for the many subsequent joint ventures which required work to be parceled out to different firms in different countries.

Breguet, the industry's only other large private firm until 1967, when it was absorbed by Dassault, was unable to match Dassault's success.

The Breguet Deux Ponts, a large transport plane, was more suitable for military than commercial use. Because no buyers could be found outside France, only twenty-seven were built.

Sud-Est's chief "competitor" among the nationalized firms was the SNCASO or Sud-Ouest, which had a very competent engineering team. When the government decided to develop an intermediate-range jet, Sud-Ouest prepared a proposal. But Sud-Est also submitted a design and ultimately won the competition. Full-scale development of the Caravelle then began. Later in 1957, when it became evident that the Caravelle would be an export success, Sud-Est absorbed Sud-Ouest, forming Sud-Aviation. The nationalized French industry had further consolidated, not because of astute planning but primarily as a result of entrepreneurial leadership and inadequate funds. The role played by government in rewarding the successful entrepreneur was a significant factor in strengthening the industry.

At the end of 1958 the French aircraft industry was heavy with success and hope. Dassault's constantly evolving Mystère and Mirage series of military aircraft were eminently successful. At the newly merged Sud-Aviation, Héreil had consolidated his power and forged a team. Sud's Caravelle, which had been flying for three years, was in production; not only Air France but the hard-headed Scandinavian Airlines System (SAS) had ordered it. True enough, there was a large overall drop in orders for heavy aircraft due to the end of U.S. procurement in Europe, as well as the budgetary drain of the Algerian war. But these pressures only served as an added incentive for the industry to keep up its policy of bold design, quick construction of flying prototypes, and aggressive marketing.

De Gaulle's rise to power in 1958 gave the aircraft industry of France new impetus. Having learned from experience the value of making bold technological jumps while avoiding head-on competition with the U.S. manufacturers, Sud's engineers concentrated on a supersonic airliner or SST which would serve the same medium-range market as the Caravelle. It was appropriately dubbed the Super Caravelle. While French engineers as a group were less experienced than their British counterparts, the situation had changed dramatically since 1950 when the French had been learning to build British jets under license. Sud's engineers, the Caravelle under their belt, had designed, built, and flown several supersonic planes. In Britain, BAC was also hard at work on an SST design, and the company was being pressed by the government to find a U.S. or European partner. After the Paris air show of June 1961, where Sud displayed a model of the Super Caravelle, serious talks were held between French and British officials at both government and industry levels. Strong British overtures to U.S. manufacturers had received no response. Héreil, too, failed to bring off an agreement whereby the

United States would concentrate on the large, long-range SST and France on the smaller, medium-range SST.[23] In the end the British and French joined forces and the Concorde project was born. When, because of understandable British opposition, Héreil was refused unquestioned control of the Concorde development, he resigned.

It is a truism that the costs of aircraft development rarely fall within original estimates. Yet not even the most pessimistic French or British civil servant would have dreamed that the Concorde costs would sky-rocket as they did. The initial estimate was from $420 million to $480 million, including funds for tooling, flight tests, and so on.[24] In early 1973 the development costs alone were officially estimated in excess of $2.4 billion. Tooling and funds for aircraft in production but not yet ordered amounted to hundreds of millions more. In launching Concorde, France and Britain unwittingly committed themselves to vast public expenditures.

France, pursuing her long-range plans, also found the means to fund the A-300B airbus and the smaller 150-passenger short-range Mercure, whereas Britain had only the Concorde as a future product. On the other hand, had it not been for Dassault's remarkable success in selling the Mirage series abroad, the French production picture from 1955 to 1972 would have been poorer than Britain's. In early 1973, as the last Caravelles rolled off the assembly line, an alarmed French industry announced that the export orders for 1972 (about 80 percent military) had slipped to 3.7 billion francs (U.S. $740 million) compared to 5 billion francs ($1 billion) in 1971 and 5.5 billion francs ($1.1 billion) in 1970. The assumptions of the Sixth Plan, based on a "conservative" increase in exports of 12 percent per year, were imperiled. Without substantial additional orders for the Concorde, A-300B, or Mercure, the industry faced a near-catastrophic reduction of activity.[25] It was at this point that Pan American and TWA rejected the Concorde, plunging French industry into a period of even greater uncertainty.

Conclusions

The evolution of the British and French aircraft industries prior to the Concorde program reveals two distinct patterns. Though both industries have a history of gradual consolidation, the resemblance is superficial. France developed a single major manufacturer of commercial transports via the route of entrepreneurial success in an environment characterized by competition and skimpy funding. Because the French industry was largely nationalized, it proved relatively manageable, permitting timely mergers and liquidations at the behest of a reasonably knowledgeable government bureaucracy. Britain, on the other hand, had quite another pattern. Starting with the advantages of size, technical superiority, the opportunity to plan strategically, and a government willing to finance airliner ventures, Britain saw those resources squandered. The reasons can be summed up in this way: first, an indecisive on-again off-again government which started and stopped too many programs; second, reliance on the captive markets of BOAC and BEA for inspiration and advice, accompanied by a failure to appreciate the subtleties of the world market; and third, a failure to force a real and well-timed consolidation of the fragmented industry.

It is perhaps too much to say that the relatively greater French success was the result of better planning on the part of government and industry. Yet it was certain by the early 1970s that France's series of five-year plans had been beneficial for its aircraft industry. Instead of a stream of committees, commissions, and white papers, and the indecisiveness characteristic of economy-minded British governments, the French industry enjoyed the stability of a single government with a consistent policy for over fifteen years. Equally important was France's adherence to the program objectives rather than the plan's financial ceilings. The ceilings were seldom met, even with the built-in provisions for inflation.

Nevertheless, planning was not the principal reason behind France's resurgent industry. Dassault's success was clearly due to excellent engineering combined with the superb leadership of an outstanding entrepreneur. Héreil's success in creating Sud-Aviation and launching the Caravelle was due also to leadership capabilities. Fortunately for France, an early lack of funds had forced a drastic limitation on prototype development. Similarly, the French decision in 1952 to initiate a small, medium-range jet when Britain had just put the four-jet Comet into service was the result of her inability to fund a larger aircraft rather than of a carefully planned strategy. So chance played a part as well.

It is clear that the emergence of two major airframe firms in both Britain and France was not the fruit of deliberate policy. With one exception—the merger in 1971 of Sud-Aviation, Nord Aviation, and SEREB, the government enterprise formed to develop and produce ballistic rockets—a series of simple and onerous political and economic circumstances forced the consolidations. It was what lay behind the economic circumstances that was important. There were of course the recurring national crises which limited available funds. But to a much greater extent the economic constraints were due to the evolving technology which constantly increased the price of maintaining a self-sustaining industry.

The coupling of technology and a large national market allowed the U.S. industry to set a very fast pace.[26] From 1942 to 1957 the British assumed that they could capitalize on their technology and experience to compete successfully with the United States. But their centralized technological planning apparently lacked an accompanying marketing study and plan. Moreover, the government lacked the will or the strength to force consolidation of the industry. Instead, the government succumbed to the pressures, urgings, promises, and hopes of the all too numerous firms, and it frittered away its dwindling resources. Britain's early lead in jet aircraft was such that many British industry spokesmen felt that had it not been for the technological misfortune of the Comet 1, Britain would have been assured of a position in the world market. The inadequacy of this hypothesis is shown in the failure of the French industry to sell enough Caravelles to break even, and Britain's later failure to sell the Hawker-Siddeley vertical take-off fighter on a permanent basis. One is led to the inescapable conclusion that the basic factors in developing a successful aerospace industry are the size of the home market and more fundamentally the bedrock of government support.

It may be true that external technological change forced firms to either grow in size or disappear.[27] The data presented bear this out. But a firm cannot grow independently of its home market over the long term. For the Europeans this implies creating a truly common market, including a common military market, as a necessary condition to successful competition with the United States. But an adequate base market alone is not a sufficient condition for success. My analysis has shown that only the most astutely led firms can succeed. A corollary is that government bureaucracies had best leave the management of individual programs and firms to the entrepreneur, and stick to the elaboration and maintenance of long-range policy. Europe must somehow create permanent aerospace firms, entrepreneur-managed and transnational, if its industry is to survive.

Aluminum   Zuhayr Mikdashi

Among the enterprises that have figured in the industrial policies of the governments of western Europe, aluminum has always occupied a prominent place. One reason for that prominence has been the relation of the industry to national defense; another has been the importance of the aluminum smelter and its related energy needs as a pole for industrial development. The preoccupation of governments with the development of an aluminum industry has usually found its focus in three lines of policy: helping to provide the capital that was needed for the large lumpy investments; helping to develop the enormous quantities of energy demanded by such installations; and promoting security of access for their enterprises to foreign raw materials, notably bauxite. As a result, during the 1960s and early 1970s practically every major country in western Europe established some sort of working relationship with its own aluminum enterprises. These enterprises, for their part, evolved their own strategies in relation both to one another and to their respective governments. The network of strategies and cooperative ties, which began at the national level, in some cases reached the European and even the international level.

By the early 1970s, however, it was not clear that any recognition of a collective European interest actually existed in the industry. Once the joint global concerns of the companies had been identified and once their distinct national interests had been accounted for, there was little left at the European level to identify or explain.

Western Europe's position in the primary aluminum-producing industry was prominent. Early in the 1970s, it was the second largest producing area in the world after North America. Moreover, as Table 1 shows, planned production capacity in western Europe was scheduled to rise substantially from 3,169 million short tons at the end of 1971 to 4,194 million at the end of 1976, or by 32.3 percent. The projected rise for North America was relatively smaller: from 5,880 million to 6,232 million, or not quite 6 percent.

Governmental Interests

Ever since the Frenchman Paul Hérault and the American Charles Martin Hall introduced the low-cost electrolytic method of smelting

Zuhayr Mikdashi is a member of the Faculty of the American University of Beirut.

Table 1. Primary aluminum ingot capacity by geographic area, 1971–1976[a]

Region	Thousands of short tons					
	1971	1972	1973	1974	1975	1976
Common Market	1,762	1,805	2,152	2,299	2,414	2,563
Other Europe	1,407	1,472	1,526	1,587	1,631	1,631
Western Europe Total	3,169	3,277	3,678	3,886	4,045	4,194
North America	5,880	5,900	6,085	6,085	6,085	6,232
Latin America	241	265	292	314	412	494
Africa & Middle East	323	428	461	491	529	662
Asia & Oceania	1,832	1,969	2,097	2,312	2,808	3,010
Total	11,445	11,839	12,613	13,088	13,879	14,592

Source: Stewart R. Spector, *Aluminum Industry Report Semiannual Review, Mid-Year Survey of Free World Primary Aluminum Capacity 1971–1976* (New York: Oppenheimer & Co., 1972), pp. 20 and 22.

[a] Figures are for actual capacity in 1971 and for planned capacity in 1972–1976. Socialist countries of eastern Europe and China not included.

aluminum in 1866, governmental interest in that metal has been keen. From the late 1930s on, governments considered aluminum a strategic commodity, largely because of its use in military aircraft and rockets. For both military and civilian purposes it offers more desirable qualities than any other basic material. It is light, weighing about one third as much as steel or copper for the same volume. It is antimagnetic, and yet it is an excellent conductor of electricity with a yield twice as large as that of copper per unit of weight. It also offers a high degree of durability, thermal conductivity, mechanical resistance, malleability, resistance to corrosion, power of reflection, power as a reducing agent, resistance to low temperatures, low fusion point, non-toxicity, and ease of fabrication.[1] To the technical qualities of aluminum should be added its commercial quality of being comparatively economical. Its price in 1972, compared with copper—a chief competitor—was about a third on a per unit of weight basis, or a tenth on a per unit of volume basis. Moreover, the leading raw material for aluminum—bauxite—was available in abundant quantities in several countries.

By 1972, aluminum usage had become so diffuse that it pervaded the major sectors of modern industrial society, almost in the same manner as steel or energy did. Besides defense industries, the major industrial groups of aluminum users were transport and space, electrical and communications, building and construction, consumer durables, containers and packaging, and machinery and equipment. The growth of consumption of aluminum products was highest among the major metals, averaging an annual compound rate of 8 percent after the end of World War II.

Governmental interest in the aluminum metal naturally led to governmental interest in the input requirements of aluminum production. One major element of input is access to raw materials, bauxite or alumina. Bauxite is found in limited quantities in Europe, while ample supplies are mostly in tropical areas; yet a tight oligopolistic structure which existed in the world aluminum industry until the late 1960s, coupled with a web of joint ventures and other forms of partnerships, effectively erected barriers to access to raw material by enterprises outside the oligopoly. By 1973, however, the number of suppliers had increased, thus broadening the access to raw material. Another important input is technology. Technology (especially for smelting) was crucial in the early stages of the industry's development. It became more diffuse in the late 1960s and early 1970s, thus eliminating the competitive gap some European national enterprises faced vis-à-vis other enterprises—notably those of North America.[2]

Two other essential inputs are capital and power. The construction of smelters requires big lumpy investments; and cheap, abundant power is needed for the reduction of alumina into aluminum metal. It is reckoned that aluminum smelting in western Europe has called for fifteen to twenty times more investment than steel for the same quantity of metal.* In 1971, capital amortization and other financial charges for aluminum in western Europe reached the high figure of 39 percent of total costs,** with energy accounting for 28 percent of the total cost of producing aluminum ingots.[3] The bulk of the energy used is consumed in the process of converting alumina into aluminum by electrolysis at the rate of about 14,000 kilowatt-hours per ton of metal. This explains the location of aluminum smelters next to abundant and cheap sources of power. Government played an active role in providing the requisite heavy infrastructure investments, especially in the form of large-capacity power plants or means of transporting energy to certain locations, with a view to promoting *pôles de croissance,* or centers for industrial regional development.

The strategic importance of aluminum for defense and civilian purposes, and its special input requirements and methods of production—as compared with textiles, for example—caused European governments to become increasingly involved in the industry. With raw materials mostly

* The investment ratio given here seems high if compared to the frequently quoted U.S. ratios of three to five times; the West European figure may include the investment cost of power plants.

** In breaking down the total cost of producing aluminum ingots, raw materials (including bauxite-alumina) and labor accounted for 17 percent and 16 percent respectively.

available outside national territories, several governments sought the protection of "security of supplies" largely through nationally owned producers, with integrated operations from markets and fabricating plants to sources of raw materials. Moreover, given the high investment costs of smelting and power generation plants in aluminum production in which they shared directly or indirectly, European governments found it necessary to keep abreast of the latest technological developments in aluminum production. The adoption of advanced technology and the construction of large-scale plants contributed to a substantial reduction in the unit cost of producing the metal.

Not all West European governments have articulated interests and objectives with respect to their aluminum industry; and when these objectives have been stated, they have not always been consistent or uniform. Furthermore, governments have valued differently the social benefits or social costs associated with aluminum, partly because of the pressures of events and partly because of the ideology of ruling groups. For example, the governments of the Fifth Republic in France have, on balance, favored the development of national champions and, more recently, the protection of "security of supplies" for raw materials. The balance-of-payments factor loomed large with the British government after the late 1950s, and especially with the Labour government of the latter half of the 1960s, which favored the establishment in Britain of aluminum smelting capacity at least partly owned by national interests. The main concern of Norway's aluminum policy was the protection of employment and wage income in depressed areas, in preference to growth in profits and markets.[4] Spain and Italy were also largely concerned with government-supported industrial regional development. Other countries, notably Germany, the Netherlands, and Switzerland, generally favored an open-door competitive policy with relatively little governmental interference.

Governmental Policies and Programs

To implement their objectives, West European governments became involved in aluminum in numerous ways. Direct governmental action was taken mostly through state ownership and management of aluminum-producing enterprises, of enterprises supplying important inputs (for example, power companies or credit institutions), or of major enterprises which used aluminum products (such as the defense, aerospace, and transport industries). In addition, governments used administrative measures to aid in such developments as mergers, or to control prices of aluminum inputs or output. Indirect influences showed up through protection from import competition, tax incentives, and financial and technical assistance. Considerable variation existed from country to country both in the perception of priorities and in the preference for instrumentalities.[5]

Norway. Norway presents an interesting case of governmental response. Its aluminum industry was both privately and publicly owned. The country offered private investors an attractive location with abundant and cheap hydroelectric power and relative proximity to major West European markets. Governmental ownership of aluminum smelters happened accidentally, not out of design. In 1945, following the withdrawal of German occupation forces, the Norwegian state inherited an uncompleted modern smelter. The size and importance of the venture inspired the Norwegian parliament to call on the government to complete the project under state ownership since no private Norwegian industrialist had the capacity to own and operate it. A Norwegian state-owned company, A/S Ardal og Sunndal Verk, was formed, and by 1963 Ardal had become Norway's largest aluminum smelting company.

An assured access to sources of raw material as well as to market outlets—in short, vertical integration—has generally been considered desirable by aluminum smelting enterprises, whether privately owned or state-owned. Ardal, however, was not vertically integrated. In 1947, it reached a 15-year barter agreement with a Canadian-based international company, Alcan Aluminium Ltd., whereby it received alumina in exchange for aluminum metal; other similar agreements were negotiated with Alcan in 1951, 1958, and 1965. Ardal also obtained loan financing from Marshall Plan funds in 1951 and from Alcoa in 1955, to be repaid in aluminum. The balance of Ardal's production of aluminum metal was sold on the open market to independent (not vertically integrated) producers of semimanufactures and finished products. In the 1960s, however, Ardal experienced increasing difficulties in securing alumina for its smelters in Norway and in disposing of its aluminum ingots on the open market at attractive prices. It was especially hit downstream through the takeover of nonintegrated fabricators which had hitherto been Ardal's main customers. Moreover, it had no guarantee that its barter agreement with Alcan would be renewed on satisfactory terms beyond the expiration date of 1971.

There were two ways in which the Norwegian government could achieve vertical integration to sources of raw materials and to consumer markets for fabricated products. It could develop Ardal into an independent, integrated producer, or it could let Ardal join an established international producer. The second option was favored on the ground that it was less risky. As a result, the Norwegian government entered into negotiations with its supplier of alumina, Alcan. The outcome was an agreement, effective January 1967, in which Alcan and Ardal merged their Norwegian interests (largely Ardal and Sunndal) on a 50–50 basis.* Alcan appointed half the directors of the merged group, although the Norwegians had the deciding vote. For this merger, the Norwegian government obtained as quid pro quo a large block of common shares (about 3 percent) in Alcan Aluminium Ltd., enabling a Norwegian government representative to sit on the board of directors at headquarters in Montreal, and enabling one representative of Ardal to sit on Alcan's bauxite-alumina subsidiary (Alcan Jamaica, Ltd.) and one each on Alcan's British and German fabricating subsidiaries (Alcan Industries, Ltd., and Alcan Aluminum-Werke GmbH). As a result of this merger, the Norwegian state-owned company entered the integrated aluminum industry.[6]

France. The French government, by contrast, favored vertical integration through the establishment of a nationally owned champion, Pechiney. In 1967, with governmental support, Pechiney took over Tréfimétaux, the leading French fabricator of nonferrous metals in the European Economic Community. To promote the merger, governmental support to Pechiney came in the form of low-cost loans or grants, big research contracts, and orders from the large state-owned companies, such as the aircraft manufacturers. The French government apparently went to the limit of direct intervention in order to consummate the merger, and "Tréfimétaux was practically thrown into Pechiney's embrace." By thwarting competition between these two national and privately owned enterprises, the French government avoided a possible takeover of one of them by a foreign enterprise. (Tréfimétaux had wanted to reduce its heavy dependence on Pechiney for primary aluminum by considering a joint venture smelter in Curaçao with a U.S. international major, Kaiser). At both the ministerial and civil service levels the French state opposed excessive competitiveness and an overwhelming drive for profit. Both of these practices were "regarded with suspicion by Government officials and—to a lesser degree—by leading businessmen as well." Higher priority was often given to promoting physical productivity and advanced technology.[7]

In its concern for security of supplies, the French state, acting through the state-owned Bureau de Recherches Géologiques et Minières

* Harvey Aluminum, Inc. (U.S.), which had sought a participation in Ardal, would have offered cash which could have been used by the Norwegian government to look for other desirable or profitable investments. Unsuccessful in its bid for Ardal, in 1963 Harvey joined with Norsk Hydro-Electrisk Kvaelstofaktieselskab (Norsk Hydro), a government-controlled power company. The new joint venture, known as Alnor Aluminium Norway A/S, was owned 51 percent by Norsk Hydro and 49 percent by Harvey. The Norwegian government had held 48 percent ownership of Norsk Hydro; French and Norwegian private interests had held 27 and 25 percent respectively. (See Arthur Stonehill, "International Mixed Ventures in Norway," Monograph Working Paper, MIT Sloan School of Management, Cambridge, Mass., August 1969, pp. 70–72.)

(BRGM), subsidized the research and exploratory efforts of French firms searching for minerals overseas. No doubt Pechiney, the largest industrial user of copper, was slated in 1972 to be a leading beneficiary of the 300 million francs to be given over a five-year period for carrying out overseas prospecting.[8] It was the view of the French government in the early 1970s that vertical integration to raw material sources was needed to cover at least one third to one quarter of the country's requirements.

In addition to the general fiscal and trading measures setting the environment for all industries, the French government had at its command important instruments pertaining to state financing and state trading. For example, the French state owned a large number of major financial institutions: commercial banks, savings banks, investment companies, and other credit institutions. Besides dominating the money and capital market, the state controlled the energy market: the gas, coal, and hydroelectric industries were nationalized, and the petroleum sector was partly government-owned (by Compagnie Française de Pétroles and Entreprise de Recherches et d'Activités Pétrolières, or ERAP) and totally government-guided under the "monopole délégué" regime, which empowered the state to allocate market shares to operators at its discretion. Aluminum producers were thus dependent on the good will of the government for credit and for energy at favorable terms. Indeed, Pechiney's growth could be adversely affected if the government rationed electric power or provided it at irregular periods, as it did in 1949. The French state, moreover, owned big users of aluminum products in such sectors as aeronautical construction, building, electricity, and transport. State purchases were so important that the aluminum industry was obliged to heed governmental wishes. State purchases furthermore were effected through a union of government purchasing organizations (Union des Groupements d'Acheteurs Publics—UGAP) under central directives. The French government also had a powerful weapon in its authority to set aluminum prices through the Direction Générale des Prix (Office of Price Control). Such a prerogative put aluminum producers at the mercy of governmental policy.[9]

The French government's effort to promote the concentration of the aluminum industry proved successful in that it led to Pechiney's virtual monopoly of the domestic market. Another inescapable outcome, however, was that the fortunes of the business went up and down with political fortunes. In the spring of 1972, when Pechiney was on the verge of getting an operator contract to produce the rich Iranian copper deposits of Sar Cheshmeh, the contract suddenly fell through. According to *The Economist,* this happened "mainly because President Pompidou snubbed the Shah and refused to attend his mammoth party [on the anniversary of the Persian Monarchy] last year." Instead, the Anaconda

Company (U.S.) stepped in to offer its technical assistance to the Iranian government.[10]

Great Britain. In Great Britain, the Labour government of Harold Wilson strove to create a domestic aluminum smelting industry and influenced the construction of three aluminum smelters with a total planned capacity of about 400,000 short tons per annum. These smelters were built over the period 1968–1973 with the support of a heavy subsidy from the British government. The subsidy cost the country £ 60 million (U.S. $150 million), notably in the form of investment allowances. Power, too, was subsidized. The benefits sought by the Wilson government were essentially import savings—an understandably dominant objective in the minds of Britain's leaders, given the weak balance-of-payments position of the country at the time. Import savings were valued at £ 60 million per year, while employment benefits for a capital-intensive industry like smelting were relatively small—just over 3,000 permanent jobs.[11] Canadian and Norwegian producers, the major suppliers of aluminum to the United Kingdom, had to bear the brunt of the British government's policy of subsidization.

Germany. The government of West Germany, probably the country closest to a market economy in western Europe after World War II, had attempted to promote competition in aluminum. For example, in November 1971 the governmental Cartel Office imposed a fine of DM5,000 on eighteen producers of semifabricated aluminum on the ground that they had participated in an exchange of market information in violation of German fair competition laws. The German government, furthermore, reacted against other governments' interventions which tended to distort the operation of free market forces. In 1971 it complained to the OECD that "certain countries" (notably Britain) were heavily subsidizing aluminum primary producing capacity at a time when the market was suffering from excess capacity. In response to the German and Canadian governments' complaint, the OECD agreed to form a working group aimed at studying the prospects of coordinating future primary aluminum expansion on "a strictly economic basis," without governmental distortion of economic conditions.[12] The German government itself had a large direct stake in the aluminum industry through a state-owned producer, Vereinigte Aluminium-Werke AG (VAW). But there is no evidence that VAW was the beneficiary of any special favors from the state.

Italy. Italy, the fourth largest consumer of aluminum products in western Europe after the United Kingdom, West Germany, and France, was an importer of aluminum metal. Having lagged behind the three other countries in developing a nationally owned aluminum industry, by 1972 the Italian authorities considered it desirable to achieve a trade balance in aluminum. To do so, the Italians wanted the EEC to allow "import quotas to help individual countries set up their own industries." Like the French government, the Italian government in the 1960s and 1970s sought—though probably less vigorously and overtly—the development of national champions in key sectors of the economy. It also aimed at protecting existing enterprises in these sectors from bankruptcy or foreign takeovers.

The history of the Italian government's involvement in national enterprise went back to 1933 when the state holding company, Istituto per la Ricostruzione Industriale (IRI), had been created to rescue enterprises from default and bankruptcy during the Great Depression.* IRI was meant to be a temporary organization, with the aided enterprises eventually being resold. In 1936, however, the government decided to use IRI to control strategic industries and implement economic policy. After 1957, IRI, along with other state-owned or state-controlled enterprises, was required by law to promote the industrial development of the South by locating at least 40 percent of its new industrial plant investment there (Act No. 634 of 1957).[13]

Another dominant social goal for the Italian government of the 1960s was to keep in national ownership the key industries that were encountering difficulties. In 1969–1971, IRI joined another state-owned Italian company, Ente Nazionale Idrocarburi (ENI), to buy in the open market the shares of an ailing business, Montedison. Formerly Montecatini Edison, it was the largest Italian aluminum producer and a leading enterprise in chemicals and power generation. Early in 1973, IRI and ENI owned 19.6 percent of Montedison shares, with the balance of shares widely held. As the largest owner through the IRI and ENI shareholdings, the Italian state had decisive influence over Montedison's policies and management. In fact, the state holdings were used to enable a president of ENI to resign and to assume the presidency of Montedison in May 1971. The Italian government was also concerned with the failure of enterprises that were considered to belong to key sectors, such as aluminum, or which were operating in depressed areas, such as the South. For example, in January 1972 the government, through the state-owned Ente Finanziario per le Industrie Meccanichel (EFIM), a member of the IRI group, intervened to buy a 50 percent interest in Società Alluminio Veneto per Azioni S.p.A. (SAVA), an aluminum smelting venture hitherto owned by Alusuisse. The Alusuisse disposal of SAVA was prompted by its loss of faith in the prospects of its affiliate, largely because of Italian labor difficulties.[14]

Spain. Forms of intervention akin to Italy's were also known in other West European countries. Spain created a state-owned Instituto Nacional de Industria (INI) in the late 1930s. This was a giant holding company which controlled some 60 percent of the country's aluminum

* See Stuart Holland's chapter in this volume.

production in 1971–72, through Empresa Nacional del Aluminio S.A. (Endassa). But statism in Spanish business did not arise out of a socialist bent; the contrary was the case. At the end of the civil war in 1941, when the country's economy was in ruin, General Franco judged that the only way to move rapidly toward economic reconstruction was through the creation of state-owned or state-supported ventures, especially "where private enterprise was put off by heavy capital costs [as in aluminum] or a low rate of profit." Through grants and debentures the government supplied capital at favorable terms to the state-owned enterprises, including aluminum. These debentures were forced on private savings institutions, which took more than 95 percent in 1969. According to report, the interest rates were "not generous."[15]

Company Strategies

The Industry Pattern. In the early 1970s, the aluminum industry in western Europe and throughout the world was noted for its oligopolistic and largely vertically integrated structure. As shown in Table 2, six firms and their affiliates owned some 60 percent of world primary ingot capacity, outside the socialist countries of eastern Europe and China. The North American firms—Alcan, Alcoa, Reynolds, and Kaiser—tended to have the bulk of their ingot capacity well concentrated in their home countries. The Europeans—Pechiney and Alusuisse—were more international, in the sense that considerable proportions of their ingot capacity were situated away from the home country.

Despite the high degree of concentration in the industry, it is evident from Table 3 that by the end of 1971 newcomers, including state-supported firms, were gradually expanding their sales and their market shares at the expense of the majors.[16] Their appearance generated a source of instability that threatened the old, established enterprises. Pressed by creditors or lured by the prospect of larger sales receipts and greater profits, the newcomers joined some of the smaller existing firms in price shading. This price strategy—branded "immature" by the majors—could not remain secret. Once knowledge of price discounts became public, competitors were bound to retaliate, causing prices to drop throughout the industry.

The pressure for sales outlets also contributed to business instability. North American companies established a large producing capacity in western Europe, and East Europeans pushed for the export of metal in their drive to earn hard currencies, with little regard for cost-price relationships. In the late 1960s several newcomers appeared from overseas: some Japanese firms, some enterprises of bauxite-producing countries, and some producers that did not control their own bauxite sources, located in countries with relatively cheap and abundant energy supplies,

Table 2. The aluminum oligopoly: Major companies' equity share of world primary ingot capacity, 1971–1976[a]

	1971		1972		1973	
Company	Thousands of short tons	Percentage of world	Thousands of short tons	Percentage of world	Thousands of short tons	Percentage of world
Alcoa	1,717	15.0	1,717	14.5	1,782	14.1
Alcan	1,582	13.8	1,688	14.3	1,766	14.0
Reynolds	1,276	11.1	1,285	10.9	1,348	10.7
Kaiser	1,021	8.9	1,041	8.8	1,055	8.4
Pechiney	886	7.7	895	7.6	892	7.1
Alusuisse	476	4.2	491	4.1	491	3.9
Subtotal	6,958	60.7	7,117	60.2	7,334	58.2
Other World	4,487	39.3	4,722	39.8	5,279	41.8
total	11,445	100.0	11,839	100.0	12,613	100.0

such as Bahrain and New Zealand. In attempting to protect themselves against the newcomers, aluminum enterprises in western Europe used several approaches simultaneously: vertical integration both within and without Europe; partnerships, mergers, or cartel-like arrangements with competitors (European and non-European); countervailing threats through foreign investment in markets serviced by their competitors; and the soliciting of antidumping and other protective measures from governments.[17] The first two approaches were noteworthy.

Vertical integration. The trend toward vertical integration increased in the late 1960s and early 1970s. Although the degree of integration among aluminum companies varied widely, all companies were approaching the point at which they were not only fabricating aluminum products but also becoming direct major end users of these products in home or office construction or the manufacturing of various types of transport equipment. It is estimated that aluminum products supplied by the independent nonintegrated fabricators in Europe fell from 50 percent in 1958 to about 25 percent in 1967, and a further decline in their share was expected. In 1971, the president of the European Primary Aluminum Association estimated that "only 20 percent of the entire aluminum market of the western world" was outside vertically integrated channels.[18]

Vertical integration at the manufacturing end came about either through the takeover of independent companies or through the construction of new plants.[19] On the other hand, a fabricator might integrate backwards to primary production, and eventually to the raw materials, such as bauxite. Behind vertical integration lay the enterprise's concern

Table 2. (continued)

Company	1974		1975		1976	
	Thousands of short tons	Percentage of world	Thousands of short tons	Percentage of world	Thousands of short tons	Percentage of world
Alcoa	1,784	13.6	1,787	12.9	1,847	12.7
Alcan	1,809	13.8	1,873	13.5	1,873	12.8
Reynolds	1,398	10.7	1,398	10.1	1,398	9.6
Kaiser	1,058	8.1	1,093	7.9	1,093	7.5
Pechiney	992	7.6	997	7.2	1,046	7.2
Alusuisse	496	3.8	496	3.6	496	3.4
Subtotal	7,537	57.6	7,644	55.2	7,753	53.2
Other World	5,551	42.4	6,235	44.8	6,839	46.8
total	13,088	100.0	13,879	100.0	14,592	100.0

Source: Spector, *Aluminum Industry Report*, pp. 20, 28–33.
[a] Figures are for actual capacity in 1971 and for planned capacity in 1972–1976.
Capacity jointly owned has been attributed to each company according to equity share in joint facilities. Socialist countries of eastern Europe and China not included.

for security of raw material supplies and unforeclosed outlets, as well as the desire to improve on profits and the coordination of various phases of the industry through cutting down on intermediaries. The development of vertical integration through the strategy of taking over existing facilities instead of developing new ones was likely to have a dampening effect on competition because it reduced the number of nonintegrated operators. By comparison, the development of vertical integration through the creation of additional independent facilities (fabricating, smelting, or raw material production) could intensify competition with the established firms. The independent operators existed mostly at the manufacturing end, largely because barriers to entry in the form of capital investment and know-how were relatively low. The two strategies, that of merger-participation with existing firms and that of independent creation of productive facilities, were followed by various enterprises.

Cooperative measures. Aluminum enterprises also formed partnerships, mergers, or associations with competitors, both in Europe and on a world-wide scale. As illustrated in Tables 3 and 4, this strategy was used mostly in the phases where lumpy and indivisible investments were required; that is, in bauxite-alumina production and in metal smelting. The growth of partnerships and mergers was prompted essentially by the desire to share heavy research and investment costs, to distribute busi-

Table 3. West European primary aluminum capacity by country, 1971 year end

Country	Ownership	Company capacity in short tons[a]	Country capacity in short tons[a]
Austria			
Vereinigte Metallwerke Ranshofen-Berndorf AG (VMRB)	Government-owned	89,000	
Salzburger Aluminium GmbH (SAG)	Alusuisse 100%	12,000	101,000
France			
Pechiney–Ugine-Kuhlmann	General public	476,000	476,000
West Germany			
Aluminium-Huette Rheinfelden GmbH	Alusuisse 100%	75,000	
Vereinigte Aluminium-Werke AG (VAW)	Government-owned	325,000	
Leichtmetall-Gemeinschaft	Alusuisse 50% Metallgesell-schaft 50%	139,000	
Gebrügder Giulini, GmbH		24,000	
Kaiser–Preussag Aluminium GmbH	Kaiser 50%	71,000	
Reynolds Hamburg	Preussag 50% Reynolds 90%	0[b]	634,000
Greece			
Aluminium de Grèce S.A.	Pechiney 77% Government 23%	160,000	160,000
Iceland			
Icelandic Aluminum Co. Ltd. (Isal)	Alusuisse 100%	48,000	48,000
Italy			
Alcan Alluminio Italiano S.p.A.	Alcan 100%	6,000	
Montecatini-Edison		134,000	
Società Alluminio Veneto per Azioni S.p.A. (SAVA)	EFIM 50% Alusuisse 50%	66,000	
Alluminio Sarda (Alsar)	EFIM (Govt) 52% Montecatini-Edison 24% Société Générale de Belgique 24%	0[c]	206,000
The Netherlands			
Aluminium Delfzijl N.V. (Aldel)	Hoogovens 50% Alusuisse 33% Billiton 17%	106,000	
Pechiney Nederland	Pechiney 90%	91,000	197,000

Table 3. (continued)

Country	Ownership	Company capacity in short tons[a]	Country capacity in short tons[a]
Norway			
A/S Ardal og Sunndal Verk (Ardal)	Government 50% Alcan 50%	358,000	
Det Norske Nitrid A/S (DNN)	Reynolds 50% Alcan 50%	45,000	
Alnor A/S (Alnor)	Norsk Hydro 51% Martin Marietta 49%	127,000	
Elektrokemisk Aluminium A/S	Alcoa 50% Elektrokemisk 50%	155,000	
Soer-Norge Aluminium A/S (Soral)	Alusuisse 67%	75,000	760,000
Spain			
Empresa Nacional del Aluminio S.A. (Endasa)	Government 75% Alcan 25%	91,000	
Aluminio de Galicia (Alugasa)	Pechiney 67.6% Endasa 10%	75,000	166,000
Sweden			
Gränges Essem AB	Alcan 21% Svenska Metall- werken 79%	94,000	94,000
Switzerland			
Swiss Aluminium Ltd. (Alusuisse)	Investors 100%	96,000	
Usine d'Aluminium Martigny SA	Giulini 100%	11,000	107,000
United Kingdom			
British Aluminium Co. Ltd. (Baco)	Tube Investments 49½% Reynolds Metals 48%	155,000	
Anglesey Aluminium Ltd.	Rio Tinto Zinc (RTZ) 10% RTZ-BICC Aluminium Holdings Ltd. 60% Kaiser 30%	112,000	
Alcan Aluminium (UK) Ltd.	Alcan 100%	132,000[d]	399,000

Sources: American Bureau of Metal Statistics *Yearbook,* June 1972; Spector, *Aluminum Industry Report,* pp. 22–24, 28–33; Government of Australia, Senate Standing Committee on Foreign Affairs and Defence, Submission by Department of National Development presented by T. B. R. Livermore, D.F.C., Canberra, March 1972, pp. 30–33; Walter R. Skinner, *Mining International Yearbook 1972–73* (London: FT Business Publications Ltd., 1972); U.S. Department of the Interior, Bureau of Mines, *Mineral Trade Notes,* 1971–1973 issues; and annual reports of the individual companies.

[a] Small discrepancies exist among various sources.
[b] Planned capacity, 112,000 tons.
[c] Planned capacity, 138,000 tons.
[d] As of January 1973.

Table 4. Examples of partnerships in bauxite alumina, 1972

Country	Operating company	Ownership	Percent
Ghana	Bauxite Alumina Study Co. Ltd. (Bascol)	Kaiser[a]	50
		Reynolds	30
		Aluminum Resources Development Co. Ltd.[b]	20
Australia	Admiralty Gulf	Amax[a]	52.5
		Sumitomo Chemical	17.5
		Sumitomo Trading	5.0
		Showa Denko	12.5
		Marubeni Iida	2.5
		Holland Aluminium[c]	10.0
Australia	Queensland Alumina Ltd.	Kaiser	37.3
		Alcan	22.0
		Pechiney	20.0
		CRA[d]	9.4
		Comalco[e]	11.3
Guinea	Compagnie des Bauxites de Guinée	Guinea Government	49
		Halco (Mining) Inc.[f]	51

Sources: See Table 3.

[a] Project manager.

[b] Consortium of five Japanese firms: Nippon Light Metals Co. Ltd.; Showa Denko K.K.; Sumitomo Chemical Co. Ltd.; Mitsubishi Chemical Industries, Ltd.; and Mitsui Aluminum Co. Ltd.

[c] Owned by Billiton N.V. (35%), Kon. Ned. Hoogovens (35%), and a Belgian group (30%).

[d] Conzinc Riotinto of Australia, Ltd. (CRA) was owned 80.65% by Rio Tinto Zinc (U.K.) and 19.35% by Australian public.

[e] Comalco Industrites Pty. Ltd. was owned by Kaiser (45%), CRA (45%) and Australian public (10%).

[f] Halco is owned by Alcan (27%), Alcoa (27%), Harvey (20%), Pechiney (10%), VAW (10%), and Montedison (6%). Harvey was 82% owned by the U.S. corporation Martin Marietta.

ness and nonbusiness risks, and generally to equalize input costs and market opportunities among competitors.

Pechiney, the leading European aluminum concern, drew up a persuasive statement of company strategy in the attempt to justify its merger with Ugine-Kuhlmann in December 1971. It argued that the merger had been prompted by management's wish to pool resources in order to meet competition from other oligopolists, to diversify its business, and to internationalize its activities. The document stated the reasons for the merger as follows:

1. In a field of traditional cooperation such as aluminum any arrangement which maintains the duality of companies, and hence a dividing of

responsibilities, results in a correspondingly weaker position vis-à-vis
. . . international competition—even assuming maximum efficiency . . .

Moreover, in those sectors where the activities of Ugine Kuhlmann
and Pechiney are complementary, the development of international competition prohibits any dispersion or duplication of efforts . . .

2. In addition to these reasons . . . there are other equally essential considerations:

(a) . . . Pechiney, whose current activities are mainly directed towards aluminum and copper fabrication, is seeking to diversify.

Ugine Kuhlmann, on the other hand, is a company with varied
activities. The merger of Pechiney and Ugine Kuhlmann is an exceptional opportunity for constituting a powerful and widely diversified
industrial group.

(b) Ugine Kuhlmann has few industrial footholds outside of France
. . . Its merger with Pechiney provides it with a wide international
base.[20]

Despite the efforts of each firm to achieve internal balance through
vertical integration and partnerships or mergers, the aluminum industry
has repeatedly been faced with problems of overproduction. As a result,
oligopoly leaders have made attempts to coordinate with one another
more effectively. Hence, three cooperative schemes have been launched
at the European level: a succession of agreements concerning the sale of
East European aluminum to a West European consortium; stockpile
financing for a group of West European companies; and a European
aluminum producers' association.

The Gentlemen's Agreement. In the 1960s, the major aluminum
companies in western Europe joined forces to absorb aluminum exports
from the USSR, Czechoslovakia, Poland, East Germany, Hungary, and
Romania. A metals brokerage firm helped in the initial negotiations.*
The successive sale-purchase agreements between the two groups, generally referred to as the Gentlemen's Agreement (also known occasionally as the Club) have extended over periods varying between one and
five years. The Gentlemen's Agreement contained a quota system of
metal exports from East European to West European countries, and
intermittently to other countries as well (notably Japan). Thus the
quota of Soviet metal to Japan for 1968, according to one source, was
set at 13,000 tons; and for 1970, according to another source, at 11,056

* Bulgaria did not produce primary aluminum, while Romania reportedly resisted participation in an export plan falling under Soviet hegemony (*Metal Bulletin*, February 14, 1969, p. 19). Nevertheless, Romania sold its aluminum
separately to the same group of Western companies. The metals brokerage firm
was Brandeis, Goldschmidt & Co. Ltd., a subsidiary of S. G. Warburg, which had
been established as a metal merchant in 1923. A founder member of the London
Metal Exchange, it dealt in a wide range of metals (*ibid.*, August 3, 1971, pp.
11, 14).

tons.[21] Export quotas were to be set annually; prices would be set from time to time depending on changes in market conditions. West European governments generally supported the Gentlemen's Agreement, for it spared them from entering into direct negotiations with East European governments.

The Gentlemen's Agreement provided for the sale of East European aluminum ingots at a discount expressed in a certain percentage from Alcan's published "international" list price. Alcan's list price, like the posted price in the international petroleum industry, was a standard of reference. "Shading," or discounting the list or posted price, was common in periods of excess supplies. In normal periods, discounts were offered on large-volume, long-term sales contracts to third parties, or on sales to affiliates to enable them to compete with outsiders. The discount on East European aluminum in 1968 was about 1¾ cents per pound, or about 7 percent. In later years, discounts on ingot (and even more on semifabricated products) were general, larger, and widespread. Late in 1971 the president of Consolidated Aluminum Corporation (Conalco) bluntly conceded the artificiality of the published ingot prices. He said: The "published price is being withdrawn because the disparity between the domestic producers' published base price and actual selling price has reached ridiculous proportions—in excess of 25 percent in many cases—and consequently the 20-cent published price is completely fictitious." The chairman of Alcoa (the world's largest producer), reportedly stated that his company had considered dropping the list price of ingots; the key prices for his company were those of aluminum mill products, since most sales were sales of products, not of ingots.[22]

Industry sources admitted that the Gentlemen's Agreement, in accordance with its objective, had helped protect the price structure of aluminum. It was surmised that if the East European suppliers had been left on their own to enter western markets, they would have had to incur substantial selling expenses, and aluminum prices would have been lower than they actually were. Both parties, the major western companies and the Soviet Union, welcomed measures to restrict the flow of aluminum from countries outside the Gentlemen's Agreement. The distribution of the eastern metal quotas among the West European producers did not present the problems encountered by the Organization of Petroleum Exporting Countries (OPEC). The major aluminum companies, with their vertical integration and multinational facilities, did not find it difficult to arrange for quota distribution among various markets through their worldwide network of producing and marketing affiliates or associates. The shares of eastern metal were established in accordance with the sales made by the European producers in western

Europe. This did not, however, preclude attempts to crack the Gentlemen's Agreement, for independent metal dealers did try to buy Russian metal outside the framework of the agreement.[23] One great merit of the Gentlemen's Agreement was flexibility; it provided for meetings to be held at least once a year, to renegotiate total quantities, quotas, and prices in the light of changing market conditions. Furthermore, the Agreement was apparently run on a commercial nonpolitical basis to the extent that quantities and prices were set in response to market forces. In fact, the East European state concerns have shrewdly used an old established West European business firm, readily informed about metal market conditions and opportunities, as a collective agent.

Stockpile financing. As a result of specific problems faced by the aluminum industry, cooperation has gone beyond trade into the field of finance. A slackening in world demand for aluminum products in 1970–1972—coupled with continued expansion of the established firms' productive capacity, the advent of newcomers, and the resulting price weaknesses—prompted the European leaders to finance the accumulation of inventories of aluminum metal. This method of fighting price weakness was devised to supplement the usual procedures or simultaneous cutbacks in production and deferments of expansion programs to which the world aluminum industry had often resorted. In June 1971 the West European members of the Aluminum Club (Alusuisse, Pechiney, VAW, British Aluminum, Montedison, Ranshofen-Berndorf, Holland Aluminum, and Giulini) established Alufinance & Trade Ltd., with the help of a merchant banker, S. G. Warburg. Warburg's function was to arrange medium-term credit to Alufinance through a consortium of nine leading European banking firms, in order to permit Alufinance to hold metal on behalf of the participating aluminum producers. The stockpile would take the metal "outside the market" when prices were weak and would not disclose it in the aluminum companies' balance sheets.[24] By keeping the stockpile apart from the commercially available supplies, it was hoped that the bearish impact of the stockpile on the market would be reduced.

The reasons underlying the creation of Alufinance were put succinctly by a spokesman of a major European participant (Alusuisse), who declared:

Production cuts are usually only made when stocks have increased beyond the ordinary level, and then stocks keep pressing on the market in spite of production having been brought in line with demand. Some producers can finance their stocks, but others, already heavily indebted, find it difficult and are having cash-flow problems. Therefore—unless production cuts and the financing, or freezing, of surplus stocks [are] carried out simultaneously—the market will not find its equilibrium. Therefore, the European aluminum industry jumped at the offer of a banking consortium to finance part of their surplus stocks (plus the bonus of this being off-balance-sheet financing).[25]

The aspirations of Alufinance extended beyond the boundaries of Europe. Its members hoped to develop a worldwide organization for the purpose of protecting prices. They approached Japan's primary aluminum producers with the proposal that a Japanese joint body similar to Alufinance be established, and the Japanese response was initially favorable. This attitude was reversed, however, when Japan's Fair Trade Commission prohibited such an arrangement. The Japanese producers also considered participating in Europe's Alufinance but feared they would be accused of forming an international cartel.[26]

The United States was another country that avoided the collective approach to stockpiling as a remedy for price deterioration. Stockpile financing would probably have been dangerous for U.S. firms to emulate because it might have raised antitrust objections on the part of the government. Major U.S. firms, acting in response to depressed prices, preferred to resort to the usual measures of production cutbacks and expansion delays. Very likely, these measures were adopted in full awareness that every other major firm in the U.S. market would, in the common interest, heed the cutback of the pacemaker. Industry sources admitted that some aluminum producers in the United States or elsewhere were "more public-spirited than others"—meaning that they had resorted to larger cutbacks. And, in fact, major U.S. aluminum producers, followed by European, Japanese, and Australian producers, cut back their production in 1971 by 10 to 20 percent of capacity, while most small producers kept their operations at close to 100 percent of capacity.

It was difficult for small producers to cut back production because their financial resources were weak and they needed sales proceeds to meet current costs. In Europe, special conditions existed that made production cutbacks more difficult or less necessary than in the United States. Partly because labor unions sought to keep up employment levels, some European firms did not have the same degree of flexibility as U.S. firms. (Norway was an exception: there the aluminum industry cut back production in 1971 but did not dismiss workers.) In addition, western Europe, thanks to the installation of new equipment, especially in the United Kingdom, West Germany, the Netherlands, and Italy, was gradually becoming a self-sufficient area in metal rather than a net importer. Accordingly, the Europeans were not in a hurry to cut back production.[27] Nevertheless, they did resort to cutbacks, though on a smaller order of magnitude than U.S. producers.

Both stockpiling and production cutbacks might have proved costly to the participating firms if these measures had encouraged the entry of newcomers. Major firms were confident, however, that in depressed price circumstances investors were not likely to enter, and "defection" of participants was not to be expected since all were "gentlemen" working in their own long-run interest. The industry had also been vertically integrated on a large scale, and most sellers of final products were associates or affiliates of the smelting companies, with their "tied" sources of raw materials. Nevertheless, there was one major threat to stability. Certain noncooperating firms (both European and non-European), hoping to increase their share of the market, might have taken advantage of the major producers by making metal available at cheaper prices. This possibility was foreseen by industry officials, who expected that their parent governments would insulate them from outside competition through antidumping actions. As an Alusuisse executive put it:[28] "It is unfortunately a fact that self-denying actions of reasonable producers may be an advantage for 'maverick' producers such as Romania, Alba [in Bahrain] or even Bluff [in New Zealand]. However, leave it to the Europeans to defend their market [sic]; after all there are such things as antidumping actions."*

The European Producers' Aluminum Association. Another form of cooperation among West European aluminum producers—noteworthy though less publicized than the Gentlemen's Agreement and Alufinance —was the European Producers' Aluminum Association (EPAA), established in 1971. Representing all west European aluminum producers, its objective was to exchange information on subjects of mutual concern, particularly plant capacity, and to achieve a balance between production and consumption. It was not anticipated, however, that EPAA would have strict cartel rules regarding market allocations and price standards, as had been the case with the "entente" of 1924–1939 among European aluminum producers.[29]

The strategies adopted by the aluminum companies could only have appeared in a highly concentrated and international industry, in which the component parts were deeply aware of their interdependence. This awareness, coupled with a web of joint ventures, made competition softer than it would have been in a less concentrated industrial structure. This does not mean that competition did not exist. On the contrary, sporadic competition and uncoordinated expansion of capacity

---

* The Alba Smelter was owned by a consortium comprising the Bahrain government (19%), Amalgamated Metal Corp. (17%), General Cable Corp. (17%), Kaiser (17%), Electrokopper (12%), Breton Investments (9.5%), and Western Metal (8.5%). Amalgamated Metal Corp. was an affiliate of Consolidated Tin Smelters Ltd., and General Cable was partly owned by American Smelting and Refining Co. The Bluff Smelter was owned by Showa Denko and Sumitomo of Japan (25% each) and by Comalco (50%).

were responsible for price cutting and the drastic decline in profits of all companies in 1971. EPAA, in fact, was set up to harmonize the expansion of productive capacity with the increase of consumption in western Europe, thereby protecting company profits.

Toward a New Equilibrium

In the 1960s and early 1970s, individual enterprises, one at a time, went international. Gradually the European companies came to realize that their national aspirations could not be achieved through a policy of autarky in relation to inputs or outputs.[30] Even privileged European countries, such as France and the USSR, endowed with relatively abundant hydroelectric power and sizable bauxite deposits, acknowledged the economic advantages of opening their borders to imports of cheap raw materials and to an interchange of technological skills and know-how. Moreover, countries that were well endowed with the needed resources, such as abundant hydroelectric capacity, were propelled into the international market. Having established large-scale smelters with a capacity in excess of domestic needs, they found themselves obliged to seek outlets beyond their domestic markets. In opening their borders, West European states girded themselves for transnational competition largely through the development of national champions, equipped to compete or cooperate in domestic or foreign markets with the champions of other states and with the international enterprises.

Not only did individual enterprises go international, but a collective international pattern began to evolve. One path the enterprises took was to form mergers. Another was to establish partnerships or cooperative schemes among independent operators in certain functions of aluminum production, notably the mining of bauxite, its transformation into alumina, and its further transformation into metal ingots. The purposes of such cooperation were two: to set up efficient large-scale plants requiring joint shouldering of the necessary heavy investments; and to search for business stability in a competitive industry characterized by high fixed costs. The search for stability in the aluminum industry also contributed to the multinational spread of nationally based enterprises, and to pan-European, cartel-like arrangements with respect to joint stockpiling, market sharing, and coordinated cutbacks of productive capacity. Added to this were the extra-European ties: to North America, Japan, Australia, and other areas. The least stable elements in these arrangements were the newcomers, especially those from some bauxite-producing countries and from some energy-surplus countries where aluminum smelters had been implanted. Leading examples of West European interrelatedness were the joint stockpile financing of "surplus" metal and the European Producers' Aluminum Association.

These schemes would have failed, however, had it not been for the cooperation of East European countries through the Gentlemen's Agreement, and especially the cooperation of the non-Europeans through their numerous joint interests and partnerships. The community of interests among major international aluminum producers took on a definitely global dimension.

Although the various West European companies cooperated with one another for specific purposes, their governments had adopted distinctive philosophies over the years and had resorted to different instrumentalities in pursuing their relationships with industry. These philosophies and instrumentalities were partly the product of the separate histories and cultures and partly a function of the ideologies of ruling elites and the problems they encountered. West European governmental ideologies ranged widely from one extreme, where government was at the service of private enterprise, to the opposite extreme where governmental control was strong. Contemporary socio-political problems had a determining effect in shaping such ideologies. West European governments also varied in their ability to achieve their goals. Some built national champions by improving the competitive position of one firm or a few firms, and by fostering their growth; but others were much less successful. The instruments of governmental action covered a wide range. They included guided national planning, nationalization, enforced mergers of national enterprises, research and development subsidies, tax rebates or holidays, credit facilities, guaranteed purchases.

Yet governmental actions had their limitations. The merger of national firms posed new problems for national governments. By their mere size and their web of relationships with other members of the international aluminum oligopoly as well as with other enterprises, national enterprises reached a stronger bargaining position vis-à-vis government. Their enhanced size and power enabled them to withstand pressures from ministries or to demand their support on the ground that the enterprises' preeminent status in the national economy entitled them to special favors: after all, what was good for the national champion should be good for the national economy. Governmental policy therefore tended to serve the ends of enterprise in countries where national champions were economically dominant. On one occasion, Pechiney influenced the French government to act in opposition to all other EEC members in blocking the reduction of the common import tariff on unwrought primary aluminum. (In the GATT negotiations of 1966, France prevented reduction of the EEC tariff from 9 percent to 7 percent.) Pechiney's line of reasoning was that a high tariff rate would protect the further rapid growth of aluminum production within the European Community and thus lead to a reduction in imports from outside the Community; and since France was the leading aluminum producer of the EEC—owing to its relatively more abundant hydroelectric power—the EEC protectionist policy would particularly favor Pechiney.[31]

An enterprise's influence on, or obedience to, the governmental policies of its home country did not necessarily derive from state ownership. According to a study of selected West European economies, "the larger the public sector, the larger *ceteris paribus* is likely to be the degree of government intervention. But it is control rather than ownership that is relevant, and public ownership does not always increase effective State control in an individual enterprise or industry." Even in countries like Norway and Germany, where the public sector dominated the aluminum industry, the state did not necessarily run its enterprises in a manner different from that followed in a free-enterprise system. Norway's state enterprises showed a remarkable degree of autonomy, as well as a concern for profit making and business stability. In West Germany the government hesitated to espouse the interests of the state-owned aluminum company, VAW, at the expense of the privately owned, independent German aluminum fabricators who were organized in Aluminium Zentrale. Instead, in response to the interests of the independents and in keeping with the social goal of a competitive open economy, the West German government actually favored the reduction of EEC import tariffs on unwrought primary aluminum.[32]

In western Europe there was a general tendency for governments to favor big business. This type of governmental favoritism was due not only to the enterprises' ability to lobby effectively but also to the concern felt by both governments and enterprises for business stability. On the part of government, this concern stemmed from the three roles it played in relation to the aluminum industry. It was both a supplier of inputs, notably energy, and a buyer of output, including strategic usage. In addition, as the regulator of the national economy, it sought income, price, and employment stability in aluminum and its related industries. Furthermore, the definitions of socially desirable objectives held by the various governments in western Europe were undergoing change in the 1960s and early 1970s. The state increasingly insisted on profits for its nationalized enterprises comparable to those derived by the private sector, and the criterion of public service tended to diminish.[33]

Despite the different positions of the various countries of Europe, two future trends can be foreseen for the West European aluminum industry from the vantage point of early 1973: a greater harmonization of national policies and regional regulations through the EEC; and a further expansion of arrangements on a global scale. Neither of these developments will set a new direction for the industry. Both will mark out further progress along familiar lines. It appears, in fact, that in terms of purposes and directions the decade of the seventies will be less innovative than the decade of the sixties, when the pre-1960 predominance of nationalism began to give way to regional and international agreements and activities.

In the coming decade, the membership of the European Economic Community will probably put forth some common rules for business behavior. Aluminum enterprises in the Community, private or state-owned, will then be increasingly faced by uniform measures regarding competition, industrial policy, and labor relations. Indeed, the EEC Commission in its continuous reviews of restrictions to competition and trade (including governmental aid) already offers guidelines for business behavior. The decisions of the Commission and the verdicts of the Community's Court of Justice in interpreting the articles of the Treaty of Rome will increasingly provide a body of rules which member governments and European enterprises will have to abide by. It is unlikely that West European national governments will relinquish all their power to the Commission in basic industries such as aluminum. Nevertheless, the Commission already appears to be gaining in responsibility and influence. It also seems that those state-owned and private enterprises (including aluminum) of the Community which have been organized in separate groupings—the European Centre for Public Enterprise and the Union of National Industries for the European Community, respectively—will continue to be consulted and treated on an equal footing.[34] Apparently no favoritism will be shown to any type of business organization.

But the impact of EEC rules on the West European aluminum enterprises should not be exaggerated. The behavior of these enterprises cannot be viewed realistically in the context of a strictly European regime, in isolation from non-European enterprises (particularly the North American, Japanese, and Australian), or separate from world market forces. The behavior of the West European enterprises, like that of other members of the international aluminum oligopoly, must be seen against a global background. All enterprises share a desire for profits, growth, and stability, and all experience the consequent pressures to integrate vertically from raw material sources to fabricated products, as well as to diversify geographically among various major areas, and functionally in allied, substitute, or complementary products. In the end, the important unit for an international aluminum enterprise—whether based in western Europe, America, Japan, or elsewhere—is the world market. Further developments in the web of relationships among international enterprises can be expected in the coming decade: links in the form of partnerships, reciprocal trading, long-term supply contracts, or exchange of technical know-how. All these forms of interrelatedness will fortify the oligopoly, inhibit competition, and reduce the disturbance to profits and growth.

In keeping with this global approach, the leading members of the aluminum oligopoly have already created an institutional framework: the International Primary Aluminum Institute (IPAI). One major purpose of the institute, established in April 1972, is to coordinate the members' investment activities in order to avoid surplus productive capacity. It thus offers an effective alternative to the European association, the EPAA. The twelve members of the Executive Board of IPAI have been drawn from Pechiney–Ugine-Kuhlmann, Alcoa, Alusuisse, Alcan, Reynolds Metals, Kaiser, Ardal, Nippon Light Metals, VAW, British Aluminium, Comalco, and CVA of Brazil. An official spokesman for the Institute, commenting on its creation, said, "We need this channel of communication if we are to face successfully the problems that confront the aluminum industry around the world."[35] The uncertain question for the future is whether cooperation with producers outside of Europe can be kept compatible in aims and instrumentalities with the role of the champions inside the European economy.

Computers

Nicolas Jéquier

The computer industry is in a sense a modern version of Thucydides' history *The Peloponnesian War:* a very small segment in the history of a nation, but one which epitomizes the best and the worst of human intelligence and presents in a microcosm many of the big issues that face a society in transition. The inability of European computer firms to stand up to American competition, the efforts made by several governments to promote the development of a symbolic national champion, and the emergence of a national computer policy can be viewed primarily as an illustration of Europe's industrial and technological development. But these phenomena, interesting as they are, have a deeper meaning: they reveal, in an acute and somewhat exaggerated form, a number of social, political, and historical problems which condition the policymaking process in a subtle and often unconscious way.

One of these problems is that of power. Rightly or wrongly, computers have come to symbolize the essential power of the second industrial revolution; and the efforts of countries like France, the United Kingdom, and, to a lesser extent Germany, to preserve a national computer industry in the face of immense technological and economic odds are not so much a fight against the apparent rationality of industrial specialization as an attempt to retain some form of real power by preserving the symbol of power. The less the real power, the more important the symbol. In this perspective, psychoanalysis might provide a better understanding of European policies vis-à-vis the computer industry than a Cartesian approach based on pure logic.

Another problem is that of the American industrial and technological "model." An implicit assumption in the European desire to maintain a national computer industry is that the trends set by American technology and by American forms of industrial organization are, by virtue of their success, those which must inevitably be followed and emulated. This linear view of technological development and social organization may not be entirely unjustified, but its universality can, and should be, questioned.

The fascination with the American model and the importance of power symbols have been two of the main leitmotivs of European governmental policies vis-à-vis the computer industry. These leitmotivs, how-

Nicolas Jéquier is a member of the Faculty of the Centre d'Etudes Industrielles, Geneva, Switzerland.

ever, were never recognized for what they really were, namely, the basic rationale or motivation for such policies. The unwillingness to look into these motivations appears to stem in part from the fact that, had this been done, the logical answer to the main question—do European countries really need to have an independent computer industry—might well have been negative. Hundreds of millions of dollars have been spent to support the industry, but there has been little if any public debate as to whether the methods of support were adequate and the objectives reasonable.

This situation has parallels in other high-technology industries. In the case of supersonic air transportation, for instance, it was only after the cancellation of the American SST project by Congress that the Europeans began to ask the real questions about Concorde, and by that time it was probably too late to step back. The assumption had been that if the United States were committed, the Europeans should also be committed. The involvement of American industry was a means of legitimizing the support given by European governments to a key industry. In terms of national policymaking, the computer industry is an easier case. European policies have been fully legitimized by the leadership of the United States in this sector, and policymakers could therefore refrain from asking the real questions. One sees no possibility of the United States deliberately renouncing its position of leadership, as had happened, perhaps only temporarily, in the case of supersonic air transportation. In the European view, the prosecution of IBM by the Department of Justice, and the possible break-up of that firm, has been in fact an additional source of legitimacy for national computer policies in that it has confirmed what policymakers, trade unionists, and journalists alike had been saying for years about the dangers of American "domination" in general, and of IBM's position in particular.

What have been the forms of support granted by European governments to their national firms? What have been the objectives of these policies? How effective has government action really been? Underlying these questions, one finds a number of recurrent themes. One is that of a "national champion," that is, a big and successful firm symbolic of national ambitions and the carrier of a country's industrial image. A second theme is that of size, considered as the precondition for success. And a third theme is that of a "European solution" to the problems of the computer industry in Europe.

Before attempting to answer these questions, it may be useful to recall some of the constraints under which national policies have been operating in Europe. The actions of governments and companies alike have been determined by what was possible, given the circumstances, and not by what was desirable; and the hard facts of life in the computer industry have tended to limit the number of strategic options open to public and private policymakers.

The Hard Facts of Life

The most conspicuous of these hard facts for Europeans is that since the early 1960s the computer industry has been essentially an American affair. At the beginning of 1973, American firms and their foreign subsidiaries accounted for some 95 percent of the cumulative value of computers installed in the non-communist world, a figure unchanged from what it had been seven years earlier.[1] The overwhelming position of U.S. industry seemed unlikely to be modified in the foreseeable future, considering the fact that in 1973 the shipments of Japanese- and European-owned firms came to less than 10 percent of the world total.

The weakness of European and Japanese firms appeared somewhat less dramatic if one looked at regional rather than world markets. In their home market, the six Japanese manufacturers accounted for some 50 percent of shipments in 1973; and in western Europe, locally owned firms supplied close to 20 percent of shipments. These regional markets, furthermore, were growing, and seemed likely to continue to grow, more rapidly than the American market: according to one reliable estimate, sales of computer equipment on the West European market could grow by some 62 percent between 1973 and 1976, as against 50 percent for Japan and 37 percent for the United States.[2] Perhaps more significant than these differences in rates of expansion was the fact that by 1973 shipments to European users had finally reached the same total—some $6 billion—as shipments to customers in the United States. Considering the higher growth rate of the European market, this suggests that, in quantitative terms at least, the center of gravity of the computer industry will be shifting from the United States to western Europe in the second half of the 1970s.

The problem facing European governments and locally owned companies could thus be stated in the following terms: Will this probable shift from the United States to Europe help to strengthen the independent European manufacturers, or will it, on the contrary, benefit primarily the subsidiaries of American firms established in western Europe? Or, to put the question in a different way, can European companies overcome the structural weaknesses which, in the past, have allowed American firms to capture more than 90 percent of the world market?

These questions can best be approached by looking at the history of IBM, the *Wunderkind* of the industry, which accounts for some two thirds of the value of the computer systems installed in the noncommunist world and for more than half of the yearly shipments.* How did IBM come to acquire such a prominent position?

Among the many reasons that can be suggested, the most important is probably that this company in effect created the computer industry as we know it today. This is not to say that IBM invented the computer. Like the automobile, it was a collective creation, and if IBM played a part of some importance in the formative period of the industry between 1936 and 1950, the people who contributed to the development of computing technology were active primarily in government laboratories and universities rather than in industry. What IBM did in the 1950s and early 1960s was to take the computer out of the ghetto of the scientific world and propose it to its customers as a substitute for the punched-card equipment they had been using for their commercial data processing services. As things turned out, this was a revolutionary innovation in marketing which took everyone by surprise, including many people at IBM.

The first computers which came on the market in the 1950s were used primarily for scientific purposes. They were cumbersome, expensive, and difficult to use; at the time it seemed only natural that the few potential customers would be the armed services, some universities, and a small number of government departments. By what appears retrospectively as a stroke of luck or a flash of genius, IBM proceeded to develop what might be called the layman's computer.† In essence, this commercial computer of the 1950s was not different from the one used by the scientist; it was, if anything, a little less complex from a technological point of view. But selling it to the customer was a more difficult affair. The commercial user, unlike the scientific user, was in most cases incapable of writing the instructions (the software) needed to operate the machine, let alone of performing the necessary maintenance and repair work. Unlike its competitors, which saw little if any future in mundane commercial applications such as payroll preparation or stock control, IBM gained an unrivaled experience in this less glamorous sector of commercial data processing.

The investments made by IBM in the commercial field during the 1950s were to pay off handsomely in the 1960s, when the first-generation computers using vacuum tubes were superseded by the more reliable, cheaper, and smaller transistorized computers of the second generation. IBM's 1401 machine, which reached the market in 1960,

---

* IBM's exact market share has been one of the greatest subjects of controversy in the computer world, and the figures above have deliberately been given in a very rough form. Suffice it to say that between 1966 and 1973, IBM's relative market position declined by a few percentage points.

† It may be worth recalling here that IMB's entry into the computer industry on a large scale took place at the time when the senior Thomas Watson was replaced as president of the firm by his son, T. J. Watson, Jr.

turned out to be the computer industry's equivalent of the Ford Model T, and definitely established its manufacturer as the Great Power in the industry. Looking back at history with the wisdom of hindsight, one might say that the cards of the industry had been played once and for all by 1960–1962, and that by 1965, European firms had already lost the game. The available figures on market shares bear this out very clearly: in 1959, British companies held 100 percent of their home computer market, but by 1965, American firms accounted for more than 50 percent of the cumulative number of computers installed in the United Kingdom.[3]

These figures are all the more revealing if one considers the enormously important contributions made by English research groups to the development of computing technology. They testify furthermore to what may appear as an unexpected paradox, namely, that the primary causes for the decline of the European computer industry were not technological but commercial. This statement is in complete contradiction with the conventional wisdom about the nature of the "American challenge" and the "technological gap" between western Europe and the United States. What happened in fact is that the commercial superiority established by IBM in the early 1960s laid the basis for the technological superiority which was to follow.

The enormous strength of IBM and the weakness of European firms often tend to be interpreted as the classical manifestation of the United States' massive superiority in the high-technology industries. What should not be overlooked, however, is the fact that though IBM was particularly successful, the same cannot be said of many other American computer companies. Two of the largest U.S. firms, General Electric (GE) and the Radio Corporation of America (RCA), dropped out of the industry after losing hundreds of millions of dollars on their computing activities. Indeed, of the nineteen American firms active in the computer sector in 1959, only four managed to survive until 1973.

The failures of European companies in the 1960s were not in essence very different from the failures of U.S. firms during the same period, and the causes were often similar. There was one important difference, however: none of the early European computer companies succeeded in becoming the transatlantic equivalent of IBM. Furthermore, except for Britain with ICL (International Computers Ltd.), no European country in the early 1970s had a national computer firm capable of matching even the second tier of computer manufacturers in the United States.

There were undoubtedly a number of factors which favored the development of the successful American computer companies: the large size of their national market, substantial procurement and development contracts given by the government, the innovativeness and affluence of their customers. In this perspective, European firms were placed at a disadvantage, particularly in the early years of the industry when the large U.S. firms established their position. External circumstances, however, do not explain everything, and one should not forget that even the most successful American companies have to fight very hard to maintain their position. And their future is never so secure as an outside observer would like to believe. Manufacturing and selling computers is a high-risk business, as many firms have learned at their expense.

One of the difficulties facing European and Japanese manufacturers as well as the governments supporting them is that in this industry the conditions for success, or more modestly for survival, are far from clear, and many of the strategic questions facing the industry in the 1960s remained unanswered in the early 1970s. For instance, should a computer firm manufacture its own electronic components or rely exclusively on independent suppliers? European firms favored the first solution, only to find that micro-circuits were even more unprofitable to make than computers, and this precisely at the time IBM entered the component industry on a large scale. Does a highly diversified company stand greater chances in the long term than a firm which concentrates exclusively on computers? No clear-cut answer emerges: diversified companies such as GE and RCA financed their losses in computers through their profits in consumer electronics and telecommunications but finally opted out of computers.

What many firms viewed as major strategic options were in fact often but a rationalization of circumstances beyond their control. A large diversified firm entering the computer industry had no choice but to manufacture its own integrated circuits and sell them to its computer division, while a company making nothing but computers could ill afford to spread its energies and its resources in other sectors.

Judging from the record, it would seem that there are never any strategic options for the industry as a whole, but only a series of problems which are different for each company and which each one must try to solve in its own way without making too many mistakes. The evolution of the industry is determined not so much by ineluctable trends as by the sum of individual decisions taken by the top managers in the leading firms. And the most successful companies are those which have made their major decisions in an independent way, without seeking merely to imitate and follow their competitors. Autonomy does not of course guarantee success, but it does seem to be one of its necessary conditions.

One of the problems facing European and Japanese companies has been the progressive weakening of this capacity to take decisions in an autonomous way. At first glance, this absence of autonomy would seem to result from the overwhelming strength of American computer companies on the world market. But the phenomenon probably goes much deeper: it touches upon a nation's culture, its psychology, and its political place in the world. It is probably no coincidence that the country which leads the world in terms of the computer industry is also the largest political power on the planet. In the same way, one cannot help seeing a striking parallel between the political decline of England, Germany, and France—the big powers of the prewar period—and the erosion of their leadership in computer technology in the last twenty years. Viewed in this perspective, national computer policies might be interpreted as a deliberate attempt to reverse the trend by opposing the market forces that seem to be favoring American companies.

The Elements of a Computer Policy

Virtually every government in Europe today can claim to have a national computer policy.[4] Only four countries, however—the United Kingdom, France, Germany, and the Netherlands—have a significant and independent computer manufacturing industry. Furthermore, in these countries, the industry consists largely of one big nationally owned firm, a limited number of very small companies, and one or two big American subsidiaries. National policy amounts essentially to a special relationship between government and the one big national firm.

National computer policies, however, do not concentrate solely on computer manufacturing, and it might be more appropriate to define them, as the French do, in terms of a *politique de l'informatique,* which covers not only the manufacturing of hardware but also the production of software, computer utilization, and education. A complete examination of national computer policies would have to cover the whole spectrum and not limit itself, as this chapter will, to the manufacturing of hardware in general, and of central processing units (CPUs) in particular.

There are several reasons for concentrating on the CPUs rather than on the broad range of products and services offered by the information industry. The first is that in the European countries which have an indigenous and independent computer manufacturing industry, national policy has tended, rightly or wrongly, to concentrate primarily on this sector. Countries which do not have an independent industry tend to focus on computer utilization, and one might even go so far as to suggest that the existence of a sophisticated utilization policy is often a psychological compensation for the absence or the earlier failure of an indigenous manufacturing firm. The second reason is that the CPU, as its name indicates, is the heart, or rather the brain, of an information system, even if economically it represents only a fraction of the total investment made by the user. The third reason, finally, is that the computer is both a source of power and a symbol of power. The argument that American industry enjoys a comparative advantage in the production of computers and should manufacture them for the whole world while letting other countries concentrate on the efficient utilization of computers can be defended in purely economic terms. Politically, however, it is no more appealing for other countries than the suggestion, made a hundred and fifty years ago, that Britain should exploit its comparative advantage in steam engines and remain the sole manufacturer for the whole world.

The emergence of a national policy goes back in France and the United Kingdom to the 1963–1965 period and in Germany to the late 1960s. In Japan, a country to which several references will be made later, the mid-1960s might be considered as the beginning of a national policy in this field, but one should not overlook the fact that in Japan, support of the computer industry was but one aspect of a much broader and considerably older policy of industrial and technological development.

Tradition has it that France's computer policy was the result of the famed *Affaire Bull* in 1964 and of the refusal of the U.S. State Department to grant an export license in 1966 for two of Control Data's largest computers.[5] Folklore is probably correct in attributing a major importance to these two accidents, but they were certainly not the *cause première* of France's computer policy. They triggered off the policy and gave it an aura of legitimacy, but the policy would probably have emerged in any case, as it did in the United Kingdom, Japan, and Germany, where there had been no takeover of a prestigious national firm by an American company and no dispute with the State Department.

The interesting point here is the rather striking similarity among the four countries which developed a national computer policy (as opposed to a computer utilization policy) in the 1960s. In terms of industrial potential, scientific strength, and economic size, the United Kingdom, France, Germany, and Japan fall roughly into the same category. Each of these countries, practically at the same time, developed very similar policies for the industry and based them on almost identical arguments. This suggests that the drive for an independent computer industry is closely linked with a country's size.

One confirmation of this is that none of the smaller European countries which at one time or another had a computer industry developed a policy to support it, contrary to what happened in the larger countries. Belgium let its only firm go under American control, apparently without any qualms. Denmark concentrated on computer utilization rather than on production, despite the competence of Regnecentralen, its only computer manufacturer. The Swedish government stated several times that computer manufacturing was less important to the country than the effective utilization of computers. As for the Netherlands, computer manufacturing remained the private affair of the Philips Company and had little if anything to do with government policy. Philips in fact has stated that it never received any government support for its computer activities.

Italy is a rather particular case which falls halfway between the "small" and the "large" countries, and there are reasons to believe that, given a sufficient commitment on the part of the government, it could have attempted to pursue the computer strategy of a large country. As things turned out in the mid-1960s, when the financial difficulties of Olivetti compelled it to accept a major financial participation of General Electric, the Italian government in effect opted by default for a small-country strategy, thus implicitly accepting the fact that Italy would in future be totally dependent on foreign computer suppliers.

The practically simultaneous emergence of national computer policies in the United Kingdom, France, and Germany is matched by striking similarities in their objectives; the motivations, furthermore, are not very different, even if France has tended to be somewhat more outspokenly anti-American than either Germany or the United Kingdom. In these three countries, as well as in Japan, the objective of a computer policy is to maintain and develop a nationally owned industry which will also be economically viable in the long run.

The means used to foster these broad objectives have been essentially the same in the three countries. The first was, and still is, financial support to research and development (R&D) activities of the nationally owned computer firms. The second is the regrouping of national firms to form one single large company capable of withstanding competition on the world market. And the third is preferential government procurement.

Government Policy and Corporate Strategy

The interface between government policy and corporate strategy can best be approached by looking at the mergers, takeovers, and licensing agreements which took place, both nationally and internationally, in the European computer industry between 1960 and 1973. These moves have been summarized in Table 1, which also indicates in each case the government's attitude toward the move. In some instances, such as the creation of ICL or CII, it is well known that the government initiated and strongly supported the move. In others, it is common knowledge that the government's attitude was negative: the best example of this is the takeover of Bull by General Electric. There are, however, a surprisingly large number of cases where no clear-cut government position can be identified.

Table 1. Intercompany agreements in the European computer industry, 1961–1973[a]

Date	Companies involved	Type of agreement	Government attitude	Main results of the agreements
1961	NRC⟶Elliott Automation	L & S	0	Loose agreements. Some Elliott computers sold in U.S.
1961	ICT⟶EMI Computer Division	T	0	Second move in the amalgamation of the U.K. computer industry (after the formation of ICT in 1959).
1961	RCA⟶ICT	L & S	0	Facilitated ICT's entry into the second generation.
1961	RCA⟶Bull	L & S	0	The agreement was helpful to Bull but had to be cancelled when Bull joined General Electric in 1964.
1963	ICT + Bull[b]	M	?	Protracted negotiation collapsed when Bull joined GE. Plans were also made for a merger with Siemens and Olivetti.
1963	ICT + Univac	S	0	Marketing agreement covering the sale of Univac's 1004 computer in England.
1963	ICT⟶Ferranti Computer Division	T	+	Progressive phasing out of Ferranti computers, but ICT acquired useful technology. Rationalization problems.
1963	EE⟶LEO Computers	T	0	Progressive phasing out of LEO computers, but EE enlarged its customer base.
1964	GE⟶Bull	JV, later T	N	The joint company, taken over by GE in 1967, generated no profits. Progressive phasing out of Bull computers. Takeover by Honeywell in 1970 when GE dropped out of the computer industry.

Table 1. (continued)

1964	GE→Olivetti	JV, later T	0	Olivetti computers phased out. Takeover by GE in 1967 and by Honeywell in 1970.
1964	Ferranti Packard→ICT	L	0	The computer developed by Ferranti's Canadian subsidiary was at the origin of ICT's 1900 series. Very successful agreement.
1964	EE→Marconi	T	0	Takeover of all Marconi activities, including components and telecommunications.
1964	BBC→Zuse	T	0	Move undertaken under the initiative of BBC's German subsidiary. Not very successful. Zuse later sold to Siemens.
1964	ICT + CITEC[b]	A	+, N	Agreement to build a large Anglo-French computer. Project cancelled when France launched the Plan Calcul.
1965	RCA→Siemens	L	0	Siemens did not develop an independent technology. Rapid expansion. Difficulties created by RCA's exit from the industry in 1971.
1965	NCR→Elliott Automation	L	0	Licensing agreement of limited importance.
1965	Philips→Electrologica	JV, later T	0	First agreement: financial support for R&D. Full takeover by Philips in 1966. Some contribution to Philips technology, but Electrologica computers phased out.
1965	RCA→EE	L	0	Facilitated EE's entry into the second generation. EE improved RCA technology.
1965	SDS→CITEC	L	0	SDS formed one of the technological bases of Plan Calcul. Agreement renewed in 1969.
1965	SDS→GEC	S	0	Agreement terminated in 1968.

Table 1. (continued)

Date	Companies involved	Type of agreement	Government attitude	Main results of the agreements
1965	Honeywell⟶Saab	S	0	Sales agreement of limited importance.
1966	AEG⟶Telefunken	T	0	Telefunken's large computers not very successful.
1966	Philips + Siemag	JV	0	Technical cooperation agreement of limited importance.
1966	GE⟶Elliott Automation[b]	T	0	Talks between the two firms never concluded.
1966	CAE + SEA	M	++	Formation of CII under the aegis of the Plan Calcul.
1967	EE⟶Elliott Automation	T	++	EE was somewhat reluctant to take over Elliott. Move facilitated by large loan from the British government.
1967	ICT + AEG-Telefunken[b]	M	N	Merger talks failed; partly because of differences between companies, partly because of government opposition.
1967	Siemens⟶Zuse	JV, later T	0	Some contribution to Siemens' technology, but Zuse computers progressively phased out.
1968	ICT + EE Computer Div. + Plessey Computer Div.	M	++	Formation of ICL. Some problems of rationalization (noncompatible computers) and overstaffing.
1970	Honeywell⟶Bull-GE	T	N	The French government at first tried to link Bull-GE with CII when the parent company dropped out of the computer industry. Reluctantly had to agree to takeover by Honeywell. Apparent return to profitability.
1970	Siemens + AEG-Telefunken[b]	M	+	No follow-up of merger talks despite government encouragement. Two years of fruitless negotiation.

Table 1. (continued)

1970	CII + ICL[b]	M	?	No follow-up of merger talks.
1970	CII + ICL + CDC	JV	?	Formation of Multinational Data. Successful in standardization. Unsuccessful in designing a common new range of computers.
1971	CII + Siemens	A & S	?	Marketing and market-sharing agreement. Plans to have a joint range of computers by 1977.
1972	AEG-Telefunken + Nixdorf	JV	+	Creation of a joint subsidiary for the production of Telefunken's large computers. Nixdorf in the driving seat.
1973	Philips + Siemens + CII	JV, M	?	Formation of Unidata. Cooperation in marketing, planning, and R&D.

Types of agreements

A	General agreement
JV	Joint venture
L	Licensing agreement
M	Merger
S	Sales agreement
T	Takeover

Abbreviations and Symbols

Names of companies

AEG	Allgemeine Elektrizitätsgesellschaft (Germany)
BBC	Brown Boveri & Co. (Switzerland and Germany)
CAE	Compagnie Européenne d'Automatisme Electronique (France)
CDC	Control Data Corporation (United States)
CII	Compagnie Internationale pour l'Informatique (France)
CITEC	Compagnie pour l'Informatique et les Techniques Electroniques de Contrôle (France)
EE	English Electric (United Kingdom)
EMI	Electrical & Musical Industries (United Kingdom)
GE	General Electric (United States)
GEC	General Electric Company (United Kingdom)
ICL	International Computers Ltd. (United Kingdom)
ICT	International Computers and Tabulators (United Kingdom)

Table 1. (continued)

Government attitude	Abbreviations and Symbols (continued)
++ Strongly approved the move or initiated it	LEO Lyons Electronic Office (United Kingdom)
+ Favorable to the move	NCR National Cash Register (United States)
0 Neutral, indifferent, or not informed	RCA Radio Corporation of America (United States)
	SDS Scientific Data Systems, later Xerox Data Systems (United States)
? Attitude ambivalent	SEA Société d'Electronique et d'Automatisme (France)
N Opposed the move	

Sources: *Gaps in Technology: Electronic Computers* (Paris: OECD, 1969); James Connolly, *History of Computing in Europe* (New York: IBM World Trade Corporation, 1968), and *Chronology of Computing in Africa, Asia, Europe and Latin America* (New York: IBM World Trade Corporation, 1968); Christopher Freeman et al., "Research and Development in Electronic Capital Goods," *National Institute Economic Review*, November 1965; Alvin J. Harman, *The International Computer Industry: Innovation and Comparative Advantage* (Cambridge, Mass.: Harvard University Press, 1971); Christopher Layton and Y. S. Hu, *Report on the Computer Industry in Europe: Hardware Manufacturing* (Strasbourg: Council of Europe, 1971); company reports; press releases; visits to companies; and private communications.

[a] This table does not cover agreements on software, hybrid computers, and process control computers.

[b] Agreement not implemented.

The main drawback of the list in Table 1 is its failure to distinguish the various moves according to their importance. Moreover, it is difficult to obtain a complete picture of what really happened. Although most of the significant moves were well—if not always accurately—publicized, many less spectacular steps were often of considerable importance. Nevertheless, this list does offer some useful clues to governmental attitudes. The summary presented in Table 2, which distinguishes among

Table 2. European government attitudes toward intercompany agreements, 1961-1972[a]

Number of cases

Agreements	Government initiated (++)	Favorable (+)	Neutral (0)	Ambivalent (?)	Opposed (N)	Total
Mergers						
National	2	1	—	—	—	3
International	—	—	—	3	1	4
Takeovers						
National	1	1	7	—	—	9
International	—	—	2	—	2	4
Joint ventures						
National	—	1	—	—	—	1
International	—	—	1	1	—	2
Licensing agreements	—	—	8	—	—	8
Sales agreements	—	—	3	—	—	3
Other joint projects	—	1	—	1	1	3
Total	3	4	21	5	4	37

Source: Table 1.

[a] An agreement that was classified in Table 1 under two headings (e.g., a joint venture followed by a takeover) has been classified here under the more important heading (in this case, takeover).

— = None

mergers, takeovers, and joint ventures involving two or more firms of the same country (national agreements) and those in which the partners were companies of different national origin (international agreements), adds a further touch to the overall picture.

The most striking point, if one compares European with Japanese policies,[6] is the apparently total lack of interest on the part of European governments in licensing agreements. None of the eight cases identified in the 1960–1972 period seems to have been either approved or disapproved by the national authorities entrusted with the "sponsorship" of the computer industry. Some of these agreements were very important. Siemens, to take one illustration, owed much of its position on the European scene in the early 1970s to the agreement concluded in 1965 with RCA. As for ICL, many of its long-term technological options (for example, noncompatibility with IBM equipment) find their origin in the acquisition of Ferranti Packard's designs. Yet these two agreements, as well as the six others, were not subject to public debate, and national policies have operated as if the introduction of foreign technology through licensing were a private affair of industry.

Another conclusion emerging from this table is that only three moves can be directly attributed to government intervention: the acquisition of Elliott Automation by English Electric, the formation of ICL through the merger of ICT with Plessey's and English Electric's computer divisions, and finally the creation of CII under the aegis of the French *Plan Calcul*.

Interestingly enough, the three mergers, which resulted first and foremost from direct government action, involved companies of the same nationality, while all the moves which were opposed by government or which raised ambivalent feelings involved a national firm with a foreign partner. This would suggest that the scope for transnational mergers between European firms and for joint European projects is rather limited. One of the reasons is that the promotion of national champions by European governments (ICL in the United Kingdom, CII in France, and Siemens in Germany) runs contrary to the tenets of European industrial and technological cooperation. In fact, there probably is a basic conflict, if not a total incompatibility, between the support given by governments to their national champion and the often expressed need for a "European" strategy based on mergers between the remaining independent companies of France, England, Germany, and the Netherlands.[7]

Though Table 2 shows that the government attitude was neutral, indifferent, or merely passive in twenty-one out of the thirty-seven cases, it is well to note that this figure is the result of reactions in two very distinct time phases. The first, which ran until 1964–65, was characterized by the absence of any real policy in this field, and the second, from 1966 until 1972, was marked by the emergence of national computer policies. Most of the noncommittal reactions occurred before 1966. In 1966, three more cases of neutrality or passivity are registered. After that, no such cases are recorded. This obviously is a reflection of the growth of national computer policies after 1965. By the early 1970s it was widely accepted that government had its *mot à dire* in the computer industry and that national firms, while still partly privately owned, had in fact become public enterprises.

The Quest for Size

The preoccupation of the Europeans with the insufficient size of their computer firms was, when it first arose, only one manifestation among many of a growing concern about the future of European industry in general and the apparently increasing superiority of U.S. firms.[8] Why was American industry so dynamic? One obvious answer seemed to be the fact that American firms were so much larger. It would be interesting to analyze here the role played by *Fortune* magazine and its annual tables on corporate turnover. The availability of such data made international comparisons inevitable, and it was only too easy to conclude that European firms could become as competitive as the Americans if their size were greater. Little attention was paid to the view that size was perhaps a consequence rather than a cause of success, and that the American environment was in many respects very different from the European environment.

In the mid-1960s, this preoccupation with problems of size acquired a technological dimension: it began to be realized that R&D and technology were at least as important as size, and international comparisons published by organizations such as OECD clearly supported this view by showing that European countries were spending much less than the United States on R&D.[9] The assumption, here again, was that Europe should catch up and try to match American expenditures. The success of national science policies came to be measured on the basis of the expenditures of the country in question as compared with the United States.

In the industrial field, one obvious answer to the challenge of size was to foster intranational mergers and acquisitions. This philosophy, shared by industry and governments alike, led in the second half of the 1960s to a major wave of concentration, touching the automobile industry as well as the chemical industries, iron and steel as well as computers and other electronic equipment. One factor which was partly overlooked, however, is that the value of such regroupings is closely linked to the rate of growth of the industry and the size of production units. In a sector with an average annual growth rate of 20 percent (in the computer industry, it has been closer to 30 percent), turnover will double in less than four years. This means, in other terms, that a merger between two companies of similar size will result in an increase in turnover corresponding to that achieved by one company individually in four years.

That fact suggests some important corollaries. The closer to zero the growth rate of the industry, the greater the potential benefits which can be achieved through a merger or acquisition. The higher the rate of growth, the smaller the time-advantage offered by a merger or acquisition. For industries with a growth rate above 12 to 15 percent, the advantages of a merger thus appear to be questionable. Furthermore, the rate of growth of a newly merged firm is often lower than that of the two original companies in previous years: mergers are a traumatic experience, and the reorganization problems accompanying them can be formidable. This is particularly true in computers, where the technologies developed by each firm are often incompatible.

To put things in a theoretical way: the merger of two companies of similar size will immediately double their market share. But if the rate of growth of the newly formed group falls to 10 percent per annum while competing companies continue to expand at the rate of 20 percent, the advantage of larger relative size will disappear in less than eight years and the main effect of the merger will have been to reduce the number of companies in existence without increasing the relative strength of the remaining firm in a significant way. This is what seems to have happened to several European computer companies.

One might argue that the rationale for mergers and acquisitions is not only the increase in market share or size of company. In many cases, especially in Europe, these moves can be interpreted as substitutes for outright failures: a firm may find it easier to sell its computer division to a competitor than to close down its laboratories and production facilities. In fact, the only two companies in Europe which have decided to close down have been the German and English subsidiaries (SEL and STC) of an American firm, International Telephone & Telegraph. All the European firms which dropped out of the industry (EMI, EE, Plessey, Olivetti, among others) did so by selling their computer manufacturing divisions to other companies.

In a fast-growing industry, internal growth may be a more satisfactory means of development than mergers or acquisitions. What should not be overlooked, however, is the fact that many companies, especially if they are weak, simply do not have the possibility of choosing between internal growth and mergers: they are virtually forced to opt for mergers if they want to survive. This is particularly true in the computer industry, which, in addition to high rates of growth and enormous risks, poses almost insuperable marketing problems to those firms that are not the leaders. Observe, for instance, that selling a computer system to a new user is several times more expensive than selling a system to a customer who already possesses a computer from that manufacturer. A firm like IBM, because of its size, its reputation, and its enormous marketing networks, ships a very high percentage of its machines to existing users of IBM equipment. Other firms, if they are to develop, must either take away customers from IBM or sell their systems to new users. In both cases, their marketing costs will be considerably higher.

In this perspective, the advantages of a merger or an acquisition appear more clearly: they are the means of acquiring what in the industry is known as a customer base, that is, a number of customers who can normally be counted upon to turn to the same manufacturer for additional requirements. When ICT merged with English Electric, or when Univac took over the responsibility for servicing the computer systems installed by RCA, one of the main objectives was to acquire at a relatively low cost the main asset of a computer firm, namely, its customer base.

Looking back at the European computer industry in the 1960s, one sees that while governments were preoccupied primarily with the size of their national firms, the firms were taking a more sophisticated view of things and thinking more in terms of long-term survival and enlargement of their customer base through the only means available to them: mergers and acquisitions. Internal growth clearly would have been a more satisfactory solution, but in many ways it was a luxury they could not afford.

The emphasis of European industrial policies on the size of firms during the 1960s seemed to have passed its peak by the early 1970s, not only because greater size did not appear in itself to be conducive to success, but also because of the progressive realization that the problem was in fact considerably more complex than the somewhat unsophisticated figures on corporate turnover would suggest. Large size is seldom tantamount to efficiency. What is often more important than the total turnover is the average size of production units; and if there are economies of scale, there can also be diseconomies of scale.

In this respect, the computer industry provides a good illustration of the complexities of size. Turnover, or for that matter shipments, may give a good indication of the size of a firm's customer base, and hence of its relative marketing costs; but as Y. S. Hu has shown, account must be taken of production costs, which decline with the cumulative number of computer systems installed in previous years, and not simply with the number of systems produced in a given year.[10] This means that a company which has been in the computer industry for a long time and has already installed a large number of computers thereby enjoys an advantage over a younger firm with the same annual turnover but a much smaller cumulative number of installations. Empirical evidence suggests, furthermore, that this experience curve does not begin to flatten out until a firm has gained around 10 percent of the world market. In other terms, companies which fall below this figure have considerably higher production and marketing costs than their larger competitors, particularly if, as in the case of all European firms except ICL, their share of the world market is well below 5 percent. In this perspective, the quest of European computer companies for larger size might be interpreted first and foremost as an attempt to survive, and not, as government policies would often suggest, as a mere desire to match the bigness of the more successful American firms.

The Emergence of National Champions

Fostering the creation of a national champion was one of the explicit goals of European government policies in the computer industry. Though this policy has a number of parallels in other industries, there is little doubt that the existence of IBM was a decisive factor. In essence, this firm has come to symbolize the success of American industry and to play abroad the role of the U.S. national champion. Paradoxically, the attitude of the U.S. government toward IBM is somewhat negative. It is a well-known fact, for instance, that the unwritten policy of the armed services as well as of many agencies is to give procurement contracts to firms other than IBM, and the attitude of the Department of Justice is not particularly friendly, to say the least. As one perceptive observer expressed it, the Department of Justice was trying to rend asunder what the Europeans were so desperately attempting to build up, namely, a profitable national computer company.[11]

The strategies followed by European governments to foster the emergence of a national champion in the computer industry have been rather similar, despite a certain number of differences which can be attributed to national tradition. The various moves from 1960 to 1972 have been summarized in Figures 1 and 2, which cover France, the United Kingdom, Germany, and, for the sake of comparison, Japan.

France was the first of the four countries to have its champion: the creation of CII goes back to 1966, two years before the emergence of ICL in the United Kingdom. This new firm was very much the second best. When Bull was forced to come to a financial agreement (later followed by a takeover) with General Electric, it was suddenly realized that Bull was in fact the national champion. By that time, the financial position of the company was such, and the negotiations with GE were so far advanced, that a *solution française* was thought to be out of the question. Looking back at the events, there are reasons to believe that the French government could have helped Bull through this critical phase and thereby prevented a takeover. The sums of money which Bull required were at any rate smaller than the later investments made by the government in the *Plan Calcul*. The problem, however, was not only one of money: the real issue was the absence of a clear-cut policy which could have justified direct support on the part of the government and allowed decisions to be taken at very short notice.

Once Bull had passed into American hands, France had no other company which could have played the part of a national champion. One

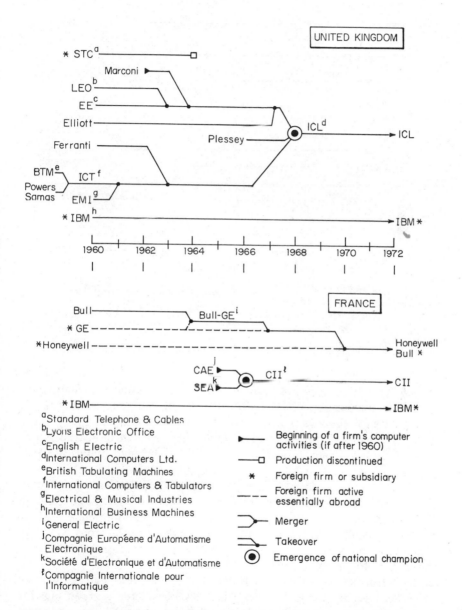

Figure 1. Emergence of a National Champion in the United Kingdom and France, 1960–1972.

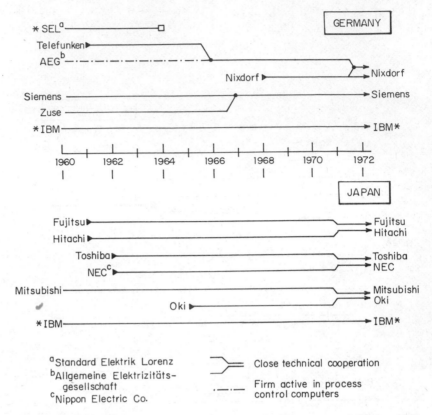

Figure 2. Emergence of a National Champion in Germany and Japan, 1960–1972.

possibility, which does not seem to have been considered, might have been a nationalization of IBM-France. Instead, the government elected to create an entirely new firm virtually out of nothing. In many ways, this move was a major innovation. Until then, French industrial policy had tended to operate through nationalizations and regroupings of existing firms.

The two companies that formed the basis of CII were extremely small. At the end of 1966 the combined market share of CAE and SEA in France was only 7 percent, and the majority of the computers sold by CII were small machines manufactured under license from SDS, an American company. In the United Kingdom, by contrast, ICT held more than 40 percent of the market at the time of the merger with the computer divisions of English Electric and Plessey. CII had neither the customer base nor the technology which are considered prerequisites for success in the industry. In addition, it had to face all the personnel problems that accompany mergers between firms with very different philosophies.

The total expenditure of the French government on the first phase of the *Plan Calcul* (1966–1970) amounted to approximately $120 million. Assessing the return on such an investment is somewhat irrelevant, since the primary objective was political, as *Le Figaro* expressed it very clearly: "Notre politique d'indépendance diplomatique n'aurait aucun sens si elle ne s'appuyait sur des capacités technologiques réelles, notamment dans le domaine essentiel des calculateurs."[12] At the beginning of 1973, CII's market share in France was not significantly higher than that of the original firms in 1966 and its exports were very modest. But the company had managed to survive, and its expansion had even been somewhat higher than originally planned at the beginning of the Plan Calcul.

In the United Kingdom, the need for a national champion was never so clearly expressed as in France after 1965. Britain, for one thing, had a relatively important computer industry which in the course of the years had made some major contributions to world technology. Its market share had declined substantially between 1960 and 1965, but the overall rate of growth was sufficient to give at least the appearance of success. After the Labour Party returned to power in 1964, the government supported industrial development through the Industrial Reorganisation Corporation. It financed the creation of firms like BLMC (British Leyland Motor Corporation) and the enlarged GEC (General Electric Company). In computers, the financial support given first to English Electric and later to ICT was one of the major aspects of Britain's emerging technological policy.

In Germany, the situation was somewhat different in that the firms of the computer industry (Siemens, AEG, Telefunken, and SEL) were primarily active in the heavy electrical and telecommunications industries. The computer industry did not emerge as an industrial sector in its own right until very late. The absence of identity might explain the difficulty experienced by government authorities in defining a policy for this industry. Another problem is that German industry, while willing to accept public subsidies, was far less amenable to government intervention than French industry. This was perhaps most obvious in the case of Siemens: several efforts were made by the government to foster *rapprochement* with other German computer firms (notably AEG-Telefunken), but without success. The problem here, however, was not only the weight of a certain German political tradition but also the psychological inability of a firm like Siemens to work in close cooperation with other computer companies.

Judging from the evolution of the late 1960s and early 1970s, the

German computer industry seemed to be evolving toward a "two-champion" structure: on the one hand Siemens, confident of its own ability and its past reputation, and on the other hand Nixdorf, a small and dynamic company which may later claim to be *the* other German computer firm.

In the large West European countries, government policies vis-à-vis the computer industry have not been so voluntaristic as certain claims make them out to be. The constraints of competition with American companies, the relative independence of certain large firms, and the difficulty of defining a coherent national technological policy have often been major limitations. Would things have been very different if European ministries had enjoyed the same influence as the Japanese Ministry of International Trade and Industry (MITI)? Japan has by far the world's most sophisticated and effective technological policy,[13] but the facts show that, in the computer industry at least, this alone is not necessarily sufficient.

In the 1950s several large Japanese firms as well as some university laboratories were active in computer research, but the commercial impact of these first computers was limited. By the late 1950s it was clear that American industry was in the lead, and the solution chosen to bridge this technological gap was to allow IBM to establish a wholly owned subsidiary, an exceptional move considering the Japanese reluctance to let any foreign firm dominate the market. Retrospectively, it seems that this decision was inspired in part by panic. Soon thereafter several Japanese companies concluded licensing agreements with other American firms. Contrary to the usual pattern, little attention seems to have been paid by MITI to the problems such tie-ups would cause: the technology of each licensor was different, thus creating a fragmentation which had not been overcome by the early 1970s. The idea was, perhaps, that some firms would decide to drop out of the computer industry after a few years; but in fact each one of the five original licensees concluded that computers were too important to be abandoned.

Several measures were taken to support the industry, notably the creation of the Japan Electronic Computer Company (JECC), which buys the computers from the manufacturers and leases them to the users, thus relieving industry of the financial burden of serving in effect as banker to the customer. Particular attention was given to Fujitsu, the only manufacturer which was independent of American licenses, both in the computer field and in components. Fujitsu was chosen as the prime contractor for the large FONTAC machine developed in cooperation with Oki and NEC, and there are signs that Fujitsu is emerging as the national champion, or at least as one among three.[14]

Contrary to what happened in the United Kingdom and in France, little emphasis was given to mergers. The view was that companies can only come together the day their technologies are compatible and their philosophies similar. Hence the major emphasis on the development of a common technology and a reluctance to force companies to cooperate against their will. Policies of this sort are long in coming to fruition. A computer generation has a life of approximately seven years, and the process of convergence initiated in the mid-1960s only began to materialize with the agreements concluded in the early 1970s between Fujitsu and Hitachi, Mitsubishi and Oki, and NEC and Toshiba. At that point, Japanese policy seemed to be evolving toward the idea of three large computer companies, thus emulating the empirical multi-firm approach of the United States and avoiding some of the risks which go with a single large firm. While Germany's two-champion concept resulted primarily from the inability of government policy to foster the creation of one single large group, Japan's three-champion structure might be more deliberate than accidental. It tends to support the view that Japan is developing a technological policy commensurate with the ambitions of a large power.

Preferential Procurement and Support to R&D

Although the promotion of mergers and acquisitions has been the most conspicuous aspect of government policies in the European computer industry between 1965 and the early 1970s, the role of preferential procurement contracts and subsidies for R&D should not be overlooked. The practical difference among these tools of national policy is not always very clear, however. The grant given to a newly merged firm may nominally be earmarked for the development of a new line of computers, but in fact it often turns out to be first and foremost an incentive for the merger. And in many cases, credits granted at short notice are in fact outright gifts, the main purpose of which is to prevent imminent financial collapse.

Bearing these problems in mind, one can nevertheless summarize in a tentative form the amount of R&D support accorded by European governments to their national computer industry over the 1966–1975 period. The figures given in Table 3 must be used with great caution. But they do suggest that government support to R&D has been comparatively much smaller in the United Kingdom than in France or Germany. Britain's absolute figures have been consistently lower, even though ICL, the main beneficiary of these grants, has an annual turnover far greater than the combined turnover of the nationally owned French and German computer companies.*

---

* The data in Table 3 do not cover military R&D, which in France and the United Kingdom has been relatively important. The only country for which official data are available is Germany. Between 1963 and 1966, the Federal Ministry of

Table 3. Government support to civilian R&D in the European computer industry, 1966–1975

(millions of U.S. dollars at current exchange rates)

Country	Yearly average	
	1966–1970	1971–1975
United Kingdom	10[a]	25[b]
France	30	48
Germany	15[c]	44
Total	55	117

Sources: Gaps in Technology: Electronic Computers (Paris: OECD, 1969); Federal Republic of Germany, Ministry for Education and Science, *Zweites Datenverarbeitungsprogramm der Bundesregierung,* 1971; Eric Moonman, ed., *British Computers and Industrial Innovation* (London: George Allen & Unwin, 1971); company reports and press releases.
   [a] 1968–1970 period.
   [b] Preliminary estimates.
   [c] 1967–1970 period.

A comparison between the support granted to European firms by their national governments in the first half of the 1970s and that given by the American government in the mid-1960s shows that in relative terms European support has not been significantly lower, especially if account is taken of the fact that a large part of the European market is in the hands of American subsidiaries which do not receive any aid from European governments. In 1965, R&D grants to the American computer industry were around $150 million. But figures of this sort can be somewhat misleading; the important thing is not how much money is spent, but how and especially when it is spent. As one of the pioneers of computing in Britain stated it, the "derisory sums" allocated to the industry should have been spent before 1960, at a time when Britain was the world leader in terms of technology.[15]

In order to measure the effective scale of government support to R&D, account should also be taken of the research performed in the universities and financed, directly or indirectly, by the government. In the United Kingdom, the contribution of the universities to industrial technology has been substantial; a number of major innovations incorporated in some of the early British computers were developed by academic scientists. This was still partly true in the early 1970s, as the close contacts between ICL and the University of Manchester would suggest.[16] In Germany the role of the universities has been much less

Defense allocated approximately $3 million to research on military computers, and the corresponding figure for the 1967–1971 period was around $15 million. (Federal Republic of Germany, Ministry for Education and Science, *Zweites Datenverarbeitungsprogramm der Bundesregierung,* 1971).

conspicuous, and it is difficult to identify one single major innovation in the computer field coming from a German university. Things might change, however, in the late 1970s and early 1980: The policy of the German government is to strengthen the scientific capability of the academic world by giving relatively large research contracts. In the second data processing plan (1971–1975), universities were due to receive approximately $10 million a year for research in computer technology, and if account is taken of all types of associated research, the yearly total would come closer to $50 million.[17]

In France, the situation has been rather different. The universities, in the computer field at least, do not have the tradition of excellence which in Britain has served as a justification for the financial assistance granted to them by the government and industry. Furthermore, unlike Germany, the French government has appeared far less anxious to build up a first-class research capability in computing in the universities. One indication of this can be found in the fact that the promotion of fundamental research was entrusted by the first Plan Calcul to a newly created organization, the Institut de Recherches d'Informatique et d'Automatique (IRIA), and not to any existing academic institutions. Coordination of the research performed in universities and other research centers was entrusted to a Comité de Recherche en Informatique (CRI), whose budget, significantly enough, amounted to only 40 percent of that of the IRIA.[18]

Insofar as one can speak of a research strategy, the situation as it stood in the early 1970s might be summarized in the following way:

(a) In the United Kingdom, continuing support to a selected number of academic centers of excellence, but on a relatively modest scale (less than $5 million a year).

(b) In Germany, a clear-cut attempt to reverse the past trend of academic insignificance by investing large sums in the universities (a move which might be attributed in part to the fact that the sponsorship of the computer industry is entrusted to the Ministry of Science and Education).

(c) In France, the development of parallel, nonacademic institutions, which have in effect bypassed the universities.

The indirect government support given to European computer firms by preferential procurement policies is much more difficult to assess than the direct and more open support accorded through R&D grants. In fact, the only country which has officially stated that government contracts would in principle be given to nationally owned firms is the United Kingdom. In 1965 a statement to this effect was made by the Minister of Technology, and in the following year it was announced that central and local government bodies would be allowed to buy British-designed computers costing up to 25 percent more than equivalent American computers.[19] In 1968, at the time of the merger between ICT and the computer divisions of English Electric and Plessey, the government introduced the single-tender principle: government procurement contracts for large computers and for smaller machines which were to be upgraded at some later stage by large computers of the same family were to be given to ICL, while for other types of computers the principle of competitive bidding was retained, subject to the reservation that at least one of the bidders be a British company.

In Germany, neither the first nor the second data processing plan made any provisions for such preferences. Both acknowledged the domination of American companies and recognized that the position of U.S. firms on the world market could be attributed in part to the indirect support of their government. But no conclusions were drawn as to the possibility of giving government contracts to German companies rather than to U.S. firms. The same situation prevailed in France, and one can find no official rulings similar to those of the British Ministry of Technology. Yet despite the absence of such statements, government procurement contracts have tended to be given both in France and in Germany to local companies rather than to American firms, and there has been a de facto preference in favor of the nationals. Such preferences, it may be added, represent a discrimination not only against American subsidiaries but also against local firms of other EEC countries, and as such they are incompatible with the Treaty of Rome, the basic charter of the European Community.

These de facto preferences have usually been enforced through "advice" and "suggestions" to prospective customers such as academic institutions and nationalized industries. Needless to say, they are seldom publicized, but they are nevertheless very real. Their effectiveness, furthermore, seems to have varied quite widely: French organizations are generally more receptive than German organizations. Moreover, pressures of this kind inevitably create tensions. The "user-oriented" departments of a government are often rather reluctant to acquire locally designed machines which may not be so good as American machines, while the "industry-oriented" departments would definitely prefer to see all important orders going to national companies whose technology they have helped to develop.

The long-term benefits to industry of preferential government procurement are difficult to assess. It may help to widen the local firms' customer basis. But there are also many drawbacks. One of them is that the user in effect has to bear the learning costs of the manufacturer, and this can mean important losses in terms of time or money. This problem may not have been unduly important in Britain, which has produced some of the world's most sophisticated computers, but in France and especially in Germany it has been far from negligible. Universities saddled with the first large Telefunken computers, for instance, have been spending large sums on writing the software which the manufacturer had failed to provide.

Another drawback is that the preference given to local firms often affects their public image in a rather negative way. Once it is known that a firm benefits from such advantages, prospective customers tend to assume that without such a preference its computers would not have been bought by the government. They may assume that the local computers are less satisfactory than comparable U.S. machines. IBM by contrast has consistently benefited from the immense psychological advantage of being the largest and most successful firm in the industry.

The similarities among the measures taken by the United Kingdom, France, and Germany to promote the development of their computer manufacturing industry may seem surprising considering the differences in political tradition and industrial philosophy. One might view this as a reflection of the fact that computer technology is largely dominated by American companies which by virtue of their size have tended to set the standards for the rest of the world. But perhaps the phenomenon goes deeper. European policies have been explicitly motivated by a desire to match what the Americans had done, and the assumption seems to have been made that the special circumstances which favored the growth of U.S. firms could be duplicated in Europe. This is perhaps most conspicuous in the case of R&D. American firms, particularly in the formative years of the industry, benefited from government development contracts, and European governments have sought to recreate similar circumstances by subsidizing the R&D activities of their firms. And today's preferential procurement practices are simply the means of creating, somewhat artificially, a government demand, just as the contracts of the U.S. Department of Defense and NASA have done in the United States. As for the promotion of mergers and the nursing of a national champion, they seem to have been largely inspired by the awesome size of American firms in general and IBM in particular.

The three large European countries have also been alike in their common neglect of alternative strategies. In the early 1960s especially, a large number of European computer firms concluded licensing agreements with American companies; yet governments showed little if any interest, and technology imports were never considered to fall within the scope of national policy. Technological independence and a certain originality are probably more valuable in the long run than a well-negotiated licensing agreement. It is nevertheless symptomatic that national policies in Europe have never even considered the arguments in favor of or against imports of American technology. Another policy tool which was neglected, perhaps for good reasons, was the possibility of enforcing some sort of limitation on the market penetration of American companies. This could have been done in the form of government-sponsored cartels between European and American companies. Such cartels would not necessarily have to be explicit: it might be sufficient for a government to state that by a certain target date (perhaps seven or ten years ahead) the market-share of nationally owned firms should amount to 50 percent. In an industry which is expanding as rapidly as computers, such an arrangement would probably not be too prejudicial to American firms; furthermore, it would allow them to concentrate on the most profitable segments of the market.

Probably the most puzzling aspect of European government policies has been their failure to encourage national firms to penetrate the U.S. market. Two British companies, Ferranti and Elliott, made a half-hearted attempt on their own to sell computers in the United States in the late 1950s, and they failed. In the early 1970s, Nixdorf, alone among all the Europeans, was trying to repeat the same experience, this time through direct investments. Yet in none of these three cases did the government seem to take any interest or give any encouragement.

There is little doubt that European policies have been deeply if subtly influenced by the fact that the industry is dominated by American companies, and all countries with a computer industry suffer from an "IBM-complex." What is perhaps not sufficiently realized is that the preeminent position of IBM on the world market is in some ways a protection for other companies. If IBM were to be dismantled by the Department of Justice and broken up into several smaller firms, as Standard Oil was at the beginning of the century, competition might become much stronger. The restraints that were imposed upon IBM by reason of its size and the threat of legal prosecution would no longer be applicable, and the competitive problems of European firms might be greatly increased.

The Emergence of a European Policy

One widely held assumption in Europe in the early 1970s was that only a "European" solution could ensure the long-term survival of the "European" computer industry. Yet such a solution seemed somewhat chimerical, given the limited powers of the EEC Commission and the inherent conflict between national computer policies and a supranational European policy.

This conflict stands out very clearly if one considers the three main themes of the emerging computer policy of the European Community. The first objective is to favor transnational mergers which, in the opinion of the Commission, will allow national computer firms to reach the same size as their American competitors. The second is to ensure that the subsidiaries of international (read: American) firms conform to the rules of fair competition set by the Treaty of Rome. And the third is to remove the restrictions on public procurement and establish a truly common market.[20]

Two of these three objectives appear somewhat contrary to the policies followed by the British, French, and German governments. The efforts undertaken throughout the 1960s to foster the creation of a national champion have largely succeeded, but the financial and political commitments in this undertaking have been such that it is difficult to imagine that the governments involved would be willing to let their champion merge with a foreign firm, even one from another EEC country. The French, for instance, signaled their attitude by the policies they adopted in the automobile industry. The proposed takeover of Citroën by Fiat was rebuffed despite the fact that France had two other national champions (Renault and Peugeot) which, in the case of a complete takeover of Citroën, could have continued to carry the national flag. Given the commitments to the one and only national computer company, CII, it is difficult to imagine that the French government would be willing to accept a merger of CII with a German or British firm, let alone a takeover.

In Germany, the situation is somewhat different. For one thing, much of the restructuring in the industry has taken place outside the framework of government policy. Furthermore, given the immense size of Siemens, a takeover by another European firm is virtually out of the question. At the worst, Siemens might decide to opt out of computers as its licensor, RCA, did in 1971. The reaction of the German government to such a move is difficult to forecast, but it is unlikely to be very positive. Perhaps the test case here will not be Siemens but Nixdorf. Given adequate financial resources and a sufficient technological interest, a firm such as CII, ICL, or Philips might conceivably decide to take it over. Would such a restructuring of the European computer industry be acceptable to Germany? Or would it be their *Affaire Bull* of the 1970s?

In the United Kingdom, the situation is somewhat clearer: in terms of turnover in computers, ICL is by far the largest European-owned company. Technologically, this firm is probably three to five years ahead of its non-American competitors, and its computers are sufficiently different from those of firms which conform to American standards to discourage any takeover bid from a European firm. ICL, however, is essentially a computer firm, and unlike Philips or Siemens it does not have the "bread and butter" activities which can finance a run of losses in the computer sector. This financial insecurity makes ICL somewhat vulnerable, and the British government may therefore be willing to

consider a "European" solution. An "American" solution would probably be unacceptable, judging from the negative reaction of the government toward the rumored takeover bid made by Burroughs in 1971.

Fostering transnational mergers and promoting the creation of *entreprises communes* might be a valid objective, but in the computer
industry today it appears somewhat unrealistic. This is not to say that
European governments would necessarily be opposed to the creation of
joint intra-European subsidiaries by their respective national champions.
Such a solution would preserve the identity of the main partners while
allowing them to benefit from certain economies of scale in R&D and in
the production of components or peripheral equipments. The creation of
Unidata, the joint subsidiary of CII, Philips, and Siemens, is precisely
such an example of new forms of cooperation which do not involve a
merger or the creation of a hypothetical *entreprise commune*. It would
seem that in the computer industry at least approaches of this type are
more adequate. It is at any rate interesting to note that this is in fact
precisely what the Japanese firms were doing in the early 1970s. Similar
arrangements could be found in the United States: for instance, the
cooperation agreements between Control Data (CDC) and National
Cash Register (NCR).

The second objective of the European Commission's policy, namely,
to encourage the subsidiaries of American companies (and notably
those of IBM) to contribute both to technological development and to
regional development, in conformity with the rules set by the Treaty of
Rome, is unexceptionable and certainly does not conflict with existing
national policies. The scope of such a policy is, however, somewhat
limited. IBM already performs a substantial amount of R&D in the
countries of the enlarged Community, has been particularly cautious not
to infringe upon national and European legislation, and has by and large
made very substantial contributions to economic development. Other
U.S. firms, notably Honeywell, have performed equally well.[21]

The third objective—the opening of public markets and a dismantle-
ment of the restrictions against firms of other EEC countries—is perhaps the most delicate of all. It runs flatly contrary to the preferential
procurement policies which have been among the main tools of European government support to the computer industry. A liberalization of
public markets would presumably apply to all firms within the enlarged
EEC, including the subsidiaries of American companies. The French
government might be willing to give preferential contracts to computers
built by Siemens and marketed by CII, but it is unlikely that it would be
prepared to dismantle a system of support aimed primarily at overcoming American superiority. Opening up public markets is undoubtedly a
very sensible objective, and in some industries, notably telecommunications, it is a precondition of effective development and greater competi-

tiveness on world markets.[22] But in the computer industry it would imply a complete reversal of what has been done ever since the mid-1960s.

To use hyperbole, one might say that the great failing of the EEC policy is that it combines certain weaknesses of national policy with the dispositions of a treaty which was not designed to deal with modern science and technology. One of the main purposes of the EEC is to create a common European market by removing the existing restrictions on trade, investment, and public procurement, while national governments, in the computer industry at least, are promoting the opposite policy on the assumption that this is the only means of ensuring the survival and development of their national champions. The conflict is obvious; nevertheless, a more sophisticated "European" computer policy might yet emerge, capable of supplementing rather than opposing national policies.

National policies and the developing European policy have both tended to focus on the computer industry as such (hardware, software, and later utilization and education). Forecasting is a very tricky affair; according to one of the most reputable American firms, it is impossible to make useful forecasts in the computer industry beyond a seven-year period. Nevertheless, if one were to look ten or fifteen years ahead, it would seem that the central issue will not be so much the computer itself as the information industry as a whole. The interaction between computers and telecommunications is becoming increasingly important, and the present dichotomy between these two sectors will progressively disappear. The Japanese have already sensed this very clearly and are in the process of developing a policy commensurate with the new information industry. The EEC might conceivably follow the same path, and in effect leap-frog directly into an information policy defined in the wider sense. This might help to solve some of the problems caused by the competition, or conflict, between European and national computer policies; but perhaps more important, it would offer tremendous opportunities for those firms which European governments are trying to keep alive.

In a shorter-term perspective, one can envisage several transitional measures which do not conflict with existing national policies. One field of action might be the components industry. Late in the 1960s, several countries attempted to foster the development of their components industry (semiconductors and especially integrated circuits), but progressively gave up in the face of strong American competition and dramatic price decreases. The EEC might well take under its wing the remnants of the somewhat unsuccessful national policies in this sector.

Another field of action might be the encouragement of new forms of intra-European cooperation. Mergers and takeovers between the existing national champions raise enormous political difficulties, but other approaches can be envisaged. One might be the creation of joint inter-European subsidiaries on the Unidata or CDC-NCR model, and another the establishment of binational firms on the Royal Dutch-Shell model or binational consortia on the Anglo-French aircraft industry model. The purpose here is not to suggest what the solutions might be, but simply to emphasize that a European computer policy can only succeed if it transcends the computer industry and goes beyond existing national policies.

Automobiles Louis T. Wells, Jr.

The governments of the major West European countries have a long history of intervention in their automobile industries. Although the national goals toward which policies were aimed have been similar from one country to another, the tools and the styles of government-business relationships have varied considerably among the principal nations.

In large part, the early government policies toward the automobile industry were designed to nurture a domestically owned industry against the threats that were posed by the American automobile manufacturers. Initially, especially before 1920, the policies were concerned primarily with protecting European firms from imports. As the American firms responded to the import barriers by setting up production facilities in Europe, some governments shifted their policies from fostering domestic production to fostering domestic ownership.

The history of government intervention in the automobile industry, therefore, goes back well before World War II. Yet it has a special relevance to the situation in the 1970s because of the way in which governments looked on the automobile industry in those early days. The automobile of the 1920s and 1930s in many respects occupied the place of the computer and the aircraft in the 1970s, as far as governments were concerned. The automobile industry provided important tools of war and a visible measure of the technological capabilities of the nation.

After 1945, new goals were evident in the government policies toward automobiles. Official policies were increasingly oriented toward regional development, price stabilization, and exports, for example. By the late 1960s, the challenge to the European industry was not from the technology and marketing skills of the Americans; the Europeans had mastered these skills and had even moved ahead of the Americans in certain areas. The growing threat was rather imports of automobiles and parts from low-wage countries. The traditional government tools for dealing with foreign challenges had been weakened by the lowering of trade barriers in Europe. New policies were tried in some cases in the postwar period. However, by the early 1970s it began to be evident that the idea

Louis T. Wells, Jr., is an Associate Professor at the Harvard Business School, Boston, Massachusetts. The research for this paper was financed by the Harvard Center for International Affairs, through a grant from the Thyssen Foundation, and by the Harvard Business School Division of Research. Professor Wells is grateful to Howard Kailes for his assistance in the library search.

of a national automobile industry in the advanced countries was becoming illusory. The internationalization of the original national champions, especially their growing business in the U.S. market, was serving as a brake on the actions of any nation. The major European automobile firms were no longer supportive of protectionist attitudes or very sensitive to the national policies of the governments that had nurtured them through their childhood. Their interests were multinational, like those of the firms against which they had originally done battle.

The internationalization of the industry by 1973 was largely the product of the policies and processes of the past. To understand the development of the relationships between European governments and their automobile industries, therefore, one must turn the calendar back well before World War II, back to the time when it appeared that the challenge to the automobile industry in most of Europe might be coming from Germany rather than from the United States.

Mass Methods over German Ingenuity

Although interest in self-propelled road vehicles existed in several countries of Europe as early as the eighteenth century, the credit for the first commercial automobiles must certainly go to the Germans. The automobiles of Benz and of Daimler appeared on the road in 1886 and 1888. Commercial production followed almost immediately, and Benz and Daimler soon had subsidiaries and licensees in the major world markets.[1] Peugeot, as well as Panhard and Levassor, early French manufacturers, were licensees of Daimler. Benz products were also among the earliest cars in Britain. In 1893, the Daimler Motor Syndicate, Ltd., was organized in England, eventually to become independent of its German ties.

In the smaller European markets, the German strength was also evident. In 1899, Daimler established an Austrian assembly plant, which survived until 1935 and was a forerunner of Steyr-Daimler-Puch, A. G., the current Austrian producer. Benz was also active in Austria, having licensed a firm which was the forerunner of the present-day Czechoslovakian "Tatra" factory. In fact, of the countries that were to become major European manufacturers, only the Italian industry was not to be strongly influenced in its early development by the Germans. There, the influence was only very indirect. The German products served as a stimulus and as models to the founders of Fiat.[2]

The Germans even invaded the U.S. market. In 1888, the Daimler Motor Company was founded in New York. The principal American partner was Steinway, of piano fame. The company imported Daimler cars and the automobiles of Panhard and Levassor to America. Then it brought out the "American Mercedes," which was 25 percent cheaper than the imported version. In 1913, after a fire, the U.S. plant was closed. The Mercedes plant, Rolls Royce's venture in Springfield, Massachusetts, and a Fiat factory in Poughkeepsie, New York, were to be perhaps the only foreign-owned automobile plants in the United States for a number of decades.[3] Not until the late 1950s were the European firms seriously to renew their interest in the construction of plants in the United States.

Soon after the new century began, it was the turn of the Americans. Although American innovation and influence had begun a bit earlier, the American strength came when, in the words of a Daimler Benz history, "the automobile market had split into two parts: on one side, the inexpensive vehicle, produced by the new mass production techniques, and on the other side, the high-quality level, high-performance car." In response to the large market that existed in America for inexpensive vehicles, the American firms developed their special kind of automobiles and marketing skills. By 1907, the United States had twelve times as many automobiles as did Germany.[4] No European manufacturer found a potential market of the scale that American manufacturers found. By the time the European markets were large enough to support a home industry that could cheaply manufacture cars for the masses, the U.S. lead was a difficult one to overcome. It was to be the goal of much of the government policy toward the automobile industry to assure that European firms could survive against this lead.

The U.S. innovations were numerous. For example, in 1911 came the first successful electric starter from America, from a market "where the driver-owner dominated—in contrast to Europe where the chauffeur was usual."[5] But it was Ford's assembly line and marketing techniques that were to lay the solid foundation on which the American challenge was built.

German domination was doomed as the cheap car became the important product in world markets. The German manufacturers concentrated on luxury cars, since the German middle class was not large enough to support the scale needed for the innovation and manufacture of an inexpensive automobile. The American Mercedes still sold for $7500 when the mass-produced American cars were being sold for under $500. Although the German domination would almost certainly have ended in any case, the First World War severely crippled the industry. Germany did not become a major factor in the world markets again until the 1950s, when its comeback was launched on the basis of the Volkswagen, the "People's Car" that had been started by the German state in the 1930s.

Policies for Protection

In every country, the automobile industry has been very dependent on government policies. The demand for automobiles has been greatly influenced by expenditures on highway construction, the taxation of vehicles and fuel, and policies influencing consumer credit. Though policies of these sorts ordinarily do not distinguish between automobiles manufactured locally and those made abroad, or between locally owned producers and foreign-owned plants in the country, the history of the industry demonstrates that they can be adapted to the purpose if necessary. The threat to the survival of a local automobile industry that was posed by the American products led to policies in Europe that were designed to discriminate between locally owned plants and those of foreigners.

National prestige and military strength both played a part in motivating the Europeans to protect their automobile firms in the early days of the industry.[6] During World War I, firms such as Renault, Citroën, and Fiat proved their worth as builders of tanks, trucks, and aircraft engines. In the interwar period, import restrictions of the prewar period were generally retained and strengthened.

American firms soon began to consider building plants in Europe to bypass the import barriers. Ford, which had already established assembly operations in the United Kingdom in 1911 and in France in 1913, set up a plant in Germany in 1926, though the company was rebuffed by Italy in 1929. The Europeans responded by developing a system of taxes that discriminated against the kind of cars the Americans were best at building. Gradually, the Americans adapted their European cars to the requirements of taxes, as well as to the roads of Europe. In some instances, American models were simply equipped with a smaller engine. In other cases, the U.S. firms applied American production and marketing methods to a European automobile, often a model that they had obtained by purchasing a European manufacturer.[7] In response to the American imports and investment, each country followed its own distinctive style.

The British reaction to the American challenge was slow in coming and somewhat muted in form. It was 1915 before the British automobile industry received tariff protection. By 1919, the British Board of Trade calculated the prevailing protection from duties and differential taxes to be 88 percent of the value of an imported car.[8] The high protection fostered a strong domestic industry, capable of showing its strength even in the international markets. For example, Austin, a British pioneer in the market for inexpensive automobiles, soon extended its overseas activities through licensing arrangements in the United States and in Germany.

The policy of protection against imports also led to an increase in U.S. investment, as Ford expanded and Chevrolet assembled its U.S. models in Britain and acquired Vauxhall in 1925. The British were characteristically slow to react. Indeed, the government did not show strong concern about U.S. investment in the industry until 1966, when Chrysler began its attempt to take over Rootes.

While the British probably represented one extreme in business-government relations in the automobile industry, that of comparatively little interference and almost total reliance on general legislation and open discussion, the Italian industry probably represents the other extreme. Government policy was generally ad hoc and directed to specific enterprises. In fact, it is difficult to determine, in much of the history of Italian automobile policy, whether the government was responsive to a perceived national interest, or whether the policies were simply responses to the requests of the leading automobile manufacturer.

There is no other European country in which one automobile firm has been so dominant as Fiat has been in Italy. Minor firms have served special segments of the Italian market, but not even the state-owned Alfa Romeo had seriously managed to challenge the dominance of Fiat up to the early 1970s.

Fiat was founded in 1899, as the Fabbrica Italiana Automobili Torino. It proved its importance to the country in the manufacture of submarines, airplanes, machine guns, and other weapons in various wars. By 1922, the firm had become the country's largest automobile producer. And in 1923, Giovanni Agnelli, Fiat's chairman and managing director, was nominated by Mussolini for lifetime membership in Italy's Senate.[9]

The Italian market was tightly guarded against outside competition. After World War I, duties on imported cars ranged between 122 percent and 212 percent. The high duties on parts finally drove out even the few European firms, such as Citroën, which had been tolerated with their small assembly operations in Italy. The sanctions imposed on Italy by the League of Nations after the Ethiopian War apparently encouraged Mussolini further in his objective of building Italy's economic independence.[10]

The growth of the Italian market led American firms to consider setting up plants in Italy as a way around the high tariffs. In 1929, Ford purchased land at Livorno, to build an assembly plant. In response, Fiat's Giovanni Agnelli protested directly to Mussolini, who suggested to Ford that they reach an agreement with Fiat. Within a few months, a royal decree was issued requiring government permission for the establishment of foreign-owned assembly plants. Mussolini said that "it was not the desire of the Italian Government to permit any big volume of imported automobiles, but rather to foster a 100 percent Italian manufacture thereof."[11] After a number of unsuccessful efforts to purchase an Italian automobile firm again in the 1960s, Ford finally acquired a tiny toehold in Italy in the 1970s.

Though the Italian government had acquired an automobile firm, Alfa Romeo, in the early 1930s as the by-product of an action to save firms from bankruptcy, its national champion was privately owned Fiat. Not until regional development policies became an important goal of the government in the post-World War II period was Alfa elevated to prominence as an important instrument of government policy.

While the British government was comparatively unprotective of its industry and the Italian government very protective, French policies toward the automobile industry were subtle and flexible. Subject perhaps to an overriding objective of retaining a major French-owned industry, even American investment could be tolerated if the investment brought substantial benefits. In fact, the most serious dispute between government and industry seems to have been with a French-owned firm, Renault. When the government was anxious to gain control of key industries immediately after World War II, it nationalized Renault, not a foreign firm, on the ground that it was a Nazi collaborator. The company's refusal throughout the 1920s and 1930s to cooperate with the government in the typically close relationship expected of a French firm was probably as important as any collaboration with the enemy in the decision for nationalization.[12]

Like Italy, the French government imposed high tariffs on imported cars and constructed a tax system that discriminated against American automobiles. In addition, the French maintained a quota on imported cars until 1959. The three firms that were to dominate the French automobile industry, Renault, Peugeot, and Citroën, all got their start before 1920. Peugeot and Citroën were particularly innovative in the production of light cars behind the protective tariffs. However, the price remained high by American standards. In 1919, when production by Citroën had reached one hundred cars daily, a small car cost in the neighborhood of $1000. At that time, the Ford Model T was selling for less than $500 in the United States.[13]

When foreign investment appeared in France, it met with a mixed reception. The investment of Ford in 1913 and the establishment of assembly operations by Fiat in 1934 were not resisted by the French. General Motors, however, did encounter resistance in 1919 when its attempt to take a half-interest in Citroën was opposed by the French government.[14]

It was 1963 before the Americans really came to France in force. Ford's early efforts had petered out, and its last foothold, a share with Fiat in Simca, was sold to Chrysler in 1958. The attempt of Chrysler to increase its holding in Simca in 1963 was to provide one of the first major tests of French protective policy after the Common Market was formed.

The Second World War brought not only the nationalization of Renault but also the end of another famous, but small, private French automobile manufacturer, Bugatti. This firm had contributed much to the artistic image of French automobiles. However, the French automobile industry in the postwar period was to be built not on art but on inexpensive mass-produced cars. And Renault, as a state-owned firm, was to play a major role in this direction.

German policy toward the automobile industry has varied from neglect to strong intervention, according to the prevailing philosophy of the times. In the period before World War I, the industry was strong and needed no support. Such a role as the government played, including relatively large purchases of vehicles for the well-developed German post transportation system, was probably not designed as an explicit tool of support.

After the virtual destruction of the industry during the First World War, the Weimar Republic seemed to show little interest in its restoration. In fact, the government probably had few tools and little freedom to nurture the industry even if it desired to do so. The German market was open to imports. Cars came first from Austria and Italy, then from the United States. Horch, a German manufacturer, commented on the American invasion: "But bad it was for us when in 1923–24 the American car came to Germany."[15] By 1925, American cars had supposedly flooded the market.

During the 1920s, most of the German automobile firms faced one crisis after the other. In 1925, for example, Audi was in financial trouble. Despite a strong appeal for government help, no help was forthcoming. Only occasional assistance to the industry came through such support as a research contract of 50,000 marks (U.S. $12,000) lent by the Reichsverkehrsministerium for work on light metal cylinders.[16]

The German industry tried without great success to stem the inflow of inexpensive American automobiles. A number of manufacturers attempted to produce light, cheap cars in Germany, but the prices remained at something like twice those of an equivalent imported U.S. car, after payment of tax. In 1927, the tariff was increased.[17] In the end, however, the German firms felt forced to merge. In 1932, Audi, Horch, DKW, and eventually Wanderer were reconstituted into the Auto-Union.

Meanwhile, the Americans had begun to manufacture in Germany. Ford established an assembly plant in Berlin in 1926 and a factory in Cologne in 1931. General Motors acquired the ailing Opel in 1929. Even Fiat moved into the German market with the purchase of a

German firm in 1928. None of these moves appears to have generated government opposition. In fact, Ford was welcomed with the claim that the industry "need[s] some fresh air."[18]

From an era of limited government interest, the period of the 1930s represents a sharp reversal. The automobile industry, symbol of technological competence in that era, became a tool for political ends and for building the country's image abroad, as well as for developing the nation's military capabilities. In 1937, Hitler stated his policy clearly: "It is my irrevocable decision to make the German automobile industry one of our greatest industries, independent of the insecurity of international importations, and place it on a solid and sure basis. And let there be no doubt; so-called private business is either capable of solving this problem, or is not capable of continuing as private business."[19]

Even during the Hitler days, foreign firms were acceptable in Germany as long as they cooperated with the government. They could probably not have been the bearers of the German flag in international racing competition. Nevertheless, Opel, owned by General Motors, held 29 percent of the domestic market in 1931 and 43 percent by 1935. Ford had another 8 or 9 percent in the 1930s. In fact, Henry Ford was awarded the Grand Cross of the German Eagle by Hitler, and in 1939 the Ford company asked for and received an appropriation to produce and store tractors for the government.[20]

In the 1930s, German government intervention took many forms. Interchangeable parts were demanded from the industry. Exports were required and rose from about 8 percent of production in 1934 to 24 percent in 1938.[21] To build the German image abroad, the racing activities of Daimler Benz and Auto-Union were subsidized by the government for several years.

The most significant government step in this period, however, was the creation of Volkswagen through the German Workers Front. Although most private domestic manufacturers rejected the feasibility of a car priced under 1000 marks (about U.S.$400) in the German market, General Motors, through Opel, is said to have offered to build the car. And the government was apparently interested at one time in working with Ford on the manufacture of the people's car. But the decision was made that the car was not to be manufactured by a foreign firm. Ford was directed to surrender the name "Volkswagen," which it had already used on one of its show automobiles, and both the American companies were instructed to raise the prices of their 1937 low-priced models so that the state car would not face foreign competition.[22]

The Volkswagen never saw commercial production before the Second World War, but the plant did manufacture vehicles for the military during the war. After the war, the plant came into the hands of the

British forces. Since no British firm was interested in taking up production of the car, the factory was returned to the Germans in 1949.

The efforts to save German firms in the postwar years appear to have been limited to the actions of some of the German states. When BMW was in financial trouble, Bavaria intervened and acquired some shares; and Bremen tried in vain to save Borgward. The thrust of German automobile policy after the war was not protectionist, but the degree of intervention, primarily in the state-owned Volkswagen, was a subject of constant dispute between the representatives of the different ideologies in Germany. This dispute is well illustrated in the management of the Volkswagen operations in the postwar period.

The Postwar Period: New Policies and Additional Goals

From the end of World War II through most of the 1960s, European governments attached increased importance to a number of policy goals. The automobile industry was seen as an instrument to improve the balance of payments, to develop backward regions of the country, and to help in efforts to stabilize the economy. Government policies toward the industry were to be concerned not only with the survival of a national industry but also with the potential contribution of the industry to a broadly conceived concept of national welfare.

The need for protection did not disappear. Nevertheless, the significant lowering of trade barriers that began in the late 1950s greatly restricted the ability of European governments to apply the traditional protective tools. The common external tariff of the European Economic Community began at 17 percent for automobiles but later fell to 11 percent for cars and 7 percent for parts. Automobile trade within the Common Market was to be free of tariff restrictions. When imports could not be limited, restrictions on foreign investment also became counterproductive. If one EEC country restricted foreign investment, the foreign firm could set up its facilities in another Common Market country and ship into the difficult nation, unless, of course, there was a common policy toward foreign investment. The machinery to implement such a policy had not yet appeared by 1973. In the face of limits on traditional policies and the increased concern with broader objectives, governments responded with new tools in their relationship with the automobile industry. However, distinctive national styles in the application of these tools tended to persist.

The case of France illustrates both the limits of the traditional tools and the nature of the new approaches. The realization that national restrictions on foreign investments were not very useful without a European investment policy was driven home to the French in 1963. In that year, Chrysler moved to increase its ownership of Simca, France's fourth largest auto manufacturer, beyond the 25 percent that it had obtained from Ford. The move came at a particularly bad time for French sentiment; Remington had just shut down a typewriter plant, and General Motors was laying off workers at a refrigerator factory in France. The government reacted sharply to Chrysler's move, with the finance minister suggesting that the Common Market itself impose curbs on foreign investment.[23] French policy could no longer contain such investment. Nothing came of the proposed EEC regulations, and Simca fell under the control of Chrysler.

Soon the difficulty was to arise again. In 1964, de Gaulle apparently rejected General Motors' plans to put up an assembly plant in Strasbourg. An automatic transmission plant was accepted instead, and General Motors put an assembly plant in Belgium.[24]

Although the French found their ability to restrict imports and foreign investment to be more constrained than it had been in the past, the nationalized Renault provided a new tool for government policy.

The formal structure of Renault after it was nationalized gave only hints of the ability of the French government to use this enterprise to influence the development of the automobile industry.[25] The Ministry of Finance had the power to appoint the president-director general of the firm, and the Administrative Council included representatives of the various ministries. In 1973, for example, the president of the council was the Inspector General of Industry, and the ministries of Industrial Development and Science, Economy and Finance, Labor, Defense, Logistics, and Transportation were represented. The government appointed a review board, and a parliamentary commission was responsible for supervising state-owned firms.

In spite of the extensive formal rights of intervention, the government's role seems to have been exercised more in the policy area than in day-to-day management activities. Subtle, characteristically French tools have linked the firm to the national interest without involving official interference in the details of implementation. The first two chief executives, for example, were government officials with experience in national planning. The usual techniques of indicative planning were supplemented by informal elite links and were reinforced by the desire of management to avoid more government control of day-to-day operations.

With such subtle means of control, it is not always easy to point out the exact effect of government policies. Executives of the company and industry observers, however, have provided a number of illustrations.

Some executives have linked Renault's strong export push with the importance of exports to the national interest. In 1958, Renault provided 59 percent of France's automotive exports outside the franc zone.[26] Executives stress that the early exports were undertaken in spite of the fact that the home market was seen as more profitable than foreign markets and home demand could not be met. Soon, export quotas were established for all the automobile firms and domestic price controls were tied to export performance.

It has been suggested that the government induced Renault in the immediate postwar era to concentrate on models aimed at lower income groups.[27] The actions of Renault then led to reactions by other French firms. For example, Citroën responded to Renault's development of the small four-horsepower car with a two-horsepower model.

The government's influence has also been apparent in the decision as to where to locate new plants.[28] The result of pressures to move into regions with low income has been a scattering of facilities that would be unlikely to have been chosen by a privately owned business.

In addition, Renault has been credited with exercising more restraint in price increases than have the private firms.[29] And in recent years, Renault has apparently been used as a testing ground for wage settlements. The patterns resulting from Renault's labor contracts seem to have spread quickly in French industry.

Renault's profit performance has not been outstanding. Yet, the firm's management appears to have viewed the maintenance of an adequate cash flow as critical in retaining independence from government intervention on day-to-day decisions. This desire for independence has probably acted as a constraint on the firm in cutting prices, for example.

The firm has led the industry in investment, sometimes in spite of government desires. It accounted for 41 percent of the total of the four leading French automobile firms from 1947 to 1955. The large degree of state control over financial institutions insured that the investment was forthcoming, even in that uncertain period. In fact, a significant portion came from the state itself, both through direct injection and through the acceptance of what by French standards have been low dividends.[30]

Like the French, the Germans also entered the postwar period with a state-owned firm which could be used as a policy tool in influencing the development of the national automobile industry. Nevertheless, the management of Volkswagen stands in sharp contrast to that of Renault. The French were able to direct the long-run policies of Renault to conform with what the government perceived as the national interest. At the same time, the government generally avoided interference in day-to-day decisions. The German government, on the other hand, was much more erratic in its relationship with Volkswagen. With occasional exceptions, intervention was confined to petty matters. There was rarely a carefully conceived sense of the national interest in the relationship. Part of the reason was almost certainly the lack of a national planning process that generated clear national objectives, and of a consensus about the proper relationship between government and business. Accordingly, Volkswagen was frequently a victim of the conflict of ideologies on this sensitive issue.

The ideological differences are well illustrated by the program to denationalize Volkswagen that began in 1961. The idea of denationalizing Volkswagen apparently came from the Free Democratic Party (FDP), the coalition partner of Adenauer's Christian Democratic Union (CDU) in the Federal government. The CDU picked up the idea and added the notion of selling shares at special prices to low-income Germans. One difficulty with the plan was that the state of Lower Saxony claimed that it owned Volkswagen. Its strong German Socialist Party (SPD) was opposed to the transfer of the firm to private hands.[31]

To settle the dispute, the Federal government decided to let Lower Saxony have 20 percent of the shares and to keep another 20 percent under its own control. The two governments retained domination of the enterprise with their 40 percent of the equity. No other shareholders could vote more than one ten-thousandth of the outstanding shares. And no single bank could represent more than 2 percent of the shares. In 1971, the restrictions on voting were relaxed, but the government still had effective control.

During the 1950s, before the sale of shares to the public, government interference in small matters had been frequent. The controller's office questioned matters such as expenditures on rugs for executives' offices and hunting trips for important visitors to Volkswagen. After the sale of public shares, the Board of Managers began to defend itself against such incursions on what it considered to be its prerogatives. It refused to divulge more information to the government than it gave to other shareholders, appealing to the provisions of German law requiring equal treatment of stock owners. Government intervention became less frequent.

After the sale of shares to the public, Federal intervention tended to be limited to occasional negative reactions. If there was a rumor that workers might be laid off, management would receive a telephone call from government officials, for example. An open dispute occurred in 1963 when Erhardt tried unsuccessfully to persuade Volkswagen not to raise prices. Later, speeches in Parliament condemned a Volkswagen promotional scheme that publicized the "Black and Yellow Racer." Management was told that a state firm should not be promoting such racing images in German youth.

In general, under the CDU government from 1945 until 1969, the philosophy of not intervening in industry tended to be overriding. In most cases, government influence was limited to relatively minor matters. However, Federal and especially state influence seems to have been strong in the decisions as to where new plants should be located. Some executives have suggested that influence by the Federal government was the principal reason behind the decision to build a plant in 1958 in Kassel, where there was a large unemployment problem. Volkswagen received subsidies from the state government and was apparently strongly influenced by the state in its expansion in two locations in Lower Saxony.

The early 1970s, however, brought signs that government intervention would be of a somewhat different nature in the future. The increase in power of the German Socialist Party in 1969 changed the ideological balance. Although the party had given up its objective of creating a socialist state, it had no philosophical inhibitions about using its equity interest in industry for national ends. In 1971, a new Supervisory Board was elected for Volkswagen. The Federal and state governments used the opportunity to place SPD members in the positions that were reserved for government appointment. The new Supervisory Board replaced the personnel manager with an active SPD member who had industrial experience. At the same time, the chief executive officer of Volkswagen, who had been closely connected with the CDU, was replaced by another manager from within the enterprise.[32]

Meanwhile, the Ministry of Finance had commissioned a review of governmental policies regarding its holdings in industry. The Potthoff report, when it emerged, recommended that the government use its holdings in industry for social ends much more than it had in the past.[33] As of 1973, the recommendations of the Potthoff memorandum had not been acted upon. The reasons for inaction were not ideological but rather technical. The recommended holding company for the state enterprise was viewed by the Ministry of Finance as a way to escape the periodic capital injections demanded by the firms.* However, it was realized that the proposed holding company would not be strong enough to go to the public for funds. By 1973, another report had been commissioned to search for new approaches to the state enterprises.

The differences between German policies and French policies in 1973, therefore, were no longer ideological. The forces that were in control of German policy toward the automobile industry did not object to intervention. They were constrained, nonetheless, by the fact that a large portion of the shares of Volkswagen were publicly held. These shares had been widely distributed in an attempt to promote "people's capitalism." In 1973, there were some 900,000 public shareholders. Accordingly, policies that would clearly lower the profitability of Volkswagen could be expected to meet with wide-based resistance. More important, the German government did not have the planning apparatus of the French. It seemed unable to communicate even to the manage-

* See the section on second-generation public enterprise in Stuart Holland's chapter in this volume.

ment of state-owned enterprises a sense of priorities and national objectives that would guide long-term policy. The change in dominant ideology, therefore, was insufficient to lead the Germans to the French pattern.

The Italians also entered the postwar period with a state-owned automobile firm, Alfa Romeo. Like the Germans, the use of this firm for national ends was limited by the lack of a national consensus about priorities and objectives. The use of Alfa Romeo by the government was confined to the one clear objective it espoused, the development of the South of Italy. Unlike Volkswagen, Alfa Romeo was insulated from interference by government ministries in daily management through the powerful holding company, IRI, which held the firm's stock.

Alfa Romeo, originally the subsidiary of the French Darracq firm, had remained a rather small manufacturer of high-priced automobiles and racing cars. Partly as a result of a 1957 law obliging IRI to place 40 percent of its total investment in the South, plans were approved in 1968 for Alfa to manufacture 300,000 popularly priced cars per year in southern Italy. The idea of an automobile plant in the South was not new, but earlier plans had been abandoned because of the uncertainty created by the threatened imports of cars from the rest of the EEC. The Alfa project had the desired effect on the industry. The announcement of the project led Fiat to expand its investment in the South after it first opposed the government project. Pirelli followed Alfa Romeo and Fiat with the construction of a tire plant in the region.[34]

Although the Italian government was able to use Alfa Romeo successfully in its regional policy, it struggled unsuccessfully with the problem of protecting the industry from imports. In the prewar and immediate postwar period, the Italians, to keep out imports, had relied on high tariffs and on direct quotas running at about 3 percent of domestic production. Not surprisingly, only four out of every thousand cars in Italy were imports in 1957.[35] The Treaty of Rome meant that the tariff on automobiles from other EEC countries would fall to zero and that imports could not be limited by quotas. Moreover, the EEC's external tariff of 17 percent at the time was below the existing Italian rates, which ranged up to 45 percent.

As the lowering of tariff barriers in the EEC threatened to bring unwanted competition, the Italian reaction was strong. A series of harassing steps was launched to restrict imports in spite of the EEC. *La Stampa,* the newspaper Fiat had once owned, waged a campaign against foreign cars. In early 1964, a special purchase tax was instituted that supposedly was weighted heavily against imported cars, including those from other EEC countries. And two months later, regulations were changed so that automobile importers had to pay foreign exchange within 30 days of importing rather than 360 days, as previously allowed.

In 1965, foreign firms complained that they could not buy advertising time on government-owned television.

Such restrictive measures could be effective only for a limited time before pressure was applied by the other Common Market members. By the 1970s, the Italian market had been opened to cars from the rest of Europe. In 1971, imports captured more than a quarter of the new car sales in Italy. Japanese automobiles, however, remained subject to an import quota of a thousand cars per year in 1973. And the tax in Italy still increased with engine size more rapidly than in any other country in Europe, thus favoring the small Fiat engines. The attempts to keep out foreign competition to the extent possible were likely to continue. As one Italian executive put it in a private interview: "The automobile industry may no longer be at the forefront of technology, but it is the only strong industry Italy has."[36]

Although the policies of the French, Germans, and Italians toward their automobile industries were similar in style to those of the prewar period, British postwar policy appeared to represent a clean break with tradition. In the immediate postwar years, British policy toward the automobile industry was directed primarily at improving the balance of payments. Steel was rationed and was allocated according to the ability of automobile firms to meet export quotas. Ford's management complained bitterly, "They [the government officials] tell us what to do, what to make, when to make it . . . If we do not do what they want, we do not get the material." The Chancellor of the Exchequer even offered to alter the basis of taxation of cars to help exports. The "closest liaison" was to be established between the Society of Motor Manufacturers and Traders and the Board of Trade on problems with overseas sales and with the Ministry of Transport on shipping difficulties.[37] However, the rationing and quotas did not discriminate by the nationality of the firm. In fact, the U.S. companies were initially better able to export than were the British firms. But the tradition of reliance on general legislation and of avoiding discrimination among firms was beginning to crack.

The intervention of the British government in Chrysler's efforts to take over Rootes in the mid 1960s showed the new willingness to act on a case-by-case approach.[38] In 1968 this new tendency was to continue as the British government supported the merger that led to the creation of British Leyland Motors.

In 1964, the British government obtained a commitment from Chrysler that it would not attempt to gain a majority share in Rootes without government approval. In 1966, Rootes was short of cash and turned to Chrysler for help. The workers proposed that the firm be taken over by the government to prevent its falling into American hands. The government attempted to develop a plan whereby the firm could remain

British. When no practical scheme could be found, the government required of Chrysler that the majority of the directors of Rootes be British; that there be an exchange of directors with Chrysler International, S.A., Simca S.A., and Rootes; that the main Rootes plant be expanded; that exports be increased; and that the state-owned Industrial Reorganisation Corporation have a 13-percent stake in the firm. The IRC contributed £3 million (U.S. $8.4 million) and retained the right to sell its shares back to Chrysler within five years. The London *Times* labeled this "Labour's new kind of state intervention."[39]

The British government feared that more foreign takeovers would occur if the automobile industry continued to be composed of small producers. For a long time, government had called for rationalization and standardization of the industry, but in vain. Over the years, a number of mergers had occurred, but the industry remained diversified and individualistic in comparison to its foreign competitors. The drive behind the merger of British Motors Holding, itself the product of a series of mergers, and Leyland apparently came from the Minister of Technology, and it was pressed at various critical junctures by the prime minister and the chairman of the Industrial Reorganisation Corporation. This seems to have been the first automobile merger initiated by the government, although the Monopolies Commission had approved the previous mergers. The *Times* said: "Never before has a private enterprise merger been conceived with such close contact with Government, both officials and Ministers, right up to Mr. Wilson himself."[40]

Government support of the new firm, extended at birth, continued. For example, the company received a revolving credit from IRC in 1970 for the purchase of machine tools. The merger, however, did not end the government's role in the automobile industry. In 1971, the government stepped in to save Rolls Royce, which had fallen into difficulties from its aircraft operations. But the British did not acquire a state-owned automobile firm. The automobile segment of Rolls Royce was to be auctioned to the highest bidder in May 1973. Foreign bidders were welcome, but if the highest bidder should be a foreign firm, it would not be entitled to use the Rolls Royce name.

The British appeared to have modified some elements of their government-business relations by the early 1970s. Nevertheless, they retained many characteristics of the earlier style. Though the reluctance to use policies that discriminated by firm had been eroded, and though policies that discriminated by nationality of firm had been applied, the habit of keeping the relationship between business and government open to public scrutiny and debate remained.

While British policy toward the automobile industry emphasized the aggressive use of the merger technique, state-owned firms emerged as the preferred tool of government policy on the Continent. Government support of merger activities was not absent from the EEC, however. France and Germany encouraged mergers, such as the link-up of Peugeot and Renault and the acquisition of Auto-Union by Volkswagen. The Italian government appeared at least not to have objected to Fiat's acquisition of Lancia, Autobianchi, Ferrari, and other private producers, since Fiat's purchase kept them out of the hands of foreign firms.

On the Continent, a potential threat to government intervention was growing as the EEC Commission began to enforce the rules on competition in the Community. Yet when assistance to the industry took the form of government subventions, hidden or overt, the Commission's capacity to intervene was in practice fairly circumscribed. The Commission had a policy of responding only when complaints were raised by a member state and only if government support of a firm was involved. The first major case of this sort that involved automobiles or trucks seemed in the making in 1973. With the harmonization of regulations on axle weights, the French firm of Berliet was threatened with the loss of advantage that came from its comparative strength in heavy trucks. The French government announced to the Commission its intention of subsidizing Berliet if the harmonized regulations had the effect of restricting the heavy weights. Whether an issue would be made of this intervention was unclear in 1973.

The Internationalization of the Industry

Until the late 1960s, European governments appeared to have the needed tools to implement national policies in their automobile industries. State-owned firms were subject to the national will, and private firms tended to emulate the policies of the state firms. Mergers on a national scale could generate units capable of surviving.

By the early 1970s, however, the effectiveness of these tools was being eroded. Both the state-owned and the private enterprises had become international in their interests. To a great extent, overseas activities tended to be conducted independently of the policies of the government at home. Even at home, mergers that were sought by automobile firms were increasingly transnational.

Governments had made two assumptions: that the behavior of national firms would more likely be in the national interest than would that of foreign enterprises; and that the national firm would respond to national policies better than would the foreign investor. By 1973, these had both become doubtful propositions in the European automobile industry. The major concerns of the European firms were not with European government policies or with the European products of their competitors. Their major concerns were with competition from the products of low-wage countries and with the threat they posed to large sales by European firms in the North American market.

During the 1950s and 1960s, the exports of European automobile firms had grown rapidly. In addition to building up an export trade to North America that was approaching a million cars a year by 1970, European manufacturers captured a large share of the growing market in developing countries. Table 1 suggests that these European exports grew partly at the expense of U.S. automotive exports, which had been declining since 1929.

Table 1. Number of automobiles exported by the U.S. and EEC-EFTA to countries outside North America and EEC-EFTA, 1956 and 1970

Exports of	1956	1970
U.S.	103,732	28,650
EEC/EFTA	383,217	870,014

Source: Graham Bannock, *The Motor Industry* (London: Dun & Bradstreet and the Economists Advisory Group, n.d.), p. A16.

Trade within Europe also grew dramatically during this period. The lowering of trade barriers in Europe led companies to invade the automobile markets of other European countries. The increase in cross-penetration of markets is strikingly shown in Table 2.

Table 2. Percentage of automobile market in EEC countries supplied by imports from other EEC countries, 1958 and 1970

Market	1958	1970
France	1%	16%
Germany	7	25
Italy	2	28
Belgium	14	49

Sources: "Driving for Cars," *Economist*, October 7, 1972, p. 95.

To some extent, the export sales were a result of government policy. But a major portion of the export sales was accounted for by the changing shape of world demand. Small, inexpensive automobiles suited the markets of the developing countries as well as a segment of the U.S. market that was no longer supplied by U.S. manufacturers.

Success in export markets led the European firms to a vested interest in retaining the markets. In the developing countries, this meant the establishment of assembly operations and eventually manufacturing facilities, as such nations promoted policies of local production. By 1973, the firms that had been successful as exporters had moved to protect their markets in developing countries. Renault, for example, had plants in Spain, Argentina, Mexico, Morocco, Portugal, Colombia, Ivory Coast, Venezuela, Turkey, Chile, Madagascar, Algeria, Philippines, Tunisia, Malaysia, Singapore, and Trinidad. By 1972, Volkswagen's Brazilian operations and Fiat's Spanish plant had grown to the point where their output was about a quarter of the output of the parent plants in the home country.[41]

In western Europe, there had long been some investment by European firms in assembly plants in other European countries.[42] Unlike U.S. investments, these had generally not met with government resistance. The notable exception was the objection of the French government in 1968 to the efforts of Fiat to obtain a majority of the shares of Citroën, one of France's most important automobile firms. Most such investments were small and short-lived. They presented no serious threat to the domestic industry. But a few of the postwar facilities had become significant by the early 1970s. In 1973, the most important of these were probably the Volkswagen and French assembly plants in Belgium and the plants of manufacturers from the EFTA countries inside the EEC. British Leyland, before it absorbed Innocenti, had an arrangement with its Italian partner to assemble one model in Italy. Sweden's Volvo had a plant in Belgium, and the British established other assembly operations inside the EEC. However, the general pattern under the freer trade arrangements of the 1960s and 1970s was for European firms to supply other European countries from home; by 1973, for example, Fiat was closing its German assembly plant.

Indeed, European manufacturers supplied even the distant U.S. market primarily from the European home country. To be sure, there were exceptions. Volvo assembled cars in Canada for the North American market; Renault established an assembly plant in Canada, though it was to close that plant in 1973; Volkswagen went so far as to purchase land in New Jersey for a North American plant in 1957, but it decided not to proceed with the plans.[43]

In the late 1960s, it looked as though a certain degree of stability might develop in the industry. A network of intricate ties, outlined in Figure 1, was appearing among the European manufacturers, suggesting the possibility of less aggressive competition. Some of the ties reflected the need for economies of scale, generally in the distribution system. For example, Volvo and the Dutch DAF agreed to sell their noncompeting cars through a common distribution system. Nevertheless, a large number of the agreements appeared to be aimed at establishing common interests and channels for exchanging information so that each firm could be aware of the developments in other firms in the industry. The

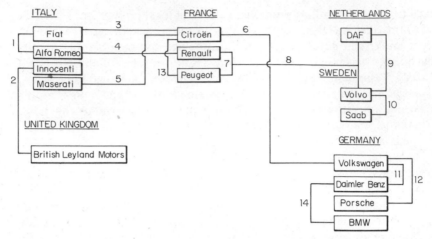

Figure 1. Some of the links among major European automobile firms, 1973[a]

1. Fiat had joint ventures with IRI, the owner of Alfa Romeo.
2. BLMC was the parent of Innocenti.
3. Fiat held 49 percent of the stock of Citroën, through a Swiss corporation.
4. Alfa assembled commercial vehicles for Renault. Some joint sales outlets existed, such as Renault Italia, S.A.
5. Citroën owned equity in Maserati.
6. Citroën had a technical agreement with NSU, a Volkswagen subsidiary. Apparently there was also a joint venture, COMOTOR.
7. A formal association existed, together with a number of ventures such as Française de Mécanique, S.A. Chausson, and Société des Transmissions Automatiques.
8. A technical collaboration agreement existed among Volvo, DAF, and Renault's Française de Mécanique.

9. Volvo held a 30-percent interest in DAF's automobile operations.
10. The firms shared a joint venture, Forss Parator.
11. The firms had a joint research group[b] and joint facilities in Spain and Indonesia.
12. The firms produced an automobile jointly.
13. The firms appeared to have a long-standing agreement to cooperate.[b]
14. The Quandt family had major shareholdings in both Daimler Benz and BMW.

[a] The links are only those that have been published, and they do not include ties through suppliers or banks.
[b] From *Industria Mondiale Nel 1971* (Turin: ANFIA, 1972).

competitive rules of the industry seemed to place less emphasis on innovation and seemed to be accepting price-leadership patterns more readily. The possibility of less intense competition among the European firms was accompanied by the apparent end of the U.S. threat to the stability of the European industry.[44] American automobiles had grown too large and too expensive for the mass market of Europe, and the European tax systems based on engine size continued to provide a special handicap for U.S. cars. To be sure, the European facilities of the U.S.

firms still provided some challenge, but it was no longer serious. The share of the American subsidiaries in the European market actually declined a little from 1964 to 1969. The Americans appeared to lose their lead in technology and marketing. In fact, the Americans were obtaining some of their technology for small cars from Europe. In addition, the production levels of the leading European firms reached such a volume that U.S. firms could no longer claim a decisive cost advantage, not even when the Americans began to merge the facilities they maintained in different European countries. Volkswagen, Fiat, Renault, Citroën, Peugeot, and British Leyland Motor Corporation all had volumes well over the mark of a half million cars per year, enough to capture the existing economies of scale.[45]

By 1973, however, the era of stability was being threatened. As equilibrium appeared to be within the grasp of the European industry, a new set of jolts was beginning to upset the balance.

The first threat was from the import of parts and automobiles into Europe from low-wage countries. The flow began with a trickle of automobile parts from developing areas which were insisting that foreign-owned automobile firms should begin to export. Mexico, Brazil, and other countries began to require that such firms export in exchange for a share of the domestic market. In 1973, Renault was using engine blocks from Spain, rubber parts from Singapore, Colombian universal joints, and Mexican wheels and upholstery in some of its French-assembled cars. Volkswagen was obtaining from Mexico some of the replacement parts for its older models still operating in the United States and Germany. In both Germany and the United States, Volkswagen was marketing Mexican "Safari's," a special model with limited demand in the advanced countries. While investments in the developing countries were growing, a number of the major automobile firms were setting up plants in eastern Europe, generally with home government support, either in the form of guarantees for credits or, in some cases, full financing on a government-to-government basis. Renault entered Romania, Yugoslavia, and Bulgaria; Fiat set up plants in Poland, where it had manufactured before World War II, as well as Yugoslavia, Russia, and Romania. Of the continentals, only the Germans lagged in entering eastern Europe, perhaps for the reasons given by one German executive in the course of a private interview: "Our détente with the eastern bloc was slow in coming, and the Russians had nothing to gain from an agreement with a state enterprise from a country in which the Communist Party was illegal."

Investments in the eastern bloc began to increase the flow of automotive imports into western Europe in the early 1970s. The arrangements typically called for the western automotive firms to receive payments for their know-how and plant in the form of components or cars. Fiat, for example, was to be paid for part of its operations in Poland in the form of engines to be incorporated in Italian models.

The imports of parts and cars from the low-wage countries faced few restrictions in Europe. Up to certain quantities, the imports from developing countries were free of duties, under EEC rules giving preferences to manufactured goods from such nations. The quotas under these rules were sufficiently high that they had not yet been approached in 1973. And the few remaining quotas on East European automobiles, such as those in Germany on Polish and Czech cars, affected an insignificant part of the trade.

By 1973, major automobile firms were beginning to establish plants in low-wage countries that were designed specifically to supply export markets. At the end of 1972, Ford announced plans to build a plant in Spain, to manufacture 240,000 vehicles per year, two thirds of which were to be exported. Peugeot and General Motors were said to be interested in setting up facilities that would export from Spain, to join Ford and Chrysler, British Leyland, Fiat, and Citroën, which already had plants there. As Ford announced its plans to export from Spain, Fiat was negotiating with the Brazilians to establish a plant of a size that would almost certainly imply plans for large exports.

As long as the imports were under the control of the major European and American firms, perhaps some degree of stability could be maintained. Efforts to retain control were evident. Where the subsidiary was owned principally by the major automobile firm, the flow of exports could be kept in bounds and the effect on prices could be minimized. Even where ownership was not sufficient, other efforts to retain control were evident in many cases. For example, Fiat had arrangements whereby Polish and Spanish models would be distributed through Fiat's dealer network in western Europe. In many cases, the models produced abroad were no longer made in the home country. These could be sold in countries where demand for the old model continued and could be offered at a discount compared with the later models in various markets. Fiat, for instance, used its Spanish Seat to supply Finland with a model that had remained popular there although it had been discontinued in Italy. In Switzerland, Fiat offered an older model Polish car at a 20 percent discount in competition with an updated Italian model. Although restricting foreign affiliates to old models allowed them to serve certain market niches, it provided a brake on the amount of competition the affiliates could give the cars from the European parent.

Although a certain amount of control could be exercised by the major manufacturers over the plants that were tied to the European and American firms, there was considerable question about the ability of the major firms to work out satisfactory arrangements quickly with the

Japanese, who began to appear in the European markets in the early 1970s. After taking a significant part of the small-car market in the United States away from the Europeans, they began to tackle those European markets where the investment required for distribution was not too great. By 1972, they had captured 16 percent of the Swiss, 10 percent of the Belgian, and 16 percent of the Norwegian markets for automobiles.[46] They had also begun to set up assembly plants on Europe's low-wage periphery, in Ireland and Portugal, and were rumored to be negotiating with East European countries for manufacturing bases.

Nonetheless, it appeared that the Japanese eventually might be talked into arrangements that would assure stability. Although the president of one major European firm was still able to say in 1973 that he knew personally the presidents of all the American and European automobile firms but had never met a top manager of a Japanese manufacturer, that situation was changing. The Japanese firms were beginning to develop ties with American firms through joint ventures, and they were establishing some loose ties with European manufacturers.

Still, possible accommodations with the Japanese promised little stability for the industry as a whole. It seemed only a matter of time before independent manufacturers in other countries would begin to export significant amounts. By 1973, independent firms in Brazil and South Africa were already offering parts for the replacement market in competition with those that were coming from the affiliates of the major automobile firms. Licensing arrangements for the manufacture of cars were spreading. Fiat, among others, had licensing arrangements in a number of countries outside eastern Europe. General Motors, in a reversal of its traditional policy, announced its willingness to license know-how for some of its products in developing countries. Each of the resulting licensees represented a potential new automobile exporter. Examples of exports from untied automobile manufacturers were beginning to appear. A former Indian licensee of Daimler Benz was exporting trucks to other developing countries. An independent Brazilian firm, using Volkswagen parts, was showing its specialty automobiles at the Geneva Automobile Show in 1973, in an attempt to capture European sales.

The era when technology seemed to be a barrier to the entry of new firms in the automobile industry appeared to have ended by the early 1970s. Though the initial investment for an automobile plant was still large, the purchase of a complete German plant by Mexican investors in 1962 indicated that it was no longer prohibitive. To be sure, the complexity of the product in the eyes of the consumer and the need for parts and service meant that the trade name and distribution system still provided some protection to the large manufacturers from the advanced countries. However, it seemed only a matter of time before even such obstacles could be overcome. The Russians, for example, were achieving some success in distributing their cars, made with Fiat's help, through their own distribution system in western Europe.

A further threat to the European industry has come from the erosion of what had been Europe's low-wage advantage over U.S. facilities. In early 1973, one European manufacturer estimated that the inflation in Europe and the realignment of currency values had resulted in U.S. labor costs that were only 35 percent higher than those in German automobile plants; and further German revaluations were yet to come.

As the wage differences were being reduced and the Japanese were increasing their sales in America at the expense of the Europeans, U.S. manufacturers brought out smaller cars designed to stem the flow of imports. Two strategies were evident. General Motors at its Lordstown plant tried to push automation as far as possible, to reduce this disadvantage of higher-cost labor in the United States. Ford tried to reduce the costs of its small car by farming out some of the parts outside the United States. In early 1973, the American subcompacts were selling at prices comparable to the small European imports.

The U.S. market looked even more insecure to the European firms because of the apparent increase in protectionist sentiment in the United States. The agreement that allowed the automotive products of factories in Canada to enter the United States generally free of duty was being threatened, and Congress and the administration seemed increasingly inclined toward import restrictions on a broad front. Whether this was a temporary phenomenon was not clear, but it added to the uncertainty facing the European automobile industry.

By the early 1970s the effect of the threats from low-wage countries and the changes that could upset the European position in the American market appeared to be leading toward further internationalization of Europe's national champions. The European firms were again seriously considering assembly operations in North America. For those firms with sufficient sales in the United States, say 200,000 cars per year (the average size of a U.S. assembly plant), a highly automated North American factory promised costs almost as low as a European facility. The penalties of somewhat more expensive U.S. labor in a plant where labor amounted to less than 30 percent of costs would be partly offset by the saving of shipping costs and savings on the 3 percent tariff. In fact, Volkswagen and some Japanese firms announced that they were investigating the possibility, and Volvo was considering an expansion of its Canadian plant. It appeared likely that a number of European and Japanese firms would attempt to secure this North American market by establishing assembly plants there.

As a result of the increasing importance of suppliers in low-wage countries and the threats to the North American market, the world automobile industry seemed to be moving toward a new structure early in the 1970s. Large manufacturers would try to hold their costs down by farming out in low-wage countries some of the 15,000 or 20,000 parts that make up an automobile. The labor-intensive parts make the most obvious candidates to be farmed out. In addition, however, manufacturers have found themselves obtaining some fairly capital-intensive parts from low-wage areas. The pressures to increase local content in the developing countries have led the firms to invest in equipment that, to be economic, must be used to manufacture more parts than can be absorbed locally. Parts such as bumpers, exported from Mexico by Volkswagen, fall into this category. In addition, low-wage countries have been proving their value as sources of assembled automobiles. In some cases the models have been specialized, such as Volkswagen's "Safari," mentioned earlier. In others, they have been models discontinued at home but popular in some markets, such as Fiat's "600." In the future, the cars obtained from sources in the low-wage countries for sale in the advanced countries and in other developing countries will probably include a few price-sensitive standard models.

By the early 1970s the prospects were that the major manufacturers would continue to assemble most of their principal models for North America and for western Europe in those countries. Possibilities of further automation of large-scale assembly operations suggested that the advantages of assembling close to the market—primarily lower transportation costs and shorter lead times—would offset the penalties of higher wage rates for all but the most standardized, price-sensitive models. In addition, the manufacturers would continue to produce technologically difficult parts in the advanced nations.

There were, however, some contingencies that could block the continued internationalization of the industry. One possible contingency, though fairly improbable, was some development that would reverse the steady march of the automobile industry toward standardized, mature products. In 1973, automobiles were beginning to be viewed by many customers primarily as a means of transportation. Novelty was directed to special segments of the market. Innovation was slight and aimed mainly at meeting the pollution and safety standards that were being implemented in North America and western Europe. One French executive described the industry as "no longer a glorious one." To be sure, the sudden success of a nontraditional engine could restore the lead of a few manufacturers. Moreover, the problems of mastering the technology of safety and pollution control could give an edge to some firms.[47] In 1973, however, it looked as if no nation would gain an overwhelming technological advantage. Two Japanese and one German manufacturer had announced that they had met the most stringent pollution standards. The United States had postponed the implementation of strict standards until its industry had more opportunity to develop the required technology. But all these seemed to be transitional developments, not likely to arrest the main trends toward standardization and internationalization.

Apart from the requirements of technology, there was a possibility that labor would act as a brake on internationalization. If the labor unions were successful in equalizing labor conditions in the producing countries for the major manufacturers, as they were attempting to do in 1973, then the move might be slowed. Some success in coordinating the activities of national unions was evident in the Ford strike in Britain in 1971; the workers of Ford's German plant refused to work overtime to supply production lost in the British plant. However, three facts made extensive success highly unlikely. First, the interests of the workers in the high-wage and low-wage countries were not the same. For example, though high wages might be attractive to Mexicans, they would hardly agree to a wage level that destroyed the incentives to produce in Mexico. Second, the automobile firms were in a position to secure their needed components in countries beyond the reach of the international labor movement. In 1973, a case in point was Spain, where the only legal union was not allowed to join the international body that attempted to coordinate the activities of national unions. Another escape route was the East European countries, whose desire for exports seemed to outweigh their concern for international workers' solidarity. Third, and perhaps ultimately most important, there was no evidence that the labor movement could enlist the support of labor in the firms that were independent of the major companies.

If continued internationalization was to be the pattern of development of Europe's national champions, there was little to suggest that their behavior would be very different from that of the U.S.-based multinational firms against which they were expected to defend the national interest. Nor were they likely to be much more subject to national control than were the U.S. firms. Like the American multinationals, the European-based automobile firms were increasingly able to operate beyond the reach of national economic policies. They could raise money outside the home country, as Fiat would do for its Brazilian plant; they could move profits to low-tax countries; and they could shift production in response to wage changes or threatened labor strife. In countries such as Germany where government intervention was on the increase, the outlook for a policy that would effectively change the path of development of the national automobile industry did not look promising. Nor did the opportunities for a concerted European-wide approach appear to be rewarding. The industry was no longer European. The survival of a major firm depended on coordinated activities that could not be responsive to European interests only.

Steel

J. E. S. Hayward

As a symbol of economic and military power, the steel industry long ago surrendered pride of place to aerospace and computers. Yet as a mainstay of the metal-fabricating industries and as a heavy generator of investment and employment, steel retained importance in the eyes of most nations as a strategic commodity in the 1970s.

The Industry's Position

For centuries, first iron and then steel had exercised a remarkable fascination not only for those who produced it but for the generality of mankind. It represented social status, political influence, and military strength. Because steel once required charcoal and charcoal required the control of large expanses of land, the steel proprietors acquired the patrician cachet of the captain of industry. The landed families who launched the firms that came to dominate the European industry sought power and influence even more than profit and found it as arms suppliers to their national governments. A French historian notes: "From the time when artillery had a decisive influence in war and until it ceased to have this influence, that is, up to the Second World War, there was a necessary interaction between the men in office and the *maître des forges*. Each needed the other. It is not always possible to say which of the two had the greater share in making the major decisions. And other industrialists will always envy this very special industry, linked by its origins with the aristocracy, privileged and protected in its activities, never fully subjected to the stern law of competition."[1]

Although by the early 1970s industrial change had deprived the steel industry of its previously undisputed preeminence, it remained close to the centers of economic and political power. The national steel industries might not be the key to industrial independence or to the commanding heights within the economy. Nevertheless, these industries had been accustomed to conducting their affairs as national units, and with the help of national governments had been insulated from the pressures of the international market.

Until a few decades ago, most steel had been sold close to the point of production owing to the high transport costs occasioned by a product

J. E. S. Hayward occupies the Chair of Political Studies at the University of Hull, Yorkshire, England.

that was bulky relative to its value. Partly because of the industry's concentration, accentuated by product specialization, there was little competition between the major firms. Moreover, where competition threatened, governments were quick to sponsor measures to limit it. The international steel cartels of the interwar years were built on restrictive arrangements within the national steel industries and were based on mutual respect of domestic markets. Steel, therefore, conformed to the industrial type characterized by large-scale capital-intensiveness and traditional technology in which the emphasis is upon cooperation between the leading firms aimed at securing stability.

One should not exaggerate the stability actually achieved after 1950. Table 1 indicates that as world steel production increased nearly three

Table 1. The distribution of world steel production, 1952 and 1972

Producing country	1952		1972	
	Thousand metric tons	Per-cent	Thousand metric tons	Per-cent
USSR	34,480	16.2%	125,700	20.0%
U.S.	84,522	39.7	120,720	19.3
Japan	6,988	3.3	96,920	15.5
Federal Germany	18,629	8.8	43,705	7.0
U.K.	16,681	7.8	25,425	4.1
France	10,867	5.1	24,054	3.8
Benelux	8,753	4.1	25,554	4.1
Italy	3,535	1.7	19,717	3.1
Others	28,309	13.3	144,995	23.1
Total	212,764	100.0%	626,790	100.0%

Source: Adapted from *La Sidérurgie française en 1972* (Paris: Chambre Syndicale de la Sidérurgie Française, 1973), p. 11.

times between 1925 an 1971, there were major shifts in the relative importance of different parts of the world as sources of supply. In 1952 the U.S. and European producers together accounted for two thirds of world production; but by 1971 their combined share was about 40 percent. Among the EEC countries, the United Kingdom alone accounted for over half the relative decline. The country which achieved the most spectacular expansion in its share of world production was Japan, while the developing countries and the USSR also substantially increased their shares.

During the postwar period, therefore, the long-time urge of European states to have and hold a steel industry was pursued in an atmosphere of rapid change. The change was reflected not only in the shift in relative shares but also by major changes in steel technology, changes that altered the optimum size and optimum location of steel plants. During these years, two near-universal convictions developed in Europe's steel industries. One was that the efficiency of steel production could be improved with size. The other was that coastal locations were more efficient than inland locations in the production of steel.

As the problem was defined, it may have seemed an ideal issue for a pan-European solution. Could not the countries of Europe, operating in the spirit of an open European market, regroup their steel industries along transnational lines, placing the new facilities where desirable on waterside locations?

The answer, as it turned out, was negative. The instinct of most countries to retain a nationally controlled steel industry prevented any serious approach to a pan-European solution. The extent and direction of adjustments to the new situation were determined largely in the context of the national political process. The result was that the steel industries became no less autarchic than in the past. Their increases in efficiency were largely constrained by what could be achieved inside each national economy.

The smallest countries of Europe were able to adjust to the new imperatives more rapidly and more effectively than the large. For better or worse, their ability to maintain a national steel industry depended on their capacity to export; and that capacity in turn could brook no loss in relative efficiency. It was the Dutch, therefore, that found the ability first to commit themselves on a large scale to a waterside location, and later were prepared to accept the threat of dilution of control that went with transnational mergers. It was the Benelux companies which were among the first to push the merger process so far as to be committed in each instance to one company: Cockerill in the case of Belgium; Hoogovens in the case of the Netherlands; and Arbed in the case of Luxembourg. Hoogovens was also among the first to anchor itself to a coastal location. And when in 1966 Hoogovens saw the advantages of a merger with foreign steelmakers, it ventured into the ambiguities of a transnational merger. By 1972, Hoogovens was inextricably tied together with the German firm of Hoesch.[2]

Italy, too, was able to manage a response to the modern imperatives of steelmaking that seemed relevant and constructive. In her case, it was not the discipline of international competition, however, that was the compelling force. Italy was fortunate in the convergence of several national factors: the lack of a well-developed steel industry prior to World War II; and the fact that her modern steel complex was developed under IRI, in the flush of that institution's most creative period. The economic desirability of a seaside location could be said, despite major reservations, to coincide with the social aim of developing the South;[3] the economic desirability of scale in steel production was consistent with the fact that development was in the hands of a single entrepreneur, IRI's Finsider.

In the discussion of British, French, and German policies dealt with below, it will be apparent that all of these same tendencies were to be found in each of these countries. But the long national legacy of steel-making, coupled with unique national economic and political conditions in each of these countries, generated a slower and more qualified response. The national modifications and adaptations proved sufficiently important to generate quite separate national programs rather than a European program. The case afforded clear evidence of the great residual national power in postwar Europe of activities that had their roots in the past.

Britain: from Industrial Self-Government to Public Ownership

By 1971, Britain's problems as a world steelmaker were overwhelmingly evident, as the figures in Table 1 attest. Those problems had been evident long before the war, however. An economy of little mills, badly located, was handicapped in maintaining its place against its competitors in international markets.

Britain's earliest responses to this problem reflected some deep national preferences. A Conservative-dominated national government did not wish to participate directly in industrial planning. To promote rationalization through industrial self-regulation, the government urged the establishment of an institution which in 1934 came into existence as the British Iron and Steel Federation (BISF). The federation did little about modernizing Britain's industry, but it played an active role in negotiating market-sharing agreements with its foreign competitors. Industrial development remained piecemeal and incremental, the sum of the separate policies of particular firms. The political influence of steel industrialists ensured that public regulation worked to their private benefit.

After the Second World War, the same balance of forces prevailed. The BISF's Five Year "plan," issued in 1946, represented a hodge-podge of responses to short-term pressures, rather than a planned reallocation of resources. This triumph of the "irresistible forces of inertia" was made possible by the fact that governments were prepared to give their blessing to a piecemeal apology for a plan as being "in the national interest."[4]

The subsequent battle over steel nationalization in the late 1940s and early 1950s seems bizarre in retrospect. The Labour party's case for nationalization was undermined from the start. It did not challenge the steel industry's past performance, it approved of the industry's development plan, and it expressed its confidence that the industry would do what the government required. The weakness of the BISF and Conservative party in the struggle was that they had long since abandoned traditional market forces for at least the semblance of public control. Their proposal to restore "competitive conditions under free enterprise" was based upon the permissive premise that "in the Government's eyes all the practices established in the steel industry under the Federation could be accommodated within their concept of 'competitive conditions.' "[5]

Nationalization in 1951 and denationalization in 1953 changed little. An Iron and Steel Board was established essentially to fix maximum prices and review the industry's development plans. The head of that board, Sir Robert Shone, had been economic director of BISF and was destined to be the first director of the National Economic Development Office (NEDO) a decade later. Meanwhile, however, operating in the early 1950s, he pioneered Britain's first serious medium-term planning exercise. The board's Second Development Report was based on a forecast of British industrial production growth from 1954 to 1962, which provided the foundation for estimates of higher British steel consumption in 1962.

Shone's work on steel in the 1950s led to very little. Britain had neither the apparatus nor the inclination to turn statistical exercises of this sort into tangible action. The capacity for integrated action in the steel industry in Britain was hardly changed when a Labour government again nationalized the industry in 1967.

The 1967 renationalization of steel had been heralded in 1965 by a White Paper setting out the case. It recalled the disastrous interference by the Macmillan government in 1958, which had rejected the Iron and Steel Board's advice at the time to site a new strip mill in South Wales, to be part of a surviving nationalized enterprise. Instead, motivated largely by regional employment problems, the project had been split into two, a sure recipe for inefficiency. The revised project also had involved making a substantial loan on privileged terms to a private firm.

The financing of very large steel works, claimed the 1965 White Paper, required public ownership. After all, the Labour government pointed out, the board could not insist on schemes which individual companies for commercial reasons were unwilling to undertake. Furthermore, stated the White Paper, "there are difficulties in raising private funds for projects of this sort, which take many years to complete and which, when completed, have to go through a long commissioning period before they can earn a return on capital sufficient to attract private enterprise." The *coup de grâce* was administered by recalling that whereas the 1953 Iron and Steel Act had provided for competition as a national policy, the industry had generally observed as actual selling prices the maximum prices fixed by the Iron and Steel Board, a practice which had been declared by the Restrictive Practices Court in 1964 to be contrary to the public interest. Moreover, the board had defended these agreements before the court, "acting quite openly as a cartel office for the industry." In the July 1966 debate on the Iron and Steel Bill, the Labour Minister of Power asserted that under the aegis of the board, the industry "had neither the stimulus of effective competition nor the advantage of positive central policy formation. It has had the worst of both worlds."[6]

The 1967 Nationalization Act covered the fourteen largest steel companies. These firms, together with their nearly two hundred subsidiaries, owned all twenty integrated steel works in Britain and 60 percent of Britain's iron ore resources; they employed 70 percent of the industry's manpower; and they produced over 90 percent of Britain's crude steel. The BISF's central trading services, research association, and statistical service were also nationalized. The deliberate avoidance of a flexible holding company with management responsibilities on the lines of Italy's IRI was manifest in a requirement that the publicly owned British Steel Corporation must secure ministerial authorization to acquire shares in other firms or to diversify outside the iron and steel industry. The sponsor minister's role was laid down in the legislation as giving BSC "general directions" on policy, approving its capital and research development programs, and controlling its borrowing and debt arrangements. BSC's financial objectives were to be agreed between the minister and the BSC board within the context of a basic principle: over a five-year period, public corporations should not only cover deficits on current account but should attain an appropriate level of self-financing of their capital expenditure and a specified rate of return on capital employed.

How did the relationship between "government" and "industry" work in practice after the violent emotions of two decades of controversy died down? ("Government" is used here to mean the Department of Trade and Industry and in particular its Iron and Steel Division, while "industry" means the nationally owned BSC, its chairman and board.) The BSC started by trying to stick closely to the letter of the 1967 act, which itself conformed to the immediate postwar pattern set by the Labour government. The public corporation was to be a financially autonomous institution, run on commercial lines, headed by nonpolitical appointees who, through a minister, would be ultimately responsible to Parliament for policy decisions but not subject to close governmental control over management. BSC Chairman Melchett took the view that in a manufacturing industry the preservation of managerial autonomy was especially vital and no information should be provided to the Department of Trade and Industry other than what was required by statute. He was worried that if the normal civil service relationship should develop and if informal contacts between "opposite numbers" who talked the same language were permitted, too much information would be extracted by the DTI. However, this rigorist approach led to abrasive clashes with a new breed of senior officials who pressed for full information to enable them to get to the bottom of the industry's problems.

The advent of a Conservative government in 1970 might have been expected to strengthen the arm's length, banker-customer relationship between the DTI and the BSC which Melchett had imposed. But BSC faced a financial crisis in 1971, a crisis which would have placed it close to bankruptcy if it had been a private firm. The situation gave the DTI an opportunity to change the Melchett-imposed arm's length relationship with the BSC. The coincidence of the industry's financial crisis with national economic difficulties led to greater governmental intervention than ever before.

By 1973, though the Conservative government had accordingly maintained a fairly close supervision of the nationalized steel industry, it had not done so without a certain amount of soul-searching and some ambiguity. For one thing, it had to consider whether and how to honor its 1966 pledge once again to denationalize steel. In the depressed circumstances of 1970–71, no one would have been prepared to buy back the steel firms, so that possibility could be put off. Meanwhile, private capital was allowed to participate in the marginal chemicals and construction engineering divisions of the industry.

BSC had been allowed a major victory over the Treasury on the form of its financing. BSC started, like most other nationalized industries, with all of its capital in the form of loans. However, it pressed for the right to raise funds through equity as well as loan capital, in order to be comparable with private steel firms. The government agreed to this, and £700 million (U.S.$1,680 million) of the BSC initial capital was turned into public dividend capital (PDC), on which the BSC had to pay a dividend to the government when it made a profit.[7]

Nonetheless, the public character of BSC should not be overlooked. In 1971, the DTI minister called for a "deep-seated review" of the BSC's financial situation and investment program, an exercise which was assigned to a Joint Steering Group of the DTI and the BSC. Both the BSC's short-term financial difficulties and its long-term strategy were scrutinized. The group's main task was to examine the BSC's investment program and obtain the information denied by a management which had been sheltering itself behind its "commercial judgment." Numerous signs of DTI's distrust of the BSC's judgment became apparent in the process; for instance, DTI employed a private consultant to advise the government on potential exports, and was unable to reach agreement with BSC on long-term expansion goals. Nevertheless, after further laborious discussions, a ten-year development strategy was agreed upon, involving a public outlay of some £3,000 million ($7,200 million). While less optimistic about export prospects than the BSC, the British government was impressed with the need to arrest the decline of the U.K. share in world steel production and trade.[8] Even though the cost of pursuing a strictly national steel policy was extremely high and other claims on public funds were numerous, an ailing national champion like BSC could not be left to its fate in a world in which government assistance to steel industries had been the rule.

Federal Germany: Private Control through Finance Capitalism

Germany offers still another variant in the patterns of ownership and control of Europe's national steel industries. The German case, when added to that of Britain, underlines the fact that at least until 1973 the focus in steel was mainly national; that the dichotomy of public ownership and private ownership was less important in explaining the behavior of the different national industries than were the hard objective facts of location, markets, and the search for stability; and, that the means used to assist a key national industry such as steel were a function of national history and national politics.

Germany shared with Britain and France a long-standing iron and steel tradition based upon indigenous raw materials. What was once an advantage had become a major handicap to Germany, for in an era when a coastal location was accepted as indispensable to efficiency in basic steelmaking, the raw materials of the Ruhr committed the industry to an inland location. Also like Britain and France, Germany inherited the rivalry of steel barons. Unlike those countries, however, Germany's barons were able to suppress their rivalries, relying on their investment banks and their cartel tradition to facilitate cooperation. (The apparent exception of Krupp, rescued by the banks from financial collapse in 1967, conclusively proved the rule.) Germany's cooperative patterns also differed from those of France and Britain in the sense that the government was at great pains to remain as inconspicuous as possible.

One of the means by which the Germans organized their market was through the use of the leading German banks. "The big banks," Shonfield notes, "have always seen it as their business to take an overall view of the long-term trend in any industry in which they are concerned, and then to press individual firms to conform to certain broad lines of development. They see themselves essentially as the grand strategists of the nation's industry." The banks have tried to fulfill this ambitious function by acquiring a remarkable degree of information, and they have influenced the firms through their representation on the supervisory boards of the major companies, their voting power through proxy votes, their control of the capital market, and their "almost para-statal position, as the natural and trusted ally of public authority in managing any intervention that is to be made in the private sector of the economy." In the case of the steel industry, one bank has stood out as preeminent: the Deutsche Bank has had a director or senior staff member on the Aufsichträte (supervisory boards) of almost all the largest steel companies.[9] When in 1967 it became necessary to reorganize a virtually bankrupt Krupp, Herman Abs, president of the Deutsche Bank, with important steel interests among his multifarious directorships, headed the new management.

Shonfield attributes a major role to the Deutsche Bank, in conjunction with the long-term forecasts of the German Iron and Steel Association, in bringing about the agreements between steel companies during the early 1960s to deal with the situation of oversupply and falling profits. Agreements by the two largest firms—Thyssen and Mannesmann—in 1962 and by four firms in 1964 marked a breakthrough to long-term planning of capacity and production. Such joint planning, however, was aimed at achieving some of the advantages of larger scale while maintaining the commercial identity of the individual firms. Another point of coordination was provided by the main source of investment funds for the steel industry, the largest German insurance company, the Munchener Ruckversicherung Allianz, A.G. In the early 1960s the link with the steel industry was reflected in its supervisory board, which included such leading steel barons as Friedrich Flick, Alfred Krupp, Hermann Reusch, and Hans-Gunther Sohl, the last two at that time being linked with the leadership of BDI, the Federation of German Industry.[10]

Finally, one should note that a further link between the major steel interests was provided by Ruhrkohle A.G., which in the early 1970s produced some 80 percent of German coal output and was largely owned by the steel companies, which had to shoulder its heavy losses. Ruhrkohle had collected together some very old coal-steel groups, such as Gelsenkirchener Bergwerks A.G., whose board of directors included Hermann Abs and Hans-Gunther Sohl. Dr. Sohl was in many ways the key figure of the German steel industry in the 1960s. President of the largest steel company in Germany, August Thyssen Hutte A.G. (which had largely reconstituted the prewar Vereinigte Stahlwerke), until his retirement in April 1973, Sohl was also president of Wirtschaftsvereinigung, the German Iron and Steel Association, and president of BDI.

Thyssen, which ranked among the largest companies of Europe, produced over a quarter of its turnover for export. It was natural, therefore, that Sohl should play a leading part in the creation in 1967 of the International Iron and Steel Institute, of which he became the first chairman. In his inaugural address he proclaimed: "We do not want State interference which subjects our industry to extraneous influences, i.e., we do not want to be the spoiled darling nor the whipping boy of politics. We hope that the time when prices and wages of our industry were frequently considered a political factor or played up as such, belongs to the past."[11] This affirmation was not altogether consistent with Sohl's own role in earlier years, when his influence in the then-ruling Christian Democratic Union party had sometimes been used to protect the steel industry's interests. But as an ideological affirmation, it had a certain value.

Although not so exclusive a dynasty as Krupp, the Thyssen family was more successful in retaining control of its company. Nearly a quarter of the shares were owned directly through a holding company and a further 11 percent by the Thyssen Foundation, the rest being dispersed among 110,000 shareholders. Though tempted to develop some interests in a coastal location, Thyssen put off any direct steps to that end until 1973, when the company did take a small interest in the de Wendel–Sidelor–Usinor plant at Fos in France. It also merged its steel pipe interests with Mannesmann, Germany's second largest steel company, and in 1973 took over Rheinstahl, Germany's largest steel company. Since Rheinstahl was highly diversified in the metal-using industry, that merger enabled Thyssen to attain a certain measure of vertical integration.

Although it was the banks that organized the actual mergers of the Thyssen dynasty, the German government approved the process to a point at which few companies were left to be swallowed. Indeed, the process of merger went so far that the only nationalized firm in the German steel industry, Salzgitter A.G., was allowed to develop a strong organic tie to Thyssen. Salzgitter, through an important 1970 merger of its own, became Germany's fifth largest company. It too was a very diversified and vertically integrated company, owning, for example, the country's largest shipbuilding firm. The shipbuilding firm in turn concluded a far-reaching cooperation agreement with a shipyard firm whose majority shareholder was Thyssen.[12]

Among the steel interests transformed in the 1960s were those of the venerable house of Krupp. The fate of Krupp exemplified the demise of the traditional steel masters. Friedrich Krupp, Germany's third largest steel producer, ruled an immense and diversified empire of eighty companies in 1968, supplying about 3,500 products or services ranging from food to fighter aircraft. Far from taking the opportunity in the postwar era to switch out of steel—an unthinkable disloyalty for a steel dynast— Krupp secured Adenauer's help in escaping from the Allies' requirement that his firm divest itself of all its steel holdings. Playing off national governments and the High Authority of the European Coal and Steel Community, he managed to avoid either the dismemberment or the sale of his steel interests; instead, by the early 1960s, he had managed to double his steelmaking capacity over prewar levels. The centuries-old alliance with government enabled the Krupp company to lean heavily on official financial aid and led it to be dubbed Germany's "most favored firm."[13]

Nevertheless, Krupp finally fell on bad times. In an effort to win markets in the Soviet Union and East European countries in the middle 1960s, he offered excessively generous credit terms. Saddled by an unexpected recession and the loss of some important tax exemptions, he faced an acute credit squeeze. When the banks would no longer provide further credit, Krupp was compelled by the government to convert his sole proprietorship into a public company over which the family would cease to have control. To be sure, the government left it to the banks to reorganize the firm, with Herman Abs—a close personal friend of Krupp—as chairman. Nonetheless, the price of survival was the substitution of modern managerialism for preindustrial paternalism.[14]

Reluctance in Germany to involve the government too closely in industrial planning meant that the steel industrial association was left to make its own production forecasts and to coordinate investment plans. After 1953, the German steel industry made medium-term forecasts of production capacity, on the basis of current investment plans. This was matched by an estimate of future demand for various steel products. The exercise was conducted "very cautiously, almost clandestinely," but it "certainly played a part in encouraging some of the major steel companies to embark on joint long-term supply arrangements for particular products, in a conscious effort to avoid the creation of surplus capacity in the industry *as a whole* some years hence . . . The general point is that German *Verbände* have traditionally seen themselves as performing an important public role, as guardians of the long-term interests of the nation's industries, as they continue to do so."[15] As in France, because private ownership has been the rule, close links between investment banks and the major steel firms have been essential to mobilize the substantial investment capital required. But a crucial difference is that whereas steel industry planning has been part of national planning in France, no such comprehensive official framework has existed in Germany.

France: Public Control without Public Ownership

The year 1966 was one in which the governments of Britain, Germany, and France were all taking a strong interest in the future of their respective national steel industries. In Britain, the government was renationalizing most of its steel industry. In Germany, key parts of the industry were changing hands. In France the government and the steel industry were signing a Steel Convention to provide the private owners with the means of modernizing on exceptionally privileged terms.

At the same time, however, French steel was also being singled out for especially stringent control. The government took a hand in the transactions of the industry both as client and supplier of the transport industry and as a heavy user of coal. In addition, the government exercised direct control over steel prices (which, by the way, represented a systematic violation of the ECSC treaty).[16] The government, acting both directly and through the nationalized industries, had so firm a grip on the industry that permanent negotiations were necessary with the Ministries of Industrial Development and of Finance.

With investment funds and prices controlled by government, the question of profitability in the steel industry was deprived of much of its ordinary meaning.[17] However, the fact that the steel industry was privately owned meant that the government's objectives had to be sought by a difficult process of negotiation, owing to the government's unwillingness (for ideological and political reasons) to threaten outright nationalization. The distinction between a private and a public corporation therefore remained relevant.

Government encouragement of steel mergers was part of an explicit industrial policy. The objective, as stated in the Fifth Plan, was the creation of one or two firms of international scale in most industries, with steel being explicitly singled out. By 1973 the prospect of a duopoly and even eventually a monopoly in France was apparent, as is indicated in Figure 1. The trend to concentration, however, did not guarantee the achievement of larger production units. In keeping with various French precedents, combinations in France's steel industry were achieved by horizontal rather than vertical integration, accentuating the industry's "closed" and introverted character. Concentration took a financial rather than an industrial form, leading to the creation of larger holding companies but not necessarily to bigger production units. This process was facilitated by the fact that all the major and even some of the smaller steel companies were linked with investment banks. A prime motivation in the strategic choices of the French steel industry was the preservation of some measure of family control. This was imperiled by any form of merger, but much more by mergers of physical facilities than by financial mergers alone. Accordingly, hierarchies of holding companies and joint subsidiaries were created among the producing firms. These, together with a multiplicity of bilateral agreements sharing out markets and sources of supply, were staging points in the process of eliminating competition.[18]

The steel industry was involved in the French planning process from its very inception; its character as a basic capital-intensive industry gave it a central position in the first postwar plan. Unlike the directors of less

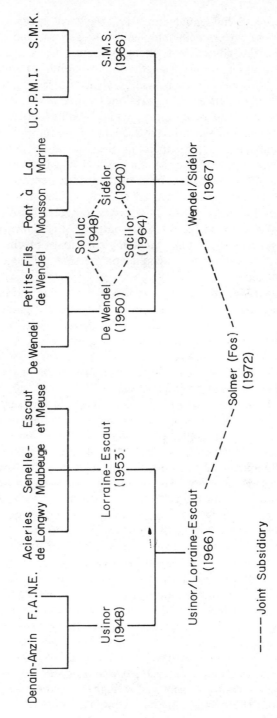

Figure 1. French Steel: The Transition From Oligopoly to Duopoly

vital and influential industries, the steel magnates had little cause to oppose government intervention in general and planning in particular. Like the government, the major steel firms wanted to dominate and control market forces rather than submit to them. Moreover, with a latent threat of nationalization always in the picture, the steel firms had a strong motive for cooperation. Desperately in need of funds for reconstruction and modernization and heavily dependent upon government for help in this task, the leaders of the steel industry expressed their willingness to participate in the indicative and consultative type of planning which Jean Monnet established in 1946. They were rewarded with the largest share of investment funds secured by any private industry. Public money financed a third of their investment program.[19] The steel industry, in fact, received especially favorable treatment, not provided for in the plan. In contrast, other industries that were entitled to priority in the plan, including chemicals, mechanical engineering, civil electronics and food, could not get that privileged treatment in actual practice.

Planning in the steel sector was particular and detailed. As a planning official declared: "The number of firms and plants being few, it is possible to have real planning, to question each firm and each plant and work out a consistent general program which is then broken down into particular programs . . . Steel is a small world; the competitors broadly know each other's position, and as a result we can achieve a coherent set of projects."[20]

Because the Chambre Syndicale de la Sidérurgie Française (CSSF) had most of the data required by the planners to undertake any serious analyses, the government's Steel Commission leaned heavily on the trade association, which returned the compliment by acting as a rationalizing and modernizing agent, explaining and securing support for government policy. The dependence of the government's planning commissariat upon the CSSF for its information was a reflection of relative bargaining power as well as a matter of convenience. For their part, the firms were undoubtedly more willing to communicate information to the Steel Commission through the CSSF. The existence of exclusive family firms, mutually suspicious and reluctant to collaborate, necessitated a powerful intermediary to reconcile internecine conflicts and act as spokesman for the industry. In the late 1960s and early 1970s, that role was personified by CSSF's President Jacques Ferry. As long as the firms were financially dependent upon the government, his position was secure.[21]

The tendency to develop detailed arrangements between trade associations and governments, partaking of some of the characteristics of an explicit contract, achieved a high in elaborateness in the Fifth Plan, 1966–1970. "In a market economy, guided by a plan," says the Plan document, "the prime responsibility for industrial development belongs to the industrialists. On their initiative depends the success of the policy whose objectives and the means of attaining them have been explained. But these initiatives should be worked out in conjunction with trade associations and the state."[22] The result of this collaboration was the 1966 Steel Agreement between the CSSF and the government.

Michel Debré, Finance Minister at the time of its conclusion, described the Steel Agreement as "the result of more than two years' thinking and work in the Ministry of Industry and Planning Commissariat as well as the Treasury Division, not to mention the steel industrialists themselves, under the arbitration of M. Jacques Ferry." How did Ferry, CSSF president and leading protagonist from the industry, present the agreement which he had done so much to make possible? Ferry stressed the coherence and continuity of the association derived from its contractual character, in contrast to piecemeal state intervention. In terms which had a corporatist overtone, he declared: "the *plan professionnel* is imperative. But instead of the obligation to undertake precise investment projects in accordance with decisions of an outside authority, the plan is built up from the schemes of each of these firms, compared, harmonized, and placed in an order of priority, subject to a framework and procedures imposed on the industry by itself."[23] The 1966 Steel Agreement led to a rapid expansion in production, higher productivity, and the attainment of a duopoly in crude steel (as shown in Figure 1). Numerous joint investment projects as well as rationalization and specialization agreements were concluded, enabling the number of steel firms to be reduced from 82 in 1967 to 66 in 1970. The number of plants, meanwhile, declined from 118 to 99. The success of the 1966 agreement in achieving its objectives demonstrated how the French government, thanks to generous financial aid, was able to secure the concentration and modernization of the industry without public ownership because it was assisted by a powerful trade association.

The European Community and the World Market

This review of national experiences suggests that in 1973 an independent national steel industry was still regarded as vital by European governments. Each country aimed at a restructuring of its steel industry on its own and at financing the new investment in large measure out of public funds. Meanwhile, what of the European ideal?

The European Coal and Steel Community, it should be remembered, was the first of the institutions that were to make up the European Community. Illusions that the creation of ECSC would overcome national identity and bring about pan-European specialization were quickly exploded. True, the ECSC did lead indirectly to a certain amount of restructuring of the steel industry. One writer noted in the late 1950s: "The ECSC treaty sought to make competition an end in itself by eliminating the barriers to interstate commerce, by subjecting cartels and new concentrations to administrative scrutiny and by establishing common commercial rules for pricing and sales. In doing so, it made the steel firms uncertain of the conduct of their rivals. The steel firms consequently decided to strengthen their position for defensive or aggressive action." Faced by the threat of increased competition, the steel firms replied with increased combination. For its part the ECSC concentrated on trying to get the national governments and firms to accept its supervision, stressing "the surveillance of collusion rather than its prevention."[24]

In retrospect, the Coal and Steel Community also disappointed the hopes of those who expected a supranational plan to regulate the industries concerned. Of the three planning organs—the High Authority, the national governments, and the big firms—the High Authority and its successor, the EEC Commission, had the least influence upon the long-term development of Europe's coal and steel industries.[25] The failure of the supranational dynamic to shift power from national governments led to a hesitant move within the EEC from competition toward planning, but the move did not go beyond a timid and ambiguous policy of "harmonization." The results were increasing amounts of unutilized capacity as well as pressure in each country to save its own steel industry at the expense of the others. As evidence of the trend, the French government, acting under pressure from the CSSF, made a number of attempts to freeze trade in steel among the ECSC countries at the 1964 or 1965 level. In July 1966 the French Minister of Industry vetoed a High Authority proposal to replace national subsidies with Community financing along the lines of the agricultural EEC agreement.

At the same time, however, there was growing realization during the 1960s that some of the steel problems of European nations might have to be dealt with on more than a national basis. In 1967, as prices fell and surplus capacity built up, the CSSF president called for an EEC steel plan on the French model. As a step to that end, Ferry proposed immediate EEC planning to prevent "abnormal" and "anarchic" trade in steel products: "In a market which has nothing in common except its name, which is in fact, after fourteen years of life, only a free trade area, where certain salutary treaty rules are no longer applied, the current brawl is only a caricature of competition." The survival of the EEC would "depend on the willingness of the members to discipline their commercial ambitions and master the disorder of their investments." Over the longer run, Ferry proposed mergers between EEC steel firms to achieve a "rapid and effective coordination through the reduction of the number of EEC [steel] decisionmakers." Ferry's vision was a worldwide organization of steel investment, production, and sales, finally banishing the scourge of "unlimited competition [which] is an absurd notion in the steel industry."[26]

The move to capture and tame the international steel market gained some support from the abrupt changes that took place in the world's iron and steel trade outside Europe. After 1968, the U.S. government from time to time pressed Japan and the ECSC countries to restrict exports to the American market. The emergence of Japan as a major exporter of steel led to restrictive countermeasures by Europe as well. While Europe continued to have a large surplus in steel trade with the United States in 1970, its adverse balance with Japan virtually counterbalanced this. In December 1971, the pressure of Japanese exports in Europe led the ECSC countries and Britain to secure a "voluntary" limitation covering the three years 1972–1974. Under this agreement (in which the European countries were represented by a delegation headed by Ferry as president of the European Steel Club) Japan's six main steel groups, with their government's approval, formed an export cartel. Ferry also headed the European delegation in tough negotiations with U.S. officials, which led the Europeans to tighten their restrictions over exports to the United States.

Table 2. European iron and steel trade with the U.S. and Japan, 1966 and 1970

(millions of U.S. dollars)

European trade	1966		1970	
	With U.S.	With Japan	With U.S.	With Japan
Exports	550	8	830	25
Imports	86	59	475	375
Trade balance	+464	−51	+355	−350

Source: Adapted from *UN Monthly Bulletin of Statistics,* April 1972, Special Table C, pp. xxxiv-v.

The growth of market restriction agreements perpetuating underutilized, unprofitable capacity indicated the danger of a coordination of strategies limited mainly to the avoidance of competition. Moreover, the increased involvement of governments in the affairs of the steel industry reinforced the tendency to prevent market forces from operating. The public servants were even more likely to espouse a "national champion" approach than were the family firms that had once provided Europe's leading steel masters. The protection of one's home market from foreign intruders remained more of a reality than the creation of a European policy for steel.

Notes   Index

Notes

Enterprise and Government in Western Europe / Vernon

1. M. M. Postan, *An Economic History of Western Europe: 1945–1964* (London: Methuen, 1967), p. 191.

2. For a useful summary, see Horst Westphal, *The Effects of National Price Controls in the European Economic Community,* EEC Commission, Study no. 9, Brussels, 1970.

3. On Britain and Germany see Andrew Shonfield, *Modern Capitalism* (London: Oxford University Press, 1965), pp. 123–125, 160–165, 239–242; Postan, *An Economic History,* pp. 38–42; E. E. Hagen and S. F. T. White, *Great Britain: Quiet Revolution in Planning* (Syracuse, N.Y.: Syracuse University Press, 1966), pp. 119–123.

On France see John Sheahan, *Promotion and Control of Industry in Postwar France* (Cambridge, Mass.: Harvard University Press, 1963), p. 29; S. S. Cohen, *Modern Capitalist Planning: The French Model* (Cambridge, Mass.: Harvard University Press, 1969), pp. 73–76; Charles de Houghton, *The Company: Law, Structure and Reform in Eleven Countries* (London: Allen & Unwin, 1970), p. 117.

On Italy see Gabriel Almond and Sidney Verba, *The Civic Culture* (Princeton, N.J.: Princeton University Press, 1963), pp. 37–39, 308–310; George Katona, Burkhard Strumpel, and Ernest Zhan, *Aspirations and Affluence* (New York: McGraw Hill, 1971), pp. 29–33.

4. Any generalization regarding the German national view toward competition and concentration is bound to stir debate among scholars. For a careful analysis, see Geoffrey Denton, Murray Forsyth, and Malcolm Mac-Lennan, *Economic Planning and Policies in Britain, France and Germany* (New York: Praeger, 1968), pp. 34–79.

5. G. H. Hildebrand, *Growth and Structure in the Economy of Modern Italy* (Cambridge, Mass.: Harvard University Press, 1965), pp. 64–73, 387–391, 404–414; Joseph La Palombara, *Italy: The Politics of Planning* (Syracuse, N.Y.: Syracuse University Press, 1966), pp. 17–62; M. V. Posner and S. J. Woolf, *Italian Public Enterprise* (Cambridge, Mass.: Harvard University Press, 1967), pp. 26–40.

6. C. P. Kindleberger, "French Planning," in M. F. Millikan ed., *National Economic Planning* (New York: Columbia University Press, 1967), pp. 287–289; de Houghton, *The Company,* p. 236; Sheahan, *Promotion,* pp. 37–41; Cohen, *Modern Capitalist Planning,* pp. 72–76; MacLennan et al., *Economic Planning,* p. 103.

7. U. G. Venturini, *Monopolies and Restrictive Trade Practices in France* (Leyden: A. W. Sijthoff, 1971), pp. 339–341; Cohen, *Modern Capitalist Planning,* pp. 62, 72–76; Shonfield, *Modern Capitalism,* pp. 73–80. On the influence of ministries, see Groupe de Sociologie des Organisations, "Le Ministère de l'Industrie et son environnement," mimeographed, Paris, January 1970.

8. Kindleberger, "French Planning," pp. 284–285; Hildebrand, *Growth and Structure,* pp. 321, 377–378; Stuart Holland, ed., *The State as Entre-*

preneur (London: Weidenfeld & Nicolson, 1972), pp. 118–124, 173–187; Posner and Woolf, *Italian Public Enterprise,* pp. 68–69, 108–112.

9. OECD, *Economic Survey: France,* Paris, July 1961, pp. 5–6, 32–34; *ibid.,* July 1962, pp. 5–6, 14–15, 45–57. For typical views, see Shonfield, *Modern Capitalism,* p. 132; Venturini, *Monopolies and Restrictive Trade Practices,* pp. 328–329, 345–346.

10. Denton et al., *Economic Planning,* pp. 111–119, 160–168; Vera Lutz, *Central Planning for the Market Economy* (London: Longmans, Green, 1969), pp. 38–39.

11. La Palombara, *Italy,* pp. 103–115, 152–157. On the Dutch and Swedes: Shonfield, *Modern Capitalism,* pp. 199–220, 294. On Germany: Lutz, *Central Planning,* pp. 128, 162; Shonfield, *Modern Capitalism,* p. 290.

12. Keith Pavitt, "Technology in Europe's Future," *Research Policy I* (Brighton, Sussex: University of Sussex, Science Policy Research Unit, 1972), pp. 211–213; J.-J. Servan-Schreiber, *The American Challenge* (New York: Atheneum, 1968), pp. 62–67.

13. Romano Prodi, "Le Nouveau Cadre Economique de la concurrence en Europe," *Reflets et Perspectives,* vol. 10, no. 4 (1971), esp. pp. 236–243. Also see P. A. Blaisse, "Growing Interaction between Government and Free Enterprise," *Economie,* vol. 35, no. 11 (August 1971), pp. 505–524.

14. For an excellent retrospective view, see Great Britain, Sixth Report from the Expenditure Committee, *Public Money in the Private Sector,* vol. 1, July 1972; Hagen & White, *Great Britain,* pp. 74–75; R. E. Caves et al., *Britain's Economic Prospects* (London: Allen & Unwin, 1968), pp. 319–322, 387–388. Helmut Arndt, *Recht, Macht und Wirtschaft* (Berlin: Duncker & Humblot, 1968), pp. 82, 84; OECD, *The Industrial Policies of 14 Member Countries,* Paris, 1971, pp. 27–37.

15. Sheahan, *Promotion,* pp. 62–65, 85–88; by the same author, "Problems and Possibilities of Industrial Price Control: Postwar French Experience," *American Economic Review,* vol. 51, no. 3 (June 1961), pp. 345–348; de Houghton, *The Company,* p. 104.

16. See, for instance, "What Sir Frank Is Up To," *The Economist,* January 18, 1969, p. 55; and "Computers: Buy British, Sell American," *The Economist,* March 7, 1970, p. 63.

17. Ingo Walter, *The European Common Market* (New York: Praeger, 1967), pp. 65–75.

18. Lutz, *Central Planning,* pp. 153, 80.

19. Venturini, *Monopolies,* pp. 349–350; Rainer Hellmann, *The Challenge of U.S. Dominance of the International Corporation* (New York: Dunellen, 1970), pp. 125–135.

20. Kindleberger, "French Planning," pp. 290–291.

21. Hellmann, *The Challenge,* pp. 262–263; Shonfield, *Modern Capitalism,* pp. 180–185, 196–198.

22. D. Swann, *The Economics of the Common Market* (Harmondsworth, Middlesex: Penguin, 1970), pp. 104–113.

23. For a convenient summary of national industrial policies in the latter 1960s, see OECD, *The Industrial Policies of 14 Member Countries;* also

Commission of the European Communities, *The Effects of National Price Controls in the European Community,* Brussels, 1970, esp. pp. 159–164.

24. For an extended discussion from an authoritative source, see Pavitt, "Technology in Europe's Future," pp. 210–273; also Eric Moonman, ed., *Science and Technology in Europe* (Harmondsworth, Middlesex: Penguin, 1968), esp. pp. 8–27. For the French case, Robert Gilpin, *France in the Age of the Scientific State* (Princeton, N.J.: Princeton University Press, 1968), esp. pp. 377–459.

25. For a bitter indictment of the French decision to go it alone in developing an extraterrestrial launching capability and a summary of prior vacillations, see "Les Mauvaises Affaires de la France," *L'Express,* November 20–26, 1972, pp. 22–25. The strength and persistence of this nationalistic tendency, even into the 1970s, are easy to document. As a striking illustration, see U.K. Select Committee on Science and Technology, *The Prospects for the United Kingdom Computer Industry in the 1970s,* vol. I, 1971, esp. pp. liv-lx.

26. Commission of the European Communities, *A Policy of the Community for the Promotion of Industry and Technology in the Aeronautical Sector* (the "Spinelli Report"), Brussels, July 19, 1972, p. 6.

27. For instance, see "Computers: Germans Glue Jobs," *The Economist,* October 9, 1971, p. 88. For a similar view, see Swann, *The Economics of the Common Market,* p. 155; Venturini, *Monopolies,* p. 356; F. M. Scherer, *Industrial Market Structure and Economic Performance* (Chicago: Rand McNally, 1970), p. 491.

28. For instance, "Fiat-Citroën Association Runs into Trouble," *New York Times,* November 7, 1972, p. 47.

29. For a discussion of Italy's IRI in such a role, see Holland, *The State,* p. 235.

30. For a similar conclusion, see Prodi, "Le Nouveau Cadre Economique," pp. 232–236.

31. Venturini, *Monopolies,* p. 349; Swann, *The Economics,* pp. 153–154; John Pinder and Roy Pryce, *Europe After de Gaulle* (Harmondsworth, Middlesex: Penguin, 1969), pp. 80–85. "Two's Company," *The Economist,* September 2, 1972, pp. 51–52. "Nucleaire: un quatrième américain entre dans la course en Europe," *Entreprise,* September 22, 1972, p. 89; see also A. J. Surrey and J. H. Chesshire, *The World Market for Electric Power Equipment: Rationalization and Technical Change* (Brighton, Sussex: University of Sussex Science Policy Research Unit, 1972), pp. 3–4.

32. Pavitt, "Technology in Europe's Future," pp. 239–244.

33. Surrey and Chesshire, *The World Market,* pp. 28–30, 153–154.

34. See, for example, "France: Our Very Own," *The Economist,* May 6, 1972, p. 98, an account of a new national effort by France at control over its raw material imports.

35. See my *Sovereignty at Bay* (New York: Basic Books, 1971), pp. 26–29; Zuhayr Mikdashi, *A Comparative Analysis of Selected Mineral Exporting Industries* (Vienna: Organization of the Petroleum Exporting Countries, 1971).

278 / Notes to Pages 22–28

36. "Governments Try to Mold European Mergers: The Meaning of Three Recent Cases," *Business Europe,* October 25, 1968, p. 337; "French Ruffled by British Deals," *New York Times,* November 10, 1972.

37. "Aluminum Companies are Planning to Join European Syndicate," *Japan Economic Journal,* November 23, 1971, p. 4.

38. For a seeming dissenting view in computers, see Consultative Assembly of the Council of Europe, *Report on the Computer Industry in Europe: Hardware Manufacturing,* Strasbourg, 1971.

Europe's New Public Enterprises / Holland

1. The degree of concentration of EEC public enterprise in basic industry and services can be seen from the sectoral breakdown of figures in two publications of the Centre Européen de l'Entreprise Publique: *Les Entreprises publiques dans la Communauté Economique Européenne* (Paris: Dunod, 1967), and *L'Evolution des entreprises publiques dans la Communauté Européenne au cours des dernières années* (Brussels: Editions CEEP, 1971). For the similar sectoral concentration of public enterprise in Britain, see Richard Pryke, *Public Enterprise in Practice: The British Experience of Nationalisation over Two Decades* (London: MacGibbon and Kee, 1971), Table 2.

2. See M. V. Posner and S. J. Woolf, *Italian Public Enterprise* (London: Duckworth, 1967), chap. 2; and Stuart Holland, ed., *The State as Entrepreneur* (London: Weidenfeld and Nicolson, 1972), chap. 3.

3. On page 81 of *Nationalization in France and Italy* by Mario Einaudi, Maurice Byé, and Ernesto Rossi (Ithaca: Cornell University Press, 1955), Byé draws attention to the fact that the number of commercial and industrial companies in France in which the state owned a majority of stock grew from 11 in 1935 and 31 in 1944 to 103 in 1946. For a brief summary of the Sociétés d'Economie Mixte, see also William A. Robson, "Mixed Enterprise," *National Westminster Bank Quarterly Review,* August 1972.

4. In Britain this skepticism about further extensions of public ownership found its most comprehensive expression in Anthony Crosland's, *The Future of Socialism* (London: Jonathan Cape, 1956), esp. chap. 19, "The Forms of Public Ownership."

5. The German Federal Republic was an exception in this respect, at least until the late 1950s. Andrew Shonfield shows in *Modern Capitalism* (London: Oxford University Press, 1965), that Finance Minister Schaeffer in the mid-1950s introduced what amounted to an accidental Keynesian deflationary policy by salting funds away on the simplistic assumption that the money so saved could later be spent on German rearmament. The Federal Finance Ministry became more explicitly Keynesian during the Schiller period in the 1960s.

6. The argument that public enterprise would be better able to plan its own resources than private enterprise should not be confused with the case for its utilization as a national planning instrument. It was the former policy

which partly lay behind the British nationalizations of the postwar Labour government. See H. A. Clegg, "Nationalised Industry," in G. D. N. Worswick and P. H. Ady, eds., *The British Economy 1945–1950* (London: Oxford University Press, 1952).

7. For an analysis of such difficulties in the monopolistic British public-sector coal industry, see W. G. Shepherd, *Economic Performance under Public Ownership* (New Haven: Yale University Press, 1965).

8. See Jean Bénard, "Le Marché commun et l'avenir de la planification française," *Revue économique,* September 1964; and Bela Balassa, "Whither French Planning?" *Quarterly Journal of Economics,* November 1965.

9. EEC Commission, "Les Investissements directs des pays tièrs dans la CEE," mimeographed. Brussels, 1969.

10. On the role of multinational companies in the EEC economies, see Wayland Kennet, Larry Whitty, and Stuart Holland, *Sovereignty and Multinational Companies* (London: Fabian Society, 1971).

11. Posner and Woolf, *Italian Public Enterprise.*

12. See Stuart Holland, *Regional Under-Development in a Developed Economy: The Italian Case,* vol. V (London: Regional Studies, 1971).

13. See Carlo Monotti, "Les Investissements de Westinghouse en Italie bloqués par l'Institut pour la Reconstruction Industrielle," *Le Figaro,* September 9, 1970.

14. Carlo Monotti, "L'Institut pour la reconstruction industrielle poursuit sa politique de dissuasion à l'égard des investissements étrangers," *Le Figaro,* September 15, 1970.

15. See Pierre Naville, Jean-Pierre Bardou, Philippe Brachet, and Catherine Levy, *L'Etat entrepreneur: Le cas de la Régie Renault* (Paris: Editions Anthropos, 1971), pp. 54–60.

16. Nora Report (Rapport au Comité Interministériel des Entreprises Publiques), mimeographed, Paris, April 1967, p. 5.

17. *Ibid.,* Introduction.

18. Nora report, pp. 27–43 passim.

19. *Ibid.,* pp. 126–130.

20. See also Stuart Holland, "Memorandum on European Para-Governmental Agencies," in *Public Money in the Private Sector,* Sixth Report from the Expenditure Committee, vol. III, July 1972.

21. *Programme commun de gouvernement du Parti Communiste et du Parti Socialiste* (Paris: Editions Sociales, 1972), pt. II, chaps. 2 and 5.

22. See Adrian Dicks, "Left-Wing Coalition Would Nationalise 13 Big French Companies," *Financial Times,* June 28, 1972; and Patrick Brogan, "Socialist Communist Alliance Transforms French Political Scene," *Times,* June 28, 1972.

23. Stuart Holland, *Memorandum on European Para-Governmental Agencies;* and Société Nationale d'Investissement, *Rapports Annuels,* Brussels, 1970–71 and 1971–72.

24. See also "Bundesholding VIAG," *Der Spiegel,* no. 41 (1970); and "Erst Gelbes Licht für eine Bundesholding," *Handelsblatt,* no. 157 (1970).

25. See also "Sweden Eyes Big Business," *International Management,* March 1969; and "Le Gouvernement suédois décide de réorganiser le secteur public," *Le Monde,* January 25, 1969.

26. See Industrial Reorganisation Corporation, *Report and Accounts* (London, 1968–1970).

27. Labour Party, *'Into the Seventies': Labour's Economic Strategy* (London, 1970).

Italy / Prodi

1. By the eighteenth century, the Neapolitan economists were justifying public intervention on the basis of their inferiority in production in comparison with Spain. Every period obviously has different terms of reference.

2. Italy, Ministero del Bilancio e della Programmazione Economica, "Relazione della Commissione Generale per la politica dell'Industria e dei Servizi," Programmazione, N. 3, November 1972, pp. 57–80.

3. Giorgio Ruffolo (Segretario Generale della Programmazione Economica), "Rapporto sull'esperienza di Programmazione," mimeographed (Rome: Istituto di Studi per la Programmazione Economica [ISPE], 1973), p. 129.

4. ISPE, "Programma di Promozione dell'Industria Chimica," mimeographed, ISPE Papers, Rome, 1971.

5. The survey carried out by *Vision* on the profitability of large European firms in 1971 lists only one firm in Italy among the profit leaders, IBM-Italia —obviously not a very Italian firm.

6. Belgium is the notable exception. Its strategy has been to become the geographical base of American industry in Europe.

7. This opinion is clearly illustrated by Andrew Shonfield in *Modern Capitalism* (London: Oxford University Press, 1965).

8. Paul Einzig, *The Economic Foundations of Fascism* (London: Macmillan, 1934).

9. Stuart Holland, ed., *The State as Entrepreneur—New Dimensions for Public Enterprise: The IRI Shareholding Formula* (London: Weidenfeld and Nicolson, 1972), pp. 288–293.

10. Pasquale Saraceno, *Lo stato e l'economia* (Rome: Cinque Lune, 1963), and *La produzione industriale* (Venice: Libreria Universitaria, 1967). Giuseppe Petrilli, *Lo stato imprenditore* (Bologna: Cappelli, 1967).

11. Shonfield, *Modern Capitalism,* p. 241.

12. Beginning at the end of the 1950s, strong pressure was applied in order to increase the level of public contribution to the financing of public enterprises. See M. V. Posner and S. J. Woolf, *Italian Public Enterprises* (London: Duckworth, 1967), pp. 100–120.

13. Ministero delle Partecipazioni Statali, *Relazione Programmatica sugli Enti di Gestione: Stato di Previsione per l'anno 1973,* 1972.

14. In regard to the difficulties of reconciling the objectives of public enterprise with the need for profits, *Business Week* (March 3, 1973, p. 68) reports that the chairman of ENI "is like a man who is trying to run NASA

at a profit with some responsibility for Indian Affairs and economic development, and he is working with a regulatory structure as backward as those you find in Latin America."

15. The difficulty of separating financial control (in the hands of the Treasury) from economic control and the necessity of unifying the departments in charge of industrial policy were adduced in Great Britain as reasons for resisting the proposals for the establishment of a Ministry for Public Holdings. See David Coombes, *State Enterprise: Business or Politics* (London: Allen & Unwin, 1962), pp. 86–122.

16. For a sketchy picture of credit incentives existing in Italy, see "Troppi dodici modi per finanziarsi," *Successo,* December 1972, pp. 37–38.

Germany / Küster

1. Ralf Dahrendorf, *Gesellschaft und Freiheit* (Munich: Piper & Co., 1962), p. 297.

2. Jörg Huffschmid, *Die Politik des Kapitals* (Frankfort on the Main: Suhrkamp, 1969), p. 138 (source of first quotation); Andrew Shonfield, *Modern Capitalism* (Oxford University Press, 1965), p. 240 (second quotation).

3. Alfred Müller-Armack, *Wirtschaftsordnung und Wirtschaftspolitik* (Freiburg: Rombach, 1966), pp. 293–315; *Verhandlungen des Europäischen Parlaments, Ausführliche Sitzungsberichte,* no. 21, Session Nov. 20, 1962, pp. 870–886.

4. Huffschmid, *Die Politik des Kapitals,* pp. 111–114.

5. Karl Schiller, "Zukunftsaufgaben der Industriegesellschaft," in Andrew Shonfield, *Geplanter Kapitalismus,* trans. Margaret Carroux (Cologne: Kiepenheuer & Witsch, 1968), pp. xx, xxi. (source of quotation); Karl Schiller, *Konjunkturpolitik auf dem Wege zu einer Affluent Society,* Kiel Lectures, New Series 54 (Kiel, 1968), p. 15.

6. Karl Schiller, *Preisstabilität durch globale Steuerung der Marktwirtschaft,* Lectures and Treatises of the Walter Eucken Institute, XV (Tübingen: Mohr, 1966), p. 21.

7. Horst Hinz, "Konjunktur und Herrschaft," *Konjunkturpolitik* 13 (1967), 298; Urs Jaeggi, *Macht und Herrschaft in der Bundesrepublik* (Frankfort on the Main: Fischer Bücherei, 1969), p. 27 (source of quotation).

8. Wilhelm Krelle, Johann Schunck, and Jürgen Siebke, *Uberbetriebliche Ertragsbeteiligung der Arbeitnehmer* (Tübingen: Mohr, 1968).

9. Schiller, "Zukunftsaufgaben der Industriegesellschaft," p. xxi.

10. Karl Schiller, "Wirtschaftspolitik," in *Handwörterbuch der Sozialwissenschaften,* XII (Göttingen: Vandenhoeck & Ruprecht, 1965), p. 215.

11. Shonfield, *Modern Capitalism,* p. 294.

12. For a detailed discussion see Alex Möller (ed.), *Gesetz zur Förderung der Stabilität und des Wachstums der Wirtschaft, Kommentar* (Hanover: Verlag f. Literatur und Zeitgeschehen, 1968); Klaus Stern and Paul Münch,

Gesetz zur Förderung der Stabilität und des Wachstums der Wirtschaft, Kommentar (Stuttgart: Kohlhammer, 1967).

13. K. H. Biedenkopf, "Rechtsfragen der konzertierten Aktion," *Der Betriebsberater,* 23 (1968), 1006.

14. Expert Council for the Assessment of the Overall Economic Development, *Jahresgutachten 1965–66: Stabilisierung ohne Stagnation* (Stuttgart: Kohlhammer, 1965), pp. vii, 109–122.

15. Herbert Giersch, "25 Thesen zur Stabilitätspolitik," *Handelsblatt,* January 27–28, 1967, p. 12.

16. For excellent surveys of the social aspects of the concerted action, see Josef Molsberger, "Zwischenbilanz der konzertierten Aktion," *Ordo,* 21 (1970), 167–191; H. H. Rupp, "Konzertierte Aktion und freiheitlich-rechtsstaatliche Demokratie," in Erich Hoppmann (ed.), *Konzertierte Aktion* (Frankfort on the Main: Athenäum, 1971), pp. 1–18; Joachim Klaus, "Die konzertierte Aktion als Instrument der neuen Wirtschaftspotlitik," in Ernst Dürr (ed.), *Neue Wege der Wirtschaftspolitik* (Berlin: Duncker & Humbolt, 1972), pp. 11–51. For the quotation see Schiller, *Konjunkturpolitik,* p. 12.

17. K. J. Gördel and M. M. Schöpf, "Antwort auf Biedenkopf," *Der Volkswirt,* vol. 22 (1968), no. 31, p. 24.

18. *Ibid.*

19. K. H. Biedenkopf, "Ordnungspolitische Probleme der neuen Wirtschaftspolitik," *Jahrbuch für Sozialwissenschaft,* 19 (1968), 323.

20. *Ibid.,* pp. 319–320, 321.

21. Klaus, "Die konzertierte Aktion," p. 43; Rupp, "Konzertierte Aktion," p. 14 (first quotation); Huffschmid, *Die Politik des Kapitals,* p. 127 (second quotation).

22. For surveys see Hoppmann, *Konzertierte Aktion;* Bert Rürup and Axel Siedenberg, "Ist der Welt bestes Konjunkturgesetz noch etwas wert?" *Wirtschaftswoche,* vol. 27 (1973), no. 4, pp. 58–61.

23. The Federal Minister of Economic Affairs, "Grundsätze der sektoralen Strukturpolitik," *Wirtschaft und Wettbewerb,* vol. 17 (1967), no. 3, pp. 197–200; The Federal Minister of Economic Affairs, "Grundsätze der sektoralen Strukturpolitik" (rev.), in Otto Schlecht, *Strukturpolitik in der Marktwirtschaft* (Cologne: Heymanns, 1968), pp. 43–46; see also OECD, *The Industrial Policies of 14 Member Countries* (Paris, 1971), p. 17.

24. Schlecht, *Strukturpolitik,* pp. 22–24; H. R. Peters, *Grundzüge sektoraler Wirtschaftpolitik* (Freiburg: Rombach, 1971), pp. 43–72, 103. The Federal Minister of Economic Affairs, *Strukturbericht 1969 der Bundesregierung,* Bundestag Papers (Bundestags-Drucksache), period V, no. 4564 (Bonn: Hegner, 1969), p. 4.

25. For a more detailed discussion see The Federal Minister of Economic Affairs, *Strukturbericht 1969,* pp. 5–16; Schlecht, *Strukturpolitik,* pp. 24–28; OECD, *Industrial Policies,* pp. 18–37.

26. J. H. Kaiser, "Industrielle Absprachen im öffentlichen Interesse," *Neue Juristische Wochenschrift,* vol. 24 (1971), no. 14, p. 588.

27. Biedenkopf, "Ordnungspolitische Probleme," p. 319.

28. Biedenkopf, "Rechtsfragen," p. 1113.

29. Karl Schiller, "Vorwort," in The Federal Ministry of Economic Affairs, *Die Kohle und die Reviere haben eine Zukunft* (Bonn, 1970), p. 4.

30. For a detailed discussion of the hard coal act see H. O. Lenel, "Das Kohleanpassungsgesetz," *Ordo,* 20 (1969), 157–180; Biedenkopf, "Ordnungspolitische Probleme," pp. 325–329; Peters, *Grundzüge sektoraler Wirtschaftspolitik,* pp. 138–146.

31. Biedenkopf, "Ordnungspolitische Probleme," p. 311.

32. *Ibid.,* pp. 327, 328 (quotation).

33. The Federal Minister of Economic Affairs, *Strukturbericht 1969,* p. 15; OECD, *Industrial Policies,* p. 36.

34. The Federal Minister of Economic Affairs, "Große Anfrage der Fraktion der CDU/CSU betreffend sektorale und regionale Strukturpolitik. Antwort des Bundesministers für Wirtschaft, Prof. Dr. Karl Schiller," in Schlecht, *Strukturpolitik,* p. 54.

35. The Federal Chancellor, *Jahresbericht 1968–69 der Bundesregierung zur Luft- und Raumfahrtindustrie,* Bundestag Papers, period VI, no. 1044 (Bonn: Hegner, 1970), pp. 1–4. The Federal Minister of Economic Affairs, *Strukturbericht 1969,* pp. 12–13; OECD, *Industrial Policies,* pp. 30–33.

36. The Federal Chancellor, *Stellungnahme der Bundesregierung zum Tätigkeitsbericht des Bundeskartellamtes für 1967,* Bundestag Papers, period V, no. 2841 (Bonn: Hegner, 1968), p. 2.

37. Karl Schiller, *Sozialismus und Wettbewerb* (Hamburg: Verlagsgenossenschaft deutscher Konsumgenossenschaften, 1955), p. 28.

38. Erhard Kantzenbach, *Die Funktionsfähigkeit des Wettbewerbs* (Göttingen: Vandenhoeck & Ruprecht, 1966). For quotations see pp. 13, 138.

39. See for instance Erich Hoppmann, "Das Konzept der optimalen Wettbewerbsintensität," *Jahrbücher für Nationalökonomie und Statistik,* 179 (1966), 286–323; Erhard Kantzenbach, "Das Konzept des optimalen Wettbewerbs. Eine Erwiderung," *Jahrbücher für Nationalökonomie und Statistik,* 181 (1967), 193–241; Erich Hoppmann, "Die Funktionsfähigkeit des Wettbewerbs. Bemerkungen zu Kantzenbachs Erwiderung," *Jahrbücher für Nationalökonomie und Statistik,* 181 (1967–68), 251–264.

40. The Federal Chancellor, *Stellungnahme der Bundesregierung zum Tätigkeitsbericht des Bundeskartellamtes für 1967,* pp. 2–3.

41. German Bundestag, *Bericht über das Ergebnis einer Untersuchung der Konzentration in der Wirtschaft,* reported by the Federal Office for Commerce in Frankfort on the Main, Bundestag Papers, period IV, no. 2320 (Bonn: Hegner, 1964). Expert Council for the Assessment of the Overall Economic Development, *Jahresgutachten 1971–72: Währung, Geldwert, Wettbewerb* (Stuttgart: Kohlhammer, 1971), pp. 125–126.

42. A 'big merger' has been defined by the Federal Cartel Office as a merger in which the bought-up companies have a balance amounting to more than 25 million DM (150 million DM for banks).

43. Aloys Schwietert and J. J. Middeke, *Unternehmensgröße und internationale Wettbewerbsfähigkeit* (Basel: Prognos, 1968); see also H. O. Lenel,

"Unternehmensgröße und internationale Wettbewerbsfähigkeit," *Ordo*, 21 (1970), 145–165. The quotation is from Schwietert and Middeke, *Unternehmensgröße*, p. 10.

44. Helmut Arndt, *Recht, Macht, und Wirtschaft* (Berlin: Duncker & Humblot, 1968), p. 84. Hartmut Berg, "Integrationsprozess und Strukturflexibilität," *Jahrbuch für Sozialwissenschaft*, vol. 22 (1971), no. 3, pp. 286–299.

45. Schlecht, *Strukturpolitik*, pp. 31–32. For more details on the special financial and advisory programs, see The Federal Minister of Economic Affairs, *Strukturbericht 1969*, pp. 6–7; OECD, *Industrial Policies*, pp. 18–22. The study referred to is Heimfried Wolff, *Die öffentliche Förderung kleiner und mittlerer Unternehmen* (Basel: Prognos, 1971), pp. 24–26.

46. The Federal Chancellor, *Stellungnahme der Bundesregierung zum Tätigkeitsbericht des Bundeskartellamtes für 1968*, Bundestag Papers, period V, no. 4236 (Bonn: Hegner, 1969), p. 3.

47. Expert Council for the Assessment of the Overall Economic Development, *Jahresgutachten 1971–72*, p. 126.

48. The Federal Chancellor, *Stellungnahme der Bundesregierung zum Tätigkeitsbericht des Bundeskartellamtes für 1969*, Bundestag Papers, period VI, no. 950 (Bonn: Hegner, 1970), pp. 2 (source of quotation), 3.

49. H. O. Lenel, "Haben wir noch eine soziale Marktwirtschaft?" *Ordo*, 22 (1971) 37; Huffschmid, *Die Politik des Kapitals*, pp. 127–132.

50. R. A. Dahl and C. E. Lindblom, *Politics, Economics, and Welfare* (New York: Harper & Row, 1953).

51. Anthony Downs, *An Economic Theory of Democracy* (New York: Harper & Row, 1957).

52. *Ibid.*, p. 256.

53. Mancur Olson, *The Logic of Collective Action* (Cambridge, Mass.: Harvard University Press, 1965).

54. Peter Bernholz, "Einige Bemerkungen zur Theorie des Einflusses der Verbände auf die politische Willensbildung in der Demokratie," *Kyklos*, 22 (1969), 282–284.

55. *Ibid.*, pp. 284–286.

56. Schiller, *Konjunkturpolitik*, p. 14.

57. Downs, *Economic Theory of Democracy*, p. 256. Klaus, "Die konzertierte Aktion," p. 33.

58. Gerd Fleischmann, "Ungleichheit unter Wählern," *Hamburger Jahrbuch für Wirtschafts- und Gesellschaftspolitik*, 12 (1967), 134.

59. H. R. Peters, "Strukturanpassungsgesetz gegen wuchernden Branchenprotektionismus," *Wirtschaftsdienst*, vol. 51 (1971), no. 12, pp. 647 (source of quotation), 648–651.

60. Peter Bernholz, "Economic Policies in a Democracy," *Kyklos*, vol. 19 (1966), no. 1, pp. 49–80.

61. Joachim Hirsch, "Zur politischen Ökonomie des politischen Systems," in Gisela Kress and Dieter Senghaas (eds.), *Politikwissenschaft: Eine Einführung in ihre Probleme* (Frankfort on the Main: Europäische Verlagsanstalt, 1969), p. 208.

The United Kingdom / Smith

1. Samuel Brittan, *Steering the Economy* (Harmondsworth: Penguin Books, 1971), pp. 193–194.

2. For a sympathetic description of these critics see John and Anne-Marie Hackett, *The British Economy: Problems and Prospects* (London: Allen & Unwin, 1967), pp. 23–43. For a less favorable view see Trevor Smith, *Anti-Politics: Consensus, Reform and Protest in Britain* (London: Chas. Knight, 1972), pp. 11–44.

3. There was evidently some difference of opinion over the creation of the DEA. George Brown, its first minister, saw it as an economic overlord to which the Treasury was subordinate, while Harold Wilson, the prime minister, regarded the two as equal ministries, complementing each other in a relationship of creative tension. See Brittan, *Steering the Economy,* pp. 310–313; Harold Wilson, *The Labour Government 1964–70: A Personal Record* (London: Weidenfeld, Joseph, 1971), pp. 3–5 and 710; and George Brown, *In My Way* (Harmondsworth: Penguin Books, 1972), chaps. 5–6 passim.

4. See, for example, Samuel Brittan, *Inquest on Planning in Britain* (London: Political and Economic Planning, 1967).

5. See, for example, "A Good Beginning," *Times* leader, November 27, 1964; and Hilary Rose, "Science in the new Britain," *Guardian,* January 12, 1965. See also "Mr. Cousin's ministry criticised," *Guardian,* July 21, 1965. As one newspaper reported: "The Ministry of Technology was misnamed . . . It is really a Ministry for Industry in the making." *Times,* February 21, 1966. See also "Benn's Empire," *Observer* leader, November 27, 1966; and William Plowden, "MinTech Moves On," *New Society,* January 12, 1967.

6. See also "NRDC to give more help to industry," *Times,* October 19, 1967. The NRDC was currently supporting 184 projects with 176 under consideration. The Industrial Expansion Act was opposed by the CBI and castigated by a leader in the *Times* (February 2, 1968) as "a dull and useless bill." See Andrew Graham, "Industrial Policy" in W. Beckerman, ed., *The Labour Government's Economic Record: 1964–70* (London: Duckworth, 1972), pp. 195–196.

7. Great Britain, Parliament, Industrial Reorganisation Corporation Act, 1966, para. 2(1) (source of quotation). See the White Paper on the IRC (Cmnd. 2889 of 1966), paras. 2 and 7. See Graham Turner, *Business in Britain* (Harmondsworth: Pelican Books, 1971), pp. 75–80.

8. See R. E. Caves, "Market Organization, Performance and Public Policy," in R. E. Caves and associates, *Britain's Economic Prospects* (London: Allen & Unwin, 1968), p. 319. The quotations are drawn from the *Times,* January 28 and February 10, 1966. I discuss the IRC in greater detail in "Industrial Planning in Britain," in J. E. S. Hayward and M. M. Watson, eds., *Planning, Politics and Public Policy* (London: Cambridge University Press, forthcoming 1974).

9. IRC, *Report and Accounts, 1967–68,* pp. 8–11. The quotation is from IRC, *Report and Accounts, 1970–71,* p. 10.

10. The chairman is quoted in "Tory MinTech puts IRC back on razor's edge," *Daily Telegraph,* July 16, 1970. See chaps. 1–7 in J. M. Samuels, ed., *Readings on Mergers and Takeovers* (London: Paul Elek Books for the Acton Society Trust, 1972). White Paper on the IRC (Cmnd. 2889 of 1966), paras. 2, 7 (source of quotation). The merger being considered in 1973 was a rationalizing merger in the process plant industry between Simon Engineering and Davy-Ashmore; see also Keith Owen, "The synthesis for success," *Times,* January 11, 1973.

11. Relatively late in the day this point was elucidated by the government in a booklet *Mergers: A Guide to Board of Trade Practices* (1969).

12. See Turner, *Business in Britain,* pp. 79–80. See also Graham in Beckerman, pp. 191–193; and M. E. Beesley and G. M. White, "The Control of Mergers in the U.K.: An Analysis of Government Institutions and Attitudes," in J. M. Samuels, ed., pp. 125–146.

13. "The logic of monopoly," *Times,* February 20, 1968.

14. Roy Jones and Paul Jacobson, "Profit motive and the public interest," *Times,* September 28, 1967. For an account of the PIB see Allan Fels, *The British Prices and Incomes Board* (London: Cambridge University Press, 1972). Graham, "Industrial Policy," in Beckerman, p. 211.

15. "Industrial and Regional Development," Cmnd. 4942 (1972).

16. According to the *Guardian.* See "Regional Aid plan shifts direction," May 22, 1972.

17. "Three regional worries," *Times,* December 20, 1972.

18. "No competition policy . . . but better for consumers," *Guardian* leader, December 2, 1972. The paper argued that "it is non-competitive behaviour rather than non-competitive structure which does the damage."

19. See W. P. Grant and David Marsh, "The Confederation of British Industry," *Political Studies,* vol. 19, no. 4, (December 1971), pp. 403–415. For a full account of the CBI's role, and in particular the Brighton conference it sponsored in November 1960, see Brittan, *Steering the Economy,* pp. 238–245.

20. See "Whom does the CBI really represent?" *Times,* May 9, 1968.

21. According to Grant and Marsh, p. 409.

22. Reported in " 'Near to a Communist state'—Sir Paul," *Guardian,* February 21, 1966; reported in "The right to criticise," *Financial Times,* November 24, 1967.

23. To quote its first director. Cf. Arthur Shenfield, "A reply to that Callaghan smear," *Spectator,* December 8, 1967. In a Commons speech on November 22, the chancellor had said he regarded the IPG as "potentially sinister."

24. Report of the Commission of Inquiry into Industrial and Commercial Representation, ABCC/CBI, November 1972. See also "ABCC agrees in principle with Devlin," *Guardian,* January 8, 1973. Earlier, three main groups of independent grocers, who did not belong to the Retail Consortium, applied to join the CBI; see the *Guardian,* December 30, 1972.

25. See Turner, *Business in Britain,* pp. 81–82; and "More for the workers—less for the bosses," *London Evening News,* August 7, 1972.

26. On this point see the view of Charles Villiers as managing director of the IRC, reported by Philip Siekman, "Europe's Love Affair with Bigness," *Fortune,* March 1970, and reprinted in J. M. Samuels, ed., p. 252.

27. See R. J. Briston and D. G. Rhys, "Problems in the Analysis of Statistics Relating to Takeovers and Mergers," in J. M. Samuels, ed., pp. 77–78.

28. To be fair to him, Samuel Brittan—one of the leading commentators —has devoted a book to the subject the main aim of which seems to be to exorcise party politics from economic policymaking. See his *Left or Right: the Bogus Dilemma* (London: Secker and Warburg, 1968). I discuss his views in *Anti-Politics,* pp. 176–179.

29. Siekman, "Europe's Love Affair." Robert Murray, "The Internationalization of Capital and the British Economy," in J. M. Samuels (ed.), pp. 267–289.

France / Michalet

1. The same distinction is used in J. M. McArthur and B. R. Scott, *Industrial Planning in France* (Boston: Harvard University Graduate School of Business Administration, 1969).

2. See Paul Samuelson, "The Pure Theory of Public Expenditures," *Review of Economics and Statistics,* vol. 36 (November 1954), p. 387–389. See also P. A. Baran and P. M. Sweezy, *Monopoly Capitalism* (New York: Monthly Review Press, 1966); *Le Capitalisme monopoliste d'état* (Paris: Editions Sociales, 1971).

3. Andrew Shonfield, *Modern Capitalism* (London: Oxford University Press, 1965).

4. A. Barrère, "La Cohérence de l'économie publique, le plan et le marche," in *Economie Publique* (Paris: CNRS, 1968), pp. 449–482.

5. A. de Lattre, *Politique économique de la France* (Paris: Sirey, 1966).

6. J. Dony, A. Giovaninetti, and B. Tibi, *L'Etat et le financement des investissements privés* (Paris: Berger-Levrault, 1969).

7. L. Stoleru, *L'Impératif industriel* (Paris: Seuil, 1969); also McArthur and Scott, *Industrial Planning.*

8. McArthur and Scott, *Industrial Planning,* p. 358.

9. Raymond Vernon, "International Investment and International Trade in the Product Cycle," *Quarterly Journal of Economics,* 80 (May 1966), 190–207.

10. McArthur and Scott, *Industrial Planning,* pp. 364–367.

11. The merger was between Cie. Européenne d'Automatisme Electronique, an affiliate of General Electric, and the Société d'Electronique et d'Automatisme, an affiliate of Schneider.

12. M. Allegre, "Les Investissements publics et le progrès de la nation," *Promotions,* 1968, quoted in de Lattre, *Politique économique,* pp. 440–443.

13. *Ibid.*

14. Stoleru, *L'Impératif industriel,* p. 105.

15. P. Bauchet, *La Planification française du ler au Vlo Plan* (Paris: Seuil, 1970); C. Gruson, *Origine et espoirs de la planification française* Paris: Dunod, 1968).

16. Shonfield, *Modern Capitalism,* pp. 131–231.

17. P. Masse, *Le Plan ou l'anti-hasard* (Paris: Gallimard, 1965), p. 250.

18. H. Schollhammer, "National Economic Planning and Business Decision Making: The French Experience," *California Management Review,* 12 (Winter 1969), 74–88.

19. Shonfield, *Modern Capitalism,* p. 141.

20. McArthur and Scott, *Industrial Planning,* pp. 467–471.

21. A. P. Weber, *Les concentrations industrielles en France* (Paris: Bordas, 1971). See also Y. Morvan, *La Concentration de l'industrie en France* (Paris: A. Colin, 1972).

22. S. Hymer and R. Rowthorn, "Multinational Corporations and International Oligopoly: The Non-American Challenge," in C. P. Kindleberger (ed.), *The International Corporation* (Cambridge, Mass.: M.I.T. Press, 1970), pp. 57–91.

23. McArthur and Scott, *Industrial Planning,* p. 496–500.

24. Jacques Rueff, *Rapport sur la situation financière* (Paris: Imprimerie Nationale, 1958).

25. M. Aglietta and R. Courbis, "Un outil pour le plan: le modèle FIFI," *Economie et Statistiques,* no. 1 (1969), pp. 45–65 (quotation from 47).

26. R. Courbis, "Developpement économique et concurrence étrangère," *Revue économique,* no. 1 (1969), p. 44.

27. *Ibid.,* p. 61.

28. L. Stoleru, "L'Etat condamne à séduire," *Expansion,* April 1972, pp. 125–133.

29. S. Nora, *Rapport sur les entreprises publiques* (Paris: La Documentation française, 1967), p. 34.

30. *Ibid.,* p. 35.

31. Stoleru, *L'Impératif industriel,* pp. 88, 100; J. Saint Geours, "Les Problèmes de la politique industrielle," *Revue de la défense nationale,* February 1968, p. 12 (source of quotation). See also by Saint Geours, *La Politique économique des principaux pays industriels de l'Occident* (Paris: Sirey, 1969), p. 411–434.

32. J. Denizet, "Evolution récente et future de la banque," *Revue d'économie politique,* no. 3 (May–June 1970), pp. 448–474.

33. McArthur and Scott, *Industrial Planning,* p. 471.

34. France, Commission on the General Economy and Finance, Sixth Plan, *Rapport* (Paris: La Documentation Française, 1971), p. 53; Commission on Industry, Sixth Plan, *Rapport,* p. 25.

35. Commission on Industry, Sixth Plan, *Rapport,* pp. 234–239.

36. C. A. Michalet, "La Multinationalisation des entreprises françaises," *Revue Economique,* no. 4 (July 1972), pp. 648–668.

37. J. J. Bonnaud and A. Bosser, "La Politique économique des pouvoirs publics et les grandes firmes internationales en France," Colloque interna-

tional de Rennes, September 1972 (mimeograph). See also R. B. Dickie, *Foreign Investment: France, A Case Study* (Leyden: Sijthoff, 1970).

38. Bonnaud and Bosser, "La Politique économique," p. 19; interview with J. Chaban-Delmas: "La France a-t-elle une politique industrielle?" *Expansion*, December 1970.

39. Raymond Vernon, "Future of the Multinational Enterprise," in Kindleberger, *International Corporation*, pp. 389–396.

Sweden / Ohlin

1. Landsorganisationen, *Arbetarrörelsens efterkrigsprogram* (Stockholm, 1944).

2. Sweden, Koncentrationsutredningen, *Oljebranschen,* SOU 1966:21; *Kreditmarknadens struktur och funktionssätt,* SOU 1968:3; *Industrins struktur och konkurrensförhållanden,* SOU 1968:5; *Strukturutveckling och ägande inom handeln,* SOU 1968:6; *Ägande och inflytande inom det privata näringslivet,* SOU 1968:7; *Läkemedelsindustrin,* SOU 1969:36.

3. Landsorganisationen, *Samordnad näringspolitik* (Stockholm, 1961).

4. Sweden, Industridepartmentet, *Statliga företag 1972.*

5. Sweden, Riksdagen, *Kungl. Maj:ts proposition angående industripolitisk verksorganisation, m.m.,* Prop. 1973:41, February 23, 1973.

Aerospace / Hochmuth

1. One of the most widely read exponents of this point of view was Jean-Jacques Servan-Schreiber in *The American Challenge* (New York: Avon Books, 1969).

2. Commission of the European Communities (Brussels), *A Policy for the Community for the Promotion of Industry and Technology in the Aeronautica,* July 1972, Annex 1, p. 18. (Hereafter cited as EEC report.)

3. *Ibid.,* pp. 17, 31; Aerospace Industries Association of America, Inc., *Aerospace Facts and Figures, 1972–1973* (New York: Aviation Week and Space Technology, 1972). In the early 1970s the United States spent some 10% of its gross national product on defense, and the U.S. space effort varied from 0.8% to less than 0.5% of GNP. The corresponding European figures were 5% (maximum) and 0.08%. See *Aviation Week and Space Technology,* March 13, 1972; *l'Europe et l'Espace: Bilan et Perspectives* (Paris: Eurospace, 1971), pp. 26, 41; German Federal Republic, *White Paper 1970 on the Security of the Federal Republic of Germany,* 1970, p. 203.

4. *Aerospace Facts and Figures, 1972–1973,* p. 22; EEC report, annex 1, p. 3.

5. Daniel Molho and Raymond Péladan, *l'Industrie Aéronautique* (Paris: Presses Universitaires de France, 1957), pp. 13, 66; John B. Rae, *Climb to Greatness* (Cambridge, Mass.: MIT Press, 1968), p. 17; Great Britain, Com-

mittee of Inquiry into the Aircraft Industry, *Report* (Cmnd. 2853), p. 39 (cited hereafter as Plowden report).

6. Rae, *Climb to Greatness,* p. 47; France, Commissariat of Planning, Committee for the Aeronautical and Space Industry, *Sixième Plan 1971–1975* (Paris: La Documentation Française, 1971), p. 35.

7. Jack Gee, *Le Mirage* (Paris: Albin Michel, 1971), p. 15.

8. Great Britain, Committee appointed by the Minister of Technology and the President of the Society of British Aerospace Companies under the chairmanship of Mr. St. John Elstub, *Productivity of the National Aircraft Effort,* 1969, Tables 6 and 7. (Cited hereafter as Elstub report.)

9. *Les Echos* (Paris), October 16, 1972, p. 28. *Fortune,* December 1972, pp. 146, 148.

10. Elstub report, para. 51; *Les Industries aéronautiques et spatiales de la Communauté, comparées à celles de la Grande-Bretagne et des Etats-Unis,* prepared for the EEC Commission by Soris s.p.a., July 1969 (Brussels: Collection Etudes, Série Industrie no. 4, 1971), II, p. 258.

11. International Civil Aeronautic Organization (ICAO), *Annual Report of the Council, 1971* (Montreal, 1971).

12. International Air Transport Association (IATA), *World Airline Statistics, 1971* (Montreal, 1972); and *World Airline Statistics, 1951* (Montreal, 1952); *Jane's All the World's Aircraft* (London: S. Low Marston, 1951).

13. EEC report, annex II.

14. *Les Echos,* March 15, 1973, p. 6; October 31, 1972, p. 19.

15. Plowden report, p. 16.

16. *Aviation Studies International* (Wimbledon, Eng.), Aviation Report Supplement, no. 175 (1968).

17. Peter W. Brooks, *The Modern Airliner: Its Origins and Development* (London: Putnam, 1961), p. 113; De Witt C. Ramsey, speech to Washington, D.C., section of the Institute of the Aeronautical Sciences, April 1950.

18. Plowden report, p. 19; *Aviation Studies International,* no. 175, pp. 33–36.

19. Brooks, *Modern Airliner,* p. 120.

20. *Aviation Week and Space Technology,* July 21, 1952.

21. Plowden report, p. 16; C.J.E. Harlow, *The European Armaments Base: A Survey,* pt. II (London: Institute for Strategic Studies, 1967), pp. 17–19.

22. Great Britain, House of Commons, Committee of Public Accounts, *First, Second and Third Reports,* 1967–1968, p. xxviii.

23. *Aviation Week,* May 10, 1948, p. 44.

24. Great Britain, House of Commons, Committee of Public Accounts, *Special Report, and First, Second and Third Report,* 1964–65, p. xxiii.

25. *Le Monde* (Paris), May 25, 1973, p. 14; Sixième Plan, p. 26; *Les Echos,* November 14, 1972, p. 28.

26. Almarin Phillips, *Technology and Market Structure* (Lexington, Mass.: D. C. Heath, 1971), passim, esp. pp. 127–130.

27. *Ibid.*

Aluminum / Mikdashi

1. See, for example, C. J. Gignoux, *Histoire d'une entreprise française* (Paris: Hachette, 1955), pp. 178–180. For the technical qualities of aluminum, see "L'Aluminium dans le monde," *Economie géographie* (Monthly bulletin published in collaboration with the professional organizations under the sponsorship of the Conseil National du Patronat Français, Paris), March 1971, pp. 1–2; and *Mutual Substitutability of Aluminum and Copper* (Washington, D.C.: National Research Council, 1972), Appendix A.

2. See Raymond Vernon, *Sovereignty at Bay* (New York: Basic Books, 1971), pp. 43–45.

3. Guy de Carmoy, "L'Inscription de l'aluminium sur la liste des exceptions dans les négotiations du GATT," in Pierre Gerbet and Daniel Pépy, eds., *La Décision dans les Communautés européennes* (Brussels: Presses Universitaires de Bruxelles, 1969), p. 381; "L'Aluminium dans le monde," p. 3.

4. On France, see J. H. McArthur and B. R. Scott, *Industrial Planning in France* (Boston: Harvard University Graduate School of Business Administration, 1969), pp. 525–526. On Britain: "Electricity, Aluminum Today—Steel Tomorrow," *The Economist*, July 27, 1968, pp. 60–62; and Dennis Topping, "Aluminum Production with Nationalism in the Air—Alcan Plays It Cool," *The Times* (London), October 28, 1971, p. 21. On Norway: Arthur Stonehill, "International Mixed Ventures in Norway," Monograph Working Paper, MIT Sloan School of Management, Cambridge, Mass. (August 1969), pp. 33, 43–44; and *American Metal* Market (New York), January 7 and 10, 1972.

5. For a brief comparison of policies and actions that West European states have generally adopted vis-à-vis their business sector, see Pierre Bleton, *Le Capitalisme français* (Paris: Les Editions Ouvrières, 1966), pp. 173–175.

6. "Norwegian Aluminum—The Unique Marriage with Alcan," *The Financial Times*, February 6, 1967; Jarle Berge, *Norwegian Policy towards Foreign Investment* (Oslo: Norsk Utenrikspolitisk Institutt, 1972), pp. 11–12; Stonehill, "Norway," pp. 35–48; and my interview in Oslo on April 10, 1969, with governmental department for state-owned industries.

7. V. G. Venturini, *Monopolies and Restrictive Trade Practices in France* (Leyden: Sijthoff, 1971), p. 351; McArthur and Scott, *France*, pp. 212–213, 501 (source of quotation); Bleton, *Capitalisme*, p. 203.

8. *Le Monde*, May 12, 1972, p. 19; "French Plan for Metals Stockpile," *The Financial Times*, May 12, 1972, p. 29; "France—Our Very Own," *The Economist*, May 6, 1972, p. 98; "Matières Premières—Un conseil interministériel met au point un plan d'approvisionnement de la France," *Le Monde*, May 12, 1972, p. 19; and "La France consolide sa politique d'approvisionnement en matières premières à usage industriel," *Les Echos* (Paris), April 19, 1972, p. 16.

9. See Jean Masseron, *L'Economie des hydrocarbures* (Paris: Editions Technip, 1969), pp. 177–180. Gignoux, *Histoire*, pp. 193–194. See also Jacques Rivier, "La Place des entreprises publiques dans l'économie française," *Economie & Statistiques* (Paris: Institut National de la Statistique et

des Etudes Economiques, 1969), pp. 33–44; Bleton, *Capitalisme,* pp. 175–204; and OECD, *The Industrial Policies of Fourteen Member Countries* (Paris, 1970), chap. 6 ("France"), p. 189.

10. *The Economist,* May 6, 1972, p. 98 (brackets added). "Remarks of John B. M. Place, President, Anaconda Company, at the 77th Annual Meeting of Shareholders, Anaconda, Montana, May 17, 1972," typescript, p. 5; and "Agreement on Sar Cheshmeh Signed with Anaconda," *Middle East Economic Survey* (Beirut), September 29, 1972, p. 2.

11. Stewart R. Spector, *Aluminum Industry Report Semiannual Review, Mid-Year Survey of Free World Primary Aluminum Capacity 1971–1976* (New York: Oppenheimer & Co., 1972), p. 23; *1972 Mining Annual Review* (London), June 1972, p. 451; "Aluminum Smelting—Two Down, One to Go," *The Economist,* May 1, 1971, pp. 80–81.

12. "German Cartel Talks," *Metal Bulletin,* November 7, 1972, p. 17. *Metals Week,* May 8, 1972, pp. 1–2 (source of quotations).

13. The quotation is from *Metals Week,* May 8, 1972, p. 2. See OECD, *Industrial Policies,* chap. 8 ("Italy"), p. 219.

14. M. V. Posner and S. J. Woolf, *Italian Public Enterprise* (Cambridge, Mass.: Harvard University Press, 1967), p. 44; "Italy's Huge, Troubled Montecatini Edison Expects Profit Again within Three Years," *Wall Street Journal,* January 12, 1973, p. 15.

15. The quotations are from "INI's in Everything," *The Economist,* May 6, 1972, p. 98 (brackets added). See also *1972 Mining Annual Review* (London), June 1972, p. 59; and "Good Year for Endassa," *Metal Bulletin* (London), May 16, 1972, p. 14.

16. See, for example, Yvonne Levy, *Aluminum: Past and Future,* Federal Reserve Bank of San Francisco Monthly Review Supplement (San Francisco, 1971), pp. 59–60; Kuhn, Loeb and Co., *Aluminum Industry Review, 1967–1968, Survey of Free World Primary Aluminum Expansion Plans, 1967–1972* (New York), December 18, 1967, p. 19 and appendix.

17. For further elaboration of these ideas, see Raymond Vernon's essay in this volume.

18. J. H. Reimers, *Present Status of Alumina and Aluminum Production in the World and in Developing Countries: Prospects of Developing an Aluminum Industry* (Vienna: UNIDO, 1967), p. 24; *Metal Bulletin,* March 2, 1971, p. 16 (source of quotation).

19. Reimers, *Present Status,* p. 24.

20. "Merger Pechiney Ugine Kuhlmann" (English text of information note prepared with the recommendations of Commission des Opérations de Bourse, Paris, December 1972), pp. 3–4.

21. *Metal Bulletin,* April 2, 1971, p. 17; July 16, 1971, p. 17; January 30, 1968, p. 20. Alcan reported from other published sources a 4,000-ton figure to Japan for 1968. Industrial Bank of Japan, Ltd., "The Aluminum Industry," *Quarterly Survey of Japanese Finance and Industry,* October–December 1972, pp. 41, 42.

22. See International Bank for Reconstruction and Development, *Past and*

Prospective Trends in the World Aluminum Industry (Washington, D.C., 1968), Appendix A; and *Metal Bulletin Monthly* (London), April 1971, p. 13. Conalco was owned by Swiss Aluminium Ltd. (60%) and Phelps Dodge Corporation (40%).

23. M. S. Brown and J. Butler, *The Production, Marketing, and Consumption of Copper and Aluminum* (New York: Praeger, 1968), pp. 151–152; *Metal Bulletin*, March 12, 1971, p. 20; Zuhayr Mikdashi, *The Community of Oil Exporting Countries, A Study in Governmental Cooperation* (Ithaca, N.Y.: Cornell University Press, 1972, and London: George Allen & Unwin Ltd., 1972), pp. 114–134; *Metal Bulletin*, January 30, 1968, p. 20, and February 14, 1969, p. 19.

24. *Metal Bulletin*, November 12, 1971, p. 17. *Ibid.*, August 13, 1971, p. 15; see also *Mining Journal*, November 19, 1971, p. 459.

25. *Metal Bulletin*, August 24, 1971, p. 15.

26. "Japan for Alufinance?" *Metal Building*, December 26, 1971, p. 15; *ibid.*, August 24, 1971, p. 15; September 14, 1971, p. 18. "Aluminium: A Japanese View," *Metal Bulletin Monthly*, October 1972, pp. 42, 43.

27. *Metal Bulletin*, August 24, 1971, p. 15.

28. *Ibid.* (brackets added).

29. Gignoux, *Histoire*, pp. 169–170.

30. Even U.S. industrialists purchased Soviet technological know-how which could result in "substantial savings of several million dollars a year." See "Kaiser, Reynolds to Use Soviet Process," in *Australian Financial Review* (Sydney), August 29, 1972, p. 32.

31. Carmoy, "L'Inscription de l'aluminium," pp. 385–386, 390–391.

32. The quotation is from Geoffrey Denton, Murray Forsyth, and Malcolm MacLennan, *Economic Planning and Policies in Britain, France, and Germany* (London: Allen & Unwin, 1969), p. 33. See report on Norwegian aluminum producers by Jean Michelet, Director General of Ardal, in *American Metal Market*, January 7 and January 10, 1972. Carmoy, "L'Inscription de l'aluminium," p. 386.

33. Lobbying might "include everything from above-board campaigning for or against legislation to the ethically gray areas of lavish entertainment and nepotism." (See the survey on the changing relationships between governments and big companies in western Europe in *New York Times*, June 19, 1972, p. C53). See Bernard Chenot, "L'Entreprise publique dans l'Etat," *Banque: Revue Mensuelle du Banquier, de son Personnel et de sa Clientèle* (Paris), March 1972, pp. 211, 212, 214, and 219.

34. See item "Policy on Competition," in the 1972–1973 issues of *Bulletin des Communautés Européennes*, published by the Commission of European Communities, Secretariat General, Brussels. Chenot, "L'Entreprise publique," p. 218.

35. *Le Monde*, April 30, 1972, p. 23. "Aluminum Institute Reveals Little," *Metals Week*, May 8, 1972, p. 1; and "IPAI's Maiden Statement," *Metal Bulletin*, May 2, 1972, p. 12 (source of quotation).

Computers / Jéquier

1. Figure for 1973 computed from the monthly reports of International Data Corporation, Newtonville, Mass., and for 1967 from Nicolas Jéquier, "Technological Gaps in the Computer Industry," *OECD Observer*, June 1969.

2. Monthly reports of International Data Corporation.

3. *Gaps in Technology—Electronic Computers* (Paris: OECD, 1969).

4. Russell Pipe, "Toward Central Government Computer Policies," mimeographed, OECD, 1972.

5. Philip Siekman, "Now It's the Europeans," *Fortune*, August 1969; Victor Havelka, "L'Affaire Bull," mimeographed study prepared for the OECD Group of Experts on Electronic Computers, 1968.

6. Nicolas Jéquier, *Le Défi industriel japonais* (Lausanne: Centre de Recherches Européennes, 1970); Gene Gregory, "Japan Turns on the Computer Power," mimeographed, Geneva, 1972, and "Japan's Unending Miracle," *Successo*, June 1972.

7. André Charguéraud, "European Computer Firms Must Unite," *Vision*, March 1972.

8. Délégation Générale à la Recherche Scientifique et Technique, *Recherche scientifique et indépendance* (Paris, 1965).

9. Christopher Freeman and Alison Young, *The Research and Development Effort in Western Europe, North America and the Soviet Union* (Paris: OECD, 1965).

10. Y. S. Hu, "Towards a European Policy on the EDP Industry," mimeographed, University of Manchester, England, 1973.

11. Michael Merritt, 'Breaking-up IBM," *The New Scientist*, April 6, 1972.

12. "La France va-t-elle créer une industrie des calculateurs largement française?" *Le Figaro*, April 19, 1966.

13. Nicolas Jéquier, "Toward a Technological Policy—The Japanese Model," *Science Policy News*, July 1971.

14. Hanzo Omi, "Fujitsu—Japan's Independent Finds Room at the Top" (Tokyo: Fujitsu Co., 1971).

15. Stanley Gill, in a Letter to the Editor, *New Scientist*, August 24, 1972.

16. Hedley Voysey, "Dusting the Computer for Fingerprints," *ibid.*, July 6, 1972.

17. Federal Republic of Germany, Ministry for Education and Science, *Zweites Datenverarbeitungsprogramm der Bundesregierung*, 1971.

18. Polen Lloret, "Le Gouvernement va définir l'orientation de la recherche en informatique," *Le Monde*, February 25, 1972.

19. Statement by the Rt. Hon. Frank Cousins, Minister of Technology, reported in *The Sunday Times*, July 3, 1966; Great Britain, *White Paper on the Computer Industry*, 1968 (Cmnd. 3660).

20. Altiero Spinelli, "Pour une stratégie communautaire en matière d'informatique" (statement before the European Parliament), *Bulletin des Communautés Européennes*, vol. 2 (1972).

21. *New Scientist,* April 27, 1972.

22. Nicolas Jéquier, *Vers une politique européenne des télécommunications,* report to the EEC Commission (Geneva, 1972).

Automobiles / Wells

1. A concise history of the early efforts to build automobiles in Europe is contained in Carlo Biscaretti di Ruffia, *Un Po' Di Storia Dell'Automobile* (Turin: Museo dell'Automobile, 1971). The history of the spread of Daimler and Benz is contained in *75 Jahre Motorisierung des Verkehrs, 1886–1961* (Stuttgart-Untertürkheim: Daimler Benz A. G., 1961).

2. Even Italy apparently had two manufacturing companies affiliated with Daimler—Daimler Società Italiana dei Motori, which was in Milan from 1903 to 1906, and De Luca Daimler Officine S.A., in Naples from 1906 to 1910. They are listed as manufacturers in Biscaretti di Ruffia's book although they are not mentioned in the Daimler Benz history.

3. The ownership of the Daimler firm is not clear from the original brochure of 1906 describing the American Mercedes, or from the Daimler Benz history. Daimler of Germany is simply described as the "parent." The opening of the Rolls Royce plant in 1919 is described in the London *Times,* October 11, 1919, p. 19, and its 1931 closing in Ken W. Purdy, *The Kings of the Road* (New York: Bonanza Books, 1952), p. 39. The story of the Fiat plant (1909–1918) appears in *Motor Italia,* no. 90 (1970), p. 9, and in "La Fiat in America," *La Mensuelle,* no. 13 (August 1970). The factory was sold to Duesenberg Motor Company.

4. *75 Jahre,* p. 90 (source of quotation). Dr. V. Köhler, "Entwicklung der allgemeinen Motorisierung," *AMZ—Auto Motor und Zubehör* (Coburg: Verlag Karl Ihl, 1963), pt. I, p. 10.

5. *75 Jahre,* p. 160.

6. The case for protection and subsidy of the automobile industry in Europe is eloquently argued in Horace Wyatt, *The Motor Industry* (London: Pitman & Sons, 1920).

7. The early policies of Ford and General Motors in Europe are described in Arthur Pound, *The Turning Wheel* (Garden City: Doubleday, Doran, 1934); and Mira Wilkins and Frank Hill, *American Business Abroad: Ford on Six Continents* (Detroit: Wayne State University Press, 1964).

8. Wilkins, *American Business,* p. 63. London *Times,* September 23, 1919, p. 12; the *Times* of that year carried a large number of articles on the debate over increased protection for British automobile manufacturers.

9. Wilkins, *American Business,* p. 112. Agnelli's close relationship with Mussolini and his influence on government policies in the period are described in detail in Valerio Castronovo, *Giovanni Agnelli* (Turin: Unione Tipografico-Editrice Torinese, 1971).

10. "What Grandfather Built," *Fortune,* August 1971, p. 127. For the effects of the restrictions, see William G. Welk, *Fascist Economic Policy* (Cambridge, Mass.: Harvard University Press, 1938), p. 177.

11. Wilkins, *American Business,* p. 230.

12. The story of the individualistic Renault is reported in Anthony Rhodes, *Louis Renault* (New York: Harcourt, Brace & World, 1969).

13. See Economic Intelligence Unit (London), *Motor Business*, no. 22 (April 1960). On the firms see Köhler, "Entwicklung," p. 5.

14. Alfred P. Sloan, Jr., *My Years with General Motors* (Garden City: Doubleday, 1964), p. 317.

15. August Horch, *Ich Baute Autos* (Lengerich: Kleins Buch-und-Kunst Verlag, 1949), p. 175.

16. *Ibid.*, p. 224.

17. The history of these attempts is summarized in Köhler, "Entwicklung." The tariff increase and other minor efforts to provide protection are described in Klaus W. Busch, *Strukturwandlungen der westdeutschen Automobilindustrie* (Berlin: Duncker & Humbolt, 1966).

18. Wilkins, *American Business*, p. 139.

19. Walter Henry Nelson, *Small Wonder: The Amazing Story of the Volkswagen* (Boston: Little, Brown, 1967), p. 48.

20. Busch, *Strukturwandlungen*, pp. 26–29, 50; Wilkins, *American Business*, pp. 304–307.

21. Busch, *Strukturwandlungen*, p. 30.

22. Some of the information in this section comes from discussions with B. Wiersch of Wolfsburg, who is putting together a complete history of the founding of Volkswagen as his doctoral dissertation. Some parts of the history are available from Nelson, *Small Wonder*, and K. B. Hopfinger, *The Volkswagen Story* (Henley-on-Thames: B. T. Foulis, 1971).

23. For a contemporary account, see "Chilly Welcome," *Time*, February 1, 1963, p. 78.

24. The Belgian incentives that were granted to General Motors are described in "GM Shakes Europe's Automakers," *Business Week*, January 30, 1965, p. 130. General Motors had a small operation in prewar France, but it was allowed to die.

25. See Pierre Naville et al., *l'Etat entrepreneur: le cas de la Régie Renault* (Paris: Editions Anthropos, 1971).

26. John Sheahan, "Government Competition and the Performance of the French Automobile Industry," *The Journal of Industrial Economics*, vol. 8, no. 3 (June 1960), p. 211.

27. *Ibid.*

28. See "It Depends What You Mean by Big," *The Economist*, March 31, 1973, p. 62, and Naville, *l'Etat entrepreneur*, p. 105.

29. Sheahan, "Government Competition," p. 211.

30. *Ibid.*, p. 212. See Naville, *l'Etat entrepreneur*, pp. 94, 96.

31. Part of the controversy is described in "New Owners May Mean New VW's," *Business Week*, December 5, 1959, p. 102. The details of the state's case are presented in Lower Saxony, Landtag, *Schriftlicher Bericht über das Eigentum am Volkswagenwerk*, Landtag official Papers no. 1002, June 26, 1958, which was prepared by an SPD member of the state house.

32. An interpretation of the change as primarily political appears in "Sturm und Drang at VW," *Newsweek*, September 13, 1971, p. 89.

33. The report, *Studien zur Neuordnung des Industriellen Bundesvermögens,* was presented to the government in May 1971, but it had not been officially released to the public by early 1973.

34. The founding of the company, transfer to private Italian ownership, and eventual transfer to IRI, are described in Peter Hull, *Alfa Romeo* (London: Cassell, 1964). Fiat's response and offer to distribute Alfasud cars abroad, apparently to ensure that operations were complementary rather than competitive, are described in Economic Intelligence Unit *Motor Business* (London), no. 53 (January 1968), p. 41.

35. "The Onrushing Auto Makers," *Fortune,* August 1963, p. 101.

36. The harassing steps are described in "Fiat Toots New Horn at Its Rivals," *Business Week,* August 14, 1965, p. 90. These and other data on European automobile sales are available from *L'Argus de l'automobile et des locomotions* (Paris), annual automobile statistics issues. The relationship between engine size and automobile taxes and the prices of gasoline in the West European countries are shown in pp. 54–55 of the *Annual Report* of Alfa Romeo, 1971. In Italy, the tax on a 3250-cc engine was approximately seven times that on a 1116-cc Fiat 128. Italy also has the highest gasoline prices of western Europe.

37. Wilkins, *American Business,* p. 364 (Ford quotation); London *Times,* October 10, 1947, p. 4.

38. The story of the government intervention in Chrysler's takeover of Rootes and other government actions in this period with respect to the industry is presented in more detail in Economic Intelligence Unit (London), *Motor Business,* no. 60 (October 1969).

39. London *Times,* January 18, 1966, p. 1.

40. See, for example, London *Times,* October 3, 1947, p. 2; December 5, 1947, p. 2; December 4, 1948, p. 4. The series of mergers preceding the formation of BLMC and the government role in the formation of BLMC are described in the London *Times,* January 18, 1968. Many more details were published later in Graham Turner, *The Leyland Papers* (London: Eyre & Spottiswoode, 1971). The quotation is from the *Times,* January 18, 1968, p. 23.

41. The production data for the largest of the overseas plants appear in the annual publication, *Automobil Revue* (Bern), 1973.

42. There have been many plants licensed or owned by companies in other European countries besides the comparatively large Fiat operations in France and Germany that have been mentioned. More than half-a-dozen foreign-affiliated plants appear in a list of automobile plants that existed in Italy, the most protective of the European countries. See Biscaretti di Ruffia, *Un Po' Di Storia.*

43. See "VW May Set Up Plant in U.S.," *Financial Times,* March 14, 1973.

44. See Graham Bannock, *The Motor Industry* (London: Dun & Bradstreet and the Economists Advisory Group, n.d.), p. 17.

45. For data on the American subsidiaries see Rainer Hellman, *The Challenge to U.S. Dominance of the International Corporation* (Cambridge:

Dunellen, 1970), p. 61. The economies of scale in automobile manufacture are a subject of constant debate, partly because of the difficulties involved in estimating the cost-volume relationship for the large number of parts involved and partly because of the difficulties in controlling for a multiplicity of models, more or less related. The most careful estimates by an economist appear to be those of Lawrence White, in *The Automobile Industry since 1945* (Cambridge: Harvard University Press, 1971), who estimates that doubling production from 400,000 per year reduces costs by only one percent. A good summary of the literature on scale in production, research, and marketing of automobiles is contained in chaps. 3–5 of Olaf Gempt, *Zukunftsperspektiven der europäischen Automobilindustrie; Zwang zu Weiterer Konzentration?* (Göttingen: Vandenhoeck & Ruprecht, 1971).

46. "How the Japanese Figure in European Car Markets," *Financial Times*, December 28, 1972.

47. The amount of money going into research and development for automobile safety and pollution controls was described as more than that spent on space programs, in James Ensor, "A Safety Standard for Europe," *Financial Times*, November 15, 1972.

Steel / Hayward

1. Roger Priouret, *Origines du Patronat Français* (Paris: Grasset, 1963), p. 19; cf. pp. 13–19. See also J. E. Sawyer, "The Entrepreneur and the Social Order. France and the U.S.A.," in William Miller, ed., *Men in Business* (Cambridge, Mass.: Harvard University Press, 1952), p. 15.

2. See *Times* special supplement "E.E.C. Companies," December 15, 1972, pp. ix, xi. The complicated company structure preserved a strict equality between Hoogovens and Hoesch. Shares in the new central company, Estel NV, registered under Dutch law, were divided equally between a Hoogovens and a Hoesch holding company. Estel NV held the shares of the two working companies: Hoogovens Ijmuiden BV and Hoesch Werke A.G. See also Christopher Layton, *Cross Frontier Mergers in Europe* (Bath: Bath University Press, 1971), pp. 27–28.

3. Walter Kendall, in Stuart Holland, ed., *The State as Entrepreneur* (London: Weidenfeld & Nicolson, 1972), p. 230. However, see *ibid.*, pp. 78–79, 98–99. Also Kevin Allen and Malcolm C. MacLennan, *Regional Problems and Policies in Italy and France* (London: Allen & Unwin, 1970), pp. 63–65, 290–291.

4. Duncan Burn, *The Steel Industry, 1939–59. A Study in Competition and Planning* (Cambridge: Cambridge University Press, 1961), p. 109; cf. pp. 67–70, 89, 107–109; and cf. H. E. English, "British Steel, a Unique Record of Public Regulation," *Canadian Journal of Economics and Political Science*," vol. 26, no. 2 (May 1960), pp. 245–247.

5. Burn, *Steel Industry*, p. 367; cf. pp. 292, 306–308, 384; See also George W. Ross, *The Nationalization of Steel* (London: MacGibbon & Kee, 1965), passim.

6. *White Paper on Steel Nationalization*, April 1965 (Cmnd. 2651), p. 5.

Charles K. Rowley, *Steel and Public Policy* (London: McGraw-Hill, 1971), p. 259 (source of second quotation). The National Board for Prices and Incomes, May 1969 Report, *Steel Prices* (No. 111, Cmd. 4033, p. 26), declared: "The (1964) ruling of the Restrictive Practices Court brought an end to the agreement on uniform pricing, though with few exceptions the practice of uniform pricing continued." *House of Commons Parliamentary Debates (Hansard),* 25 July 1966, p. 1231 (source of last quotation).

7. Aubrey Silberston: "The British Steel Corporation," *Annals of Public and Co-operative Economy,* vol. 43, no. 2 (April 1972), p. 111.

8. Great Britain, Department of Trade and Industry, *Steel. British Steel Corporation: Ten Year Development Strategy,* February 1973 (Cmnd. 5226), pp. 6–7. For a highly critical examination of DTI-BSC relations, see First Report from the Select Committee on Nationalized Industries, session 1972–73, *British Steel Corporation.*

9. Andrew Shonfield, *Modern Capitalism* (London: Oxford University Press, 1965), pp. 261–262 (source of quotation), p. 255; see also Jean-François Besson, *Les Groupes industriels et l'Europe* (Paris: Presses Universitaries de France, 1962), p. 504; cf. pp. 92, 298, 604, 606.

10. Besson, *Les Groupes industriels,* p. 504; cf. pp. 603–604; and cf. Gerard Braunthal, *The Federation of German Industry in Politics* (Ithaca, N.Y.: Cornell University Press, 1965), pp. 48, 142–143, 276–277. *The Economist,* January 13, 1973, pp. 43–44; and *Times,* January 4, 1973.

11. International Iron and Steel Institute, First Annual Conference, *Report of Proceedings,* November 1967, p. 12. However, see Shonfield, *Modern Capitalism,* p. 275.

12. The *Times* supplement "E.E.C. Companies," December 15, 1972, p. v. For a dated but still interesting study of the ramifications of interlocking ownership in the German steel industry, see Besson, *Les Groupes industriels,* pp. 92–100, 286–313, and, on vertical integration, pp. 376–387.

13. William Manchester, *The Arms of Krupp, 1587–1968* (London: M. Joseph, 1968), p. 806; cf. pp. 833–834, 840–841, 851–853, 924.

14. *Ibid.,* pp. 898–940. See Malcolm Rutherford: "Krupp without Krupps," *Management Today,* January 1971, pp. 68–73; and *The Times,* June 23, 1972, p. 23; see also *The Times,* September 15, 1972, and December 8, 1972.

15. Shonfield, *Modern Capitalism,* p. 245; see also pp. 242–246. See also Hans-Joachim Arndt, *West Germany, Politics of Non-Planning* (Syracuse, N.Y.: Syracuse University Press, 1966) p. 73.

16. Philippe Saint-Marc, *La France dans le C.E.C.A.* (Paris: Colin, 1961), pp. 249, 263; cf. John and Anne-Marie Hackett, *Economic Planning in France* (London: Allen & Unwin, 1963), pp. 264–265; Besson, *Les Groupes industriels,* pp. 35, 369.

17. Saint-Marc, *La France dans le C.E.C.A.,* p. 263; see also pp. 251–252, 266, 269.

18. Besson, *Les Groupes industriels,* pp. 315, 347–348. For a detailed description of the domestic and foreign links of the French steel companies and their ties with iron ore companies about 1960, see *ibid.,* chart on p. 89,

list on pp. 100–106 and pp. 245–247, 257–260, 315, 427. See also Pierre Belleville, *Une Nouvelle Classe Ouvrière* (Paris: Julliard, 1963), pp. 46–57; Louis Charvet, "Note sur les concentrations realisées dans le secteur sidérurgique français depuis la Libération," Appendix 1 to Lagandré report "Problèmes posés par la concentration des entreprises," *Journal Officiel. Avis et Rapports du Conseil Economique et Social,* February 10, 1967, pp. 247–248.

19. Henry W. Ehrmann, *Organized Business in France* (Princeton: Princeton University Press, 1957), p. 289. On the application of the First Plan to the French steel industry, see Burn, *Steel Industry,* pp. 390–398.

20. Henri Bustarret in *Les Cahiers de l'hexagone,* April 1964, pp. 61, 63. On business domination of the Steel Commission and working party chairmanships and rapporteur positions, see J. E. S. Hayward, "Le Fonctionnement des commissions et la préparation du Vᵉ Plan," *Revue française de sociologie,* 8 (1967), 464–465.

21. E. Arrighi de Casanova, "Les quasi-contracts du Plan," *Droit social,* June 1965, p. 348. On the CSSF's financial arm, the *Groupement de l'industrie sidérurgique,* see John H. McArthur and Bruce R. Scott: *Industrial Planning in France* (Boston: Harvard University Graduate School of Business Administration, 1969), pp. 198–201. See also Rémy Prud'homme, *La Sidérurgie française et le 3ᵉ Plan,* Thèse complémentaire, Faculté de Droit de Paris, 1964, p. 57; cf. Besson, *Les Groupes industriels,* p. 507.

22. *Vᵉ Plan* (Paris: Imprimerie des Journaux Officiels, 1965), I, 72–73; cf. 70. On the role of contract more generally, see J.E.S. Hayward, "State Intervention in France: The Changing Style of Government-Industry Relations," *Political Studies,* vol. 20, no. 3 (September 1972), pp. 287 ff.

23. Interview of Jacques Ferry in *La Vie française,* August 5, 1966.

24. Louis Lister, *Europe's Coal and Steel Community* (New York: Twentieth Century Fund, 1960), p. 168 (source of quotation); cf. pp. 198, 225, 248, 404; and Michael Adler; "Specialization in the E.C.S.C.," *Journal of Common Market Studies,* vol. 8, no. 3 (March 1970), pp. 180, 189, 191. William Diebold; *The Schuman Plan* (New York: Praeger, 1959), p. 712; cf. Lister, p. 174.

25. Saint-Marc, *La France dans le C.E.C.A.,* p. 197; cf. pp. 224–226; Besson, *Les Groupes industriels,* pp. 407–408, 432–433, 497–498, 514–516.

26. Jacques Ferry, "Coordonner les investissements ou planifier les échanges," *Le Monde,* October 11, 1967; cf. October 4, 1967. *Ibid.,* October 9, 1967, p. 20; cf. IISI First Annual Conference, *Report of Proceedings,* 1967, p. 18. For similar criticisms of a purely market approach in matters of investment, see Ferry's speech as president of the ECSC Consultative Committee, reported *ibid.,* 27 January 1968.

Index

Abs, Hermann, 263, 265
Act for the Promotion of Stability and Economic Growth (Germany), 64, 69–70, 71, 72, 83, 86
Act against the Restriction of Competition (Cartel Act; Germany), 64, 72, 75, 81–82, 83, 86
Adenauer, Konrad, 240, 264
AEG (Allgemeine Elektrizitätsgesellschaft; Germany), 217
Aeritalia, 34, 55
Aerospace industry, 145–146; major subsectors of, 147; sales by country and sector, 147–148; wide variations in development times and costs, 148–152; military versus commercial aircraft market, 152–158; in Great Britain, 158–164, 167–169; in France, 164–167, 168
Aerospace Industry Committee, 147–148
Agency for Industrial Development (Office de Promotion Industriel, OPI; Belgium), 38
Agfa-Gevaert, 19
Agnelli, Giovanni, 233
Air France, 154
Alcan Aluminum, 174–175, 179, 186, 194
Alcoa Aluminum, 179, 186, 194
Alemagna Food Company (Italy), 34, 54
Alfa Romeo, 33, 233, 234, 242
Alufinance & Trade Ltd., 187–188
Aluminum Club, 187
Aluminum industry: governmental interests in, 170–173; governmental policies and programs for, 173–179 (*see also individual countries*); pattern of, 179–180; vertical integration within, 180–181; cooperative measures in, 181–185; Gentlemen's Agreement within, 185–187, 191; stockpile financing by, 187; and European Producers' Aluminum Association, 189–190, 194; efforts to achieve new equilibrium within, 190–194

Alusuisse, 178, 179, 187, 189
Anaconda Company (U.S.), 176–177
Anglo-Iranian Oil Company (Great Britain), 7, 11
ANTAR (France), 112
Ardal og Sunndal Verk, A/S (Norway), 174–175, 194
Armstrong-Siddeley (Great Britain), 159
ASEA (Sweden), 137, 138, 139
Association of British Chambers of Commerce (ABCC), 101–102
A-300B, 158, 167
Atomenergi (Sweden), 133, 139
ATP, *see* Supplementary Pension Fund
Audi (Germany), 235
August Thyssen Hütte A.G. (Germany), 263
Austin (Great Britain), 232
Auto-Union (Germany), 235, 236, 245
Automobile industry, 229–230; German domination of, before World War I, 230–231; government policies for protection of, 232–237; postwar policies and goals for, 237–245; internationalization of, 245–254. *See also individual countries*

BAC (Great Britain), 162, 163
BAC-111, 157, 161
Banking structure: Italian, 52–53, 56; French, 107; Swedish, 129–130; role of German, in steel industry, 262–263
BDI, *see* Federation of German Industry
BEA, *see* British European Airways
Beechams (Great Britain), 101
Belgium, new state holding agency introduced in, 37–38
Benn, Anthony Wedgwood, 93
Benz, Karl, 230
Berliet (France), 26, 245
Blue Streak project (Great Britain), 162–163

Publications Written under the Auspices of the Center for International Affairs, Harvard University

Created in 1958, the Center for International Affairs fosters advanced study of basic world problems by scholars from various disciplines and senior officials from many countries. The research at the Center focuses on economic, social, and political development, the management of force in the modern world, and the evolving roles of Western Europe and the Communist nations, and the conditions of international order.

BOOKS

The Soviet Bloc, by Zbigniew K. Brzezinski (sponsored jointly with the Russian Research Center), 1960. Harvard University Press. Revised edition, 1967.

The Necessity for Choice, by Henry A. Kissinger, 1961. Harper & Bros.

Strategy and Arms Control, by Thomas C. Schelling and Morton H. Halperin, 1961. Twentieth Century Fund.

United States Manufacturing Investment in Brazil, by Lincoln Gordon and Engelbert L. Grommers, 1962. Harvard Business School.

The Economy of Cyprus, by A. J. Meyer, with Simos Vassiliou (sponsored jointly with the Center for Middle Eastern Studies), 1962. Harvard University Press.

Communist China 1955–1959: Policy Documents with Analysis, with a foreword by Robert R. Bowie and John K. Fairbank (sponsored jointly with the East Asian Research Center), 1962. Harvard University Press.

Somali Nationalism, by Saadia Touval, 1963. Harvard University Press.

The Dilemma of Mexico's Development, by Raymond Vernon, 1963. Harvard University Press.

Limited War in the Nuclear Age, by Morton H. Halperin, 1963. John Wiley & Sons.

The Arms Debate, by Robert A. Levine, 1963. Harvard University Press.

Africans on the Land, by Montague Yudelman, 1964. Harvard University Press.

Counterinsurgency Warfare, by David Galula, 1964. Frederick A. Praeger, Inc.

People and Policy in the Middle East, by Max Weston Thornburg, 1964. W. W. Norton & Co.

Shaping the Future, by Robert R. Bowie, 1964. Columbia University Press.

Foreign Aid and Foreign Policy, by Edward S. Mason (sponsored jointly with the Council on Foreign Relations), 1964. Harper & Row.

How Nations Negotiate, by Fred Charles Iklé, 1964. Harper & Row.

China and the Bomb, by Morton H. Halperin (sponsored jointly with the East Asian Research Center), 1965. Frederick A. Praeger, Inc.

Democracy in Germany, by Fritz Erler (Jodidi Lectures), 1965. Harvard University Press.

The Troubled Partnership, by Henry A. Kissinger (sponsored jointly with the Council on Foreign Relations), 1965. McGraw-Hill Book Co.

The Rise of Nationalism in Central Africa, by Robert I. Rotberg, 1965. Harvard University Press.

Pan-Africanism and East African Integration, by Joseph S. Nye, Jr., 1965. Harvard University Press.

Communist China and Arms Control, by Morton H. Halperin and Dwight H. Perkins (sponsored jointly with the East Asian Research Center), 1965. Frederick A. Praeger, Inc.

Problems of National Strategy, ed. Henry Kissinger, 1965. Frederick A. Praeger, Inc.

Deterrence before Hiroshima: The Airpower Background of Modern Strategy, by George H. Quester, 1966. John Wiley & Sons.

Containing the Arms Race, by Jeremy J. Stone, 1966. M.I.T. Press.

Germany and the Atlantic Alliance: The Interaction of Strategy and Politics, by James L. Richardson, 1966. Harvard University Press.

Arms and Influence, by Thomas C. Schelling, 1966. Yale University Press.

Political Change in a West African State, by Martin Kilson, 1966. Harvard University Press.

Planning without Facts: Lessons in Resource Allocation from Nigeria's Development, by Wolfgang F. Stolper, 1966. Harvard University Press.

Export Instability and Economic Development, by Alasdair I. MacBean, 1966. Harvard University Press.

Foreign Policy and Democratic Politics, by Kenneth N. Waltz (sponsored jointly with the Institute of War and Peace Studies, Columbia University), 1967. Little, Brown & Co.

Contemporary Military Strategy, by Morton H. Halperin, 1967. Little, Brown & Co.

Sino-Soviet Relations and Arms Control, ed. Morton H. Halperin (sponsored jointly with the East Asian Research Center), 1967. M.I.T. Press.

Africa and United States Policy, by Rupert Emerson, 1967. Prentice-Hall.

Elites in Latin America, edited by Seymour M. Lipset and Aldo Solari, 1967. Oxford University Press.

Europe's Postwar Growth, by Charles P. Kindleberger, 1967. Harvard University Press.

The Rise and Decline of the Cold War, by Paul Seabury, 1967. Basic Books.

Student Politics, ed. S. M. Lipset, 1967. Basic Books.

Pakistan's Development: Social Goals and Private Incentives, by Gustav F. Papanek, 1967. Harvard University Press.

Strike a Blow and Die: A Narrative of Race Relations in Colonial Africa, by George Simeon Mwase, ed. Robert I. Rotberg, 1967. Harvard University Press.

Party Systems and Voter Alignments, edited by Seymour M. Lipset and Stein Rokkan, 1967. Free Press.

Agrarian Socialism, by Seymour M. Lipset, revised edition, 1968. Doubleday Anchor.

Aid, Influence, and Foreign Policy, by Joan M. Nelson, 1968. The Macmillan Company.

International Regionalism, by Joseph S. Nye, 1968. Little, Brown & Co.

Revolution and Counterrevolution, by Seymour M. Lipset, 1968. Basic Books.

Political Order in Changing Societies, by Samuel P. Huntington, 1968. Yale University Press.

The TFX Decision: McNamara and the Military, by Robert J. Art, 1968. Little, Brown & Co.

Korea: The Politics of the Vortex, by Gregory Henderson, 1968. Harvard University Press.

Political Development in Latin America, by Martin Needler, 1968. Random House.

The Precarious Republic, by Michael Hudson, 1968. Random House.

The Brazilian Capital Goods Industry, 1929–1964 (sponsored jointly with the Center for Studies in Education and Development), by Nathaniel H. Leff, 1968. Harvard University Press.

Economic Policy-Making and Development in Brazil, 1947–1964, by Nathaniel H. Leff, 1968. John Wiley & Sons.

Turmoil and Transition: Higher Education and Student Politics in India, edited by Philip G. Altbach, 1968. Lalvani Publishing House (Bombay).

German Foreign Policy in Transition, by Karl Kaiser, 1968. Oxford University Press.

Protest and Power in Black Africa, edited by Robert I. Rotberg, 1969. Oxford University Press.

Peace in Europe, by Karl E. Birnbaum, 1969. Oxford University Press.

The Process of Modernization: An Annotated Bibliography on the Sociocultural Aspects of Development, by John Brode, 1969. Harvard University Press.

Students in Revolt, edited by Seymour M. Lipset and Philip G. Altbach, 1969. Houghton Mifflin.

Agricultural Development in India's Districts: The Intensive Agricultural Districts Programme, by Dorris D. Brown, 1970.

Authoritarian Politics in Modern Society: The Dynamics of Established One-Party Systems, edited by Samuel P. Huntington and Clement H. Moore, 1970. Basic Books.

Nuclear Diplomacy, by George H. Quester, 1970. Dunellen.

The Logic of Images in International Relations, by Robert Jervis, 1970. Princeton University Press.

Europe's Would-Be Polity, by Leon Lindberg and Stuart A. Scheingold, 1970. Prentice-Hall.

Taxation and Development: Lessons from Colombian Experience, by Richard M. Bird, 1970. Harvard University Press.

Lord and Peasant in Peru: A Paradigm of Political and Social Change, by F. LaMond Tullis, 1970. Harvard University Press.

The Kennedy Round in American Trade Policy: The Twilight of the GATT? by John W. Evans, 1971. Harvard University Press.

Korean Development: The Interplay of Politics and Economics, by David C. Cole and Princeton N. Lyman, 1971. Harvard University Press.

Development Policy II—The Pakistan Experience, edited by Walter P. Falcon and Gustav F. Papanek, 1971. Harvard University Press.

Higher Education in a Transitional Society, by Philip G. Altbach, 1971. Sindhu Publications (Bombay).

Studies in Development Planning, edited by Hollis B. Chenery, 1971. Harvard University Press.

Passion and Politics, by Seymour M. Lipset with Gerald Schaflander, 1971. Little, Brown & Co.

Political Mobilization of the Venezuelan Peasant, by John D. Powell, 1971. Harvard University Press.

Higher Education in India, edited by Amrik Singh and Philip Altbach, 1971. Oxford University Press (Delhi).

The Myth of the Guerrilla, by J. Bowyer Bell, 1971. Blond (London) and Knopf (New York).

International Norms and War between States: Three Studies in International Politics, by Kjell Goldmann, 1971. Published jointly by Läromedelsförlagen (Sweden) and the Swedish Institute of International Affairs.

Peace in Parts: Integration and Conflict in Regional Organization, by Joseph S. Nye, Jr., 1971. Little, Brown & Co.

Sovereignty at Bay: The Multinational Spread of U.S. Enterprise, by Raymond Vernon, 1971. Basic Books.

Defense Strategy for the Seventies (revision of *Contemporary Military Strategy*), by Morton H. Halperin, 1971. Little, Brown & Co.

Peasants Against Politics: Rural Organization in Brittany, 1911–1967, by Suzanne Berger, 1972. Harvard University Press.

Transnational Relations and World Politics, edited by Robert O. Keohane and Joseph S. Nye, Jr., 1972. Harvard University Press.

Latin American University Students: A Six Nation Study, by Arthur Liebman, Kenneth N. Walker, and Myron Glazer, 1972. Harvard University Press.

The Politics of Land Reform in Chile, 1950–1970: Public Policy, Political Institutions, and Social Change, by Robert R. Kaufman, 1972. Harvard University Press.

The Boundary Politics of Independent Africa, by Saadia Touval, 1972. Harvard University Press.

The Politics of Nonviolent Action, by Gene E. Sharp, 1973. Porter Sargent.

System 37 Viggen: Arms, Technology, and the Domestication of Glory, by Ingemar Dörfer, 1973. Universitetsforluget (Oslo).

University Students and African Politics, by William John Hanna, 1974. Africana Publishing Company.

From Cartel to Concorde: Organizing Transnational Enterprise in Advanced Technology, by M. S. Hochmuth, 1974. Sijthoff (Leiden). *Becoming Modern*, by Alex Inkeles and David H. Smith, 1974. Little, Brown & Co.

Economic Nationalism and the Politics of International Dependence: The Case of Copper in Chile, 1945–1973, by Theodore Moran, 1974. Princeton University Press.

The Andean Group: A Case Study in Economic Integration among Developing Countries, by David Morawetz, 1974. M.I.T. Press.

Harvard Studies in International Affairs*
(*formerly Occasional Papers in International Affairs*)

† 1. *A Plan for Planning: The Need for a Better Method of Assisting Underdeveloped Countries on Their Economic Policies*, by Gustav F. Papanek, 1961.

† 2. *The Flow of Resources from Rich to Poor*, by Alan D. Neale, 1961.

† 3. *Limited War: An Essay on the Development of the Theory and an Annotated Bibliography*, by Morton H. Halperin, 1962.

† 4. *Reflections on the Failure of the First West Indian Federation*, by Hugh W. Springer, 1962.

5. *On the Interaction of Opposing Forces under Possible Arms Agreements*, by Glenn A. Kent, 1963. 36 pp. $1.00.

† 6. *Europe's Northern Cap and the Soviet Union*, by Nils Örvik, 1963.

7. *Civil Administration in the Punjab: An Analysis of a State Government in India*, by E.N. Mangat Rai, 1963. 82 pp. $1.00.

8. *On the Appropriate Size of a Development Program*, by Edward S. Mason, 1964. 24 pp. $.75.

9. *Self-Determination Revisited in the Era of Decolonization*, by Rupert Emerson, 1964. 64 pp. $1.25.

10. *The Planning and Execution of Economic Development in Southeast Asia*, by Clair Wilcox, 1965. 37 pp. $1.00.

11. *Pan-Africanism in Action*, by Albert Tevoedjre, 1965. 88 pp. $2.00.

12. *Is China Turning In?* by Morton Halperin, 1965. 34 pp. $1.00.

†13. *Economic Development in India and Pakistan*, by Edward S. Mason, 1966.

14. *The Role of the Military in Recent Turkish Politics*, by Ergun Özbudun, 1966. 54 pp. $1.25.

†15. *Economic Development and Individual Change: A Social-Psychological Study of the Comilla Experiment in Pakistan*, by Howard Schuman, 1967.

16. *A Select Bibliography on Students, Politics, and Higher Education*, by Philip G. Altbach, UMHE Revised Edition, 1970. 65 pp. $2.50.

* Available from Harvard University Center for International Affairs, 6 Divinity Avenue, Cambridge, Massachusetts 02138

† Out of print. May be ordered from AMS Press, Inc., 56 East 13th Street, New York, N.Y. 10003

17. *Europe's Political Puzzle: A Study of the Fouchet Negotiations and the 1963 Veto,* by Alessandro Silj, 1967. 178 pp. $2.50.
18. *The Cap and the Straits: Problems of Nordic Security,* by Jan Klenberg, 1968. 19 pp. $1.00.
19. *Cyprus: The Law and Politics of Civil Strife,* by Linda B. Miller, 1968. 97 pp. $2.50.
†20. *East and West Pakistan: A Problem in the Political Economy of Regional Planning,* by Md. Anisur Rahman, 1968.
†21. *Internal War and International Systems: Perspectives on Method,* by George A. Kelley and Linda B. Miller, 1969.
22. *Migrants, Urban Poverty, and Instability in Developing Nations,* by Joan M. Nelson, 1969. 81 pp. $2.25.
23. *Growth and Development in Pakistan, 1955–1969,* by Joseph J. Stern and Walter P. Falcon, 1970. 94 pp. $2.75.
24. *Higher Education in Developing Countries: A Select Bibliography,* by Philip G. Altbach, 1970. 118 pp. $3.75.
25. *Anatomy of Political Institutionalization: The Case of Israel and Some Comparative Analyses,* by Amos Perlmutter, 1970. 60 pp. $2.25.
26. *The German Democratic Republic from the Sixties to the Seventies,* by Peter Christian Ludz, 1970. 100 pp. $3.00.
27. *The Law in Political Integration: The Evolution and Integrative Implications of Regional Legal Processes in the European Community,* by Stuart A. Scheingold, 1971. 63 pp. $2.25.
28. *Psychological Dimensions of U.S.–Japanese Relations,* by Hiroshi Kitamura, 1971. 46 pp. $1.75.
29. *Conflict Regulation in Divided Societies,* by Eric A. Nordlinger, 1972. 137 pp. $4.00.
30. *Israel's Political-Military Doctrine,* by Michael I. Handel, 1973. 101 pp. $3.00.
31. *Italian Politics and Foreign Policy: Italy, NATO, and the EEC,* by Primo Vannicelli, 1974.
32. *Studies of Inappropriate Technologies for Development,* by C. Peter Timmer, John W. Thomas, Louis T. Wells, Jr., and David Morawetz, 1974.